The Isle of Man and Britain
CONTROVERSY
1651-1895

From Smuggling to the Common Purse

Best wishes Priscilla
Happy "Murray's Road" days
Kit

The Isle of Man and Britain

CONTROVERSY

1651-1895

From Smuggling to the Common Purse

C. W. GAWNE

Manx Heritage Foundation

First published by the Manx Heritage Foundation 2009
PO Box 1986, Douglas, Isle of Man IM99 1SR

Printed and bound in Wales by Gomer Press Limited, Ceredigion

© Dr C. W. Gawne and the Manx Heritage Foundation
Dr Gawne asserts the moral right to be identified as the author of this work

All rights reserved. No part of this book may be printed or reproduced or utilised in any form or in any electronic, mechanical, or other means, now known or hereafter invented, including photocopying or recording, or in any information retrieval system, without permission in writing from the publishers.

Cover design: Ruth Sutherland

British Library Cataloguing in Publication Data
A catalogue record for this book is available from the British Library

ISBN 978-0-9554043-8-2

For June

Contents

Acknowledgements x

Abbreviations xi

Illustrations xii

Introduction
    Revelation 1
    Sources 2
    Previous studies 3

Chapter 1
The Isle of Man: A Separate Identity
    Present 7
    Past 8
    The Journey 11

Chapter 2
Smuggling
    Trade 13
    'The Trade' 17
    Island passes from Derby to Atholl 23
    Manx Merchant 28

Chapter 3
Revestment
    Purchase of the Isle of Man 37
    Revestment and Mischief Acts 43
    Immediate repercussions 49
    Aftermath 51

Chapter 4
DETERMINED DUKE
- Significance of the new relationship 57
- 'Cursed crew of Taubmans and Quayles' 60
- Commissioners' Report 63
- Further compensation 67
- Bitter end 71

Chapter 5
FINANCIAL THREAT
- Calls for reforms 81
- 'A Stranger' 83
- Possible assimilation 85
- Resistance 88
- London 94
- The 'clique', the 'squib' and the 'bogey' 101

Chapter 6
FREE TRADE
- Discontent 105
- The willing Dr Bowring and the unwilling House of Keys 108
- Outspoken rival newspapers 113
- A new Act 116
- Demands for constitutional reform 121

Chapter 7
BRITAIN'S CONTINUING AUTHORITY
- Isle of Man and the Treasury 125
- Further resistance 130
- Controversial inclusion in a General Bill 132
- 'If the House of Keys had been a representative body' 135
- End of the licence system 140
- 'A palpable breach of faith' 142

Chapter 8
FISCAL AND CONSTITUTIONAL REFORM
    Governor Loch and the state of the Island 147
    Breakwater and harbour works 150
    Self-elected Keys 153
    Proposals and negotiations 156
    Double dilemma resolved 163

Chapter 9
COMMON PURSE
    Ambitions 173
    Towards further financial freedom 177
    Tea duty - Britain: 4.88 pounds, Isle of Man: 6 pounds 180
    Establishment of the Common Purse Arrangement 183
    Contrasting fortunes 190
    Extension of Arrangement and revised 'fiscal population' 193

Chapter 10
CONTROVERSY CONSIDERED 199

APPENDICES 209

REFERENCE NOTES 235

BIBLIOGRAPHY 259

INDEX 269

Acknowledgements

I take pleasure in thanking again those who supported me throughout the production of my PhD thesis as well as those who have subsequently given their assistance in the transformation of the thesis into this book.

My thanks go to Dr Peter Davey, Dr Fenella Bazin, Dr Breesha Maddrell and the staff at the Centre for Manx Studies for their assistance from the beginning of my adventure. The support given by Roger Sims, Bernard Foley and Professor John Belchem at the University of Liverpool was encouraging to the highest extent. Since the early drafts of my thesis I sought advice from William Cain, Second Deemster, 1993-98, and First Deemster and Clerk of the Rolls, 1998-2003, and Fred Kissack, Chief Secretary of the Isle of Man Government, 1989-2002. Both offered their thoughts to a degree much further than might have been expected.

My additional thanks go to Mark Shimmin, Chief Financial Officer of the Isle of Man Government; John Cashen, Chief Financial Officer, 1991-2001; Martin Caley at the Economic Affairs Division of the Isle of Man Treasury; Ray Todd at the Customs and Excise Division of the Isle of Man Treasury; Alan Franklin, Wendy Thirkettle, Pat Griffiths, Andrea Roberts and Diana Jones at the Manx National Heritage Library and Archives; Miriam Critchlow and Meic Pierce Owen at the Isle of Man Public Record Office; Geoff Haywood and the staff at the Tynwald Library; Colin Morgan and Ken Linkman at the University of Liverpool's Sydney Jones Library; the staff at the British National Archives in Kew; the staff at the National Archives of Scotland in Edinburgh; John Beckerson; Frances Coakley; Frank Cowin; Nigel Crowe; Matthew Richardson.

The project has been made possible by the support of the Manx Heritage Foundation, and I am most grateful to its administrator Charles Guard for his assistance and advice.

My special thanks go yet again to my wife June, whose support has been at the heart of this and my previous projects. June has once more put up with the changes to our life as a result of my research and writing with no complaint but with lots of encouragement and interest. She is, as she has been since we were both seventeen, my best friend and kindest critic. I dedicate this book to her with all my love.

ABBREVIATIONS

AP	Atholl Papers
BP	Bluett Papers
BHP	Bridge House Papers
GML	George Moore Letter Books
GOCB	Government Office Correspondence Books
GOP	Government Office Papers
HKJ	House of Keys Journals
HO	Home Office Papers
IOMNHAS	Proceedings of the Isle of Man Natural History and Antiquarian Society
JMM	Journals of the Manx Museum
LCJ	Legislative Council Journals
MB	Manx Books
MHK	Member of the House of Keys
MNHL	Manx National Heritage Library and Archives
MP	Member of Parliament
NA	British National Archives
PC	Privy Council Papers
PP	Parliamentary Papers
T	Treasury Papers
£ s d	pounds, shillings and pence
£1	= 20 shillings = 240 (old) pence
1 shilling	= 1/- or 1s = 12 (old) pence or 12d = 5 (new) pence or 5p
1 penny	= 1d
f.	Folio number
p.	Page number

Illustrations

Map of the Isle of Man, 1845 6
Extract from the *Chronicles of Man* 9
Manx cottage 14
'Squaresail' fishing boat 16
Castletown Bay, c.1650 19
Castle Rushen, c.1650 20
James Murray, second Duke of Atholl, ... 25
Sir George Moore MHK 30
Squadrons of Thurot and Elliott, 1760 34
John Murray, third Duke of Atholl, and Lady Charlotte, Baroness Strange 38
George Grenville MP 41
Castle Rushen, c.1760 45
Revestment Proclamation, 1765 46
Douglas, 1789 52
Peel, 1784 53
Brig *Caesar* 55
John Murray, fourth Duke of Atholl 58
House of Keys, 1790 61
John Taubman (senior) MHK 62
John Taubman (junior) MHK 62
John Quayle 62
George Quayle MHK 62
Report of the Commissioners of Inquiry, 1792 64
John Christian Curwen MP MHK 68
Bishop George Murray 73
Governor Cornelius Smelt 76
Castle Mona 78
Robert Fargher 82
Governor John Ready 86
Charles Poulett Thomson MP 88
Sir William Hillary 90
Mona's Isle 95

Letter to John Courtney Bluett, 1837 97
Douglas Customs House, 1841 106
Dr John Bowring MP 109
John Henry Thomas Manners-Sutton MP 112
Manx Sun and *Mona's Herald*, 1844 113
Douglas Market Place, 1846 119
Governor Charles Hope 122
Shipbuilding in Castletown, c.1850 126
Laxey waterwheel and mines, 1854 127
James Wilson MP 129
George Dumbell MHK 133
William Callister MHK 133
Punch magazine, 1853 136
End of the licence system, 1853 141
Dumbell banknote 148
Governor Henry Loch 149
Abernethy breakwater, 1865 152
James Brown 155
Sir George Grey MP 157
Hugh Culling Eardley Childers MP 159
Isle of Man Customs, Harbours and Public Purposes Act, 1866 164
House of Keys Election Act, 1866 168
Royal Proclamation dissolving the self-elected House of Keys, 1866 169
First public election of the House of Keys, 1867 171
Isle of Man development 174
Tynwald Court 175
Governor Spencer Walpole 178
Tea advertisement, *Isle of Man Examiner*, 1890 182
Reginald Earle Welby 184
Sir James Gell 187
Tobacco and free education, *Manx Sun*, 1892 189
Thomas Thurman, 1895 191
Douglas alms houses, c.1898 192
Governor Sir West Ridgeway 194
Summer visitors, c.1895 196
Local residents, c.1895 197

Illustrations Acknowlegdement

The author would like to thank the following individuals and organisations for permission to use images from their collections:

Page numbers:
38, 58 Blair Atholl Estate;
41, 88, 109, 129, 157, 159, 184 National Portrait Gallery, London;
112 State Library of Victoria;
126 Frank Cowin Collection;
136 Punch Magazine;
164, 168 Tynwald Library;
all other images by courtesy of Manx National Heritage Library and Archives.

INTRODUCTION

Revelation

This book is based upon my University of Liverpool PhD thesis *Development of the Fiscal Relationship between the Isle of Man and Britain: Revestment Act to Common Purse Arrangement, 1765-1895*. The term 'fiscal' is used when referring to matters relating to government finances, in particular the income from customs duties. I have revised, where necessary, my original writing, explained in more depth the earlier unique history of the Isle of Man, including the fascinating story of the smuggling trade, and, for a better balance, condensed the latter stages of the chapter on the Common Purse Arrangement.

The book investigates the issues surrounding the development of the financial relationship between the Isle of Man and Britain during the seventeenth, eighteenth and nineteenth centuries and concentrates principally on the concerns surrounding the Manx customs revenue. The main means of raising public finances for funding the costs of government and improving the infrastructure of the Island was through taxation by way of customs tariffs applied to a range of goods. The book also seeks to identify how the amounts of expenditure were decided, how the issue of the surplus revenue was handled and how the levels of customs duties were determined. It investigates what the roles of the British authorities, the British appointed Governors and the Island's ancient parliament, Tynwald, were. It considers the status of Tynwald and how Britain's imposed sovereignty over the Island had major consequences on limiting and controlling the financial prerogative of the Manx parliament. Throughout this time, the Island experienced a period of remarkable evolution, a period which saw the ending of feudalism, the beginnings of constitutional and fiscal reforms and the transformation of the Manx economy.

The issues associated with the constitutional standing between the two countries and the legitimacy or otherwise for Britain to assume financial authority for the Isle of Man's customs arrangements feature in each relevant context in this study - politics and money always being intertwined. The research bears out that it was at times an acrimonious story and featured many uneasy negotiations and mutual uncertainties at political and officer level. The bargaining carried out by the Governors with the British authorities in the latter part of the nineteenth century was more cordial. But it must be pointed out that on occasions during their dealings with the Island, even up to most recent times, Westminster and Whitehall, either ignorantly or deliberately, have frequently overlooked the fact that there has been another parliament concerned, Tynwald.

However, any considerations regarding the extent of Tynwald's powers and the relationship the two countries shared must take into account that, whilst it was not part of the United Kingdom of Great Britain and Northern Ireland, the Isle of Man was part of the British Empire and a dependency of the British Crown. Britain's imperial policy of securing beneficial rights for itself in the overseas colonies it settled and appropriated had at its heart the concept of parliamentary sovereignty. Indeed, it considered it was the supreme authority and could pass legislation for enactment throughout all the territories of the empire; an authority that was assumed to be absolute and unlimited. This meant that Tynwald Court and the Island's common law and customary rights were seen by Britain as offering no protection against the might of parliamentary sovereignty. There was never any Manx representation in the British Parliament or its policy forming institutions that, if there had been, could have directly influenced the landmark economic and political decision-making on the Island's future. The various departments of the British Government and the externally appointed Governors exercised an overwhelming dominance over Tynwald. These powers ensured that Tynwald's role in dealing with fiscal matters, though improved over time, was always weak. It had little input in the making or influencing of policies affecting customs revenue and determining the size and shape of the public economy.

The book traces and reveals the significance of the varying changes in the relationship between the Isle of Man and Britain as a result of the following events:

- The policies of the Lords of Man.
- The legal trade and the smuggling 'trade' of the Island.
- Britain's reclamation of its sovereign rights by the introduction of the Revestment Act.
- The perseverance of the fourth Duke of Atholl.
- The concerns and aims of the financial protectionists and the political reformers.
- The attempts by Britain to assimilate the Island's customs duties to its own.
- The Island's acquisition of some control of its principal public revenue.
- The democratising of the House of Keys.
- The establishment between the two countries of the Common Purse Arrangement.

Sources

The progress of the Isle of Man's fiscal situation during the seventeenth, eighteenth and nineteenth centuries has been a somewhat neglected subject. This book seeks to rectify the situation by studying and analysing the evidence of the many primary source materials relative to the circumstances surrounding the development of the customs revenue system. Access to archives which were not previously available now allows for much more detailed research of what is a quite specialised subject.

Introduction

The archives at the Manx National Heritage Library and Archives and the British National Archives are more accessible to the researcher than they ever have been, giving much better opportunities for informed and extended opinions. The research for this book has been enabled by the vast amount of archival records available at both these national repositories, and these records have been the principal sources of study. Parliamentary proceedings, statutes, reports and papers were reasonably accessible at both centres.

Official and private papers kept at Manx National Heritage have been essential tools for research, and the continuing revelation of once inaccessible records augurs well for future studies. Hand-written records of both branches of Tynwald Court and the papers and letter books of the respective Governors were most informative. The various individual and family records gave a fascinating insight into the historical events and the personalities of those involved.

Online access to the National Archives was invaluable in preparing for actual visits. Treasury, Home Office, Customs and Privy Council files kept at the National Archives often linked up with the information found at the Manx National Heritage Library and Archives. The authentication of various historical documents by connected information discovered in several sources was most important in confirming and understanding the complex circumstances of the Isle of Man's history.

Early Manx newspapers carried little local information, mainly featuring accounts of British and world affairs which appealed to a fairly narrow section of the population. However, in the early part of the nineteenth century the newspapers became more concerned with Island news, and their editors and publishers became heavily involved in calls for economic and political reforms. Various directories have proved to be useful references.

The Tynwald Library was able to provide access to copies of British Acts of Parliament. The Sydney Jones Library at the University of Liverpool was also a rewarding means of referring to official parliamentary records.

Previous studies

There are some notable contemporary accounts of events taking place in the Island which were recorded by a number of temporary residents who were writing from a variety of standpoints at or about the time of the pertinent historical happenings. Examples include the 1656 studies of William Blundell, a Royalist officer and topographer, who compiled *A History of the Isle of Man*, and James Chaloner, a parliamentarian and antiquarian, who wrote *A Short Treatise of the Isle of Man*. Chaloner had been appointed by Lord Fairfax (who had been given authority of the Island under the Commonwealth in the aftermath of the English Civil War) as one of three commissioners to look after the affairs of the Island and was subsequently appointed Governor after the restoration of the monarchy. Another commissioner, George Waldron, sent to the Island almost one hundred years later to keep watch on its trading situation, produced a study which became *The History and Description of the Isle of Man* in 1744. The entries relating to the Isle of Man in the journal kept by John Murray, the fourth Duke of Atholl, which feature in the *Chronicles of the Atholl and Tullibardine Families*, provide a most illuminating insight into the thinking of one of the principal characters in the Island's not too distant past. In her 1816 book, *History of the Isle of Man*, Mrs Hannah Bullock provides a fascinating commentary and observation on society (including 'An Example presented to the Ladies for their Imitation') and the manners of the various classes of people living in the Island. In 1845 Joseph Train, a Scottish antiquarian and correspondent of Sir Walter Scott, was resident in the Island writing *An Historical and Statistical Account of the Isle of Man*. These and many other contemporary accounts are most informative and enlightening, but care must be taken to read them critically, bearing in mind at all times the particular interests and persuasions of the authors.

Various officials of Tynwald Court have produced useful studies of both their own and previous times which provide a means of not only comprehending the past but appreciating the thinking of those directly involved in the forming of Manx history. In 1767 Charles Searle, the Island's Attorney General, gave his account of the Island's condition in *A Short View of the Present State of the Isle of Man*. 'An Abstract of the Laws, Customs and Ordinances of the Isle of Man', originally compiled by Deemster John Parr in 1690 and subsequently edited by Deemster Sir James Gell when he was Attorney General and produced in volume 12 of *The Manx Society* in 1867, is an invaluable reference work which was expanded on to give a detailed discourse on the Island's history. A most fascinating account is *Land of Home Rule: An Essay on the History and Constitution of the Isle of Man* of 1893 in which Spencer Walpole included a description of the Island's recent history and additionally wrote it from his perspective as a Governor. Walpole had been a Tory but, disillusioned by Disraeli's foreign policy, he became a Liberal well before he took up his appointment in the Island. The Speaker of the House of Keys, A. W. Moore, wrote his most informative *A History of the Isle of Man* in 1900, which stands to this day as the most comprehensive overview of Manx history. The personalities and leanings of each of these writers give interesting opinions and slants on the Island's changing affairs.

More recent historians and academics have added to the knowledge of the Island's fiscal and constitutional situations. Thomas Grindley, in his early twentieth-century works, provides a most useful study of Britain's determination to regain control of the Island from its feudal Lords and revest the sovereign rights to the British Crown. Robert Forster, the Manx born schoolteacher and historian, researched the constitutional, fiscal and social reform movements of the nineteenth century whilst at university at the beginning of the 1950s and continued this interest through his

Introduction

membership of the Isle of Man Natural History and Antiquarian Society. Forster's writings have been a crucial early reference point for this study. Ann Harrison, a previous Manx National Heritage archivist and librarian, was also interested in these aspects of Manx history and produced a number of related papers in the *Proceedings of the Isle of Man Natural History and Antiquarian Society*. It was not until 1964, when J. W. Birch's useful piece of specialist work *The Isle of Man: A Study in Economic Geography* was published, that the Island's economic history received some extensive formal academic attention. Since then there have been a number of further authoritative studies undertaken which are most enlightening, including *Devolution at Work: A Case Study of the Isle of Man* by David Kermode which analyses the more recent happenings and *The Lordship of Man Under the Stanleys: Government and Economy in the Isle of Man, 1580-1704* by Roger Dickinson which gives a detailed account of the earlier times. The chapters by John Belchem and Derek Winterbottom in *A New History of the Isle of Man, volume 5: The Modern Period, 1830-1999* are works of importance which consider the Island's relevant history during this time of great progress.

There have been a number of essays in the publications of *The Manx Society* (1858-1907), the *Journals of the Manx Museum* (1924-80) and the *Proceedings of the Isle of Man Natural History and Antiquarian Society* (1879 to date) which were invaluable starting points.

Whilst some of the opinions of modern authorities on the Island's constitutional situation are at times interestingly at variance one with another, their considerations of the complicated ramifications concerning the fiscal situation, in particular the customs arrangements which took place in the Island throughout the seventeenth, eighteenth and nineteenth centuries, have been somewhat limited, caused mainly by the extent of the breadth and particular focus of their studies. This book rectifies the situation by providing a comprehensive account of the far reaching effects on the Isle of Man as a direct result of its controversial development, the consequences of which have been in a major way responsible for the Island's fiscal situation as it is today.

John Belchem, editor of volume five of *A New History of the Isle of Man* produced in 2000, wrote in his introduction that 'the purpose of this volume is to encourage further research in modern Manx history'. This book seeks to advance this aim by exploring and explaining the Isle of Man's unfamiliar fiscal history and its intriguing development through the recent centuries, whilst at the same time revealing the nature and purposes of the various fascinating characters involved in the making of the country's unique identity.

A map of the Isle of Man drawn by R Creighton from Samuel Lewis, Topographical Dictionary of England, 1845.

Chapter I

THE ISLE OF MAN
A SEPARATE IDENTITY

Present

The Isle of Man geographically occupies a central position both in the Irish Sea and the British Isles. The Island is situated some thirty miles from England, seventeen from Scotland, thirty-three from Ireland and forty-three from Wales.[1] It is approximately thirty-and-a-quarter miles in length along its main axis from the Point of Ayre in the north to the Sound in the south (thirty-two miles to Caigher Point on the Calf of Man islet), a maximum of eleven miles wide at right angles to this axis and 227 square miles in area.[2] A range of hills stretches obliquely across it, the highest of which is Snaefell at 2,036 feet. Between these hills lie well-defined valleys. Around the flat northern plain are long sandy beaches which contrast markedly with the rocky cliffs and sheltered bays around the rest of the coastline.

The 2006 interim census revealed that the resident population was 80,058.[3] Less than half of those were Manx born (38,069, 47.6%). The major centres of population were Douglas, Onchan, Ramsey, Peel, Port Erin, Braddan and Castletown.

The Isle of Man is a self-governing territory, though subject to certain powers held by the British Crown. It is responsible for its own laws, currency, taxes, public expenditure, civil administration and social policies, all legislated for through its ancient parliament, Tynwald.[4] Tynwald is reputed to be the world's longest continuous parliament. The date of its establishment is uncertain, though it is of Norse origin and its millennium was celebrated in 1979. Tynwald Court comprises two branches: the House of Keys, which is the lower branch and the legislative chamber, and the Legislative Council, which is the upper branch and the revising chamber. The two assemblies sit separately but come together to deal with finance, policy and secondary legislation. The twenty-four Members of the House of Keys are elected by the people every five years.[5] They select a Speaker from amongst their number who chairs their debates. The Legislative Council consists of eight members elected by the Keys. It also has three ex officio members: the President of Tynwald, the Attorney General and the Lord Bishop of Sodor and Man, of whom only the Bishop has a vote.[6] The Island's legal system is headed by two Deemsters who are the senior judges for civil and criminal cases in the superior courts of law.[7] The Deemsters promulgate new Acts, the titles of which they read in Manx, one of the Goidelic group of Celtic languages, and English at an open-air ceremony on the ancient site of Tynwald Hill in St John's as part of the official proceedings which take place at the Island's Tynwald Day national celebrations each 5 July, old midsummer's day. Government in the Island is based on a ministerial system.

The Isle of Man's anomalous relationship with Britain is certainly something of a curiosity.[8] Whilst its people have British nationality, it is not part of the realm of the United Kingdom of Great Britain and Northern Ireland.[9] It is a dependency of the British Crown. Guernsey and Jersey are similar dependencies, though with different constitutional backgrounds and structures to that of the Isle of Man. Through its relationship with Britain, the Island is part of the British Commonwealth of Nations. The reigning British monarch is also its monarch. The Crown's resident representative is the Governor, charged to protect the Crown's interests but whose powers and functions have diminished considerably in recent years.[10] The Crown maintains the right to have ultimate responsibility for overseeing the Island's 'good government' - presently through the Department for Constitutional Affairs and previously through the Home Office - and in this respect acts on the advice of ministers of the British Government in their capacity as Privy Councillors. With due consultation, the Crown appoints the Island's Governor, Deemsters, Attorney General and Bishop, exercises the power of Royal Assent over all its primary legislation, guarantees its defence and assumes responsibility in law for its international relations. The Isle of Man is not represented in the British Parliament, and Acts of Parliament do not automatically extend to it.

The Island has a high degree of autonomy, enjoying domestic political and legislative competence and has a range of extended world-wide contacts. It currently has a special relationship with the European Union by virtue of 'Protocol 3 of the Act of Accession of the United Kingdom' of 1972 whereby it is neither a member state nor an associate member, though it is part of the customs territory and there is free trade in industrial and agricultural products. It neither contributes to nor receives any direct funding from the finances of the Union.

Past

The fiscal and constitutional situation of the Isle of Man has a long and interesting history. For centuries people have been attracted to this tiny but strategically sited landmass, pivotal to the important sea trade and communication routes from Scandinavia in the north and continental Europe in the south. Evidence of the Island's early history is abundant with Neolithic, Celtic and Viking sites, and over the centuries there has been a fusion of cultures which is most evident in the Island's archaeology, language and place names. Throughout most of its chequered history it has had some degree of internal self-government, whether it was under the authority of Norway, Scotland, England or Britain. The extent of that self-government has varied over the years, but at

Description in Latin of the seizure of the Isle of Man by Godred Crovan in 1079, featured in Cronica Regum Mannie et Insularum: Chronicles of the Kings of Man and the Isles.

no time has the Island been wholly integrated into any other state.

The system of government in the Island, which has lasted down the years, has its origins in Norse settlements between the ninth and thirteenth centuries. The Isle of Man together with the Hebrides became the Kingdom of Man and the Isles when Godred Crovan, a Norse-Gaelic ruler from Dublin, seized the Island in 1079 at the Battle of Sky Hill, following which he:

> granted the southern part of the island to the few islanders who had stayed with him, and the northern part to the remainder of the Manxmen, on condition that none of them

should at any time dare lay claim to any part of the land for himself by right of inheritance. Whence it has come to pass that up until the present day the entire island is the property of the king alone, and that all its dues belong to him.[11]

The Isle of Man then became the seat of power for this Viking maritime kingdom. The islanders were dispossessed of their land and became tenants at will of the king. The establishment of Tynwald Court and twenty-four Keys originates from the time of Norse rule, when 'xxiiij [24] free Houlders, viz. viij [8] in the Out Isles, and xvj [16] in your Land of Mann, and that was in King Orreys Days', were the chosen representatives of the freemen living in the Kingdom of Man and the Isles.[12]

After many years of negotiations and battles between the two countries, the Island was surrendered by Norway to Scotland in 1266. For some time following, it was fought over by Scotland and England. In 1333 England took firm possession of it, and since 1399 the Crown has claimed absolute sovereignty, with a brief period (1651-60) under the Commonwealth government established by Parliament as a result of the English Civil War. The period from 1405 until 1765, and then to a lesser extent to 1829, was principally dominated by two essentially hereditary feudal lordships: the Earls of Derby (the House of Stanley, from the north-west of England) and the Dukes of Atholl (the House of Murray, from the central Highlands of Scotland).

As a reward for his services to the Crown, the Island was given for life to Sir John Stanley by Henry IV in 1405.[13] The following year 'all the Islands, Castle, Pele and Lordship aforesaid, together with the Royalties, Regalities, Franchises, Liberties, Sea Ports, and all Things to Port reasonably and duly belonging' were granted in perpetuity to Sir John and his descendants in return for simply 'yielding to our heirs Kings of England two ffalcons upon the Coronation days of the s[ai]d heirs'.[14] The Stanleys assumed the title of King of Man, but then changed the regal title to that of Lord of Man, probably considering it politically prudent to do so in homage to the English Crown. James Stanley, the seventh Earl of Derby, later put it that 'to be a great lord is a more honourable title than a petty king'.[15] The Lords of Man possessed extensive regal powers by which they had the rights to summon and preside at Tynwald Court, appoint the Bishop, Lord's Council, House of Keys and civic officials, give assent to all statutes, be the ultimate legal authority in the courts of law (including the imposition of the death penalty) and confer ecclesiastical patronage. The Island became part of the Lords' landed property, with all the responsibilities and lucrative rights and privileges which that entailed. Their proprietorial privileges included the benefits of the revenue from the customs duties, manorial and mineral rights, rents, tithes and other similar financial advantages. The Stanley family was rewarded again when Sir Thomas Stanley was created as the first Baron Stanley in 1456.[16] His son, another Thomas Stanley, was appointed as the first

Earl of Derby in 1485 by his stepson Henry VII for allegiance in the struggle against Richard III.[17]

The Earls of Derby were succeeded as Lords of Man by the Dukes of Atholl in 1736. The detrimental effect on the British revenue by the smuggling of foreign goods into Britain from the Isle of Man led the British Government to treat with the Atholls to purchase back the Crown's sovereign rights and consequently repossess the Island by the Revestment Act in 1765. The Atholl family's interests were finally severed in 1829.

The Journey

In order to understand the circumstances which the people of the Isle of Man found themselves in from the mid-seventeenth century and on into the late nineteenth, this book uncovers the fascinating and, at times, sensational stories behind the historical events. It reveals how the Island progressed, why Britain came to take control of the customs duties and revenue for its own purposes, the different effects the economic changes had on the fortunes of the many groups of people living there, where the pressure came from to alter the Island's relationship with Britain, how the periodic difficulties were handled and who benefited from the situation and at whose expense. It traces what motivated the actions of the Lords of Man, created the smuggling 'trade', led to Britain firmly imposing its sovereignty upon the Island, brought about some much needed reforms and created the unique financial arrangement which is still the basis of the Isle of Man's financial success today.

The Isle of Man's development has been greatly influenced by the nature of the association it has with Britain. Whilst the Island's physical insularity in the centre of the Irish Sea has never totally isolated it from the influence of its near neighbour, it has undoubtedly assisted in the retention of its political separateness. The Crown has claimed sovereignty over the Island since the fourteenth century, but the Island has never been incorporated into Britain, remaining constitutionally responsible through its own legislative assembly, Tynwald. It is Tynwald which gives authority to the Isle of Man, and in any debate about its parliamentary competency and fiscal independence it needs to be borne in mind that Tynwald owes its legitimacy to an earlier tradition than that of Westminster.

There were many changes brought about by the efforts of various individuals, either acting alone or in association with others of a like mind, whose ambitions and actions over the centuries have resulted in the basis of the Island's historical situation. Whether it was the efforts of the Lords of Man to enhance their personal exchequers or the British navigation and trade Acts or the establishment of a great smuggling network operating out of the Island - which in turn would secure the fortunes of many Manx families - the early threads of this story are linked with power and money. These two factors continued to dominate the situation and feature as a continuing theme in each chapter of this book. The success of the smuggling trade, involving people like Sir George Moore, resulted in a concerned Britain buying back the rights of the Lords of Man and regaining control of the Manx customs revenue in order to protect its own financial interests. But the determination of the young John Murray, the fourth Duke of Atholl, in his attempts to limit his family's losses was an impediment to the Island's need to progress away from its recent feudal history. The ambitions of the Manx people themselves were limited by these machinations, and, whilst some individuals certainly enriched themselves as a direct result, others struggled simply to survive. The export business was inhibited by the restrictive measures placed upon it as a result of Britain not allowing full free trade between the two countries, and the ever present possibility of the assimilation of the Manx customs duties to those of Britain and even the incorporation of the Isle of Man into the United Kingdom were constant threats that the Island's inhabitants suffered. The imposition of a licence system on the importation of luxury goods benefited no one but a select few. The self-interested establishment was embodied in the self-elected Members of the House of Keys whose principal ambitions were not for their fellow citizens but for the protection of themselves. Protests against the various different but conjoined issues came from protectionists such as Sir William Hillary and John Courtney Bluett and reformers such as Sir John Bowring and the newspaper editors Robert Fargher and James Brown. The success of the summer visitor trade gave the Island a much needed lift to both its public and private economy. In the latter part of the nineteenth century the financial and constitutional problems were finally addressed and resolved by the resolute actions of Governors Henry Loch, Spencer Walpole and West Ridgeway.

Chapter 2

SMUGGLING

Trade

The story begins during the latter part of the sixteenth century and on into the seventeenth when the Isle of Man's economic situation was at a low ebb. Unfair land tenure regulations and crippling fishing dues were causing hardship amongst many of the farmers, crofters and fishermen. These impositions were a direct result of the policies of the Lords of Man and contributed in no small part to the distressed circumstances many of the Manx people lived in. The policies of Britain did nothing to help either. The Island was considered to be one of its 'dominions beyond the seas' and was therefore not permitted to be fully part of the free trading system which operated between the British ports, the so-called 'coasting trade'. As a consequence, any legitimate trade between the two countries was made very difficult. However, matters would improve, and from the latter part of the seventeenth century circumstances would begin to change and lead to a long period during which the Isle of Man used its independent laws and customs duties to benefit from a new lucrative trade - smuggling.

But whilst smuggling became a way of life for many residents, a large proportion of the population was primarily involved in farming and fishing, and these occupations were the mainstays of the fragile Manx economy. The straitened nature of the times meant that rural workers and their families lived simple lives in stone and clay cottages which had compacted earth flooring and roofs thatched with broom held down by netting and ropes.[18] The rectangular building contained one or possibly two rooms with a large open hearth at one of the gable ends where gorse sticks and peat kept the pot and the family warm, and a hole in the roof allowed the smoke to escape. In such 'mere hovels . . . doth the man, his wife, and children, cohabit, and in many places with ye geese and ducks under ye bed, the cocks and hens over his head, the cow and calf at the bed's feet'. The basic diet of the majority of people consisted of herrings, oat cakes, salted butter and milk. Some also had 'a store of bacon, fresh butter, geese, ducks, hens, capons, eggs, piggs, etc., to feed upon', and these and other items such as yarn, flax, hemp and honey were often sold at fairs and markets or exchanged with shopkeepers in the towns for iron, starch, soap, candles, pitch, tar and other necessities. Most farmers and crofters cultivated some type of corn, including rye, wheat, barley or oats, and reared cattle, goats, pigs, horses and sheep, including the coarse-fleeced loaghtyn.[19] Some sold 'rabbits at twopence the couple, a fat goose for sixpence, hens

Typical stone and clay cottage, Bride.

and ducks at threepence a piece, and usually twelve eggs a penny'.[20] The fishermen's work was more seasonal, with herring the most abundant catch, but there was also a 'great store of salmons, codds, haddocks, macarels, rayes, place, thornbecks, and more' present in the surrounding waters.[21] Shellfish were also caught to be sold, 'a large lobster for a penny, and very often a dozen of crabs'.[22]

Tenants of land belonging to the Lord of Man historically occupied their freeholds by straw tenure, a system whereby property was held indefinitely from father to son and could be surrendered, sold or exchanged by handing over a piece of straw at the manorial court where the transaction was formally recorded.[23] The tenants, although tenants at will, began to consider the estates as their own and sold and exchanged them without permission. This practice was temporarily placed in check in 1582 when any changes in tenancy became subject to the issue of a licence by the Lord or his Council.[24] The straw tenure was dealt a further temporary blow eleven years later when Ferdinando Stanley, the fifth Earl of Derby, ordered that:

> If any Person shall pretend Title to any Farme, Houses or Ground within the said Isle, and do not exhibit his Bill in Writing for the same . . . whereby it may be entered of Record within the Space of twenty-one Years next after he or his Ancestors have been dispossed thereof, that then he or his Successors claiming after him to be utterly excluded and barred from making any Title thereunto for ever.[25]

Poorer tenants suffered financial hardship because of the low prices they received for their produce, and they complained that they were 'greatly oppressed and impoverished by selling away the Corn in Winter to the richer Soart that ingross and export the same'.[26] Tithes were paid to the Church on a multitude of produce and livestock, including corn, flax, hemp, wool, eggs, butter, cheese, honey, sheep, lambs, calves, colts, geese, cockerels and hens.[27] Whilst the rights to sell or transfer estates at pleasure had been restored in 1610, insecurity was again felt in 1643 when the ancient system of straw tenure was once more restricted by being limited to twenty-one years or three generations.[28] These were not necessarily three successive generations, but rather three existing lives. Farm workers earned very low wages, ploughmen were paid 13s 4d a year, drivers 10s and horsemen 8s.[29] Times could be hard for the rural workers and their families.

The success of the herring fishery was very important in the welfare and the economy of the Island, particularly at times of poor harvests. Fishermen not only had to deal with the vagaries of uncertain catches but also had to pay significant dues to the civil and ecclesiastical authorities. The Lord historically received one-fifth of all the herring caught by each boat.[30] This portion of the catch was known as the Castle Maze because it was used for the provision of the various garrisons. There was also a customs duty of 1d for each maze of herring.[31] An additional due of a kybbonfull of herring from each catch was paid to the Water Bailiff, the official who had jurisdiction over the operation of the fishing and the collection of the customs revenues.[32] The Church also received fishing tithes, including the requirements that 'every Master of every Fishing Boat shall cause all Fish to be brought above the full Sea Mark, and there pay truely the Tyth' and 'when Herring Fishing is, the Proctor shall take his Tyth where the Boat doth ground and land'.[33] Fishermen were finding it difficult to make a profitable living, and circumstances became so bad by 1613 that Deemster Ewan Christian, Clerk of the Rolls John Halsall and two other Tynwald officials reported to Lady Elizabeth, Countess of Derby (she and her husband William Stanley, the sixth Earl of Derby, were joint rulers of the Island) that:

> because of the great Imposicon by an anncyent Statute in this Isle for paying of Customs Heyrings (called Castle Mazes) in Tyme of Heyringe Ffishinge, not onlie Strangers have refrayned to come the late Fishinge of this Isle, but also the Islanders themselves being thereby discouraged, did not shewe their willinge Minds, nor consequentlie use their industrious Paynes in and about the Fishinge.[34]

The levies not only affected the fishing community. There were problems with certain members of the higher ranks of Manx society attempting to avoid their dues. An order was issued reminding them that at 'every Herring Fishing upon the Coast of Mann, all Manner of Persons, whatsoever they be, Barrons, Officers, or Soldiers, to pay the Castle Maze and Customes as hath been heretofore used'.[35]

Example of the ancient Manx 'squaresail' fishing boat.

The townspeople lived in thatched cottages which generally had two storeys, with a loft on the upper level reached by an outside stone staircase or wooden ladder.[36] Some houses in Castletown and Douglas had tiled roofs. The loft was long and narrow with room for two beds, and 'ye walls very thick, so as these rooms commonly are not so lightsome as you may desire, but of purpose are they thus contrived and for warmth, and to keep out the bitter cold and bleake winds which in the winter season are there very frequent and boisterous'. Shops had a warehouse on the upper floor, with an additional building for the shopkeeper to store items such as 'barrels of beer, the barrl'd herrings, and powder'd beef, and for all other comodities wherewith he trafficketh, besides all his other lumber'. The upper floor of this building was let to lodgers 'for the most part every house there entertaineth lodgers, and is a kind of tavern'. It was claimed that the local merchants and shopkeepers had 'the best trade or profession', and 'these there thrive most', being able to import goods to 'sell 'em again at double the rate that they are sold [in England]'.

The levels of wages for general workers and tradespeople were laid down by Tynwald Court.[37] Artisans such as tailors, masons, carpenters, shipwrights, hoopers, slaters, thatchers and joiners, were paid 4d a day 'with meat and drink', and apprentices 2d. Some tradespeople were paid by the job: 'every woolen weaver shall have for every yard of woolen cloth for blankett sufficiently wrought an ob; for every four great hundred breadth of keare, ob qs, for every yard of medlie, Id qs', and 'every blacksmith shall have for laying of every coulter 1d, for making of every coulter 2d, for making of every new sock 2d, for making and laying of every wing an ob'.[38]

Tynwald appointed four local merchants to assist the Captains of the towns and the Water Bailiff in dealing with the non-local traders, known as 'merchant strangers', who brought in most of the commodities which were not produced locally. On certain articles the merchant strangers paid higher customs duties, often double those paid by locals.[39] The principal imports were coal, pitch, timber, iron, manufactured goods and wine, and the principal exports were cattle, hides, sheep, wool, cloth and a small amount of corn and herring.[40] Attempts were made, with limited success, to establish manufacturing industries, including linen works, brick making and mining.[41] Trade into and out of the Island was seemingly insignificant, with only low levels of ingates and outgates (revenue from the import and export customs duties) being recorded.[42]

The situation was summed up by James Stanley, the seventh Earl of Derby (known in Manx Gaelic as *Yn Stanlagh Mooar*: 'The Great Stanley'), when he wrote in 1648 to his son, Charles, Lord Strange, that 'this Isle will never flourish until some trading be'.[43] In 1653 James Chaloner, a future Governor but at that time acting as one of the commissioners looking after the Island for Lord Fairfax who was temporarily in possession of it on behalf of Parliament, included in a report a short chapter entitled 'Concerning the Trade of the Isle' in which he stated that 'the trade of this Island . . . hardly deserveth a chapter by itself'.[44]

'The Trade'

The problem of poor commerce meant that 'the trade' the Island would eventually turn to was the smuggling of goods into Britain and Ireland. 'The trade' was a contemporary euphemism used to describe smuggling. It is critical in considering this particular aspect of history to examine the imperial ambitions of Britain and the extent of the Manx smuggling. Both these circumstances impacted on the relationship between the two countries.

From 1651 various navigation and trade Acts were brought into force by Britain to encourage its commerce, establish its supremacy in the world's maritime trade, finance its international endeavours and defend its shores.[45] The costly wars with its European neighbours led to Britain forbidding any trade with its enemies, imposing high tariffs on imported goods, prohibiting or restricting the importation of foreign goods likely to be competitive and requiring merchandise coming from and going to its colonies and plantations to be carried in British ships and go through British ports. As a consequence of Britain strictly regulating its colonial trade, its naval and merchant fleets rapidly increased in size and quality, resulting in it becoming a global superpower.

The navigation and trade Acts resulted in an unforeseen repercussion which gave indirect encouragement to smuggling from the Isle of Man with its less restrictive customs laws. British customs duties on certain foreign goods were practically prohibitive. This provided a temptation to smuggle such goods in large ships into Britain's shores, but direct access was often difficult and dangerous due to the preventive measures of the customs and excise service. However, the Island's position, constitutionally and physically, made it a prime entrepôt for smuggling. British Acts did not automatically apply to the Isle of Man. It was ideally centred in the British Isles for use as a base for receiving and dispatching foreign goods. Bulk cargoes brought into the Island in large ships were required to pay only the nominal Manx customs duties, and the volumes of imports were such that the Island could well afford to undercut the British and Irish tariffs yet still enrich the Lord's revenue. A host of smaller vessels could then run parcels of contraband out of the Island, past the revenue cutters, to be smuggled into secluded parts of Britain and Ireland. The merchants and entrepreneurs, with the connivance of the various Earls of Derby, made the most of the situation. None was better or worse than the other, each was trying to make the most of an opportunity which was always at risk of foreclosure. They excused their actions by claiming that what happened to the goods after they had been legally brought into the Island, paid the proper duties and then legally left the Island, was not their concern. At this stage they were certainly acting within Manx law. The final action, however, of running the same goods into Britain and Ireland, when legal trade turned to smuggling, was against British law. This was the reality of the situation, and, call it what you will, smuggling became a very lucrative way of life for many of the Island's inhabitants and ultimately reached such proportions that it was inevitable that Britain would eventually act against it.

There was a rapid increase in smuggling during the last twenty years of the seventeenth century and the early part of the eighteenth. This period marks the beginnings of a new era in Manx history. Many local merchants who were legally trading with Europe, the West Indies and Africa were also involved in smuggling, but a lot of the illicit dealers were the merchant strangers.[46] In about 1680:

> a band of adventurers came from Liverpool and settled themselves in Douglas, for the avowed purpose of carrying on an illicit trade; and by the advantages they held out, they soon induced ships to and from the East and West Indies, as well as those engaged in the Guinea [slave] trade, to touch at the Island, where they found a ready market for part of their cargoes, which were afterwards conveyed in Manx vessels (and by those means, eluding the customs duties) into other countries, as well as Great Britain and Ireland.[47]

One of the earliest contemporary references to the situation is contained in a letter written in 1682 by Edward Tyldesley (the eldest son of Sir Thomas Tyldesley who had been a fellow royalist commander with the seventh Earl of Derby) to the Commissioners of Customs in England.[48]

Goods being transported by small boats to and from a trading ship, with the Countess of Derby, family and attendants in the foreground, Castletown, c.1650.

Tyldesley informed them that the Island 'was become a magazine of all sorts of forreign goods . . . as might from thence clandestinely be imported into any of the three Kingdomes'. Whilst William Stanley, the ninth Earl of Derby, disputed this claim - he referred to Tyldesley as 'an inveterate papist who had been disobliged in the Isle of Man and had an inventing plausible pen' - and the Island considered itself to be outside Britain's jurisdiction, officers from the English Board of Customs were sent over to watch and report back on anything which might be adversely affecting Britain's own revenue.[49] These officers, of whom Tyldesley was most probably a covert agent living locally, were able to confirm that not only were foreign goods being brought directly to the Island from abroad but that certain articles were being legally shipped from Britain to the Island and legally claiming drawback (refund) of the higher British customs duties. Both types of imports were legally paying the lower Manx duties, legally being stored in warehouses, legally leaving the Island but then illegally being smuggled into Britain and Ireland. The Earl was most indignant over the customs officers' reports, later protesting that they were groundless.[50] However, he promised to be more diligent in the future in watching for smuggling activities. Much stricter regulations were introduced, and, to assist with this, orders were given by Governor William Sacheverell that from 1692 a customs office should be based at Castle Rushen in Castletown, the ancient capital.[51]

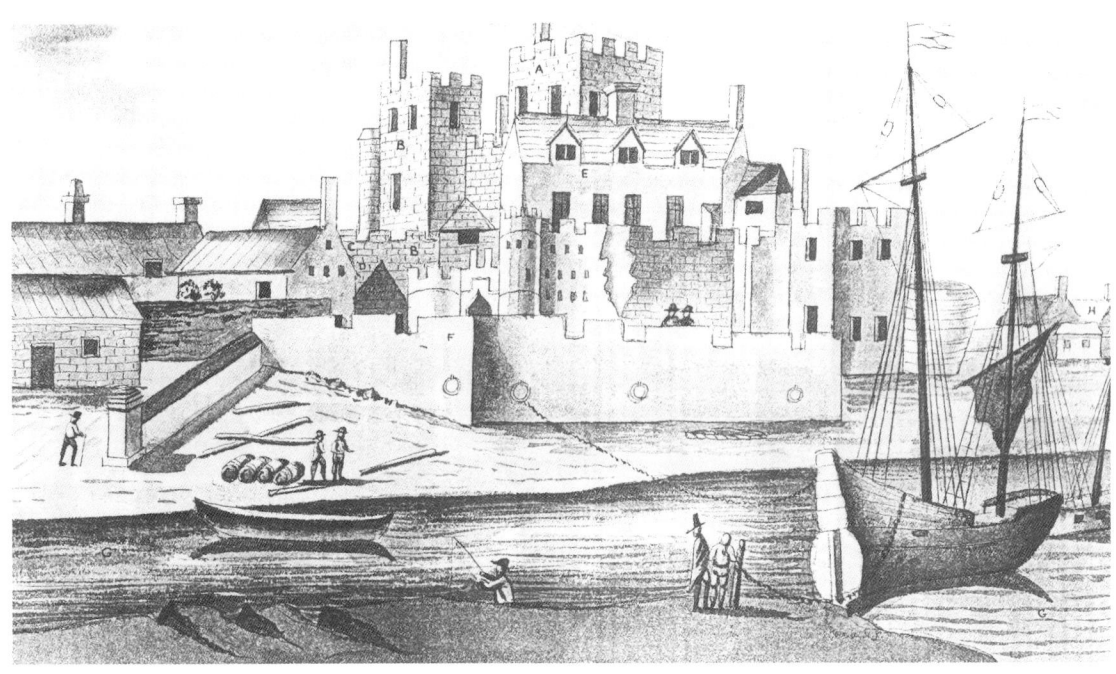

Castle Rushen, south-eastern view, c.1650.

Castle Rushen was the residence of the Lord of Man when he visited the Island. It was also the home of his Governor, as well as being the seat of government, courthouse, executive offices, gaol and garrison. The Governor, who was also chancellor and judge, presided over Tynwald Court where he was assisted by the Lord's (later, Legislative) Council to administer the Island's legislative and executive functions. The lower branch of Tynwald, the House of Keys, had legislative and judicial powers, interpreting the common law and assisting the Deemsters. The Keys were twenty-four freeholders who represented the people. The House of Keys was virtually a self-elected body, 'recruited solely from a few of the principal insular families, and, though they called themselves the representatives of the people, they really represented no one but themselves'.[52] When a vacancy occurred in the House, which only happened upon death, resignation or promotion to a position in the Council, the Keys nominated two persons to the Governor for his decision as to which one should then be appointed. This selection process gave the Keys the opportunity to propose further members of their tight knit establishment to positions of authority and gave the Governor virtually total control of Tynwald

Also in 1692 a new book of rates of customs duties was drawn up on the authority of the

Earl and enacted illegally without any consultation being made with or any consent being received from Tynwald as a whole.[53] The rates applied to 98 types of exported articles and 230 types of imported articles and imposed a 2½% ad valorem duty on all other imports. 'Ad valorem' was a percentage calculation of tax which was relative to the value of goods. Some years later the Earl wrote to Governor Nicholas Sankey urging him to direct the laws against the practice of smugglers openly discharging their cargoes into the Manx ports.[54] However, 'it is not improbable that there was a distinct understanding as to how far these instructions were to be carried out, and, indeed, it is clear that very little was done to check the practice'.[55] The financial interests of the Derbys were well served by the increased activities of the merchant strangers and the smugglers, and the lifting in 1697 of the long-standing restrictions placed on aliens (persons who were not Manx, naturalised or English) living and carrying out their businesses in the Island assisted in extending smuggling opportunities even further.[56]

Whilst smuggling was on the increase, farming was suffering as a consequence, and the Derbys were experiencing many problems with a number of the agricultural holdings. As more and more locals were becoming involved in the lucrative contraband trade they were consequently giving up their tenures. The money made from a small amount of low risk smuggling far outweighed the pittance made from working the land. Matters were not helped either by the poor husbandry methods which were making farming unproductive and uneconomic. Some tenants were reduced to giving their labour, produce or livestock in lieu of their rents. Others surrendered their properties as they could no longer afford to pay their rents in any form. The restricted and uncertain tenure of twenty-one years or three lifetimes had resulted in many of the holdings becoming neglected. The loss of income and the continuing administrative costs of maintaining the leasehold system affected the Derby family's fortune. The Manx people petitioned the ninth Earl in 1700, demanding the re-establishment of their original rights, and three years later the House of Keys drew up proposals to address the situation and sent a deputation of three of their members (Ewan Christian of Milntown and also of Unrigg in Cumberland, his relative another Ewan Christian of Lewaigue and John Stevenson of Balladoole) to England to meet James Stanley, the tenth Earl, who had succeeded to the title on the death of his brother in the previous year.[57] In consultation with the Bishop of Sodor and Man, Thomas Wilson, the Earl arranged for an 'Act for the perfect settling and confirmation of the estates, tenures, fines, rents, suits and services of the tennants' to be passed by Tynwald in 1704 to end the leaseholding system and restore the ancient customary inheritance from father to son in perpetuity.[58] Thus was resolved a long-standing grievance of the people which also ensured that the Derbys received a more certain rental income from their tenancies in the future.

The economic policies of Britain during this period were imbued with the imperative of conducting overseas trade for the benefit of its Exchequer.[59] The mercantilist framework which underpinned these policies meant that Britain needed to be competitive with other western European powers to protect its own commerce and further its imperial desires. Merchants needed government help through naval and military support and protection in the opening up and expansion of world markets. To assist in these ambitions, further navigation and trade Acts were needed. One such Act, 'An Act for better securing the duties of East India goods', was introduced in 1706 restricting the landing of goods from the East Indies into Britain only, thereby prohibiting their importation into any British possessions.[60] This legislation would have assisted in the prevention of smuggling from the Isle of Man. In a further and more specific attempt to address the situation, and shortly after the political union between England and Scotland in 1707, a proposal was made in Parliament to assimilate the Manx customs laws with those of Britain.[61] Neither the Act nor the proposed assimilation was enforced in the Island. But, worried that these two threats could be used in the future to undermine even further the Island's already limited rights, Tynwald addressed the situation in 1711 by introducing 'An Act for Preventing Frauds in Her Majesty's Customes by the Exportation of forraigne Goods from this Island'.[62] This Act was also passed in the expectation that, with Tynwald introducing heavy penalties, restricting by bond the exportation of foreign goods out of the Island to Britain and not allowing ships taking goods abroad to stop at British ports, Britain in return would permit the Manx farmers, fishermen, traders and manufacturers to export local cattle, crops, produce and articles into Britain free of duty. Britain, however, did not reciprocate the attempt by the Island in discouraging smuggling whilst at the same time encouraging free trade, so Tynwald promulgated another Act in 1714 suspending the earlier one.[63] Although the British Parliament did not support the efforts of Tynwald in attempting to control smuggling and made no effort to assist legitimate Manx interests, two decisions which would greatly affect both countries in the future, it did make various proposals to protect its own interests. Further commissioners and agents were sent over to the Island to investigate and report on matters, and revenue cutters were stationed off its coasts to watch for smugglers.

There was concern over the consequences of trading with the enemy, including any loss to Britain's revenue as a result of the importation of foreign goods into the Island, particularly from France, at the expense of the British Exchequer. 'What started the money racket soon took on a more sinister aspect, as the smugglers became the catspaw of the enemy. . . . British gold was being smuggled to the enemy by those self-same smugglers'.[64] The Island's Lord Bishop, Thomas Wilson, in a letter to his son, stated that:

> The loss to Great Britain and the gains to the French are inexpressly great. As all the sums drained from us are employed by them, in time of war, to hire troops and pay armies to

fight against us, it will be no exaggeration of truth to say, that since the peace of Utrecht [1713-15], they have drawn money from us, by means of their trade with the small Isle of Man, than was sufficient to maintain thirty thousand men with a train of artillery, during the late war in Flanders.[65]

Smuggling continued, and it increased even further from 1721 when two merchant strangers, Richard Macquire from Dublin and Josiah Poole from Liverpool, farmed (leased) the Manx customs from James Stanley, the tenth Earl of Derby, for twenty-one years at a cost to them of 1,000 guineas (£1,050) a year.[66] On their own behalf they also imported commodities, stored them in cellars and warehouses leased from the Earl and then clandestinely ran them into the neighbouring countries. Robert Walpole, first Lord of the Treasury and Chancellor of the Exchequer, had set about early on in his premiership to secure a sound and prosperous industrial and commercial Britain.[67] His economic policies would have been irritated by the losses to the Exchequer as a consequence of the Manx smuggling. Two trade protection Acts were introduced by the British Parliament. 'An Act for the further preventing His Majesty's subjects from trading to the East Indies under Foreign Commissions' in 1721 once again endeavoured to restrict any goods from the East Indies being imported anywhere other than into Britain.[68] 'An Act for the Improvement of His Majesty's Revenues of Customs, Excise and Inland Duties' in 1726 disallowed any goods other than those produced in the Island to be brought from there into Britain.[69] These restrictions were influential in the two merchant strangers surrendering their lease back to the Earl. Very importantly, the 1726 Act also authorised the British Treasury to negotiate with the Earl and his immediate heirs with the intention of purchasing back the full sovereign rights of the Isle of Man. The Treasury, the 'department of departments', was responsible for the collection and custody of public revenue, the initiation of financial legislation and the control of public expenditure.[70] The two Acts of 1721 and 1726 were not fully enforced at the time, the flow of goods into and out of the Island continued, though at a temporarily reduced scale, and the Earl of Derby remained Lord of Man. He and many others were profiting from the vast flow of wealth pouring into the Manx shores, and they were in no particular hurry to lose this valuable source of income.

Island passes from Derby to Atholl

On 1 February 1736 James Stanley, the tenth Earl of Derby, died childless. He was the last male heir in direct descent. The title of the earldom reverted to a distant cousin, Sir Edward Stanley. By separate rules of inheritance the suzerainty of the Isle of Man passed to James Murray, the second Duke of Atholl, a Scottish nobleman and heir as great-grandson through the female line of the seventh Earl of Derby.[71]

The new Lord of Man, accompanied by a large retinue, visited the Island in early summer

1736 to formally take possession of his newly acquired estate.[72] The visit was arranged to coincide with the Tynwald Day ceremony to be held on the forthcoming midsummer's day. The wind direction had prevented the Duke's ship, the *Prince William*, sailing from Liverpool until the morning of 10 June, and, although it got to within sight of the Island late that evening, gales throughout the night forced it to turn around, and it arrived at Holyhead for shelter the next afternoon. Another ship carrying the Duke's baggage, horses and servants made it to the Island by steering a more windward course. The captain of a customs cruiser offered to take the Duke and two others to the Island when the elements had calmed down, and the remainder of the party would follow later in the *Prince William*. Leaving early on 14 June, the customs cruiser arrived at Derbyhaven, the port which served Castletown, on the morning of the following day. Governor James Murray, the Duke's relative, accompanied by certain government officials, the garrison of Castle Rushen and the local militia, met with the Duke on his way to Castle Rushen. There a ceremony took place involving the firing of cannon, the surrender of his white rod by the Governor, which was duly returned by the Duke, and many speeches. That evening bonfires were lit, and punch and beer were distributed to members of the populace who gathered at Castletown, Douglas and Peel. Later in the week the Duke was visited by the merchants and principal inhabitants of Douglas and Peel, the Lord Bishop, the Archdeacon, other clergymen and the Members of the House of Keys. On midsummer's day the Duke attended the Tynwald ceremony at St John's. He, his retinue and livery-servants, two of whom carried French horns, rode by horse from Castletown to St John's, a journey of ten miles. The Duke was also accompanied by three squadrons of horse militia carrying drums and standards embroidered with the arms of the Island, the Three Legs of Man. When they arrived at St John's the horse militia formed into two lines at Tynwald Hill where the Deemsters in their gowns, the Bishop in his habit, the Archdeacon, the clergy, the officials, the Lord's Council and the Members of the House of Keys were assembled to receive the Duke. Many thousands of excited onlookers attended the colourful ceremony. The Duke alighted from his horse and was introduced to the dignitaries. The processional way from the hill to the chapel was flanked on both sides by a regiment of armed foot militia carrying colours on their pikes, beating drums and playing music. The Governor held his white rod and led the way to the chapel accompanied by a member of the Murray family bearing the sword of state, and the Duke and the various other ranks followed on behind. As they entered the chapel there was a volley of musket fire. Inside, the Duke sat on a chair of state which was covered with crimson damask and had a footstool in front of it. After the service, those assembled proceeded back to Tynwald Hill where another chair of state was placed at the top of the mound. The Duke ascended, followed by the civil and ecclesiastical officials. The ancient proclamation was made in Manx for fencing the court: a warning to all those attending not to 'quarrel, brawl or make any disturbance'. The Clerk of the Rolls called over the twenty-four

James Murray, second Duke of Atholl.

Members of the House of Keys. He then called over the six Coroners of the sheadings, the officers responsible for ensuring the carrying out of the processes of law.[73] They ascended the mound one by one, knelt at the feet of the Duke and were duly handed their badges of office. Then the Lord Bishop, as Baron of the Island, did homage to the new Lord of Man, and he, the Archdeacon and the Vicars General were sworn into office. After a proclamation was made that all owners of fishing boats should prepare to go to the herring fishery, three cheers were called for and given, hats were thrown in the air and another deafening volley was let fire by the militia. The Duke descended from Tynwald Hill and walked to Mullin-e-Cloie, a house situated a short distance away, where a grand meal was provided for the principal guests.

The new Duke had appointed his kinsman and a former Receiver General of Scotland, another James Murray, to the office of Governor and Commander in Chief of the Island, whose principal responsibility was to look after the family's newly acquired feudal asset.[74] Many other members of the Murray family would come to the Island to serve in positions of authority on behalf of their kinsman. It was soon realised that the moderate Manx customs duties and the opportunities they provided for profiting from smuggling could be turned even further to the advantage of the ducal coffers. Indeed, Governor Murray had such control of the financial situation during the eight years he was in office that 'things were so dextrously managed that there is difficulty in forming any sort of computation of the importations made into the Island'.[75] Despite later investigations by the Commissioners of Customs, the Duke confidently told his new Governor, Patrick Lindesay, that 'nothing can happen from this that can hinder our business from going on briskly'.[76]

By Tynwald's Statute Laws Act, section 14 (1-6), of 24 June 1737, the 1692 book of customs rates, which had been set by the Governor and Council and agreed by the Lord but without reference to the Keys, was legitimised, and 'no order, precept, or command, prohibiting the importation or exportation of any foreign goods, or any other goods of the growth, product, or manufacture of the Isle, shall be granted or made without the consent of the Governor, Council, Deemster and Keys of the said Isle'.[77] This section of the Act emphasised a crucial and very important part of the Island's constitution, that, although the customs duties belonged to the Lord of Man, they could only be amended by agreement between the Lord and Tynwald Court, a point which had been ignored by the Earl of Derby in 1692 and would be ignored by Britain in the future. Customs duties on exports ceased at this time, which was very important in giving both the legal export trade and smuggling a boost. Apart from smuggling, another important measure which directly affected the Manx community was brought about by this Act. Section 4 (3) stated:

> That any person prosecuted in this Isle for a foreign debt, by any accon of arrest [action of arrest] in the said Court of Chancery, shall for the future be held to bail only for his personal appearance to such accon, and for the forthcoming of what effects he hath within this Island to answer the judgement upon the same.

This enabled debtors to come to the Island with little fear of arrest for their debt, and, in consequence of this, the Island became 'the sanctuary of the unfortunate and profligate of the surrounding nations'.[78] To supply these new residents and to continue the contraband trade, huge quantities of goods were being imported, some to be broken up into smaller cargoes and then smuggled into Britain.[79] Captain Webber reported that, when he was one of the English customs officials stationed in the Island, goods were being brought there by English ships flying neutral colours and pretending to be from Portugal, Sweden or Denmark. If vessels were met by revenue cruisers in the St George's Channel and boarded and rummaged by the officials, the masters were well prepared with ploys to extricate themselves from whatever circumstances. Some surreptitiously dropped their goods overboard in bundles with floating markers to be retrieved later. Others held on to their goods, confident that they could talk their way out of the situation. Some who came from the south claimed to be bound for ports in the north and those from the north for ports in the south. To support their claims, they produced fictitious bills of lading, letters of instruction and bills of consignment. Other masters claimed that they were sailing to Shetland, the Faeroe Islands or Norway, whilst others blamed the weather for their wrong positions. As soon as the revenue cruisers left, the ships continued on their way to the Isle of Man and discharged their cargoes. George Waldron, another customs official, noted that in Douglas 'a master of a ship has no more to do than watch his opportunity of coming within the piles, and he is secure from any danger from the King's officers. I myself had once notice of a stately pirate that was steering her course into this harbour'.[80]

It was the King's officers who were responsible, by virtue of the 1726 Act, for checking the legality of goods landed and sent out again, but their powers were limited and their presence was often vehemently opposed, and open hostility was occasionally shown to visiting English customs cruisers. One such serious incident occurred when Captain George Dow brought the Whitehaven stationed revenue cruiser *Sincerity* into Douglas bay in midsummer 1750.[81] The following morning the large Dutch ship *Hope* laden with East India goods anchored off Douglas Head. Dow ordered his mate to search her, but there was fierce resistance from locals led by Paul Bridson, Captain of the town. The *Hope* hoisted her sails and, with the *Sincerity* in pursuit, headed north, where the Dutch skipper deliberately ran his ship aground in Ramsey bay. Captain Dow sent his mate and ten armed men to board the vessel, but when they ceased their rummaging and came from below decks they found themselves surrounded by a much larger party of locals led by Matthew Christian, Captain of the town. Christian cocked his pistol, warned Dow's men that he would fire at 'the first man that offered to take up a Cutlass' and then arrested them all. The Ramsey locals unloaded the cargo of tea, silks, chintzes and pepper. Christian ordered the boarding party from the *Sincerity* to be taken to the Island's gaol at Castle Rushen, where they were released on bail after making statements. One of the bailed men was Dow's son who was later caught at Derbyhaven attempting to send a message to his father 'to load his Guns, prepare Grenades'. The bailed men were re-arrested and brought to the gaol at Castle Rushen. In order to attempt to secure the freedom of his men, Dow invited Christian aboard the *Sincerity* a few weeks later, when, after taking drinks in his cabin and calmly discussing the situation, the mood changed. Dow and his mate drew their pistols and aimed them at Christian. Dow threatened to 'shoot out his brains' and blow his house to pieces with the cruiser's guns if the gaoled men were not speedily set free. But the prisoners languished in gaol for several months before being released.

An even more serious incident had occurred just a few years earlier when James Moss, an army deserter who had been imprisoned in Cardiff gaol, gave evidence in Castle Rushen on the murder and wounding of several people, including a revenue officer and some of his assistants, by William Owens.[82] The smuggler and outlaw Owens was on the run from the authorities and had been sheltering in his vessel in Cardigan Bay in the spring of 1744 when James Phillips and other armed men, including the pressed Moss, boarded the vessel to arrest him and his crew. Owens brought them to a cabin, plied them with ale and entreated them to leave, offering ten guineas if they would do so. When they refused, he cried out, 'We will not surrender and so you may fire away', grabbed his pistols, shot and killed Phillips and another man and wounded others. Moss was slightly wounded in the skirmish and was unable to escape with the other survivors, so Owens threw him into the forecastle and ordered his crew to set sail for the Isle of Man. He left Moss in Douglas, 'swore him upon bread and salt' not to report the incident and then sailed round to Peel from where he eventually disappeared before the authorities could arrest him.

The Island had been for 'many years a common storehouse for all manner of goods and merchandises' which included tobacco, tea and Dutch East Indies goods from Holland, tobacco from Dunkirk, Ostend, Norway and Britain, tea and India goods from Denmark and Gothenburg in Sweden, brandy and wines from France and Spain, and rum, the product of the slave trade, from America.[83] Vast quantities of goods were unloaded, stored in yards, sheds, warehouses or cellars, repackaged into smaller containers and then loaded into wherries and clippers from the quaysides or bays at the four main ports. Vessels of all sizes were used to transport them across the short stretch of sea to the nearby mainland. These ranged in size from two-masted wherries weighing three tons which were open and swift, with sterns as sharp as their bows for ease of manoeuvrability by crews of six oarsmen at shallow shores and in narrow creeks, through to larger sailing ships weighing eighty tons which could take great quantities of cargo to remote coves and quiet estuaries. Douglas and Castletown supplied Wales, Cheshire and Lancashire. Peel supplied the east and north of Ireland and the Highlands and west of Scotland. Ramsey supplied Cumberland, the Solway Firth and into the Scottish border near Annan.

Manx merchant

The years which followed James Murray becoming the second Duke of Atholl and Lord of Man were without doubt the greatest period in Manx maritime trading history. Capital generated from smuggling became available for investment in legal foreign trade.[84] This overseas traffic was of a complex nature, consisting of goods from America and the Mediterranean and goods and slaves from Africa - historical documentation reveals that the Island was involved in many aspects of the transatlantic slave trade. John Joseph Bacon was one of the most outstanding Manx ship owners and merchants of this period. His daughter was married to the son of George Moore, a lesser but still very successful merchant. George Moore's importance in Manx history is that he was a prolific letter writer, and two books into which copies of his outgoing correspondence were transcribed have survived.[85] They reveal that his legitimate interests were simply an extension of his involvement in smuggling. They also show the wide range of people with whom he corresponded: from merchants in Europe, Boston and the West Indies, to ship masters and bankers, from customers and contacts on the west coast of Scotland, to suppliers of barrel hoops and glass bottles, as well as the more personal exchanges associated with members of his family.[86]

George Moore was born in 1709, a member of the 'Moores of the Hills' family, the Hills being an estate on the outskirts of Douglas. After working for his father in Douglas he established an overseas trading business based in Peel. He was associated with the town for over fifty years during which time the fortunes of many of its inhabitants were very closely linked with both the legal and illegal trade. Moore's success in business attracted others with similar ambitions to come to the town, and its population substantially increased over the years: from 475 in 1726 to 1,254 by 1784.[87] Moore married Catherine Callan in 1733. They lived with their three sons and three daughters in a grand house located on a prime site situated at the corner of Castle Street and what is now Crown Street, near to the mouth of the harbour.[88] It overlooked a bowling green and, beyond that, Peel Castle and the bay. It was reputed to be the most elaborate house in the town, both outside and in, with red sandstone quoins, cut stonework around the windows and panelled rooms and staircase. A yard, storehouse and cellars were located nearby, easily accessible to the busy commercial quayside.

After a number of years living in Peel the family moved permanently to what had been their summer home at Ballamoore in Patrick, close to the west coast of the Island and less than two miles from their business at the quayside. When Moore bought the property from Margaret Wattleworth for £650 in 1750 the house was small, consisting of a parlour, two small bedrooms and an upstairs room.[89] It was adjacent to land owned by the second Duke of Atholl who had 'invited me to build a house with a good garden'.[90] Moore now set to work on constructing a much larger building containing a parlour, drawing room, kitchen, back-kitchen, four bedrooms, two water closets and attic rooms.[91] He improved the farm and created an orchard and ornamental garden which he considered needed to be 'executed in a genteele taste which perhaps would not prove more

Sir George Moore, merchant and Chairman of the House of Keys.

expensive than having my improvement in no taste or a bad one'.[92] His vessels brought bushels of acorns and pine cones from Scotland and New England, myrtles, hollies and spruce from Ireland, and grafted nut bushes from Holland, whilst his vinery was supplied with red and white grape vines from southern France.[93] He consulted with the Duke's gardener on tree planting.

Moore was an affectionate and concerned husband and father, and the captains of his ships were instructed to bring home from their far ranging voyages quantities of oranges, lemons, prunes, raisins and nuts for the family.[94] A list of incidental articles and materials purchased for him at European ports hints at the fashionable display with which his wife and daughters dazzled the matrons of Peel: boxes of artificial head and breast flowers, fans, earrings and necklaces, silver tippets and Barcelona handkerchiefs, scarlet satin and crimson velvet, yellow lutestring (ribbon) and silk paduasoy (corded fabric) in various colours, pink and silver shoes, gauze dress caps and lace for ruffles. When his son Phil was twenty-one, Moore bought him a pair of French brilliant stone buckles and a blue satin waistcoat embroidered with gold.

George Moore was well organised and highly successful in his business. His customers were merchants located in the nearby Scottish seaboard. Once a customer's need had been identified, Moore would write several letters until a source of supply had been located.[95] He would then search for an outward cargo, the proceeds of which would assist with covering the costs of the return goods. A vessel would be engaged and arrangements made for the cargo to be purchased on credit. Moore's business flourished over the years to such an extent that in 1750 he had two vessels built in Boston in America: the *Peggy* (named after his daughter Margaret, known affectionately as Peggy), 150 tons, and the *Lilly*, 120 tons. They were snows, small two-masted sailing ships, which travelled back and forth across the Atlantic at all times of the year and in all weathers. Both of Moore's vessels regularly made the crossing to the West Indies, returned via the Straits of Gibraltar to trade in the Mediterranean with France and Spain and then sailed back to the Isle of Man. A typical voyage was started in January 1751 by the *Peggy*, accompanied for most of the way by the *Lilly*. Under the command of Captain Pat Montgomerie the *Peggy* sailed from Irvine on the coast just south of Glasgow to North America with £800 worth of Glasgow and Liverpool manufactured goods.[96] These were disposed of in Boston, and her hold was subsequently filled with New England rum and 3,000 quintals (150 tons) of dry fish.[97] Moore instructed Pat Montgomerie to 'pray take care that your cargoe of fish be taken on board in dry order for the quality of ye fish depends the success of the voyage'. A course was then set for the Straits, and Montgomerie was entrusted to sell the fish in whichever port he could get a good price. Eventually they were sold in Barcelona.[98] The money was used to purchase forty pipes (5,000 gallons) of Spanish brandy, after which the *Peggy* sailed home on the last leg of her triangular voyage and arrived in Peel in April 1752, some fifteen months after leaving.[99] For the next three months another route was followed by the *Lilly* under the command of her new master, Captain Robert Montgomerie, who was most probably a relative of Captain Pat Montgomerie.[100] She called at Cork at the end of May 1752 to collect £900 worth of butter and other provisions. By the beginning of July she reached Barbados where Robert Montgomerie disposed of the cargo, bought 200 hogsheads (12,500 gallons) of rum with the proceeds at a cost of 2/- a gallon and returned to Peel in late August.[101]

Nothing could be landed at Peel without the official entry papers, and brandy or rum could not be moved from the quayside to be cellared until officially gauged. But there were times when the rules were bent. As the restricted and narrow quayside could only hold about one third of a large cargo, Moore had arranged with the deputy searcher, Captain Murray, for parts of such cargoes to be rolled across the quay into his open yard, there to be available for official scrutiny.[102] Moore's cooper, Thomas Taylor, would have small wooden barrels and casks ready to split up the contents of the hogsheads and pipes of alcohol and boxes and bags to take the contents of the chests of tea and tobacco for them to be deposited in the nearby storehouse and cellars. Governor

Basil Cochrane was concerned about these arrangements, believing that Moore and Murray were far too close, so he had Murray transferred to Castletown, 'to have him under my eye', and a new and more reliable searcher, William Lidderdale, took his place in order to ensure that the Lord's revenue was fully protected against any dubious deals which might be made to evade the necessary dues.[103] It was not long before the astute Moore and the brusque Lidderdale were in confrontation. When a large Dutch ship arrived in Peel bay in early 1759 with a cargo of brandy, wine and vinegar from Bordeaux for Moore, there were problems with bringing the ship into the harbour caused by a low tide not giving sufficient depth of water.[104] Late at night, with the possibility of a changing storm force wind threatening the ship and cargo (whose combined value was put at £5,000), her captain and Moore arranged for the goods to be unloaded in the bay, rowed ashore and deposited at Moore's premises. Moore quickly scribbled out a message asking for entry papers which he sent overnight by the Peel carrier, 'the old man', to John Quayle, the comptroller who also happened to be Moore's son-in-law. Amongst his many other responsibilities, the comptroller was the official in overall charge of the searchers, weights and measures operations and customs documents, but his office was more than twelve miles away in Castletown and authorisation would take some time to be collected and returned. In the meanwhile Moore informed Lidderdale what he had done. Lidderdale told him in very severe terms to stop the unloading and reinforced this demand by sending him an official letter stating, 'I have ordered a soldier to attend the ship entry in the morning. At the same time thought proper to acquaint you with the directions I intend giving him viz: nothing to be landed without the entry [papers]'. But before either the soldier or the papers arrived a good part of the cargo had been discharged. Moore complained to the Governor about his treatment, and Cochrane brought the two parties together and reluctantly demanded Lidderdale to make an apology, which he eventually did, though he did so equally reluctantly. Moore's actions display a man of determination and shrewdness in dealing with matters to satisfy his own interests.

The main objective of each voyage of George Moore's ships, to which everything else was subordinated, was a homeward cargo of brandy, rum, wine, tea and tobacco which were stored in his premises in Peel in readiness for the smugglers.[105] The Lord's low customs duties were duly paid, and sound economics required that the items were disposed of as quickly as possible. Moore's customers had previously sent word of their requirements. Boatmen of their own choice and hire came to Peel to take the merchandise on board their vessels for transportation to the Scottish coast. There the goods were landed, mainly at night, on a beach or in a sea loch unlikely to be visited by the revenue men. The boatmen received payment from the carriers who met them, and the goods were loaded on to horses and carts for transportation to the customers. Moore carefully avoided any direct risk of being accused of involvement in smuggling; once the goods left the Island they became the property of the purchaser, and what happened to them from then on was not Moore's responsibility. His network of customers and agents in Scotland was well established and was concentrated mainly along the coastline from Dumfries and Galloway in the south-west to Strathclyde in the southern Highlands. He visited these contacts for two months each summer in order to drum up business and sort out any outstanding debts.[106] Moore's customers were occasionally in trouble with both him and the authorities. John Orr, who owed Moore £20, had moved from Inverkip to Gourock and so had 'got out of my road when I'm in Scotland and declines from seeing me though I send for him'.[107] James Gillie was a passenger on board the smuggling vessel *Janet Knights* and was keeping an eye on his goods when it was searched for contraband brandy and rum, and, although the crew members were arrested for interrogation, he was allowed to go free after protesting that he was simply an innocent passenger.

During the Seven Years War, a worldwide series of conflicts fought from 1756 to 1763 which involved most of the major powers of Europe, the hostilities between Britain and France seriously interfered with Moore's business as it increased the dangers to ocean-going trade and left him open to the accusation of dealing with the enemy. In 1758 he wrote to Peter Berail, his long-standing supplier in Cette, now known as Séte, on the Mediterranean coast of France, instructing him to carry out an unlawful act in order to overcome the difficulty caused by trade with France, other than by special licence, being forbidden.[108] He asked Berail to hire a neutral ship from Holland, Denmark or Sweden, load it with brandy and send it to Peel. The official documentation was not to be put on board the ship but forwarded by post to Alexander Wallace, a merchant and the British consul in Bergen in Norway, 'as if the cargoe was his'. Fearful that his unlawful plan might be discovered, Moore insisted that the captain of the ship 'keeps private from the crew that the cargoe is intended to be discharged in this port [Peel]'. Later in the year Moore had second thoughts about such a venture. He was worried that the risks taken could end in disaster and warned Berail that all vessels bound for the Isle of Man with French goods on board would certainly be arrested if stopped by privateers or British warships.

The seas were crowded with privateers which were manned by desperate men, in many cases only to be distinguished from pirates by the letters of marque they carried from their respective governments.[109] A battle off the west coast of the Isle of Man between French privateers led by the smuggler and adventurer Captain François Thurot and British warships led by Captain John Elliot had a link with George Moore.[110] Captain Thurot sailed a squadron of six vessels from Dunkirk in October 1759 - ready to capture or destroy as many British merchant vessels as he possibly could during the next few months - and headed north to Gothenburg, past the Faeroe Islands and St Kilda, and was going on to Londonderry in the north of Ireland. By the latter stages of Thurot's expedition, storms and desertion meant that he only had his own ship, the *Belle Isle*, with forty-four guns and 540 men, and two others, the *Blonde*, with thirty-two guns and 400 men, and the

Squadrons of Captain François Thurot and Captain John Elliott in battle off Ballaugh coast, 28 February 1760.

Terpsichore, with twenty-six guns and 300 men. Unfavourable winds brought the ships to Belfast Lough where 600 troops landed and attacked Carrickfergus to get provisions and money. Captain John Elliot, the young twenty-five-year-old Commodore of three warships, was sheltering his squadron from a storm in Kinsale in the south of Ireland on 24 February 1760 when he got word of Thurot's whereabouts. The British squadron, made up of the *Aeolus*, with thirty-two guns and 220 men, the *Brilliant*, with thirty-six guns and 240 men, and the *Pallas*, also with thirty-six guns and 240 men, headed north to engage the French who by this time were sailing towards the Isle of Man. John Kelly, the pilot in Elliot's flagship the *Aeolus*, sighted the French just off Jurby Head at four o'clock in the morning on 28 February. With confusion over signals and responsibilities, the *Belle Isle* found itself isolated from her sister ships, but she still took on the British force. The ensuing battle, fought off the Ballaugh coast, was fierce and lasted about one-and-a-half hours before all three French ships surrendered. Captain Thurot was killed in the latter stages of the melee by a shot from a swivel gun. Over three hundred French soldiers and sailors were killed or injured. John Kelly told of the desperate scene he saw on the *Belle Isle* the day after the battle, 'turn which way I would, nothing but scattered limbs of dead and dying men presented themselves to my view. . . . Thurot's body was thrown, by mistake, overboard amongst the rest'. Only five British personnel were killed and twenty-eight injured. Captain Elliot brought all six ships into Ramsey bay where they lay for eight days whilst they were repaired during a time of 'the most perfect calm ever remembered, at that or any period of the year'. The *Belle Isle* had lost her bolt-sprit, mizen-mast and main-yard and was damaged so badly that she was in danger of sinking. The prisoners were taken away from the Island. It is unclear why Thurot's route had brought his ships so close to the north of the Isle of Man. There had been great alarm in Liverpool that the intention was to invade its rich port, and orders had been issued for all the military in the Warrington and Manchester areas to immediately march there. Twenty companies had gathered by 27 February, and 'their officers ordered the drums to beat to arms, and they marched off', with each company consisting of three sergeants, two drummers and sixty privates. There was equal alarm felt in the defenceless Isle of Man. It has been suggested that the French were sailing there with the intention of seizing ships, provisions and even hostages. Miss Maggie Kelly of Peel related an account of the battle that had been handed down in her family, which included the belief that 'the Frenchmen after plundering Carrickfergus came towards Peel with the intention of robbing Sir George Moore's house at Ballamoore'.[111] Moore himself claimed that Thurot was intending to take political hostages and possibly worse:

> Thurot's squadron w[hi]ch certainly intended us a Visit, this in all Places W[oul]d have been Severly felt, for the Names of the Principals who were to be taken Hostages have transpired. How fatal to Trade & destructive to private Property would this Descent have proved had the Intention taken Place. On W[hi]ch Intelligence our Enemies found their Intentions cannot be known of if Invited by the Defenceless state of this Isle, which it may be thought, they were acquainted with, if the Surmise be true, That they had correspondents in this Isle.[112]

Moore was seemingly suspicious of the Lord Bishop, Mark Hildesley, who he considered had preached during his Lent sermons 'in favour of a change of Mast[e]rs and dispositions' in the Island. The 'correspondents' who Moore referred to may have been, unbeknownst to him, closer to home. François Thurot certainly knew the Isle of Man from his smuggling days, and his African butler, Douglas, knew Peel and Ballamoore very well. He had previously been George Moore's servant until his master had discovered him having sex with the cook in the dairy. As a consequence, Douglas had to be quickly sold on. Moore wrote a letter to be picked up by the dependable Captain Pat Montgomerie en route during one of his trading voyages aboard the *Peggy* which informed him that 'I expect you have Disposed of my Negroe Douglass because his face I never want to see, if he be not sold, sell him in Spain for what you can get for him'.[113] That Douglas returned to the Isle of Man in such daring circumstances some six years later, most surely with the purpose of serving his new master against his old, is intriguing.

The success of merchants such as George Moore and the many others involved in the supply of luxury goods brought into the Isle of Man to be stored for a short time and quickly repackaged for onward smuggling into the neighbouring countries had repercussions which were causing great losses to Britain's Exchequer and would now seriously affect the relationship between the two countries.

Chapter 3

REVESTMENT

Purchase of the Isle of Man

It was becoming clear that the British Government would eventually be compelled to take appropriate action against the situation in the Isle of Man. The expensive wars with its European neighbours during the middle part of the century meant that Britain needed to have access to and control of as much money as it could and cut off any funds which could enrich the coffers of its enemies.[114] The smuggling activities emanating from the Isle of Man were compounding both these problems and needed to be stopped. Towards this end, throughout the 1740s, 1750s and into the early 1760s, the Treasury had been involved in negotiations with the second Duke of Atholl for the sale of the Island.[115] It was held as a feudatory dominion of the Crown of England 'so ever since from a long time past granted' and 'from time immemorial'.[116] In 1751 a proposal had been made in Parliament to purchase the Isle of Man from the Atholls in order to annex it to the Crown, and the Treasury was anxious to receive from the Duke details of his conditions for the sale, but nothing came to fruition.[117] The gross customs revenue increased from a total of £23,123 for the decade 1740-49 to £44,650 for the decade 1750-59.[118] £44,650 is now equivalent to almost £6 million.[119] The Duke kept even his most senior officials in the Island in the dark whilst all the negotiations were going on. In 1752 he had assured Governor Basil Cochrane that rumours of the sale of the Island were groundless and had repeated this denial three years later.[120] However, the second Duke had recognised the inevitability of the situation and had been making long-term plans over many years. By various deeds of conveyance in November 1737, May 1748, April 1756, November 1761 and July 1762 he had given his trustees the power to sell the Island after his death.[121] The legality of these transactions is very questionable, but the Duke obviously considered the Island as negotiable real estate.

James Murray, the second Duke of Atholl, died on 8 January 1764. His only surviving child, Lady Charlotte, Baroness Strange, succeeded him.[122] She was married to her cousin, John Murray, who now became the third Duke of Atholl as the male heir to the dukedom and also became Lord of Man through his wife's succession.[123] John Murray's indirect claims to his new titles would no doubt have caused him some concern with regard to the various benefits they brought. Indeed, the importance of the Isle of Man to the Atholls is shown when on the very day the second Duke died the new Duke and Duchess suppressed their grief sufficiently to send a petition to the British

John Murray, third Duke of Atholl, Lady Charlotte, Baroness Strange, and their children.

Parliament demanding the retention of their privileges in the Island.[124]

But smuggling was still rife, and the Treasury wanted to know its extent, so requested various reports, follow-ups to ones commissioned a few years earlier.

The earlier reports had estimated that the annual revenue losses were £200,000 to Ireland, £300,000 to England, Wales and Scotland and £200,000 to the East India Company.[125] The total of £700,000 is now equivalent to in excess of £100 million. A specific example of the losses showed that at least 700,000 pounds weight of tea a year was drunk in Ireland, yet its importation from England was only 200,000 pounds. The difference of 500,000 pounds was known to be brought from Gothenburg, Copenhagen and Holland to the Isle of Man and from there run into various ports in Ireland, causing a loss of £42,000 to the Irish Exchequer through it not receiving the customs duties of 1/8 a pound.

The new reports received throughout 1764 detailed the current situation and showed continuing losses.[126] The Attorney General and the Surveyor General presented a lengthy appraisal on the means to prevent smuggling. The Commissioners of Customs for Scotland estimated that smuggling out of the Island caused a loss of £350,000 a year to the British revenue. They explained that the smugglers used large ships of up to eighty tons to supply the west coast of

Scotland and smaller Manx wherries for the south-west. Local farmers and labourers assisted in unloading the smuggled goods and putting them on to pack horses to be taken on secluded tracks and across moorlands to various destinations throughout Scotland and into the north of England. A graphic report from Colin Campbell, the commander of a revenue cutter, told of him taking a party of armed soldiers and sailors to investigate information he had received that a large quantity of spirits had recently been smuggled into Old Kirk Patrick on the River Clyde. They searched the area and found seventy ankers of spirits.[127] But as they were loading the barrels on to the cutter they heard a church bell being rung as an alarm and soon found themselves confronted by an angry mob of armed men who attacked them with flails, pitchforks, sticks and stones. Campbell and several of his men were injured, so they shot at their assailants, wounding and killing a number. The revenue men speedily loaded the remainder of the goods on to their cutter and sailed away. From Dublin it was reported that the value of goods seized off the Irish coast amounted to £10,000 a year, and much more would have been successfully smuggled past the customs officers. Indeed, it was reported that wherries built in Rush and colliers from Lancashire and Cumberland stopped in the Isle of Man in order to collect contraband which was then brought into Ireland, some being to the value of £1,200 a sailing. The response from Carlisle was that their officers had observed large gangs of armed smugglers moving through their area. There were other reports from Liverpool, Whitehaven, Edinburgh and London. Charles Lutwidge, the Surveyor General for Cumberland, Westmoreland and Lancaster, sent an extensive report to the Treasury which included the information that luxury goods were being landed in great quantities in the Island, the principal items being tea, tobacco, brandy, rum and coffee. The countries of supply included France, Spain, Sweden, Holland, Germany and the West Indies. Lutwidge knew of one merchant who traded in smuggled silks bought at the India sales, a business worth £10,000 a year. He estimated that the net ducal revenue from all sources in the Island was £7,500 a year, of which £6,500 was from duties on goods intended for smuggling.

Whilst the accuracy of the above figures may be questionable, what is certain is that the smuggling trade out of the Island was causing a great financial loss to Britain. The estimated £350,000 annual loss to the revenue represented an amount in excess of 15% of Britain's £2.282 million customs income raised in 1764, a considerably high percentage.[128] The receipts from customs (tax on imported or exported goods) and excise (tax on locally produced goods for local consumption), 22% and 49% respectively, made up the bulk of Britain's £10.221 million general revenue. Given the large financial losses to Britain and Ireland, the extent and scale of the smuggling trade are well and truly put into perspective when the size of the population in the small Isle of Man of 20,000 is compared to that in Britain and Ireland of 11,250,000.[129]

At this time Britain was financially and militarily stretched due to its involvement in the conflicts of the Seven Years War. A significant cause of ministerial instability throughout the early 1760s was as a result of senior government ministers bickering amongst themselves over the economic consequences of these conflicts. Additionally, the ministers had a new monarch, the young twenty-two year old George III, to deal with. From the outset of his reign, George III was intent on making politicians concentrate upon public rather than private interest.[130] The ministers also had a new First Lord of the Treasury and Chancellor of the Exchequer. George Grenville, who had been in office for less than a year when the reports on Manx smuggling were being considered, was trying to resolve the financial repercussions of war by bringing in a range of economies to reduce the burdening national debt, boost the Exchequer income and avoid introducing any unpopular new taxes.[131] His policies included ensuring that Britain gained control of all possible revenues. The losses to the Exchequer through the situation created by the Island would now be addressed. After suffering the consequences of smuggling for a hundred years, Britain eventually resolved to bring it to an end, first by negotiation, then by legislation and eventually by determination to physically stop it at source.

Scarcely had John Murray an opportunity to consider his situation as the new Lord of Man, when negotiations were opened in earnest by the Treasury for the return of the sovereign rights of the Isle of Man to the British Crown, an action which would become famously known as 'revestment'. The accession of the new Lord probably provided this long awaited opportunity. In April 1764 the Treasury complained that, despite many requests, nothing had yet been received from the Duke regarding his terms to sell the Island to Britain.[132] Meanwhile, with rumour rife in the Island, the Duke was reassuring the local merchants that he and the Duchess had no intention to sell, claiming that 'no application whatever has been made to us from the Government about it'.[133] Procrastination and dubious denial did not put off the inevitable. On 25 July 1764 a proposal under the terms of the 1726 Act was made to the Duke by the Lords of the Treasury led by Grenville:

> to treat with you for the purchase of the Isle of Man, or of such part of the rights claimed by your Grace in the said Island, as it shall be found expedient to vest in the Crown for preventing that pernicious and illicit trade, which is at present carried on between the said Island and the other parts of his Majesty's dominions, in violation of the laws, and to the great diminution and detriment of the revenues of this Kingdom.[134]

The Lords of the Treasury repeated to the Duke that they were willing to receive proposals from him as to what portions of his Isle of Man property and rights he was prepared to sell and what total value he placed upon them. Frustrated with his lack of response, they threatened him that, if he would not enter into a treaty, 'we beg to be informed of it, that we may then pursue such other measures as we shall think our duty to the public requires us'. In the meanwhile, in order to emphasise their threat still further, the Lords of the Treasury had 'proceeded from strong words

*George Grenville, First Lord of the Treasury
and Chancellor of the Exchequer.*

to strong deeds'.[135] An Order in Council had been issued specifying that the laws against smuggling from the Isle of Man would be strictly enforced by Britain stationing revenue cruisers around the coasts and in the harbours of the Island, thereby treating Manx territorial waters and ports as if they were part of Britain.[136] Having received advice from his relative, friend and trustee, Lord Mansfield (William Murray, a former Solicitor General, Attorney General, Lord Chief Justice and Privy Councillor), the Duke replied to the Treasury, accepting that he was ready to negotiate for the sale of the Island, but pointing out that, as he had only been in possession of it for a few months, it was impossible for him to fix an adequate value on his property and rights, but stating his readiness to receive an estimate from the Treasury.[137] The Lords of the Treasury replied that they were unable to arrive at a value as they had no statistical information which would enable them to determine a price.[138] Yet again they asked him for full information on the value of every branch of the Manx finances. However, before the Duke could reply, and whilst in London to discuss the matter, he was informed that the British Government, no doubt totally exasperated with his lack of action, did not intend to go any further with the treaty but proposed, without any further negotiations, to purchase his lucrative rights in the Island by an Act of Parliament.[139] All of this must have convinced the Duke that his short term as Lord of Man was coming to an end.

On 21 January 1765, barely one year from the accession of John Murray to the lordship of Man, George Grenville introduced a Bill into the House of Commons to progress matters for 'more effectually preventing the mischief arising to the revenue and commerce of Great Britain and Ireland from the illicit and clandestine trade to and from the Isle of Man'.[140] The Bill empowered English customs officers to search all ships in Manx harbours and off the coast for any suspect goods, allowed for the licensing of certain goods and restricted the importation and exportation of others. But it would have been difficult for the Mischief Bill, as it was known, to be legally progressed to an Act whilst the Island was still under the lordship of the Atholls. So, Britain considered that, in order to resolve this matter, the title and regalities of the Lord of Man should be transferred to the Crown. It determined to revest the sovereign rights, using force if necessary. Annoyance had turned to threats, and threats were now to become reality through the Revestment Act.

Meanwhile, the Duke of Atholl was again under pressure, and there was a great deal of action during that February. He presented a petition to the House of Commons against the Bill.[141] He belatedly supplied the statistical information which the Treasury had demanded.[142] This showed that the revenue derived from the Isle of Man by the Atholls for the decade 1754 to 1763 totalled £72,930 (£85,085 Manx), made up of an amount of £55,043 from the customs duties, £1,078 from the herring customs and £16,809 from other revenue. Two valuations of the Duke's full rights in the Island feature in documents in the Atholl Papers: one totalled £299,773 and the other £620,360 (the larger figure was based on a different formula to the smaller one and included an allowance for additional compensation due to an estimated doubling of customs income in the future).[143]

The Treasury informed the Duke that, despite the earlier proposal not to negotiate any longer, a treaty for the purchase of his rights might yet be entered into.[144] Whilst the Duke was involved in this bargaining in London, the Members of the House of Keys had no knowledge of the proposals. When rumour of what was going on reached the Island, the Keys met in March 1765 at their chambers on the ground floor of Bishop Wilson's library, just a short walk from Castle Rushen.[145] Fearing that the interests of the Island, and, no doubt, their own, would be overlooked in the course of these negotiations, they appointed two of their members, Hugh Cosnahan and Thomas Moore, to go to London to protect the Island's constitutional rights.

However, a bargain between the British Government and the Duke had already been sealed, which the Duke declared to be, 'as matters stand, a mighty good bargain'.[146] He had originally proposed that he should be paid the value of his rights in the Island, totalling £299,773, but, concerned that his family may be stripped of the whole of its rights in the Island without any remuneration whatsoever and with the possibility of other dire repercussions - some commentators have speculated that these might have included the removal of his title and estates - the Duke eventually agreed to surrender all his regalities and customs rights for £70,000, an amount proposed by the Treasury.[147] The figure was made up of £46,000 for the regalities and £24,000 for the customs. Confused, depressed and unsure as to whether he was making the right decision, the Duke timorously informed the Treasury that his hope was that 'neither your Lordships nor the public will think the clear sum of £70,000 too great a price to be paid us in full compensation' for the rights to the regalities and customs. Importantly for the Atholls, they were to retain possession of the remaining privileges, including the ecclesiastical patronage, manorial and mineral rights, rents and various other benefits. The £70,000 (now the equivalent of £7.8 million) was invested by the Duke in his Scottish estates.[148] On 22 August, by order of George III to the Lord Lieutenant of Ireland, a settlement out of the Irish revenue of £2,000 a year pension was granted to the Duke and Duchess for their joint lives.[149] It was considered that this compensation should be made by Ireland as it too would benefit by the stamping out of the smuggling trade.

The question as to whether the £70,000 settlement represented a bargain or not to both parties is of interest. In this respect it needs to be emphasised that any claim by the Duke of Atholl for compensation as a result of the loss of his ducal customs revenue was weak because the basis of his family's principal Manx income was built on two very dubious practices: the smuggling trade and customs duties set without reference to Tynwald.[150] It is clear that £70,000 was a small amount to pay as a one-off settlement when compared to the vast amounts which had been lost annually to the British and Irish revenues over many years. But Britain, in limiting the settlement and turning down the Duke's offer to sell all of his rights for £299,773, missed out on a crucial opportunity to rid itself once and for all of the Atholl's interests in the Island.

Revestment and Mischief Acts

The Bill for giving effect to the return of the principal rights of the Island to the British Crown speedily went through all the stages of the two Houses of Parliament from 23 April to 7 May 1765, barely a fortnight. The resultant Revestment Act of 10 May 1765 returned the sovereignty, regalities and customs of the Isle of Man to the British Crown.[151] The British monarch became the Lord of Man. The Act 'vested the Island in His Majesty, his Heirs, and Successors' without any rights to transfer, thereby returning to the Crown:

the said Island, Castle, Pele and Lordship of Man, and all the Islands and Lordships to the said Island of Man appertaining, together with the Royalties, Regalities, Franchises, Liberties and Sea Ports, to the same belonging, and all other Hereditaments and Premises comprized, mentioned, and granted.

The Atholl family retained their other privileges, which were many and often colourful in description, making them worthy of listing in full:

Patronage of the Bishoprick of the said Island of Man, or of the Bishoprick of Soder, or of the Bishoprick of Soder and Man, or the Temporalties of the said Bishoprick or Bishopricks, whenever it or they shall become vacant; or the Right of Advowson, Patronage, Presentation, Collation, Donation, Domination or free Disposition, of or to any Archdeaconries, Canonries, Prebends, Colleges, Hospitals, Churches, Chapels, Rectories, Vicarages, or other Ecclesiastical Benefices or Promotions whatsoever, within the said Island, Lordship and Territory of Man, or the Dependencies thereof, or any Hundreds, Wapentakes, Manors, Towns, Vills, Churches, Monasteries, Abbies, Priories, or the Scites, Circuits or Precincts thereof, Farms, Messuages, Houses, Granges, Tofts, Cottages, Curtilages, Barns, Stables, Mills, Dove-houses, Orchards, Fruiteries, Gardens, Lands, Demesne Lands, Glebe Lands, Meadows, Leasows, Feedings, Pastures, Woodlands, Woods, Underwoods, Trees, or Soil or Ground thereof, Wastes, void Grounds, Roads, Paths, Heaths, Furzes, Moors, Marshes, Mines of Lead or Iron or other base Metals, Collieries, Quarries, Inland Waters, Pools, Fish-ponds, Watercourses, Streams, Rivulets, Aqueducts, Rents, Arrearages of Rent, Rent Services, Rent Charges, Rents Seck, Rents reserved, Annual Farm Rents, Fee Farm Rents, Rents of Assize, Annuities, Heriots, Services or Works of Tenants either free or customary, Rectories, Tythes, or Impropriations of Tythes, either Great or Small, Predial, Personal or Mixed, Portions of Tythes, Pensions, Oblations, Obventions, Commons, Frankfolds, Estovers, Commons of Estovers, Turbaries, Ways, Passages, Easements, Forests, Parks, Liberties of Parks, Chases, Lawns, Warrens, Assarts, Purprestures, Chiminages, Hawkings, Huntings, Piscaries, Fishings, Fairs, Fair Days, Markets, Stallages, Tolls, Multures, Waifs, Estrays, Deodands, Wrecks of the Sea, Assize or Assay of Bread, Wine or Beer, Fealities, Reliefs, Escheats, Forfeitures, Goods and Chattels of Traitors, Felons, Clerks, Convict, Fugitives, Persons convicted, attained, condemned, outlawed, put in Exigent or standing mute, Suits of Tenants, Courts Baron, Profits or Perquisites of Courts Baron, Fines, Amerciaments, or any Thing to Courts Baron appertaining, or any Profits, Commodities, Advantages, Emoluments or Appurtenances, Spiritual or Temporal, to the said reserved and excepted Premises, or any of them, belonging, incident, appendant or in any wise appertaining, or any Interest therein in Possession, Remainder or Reversion, within the said Island of Man, or any of the Islands and Dependencies to the same belonging.

Castle Rushen, north-eastern view, c.1760.

The Mischief Act, legalised by the Revestment Act, became effective five days later.[152] This was followed up by a Royal Proclamation bearing the great seal being issued by George III on 21 June setting out that all powers were now to be exercised by the authority of the Crown and that all existing officials, other than those who had been responsible for the collection of the revenues, would continue in their posts.[153]

An official ceremony to mark revestment was held in the Island on 11 July.[154] This started in the morning when the Manx flag was hoisted over Castle Rushen and troops were drawn up in the market square. At eleven o'clock the numerous officials gathered in the hall of the Governor's house and formed a procession. Four soldiers with fixed bayonets led the way out, followed by the Captains of the garrisons, towns and parishes, the clergy, the Members of the House of Keys, their Chairman, the two Vicar Generals, the Archdeacon, the two Deemsters and the Attorney General. The Constable of Castle Rushen was next in line, carrying two wooden boxes containing the Royal Proclamation and the Governor's commission. Finally came Governor John Wood and his guard.[155]

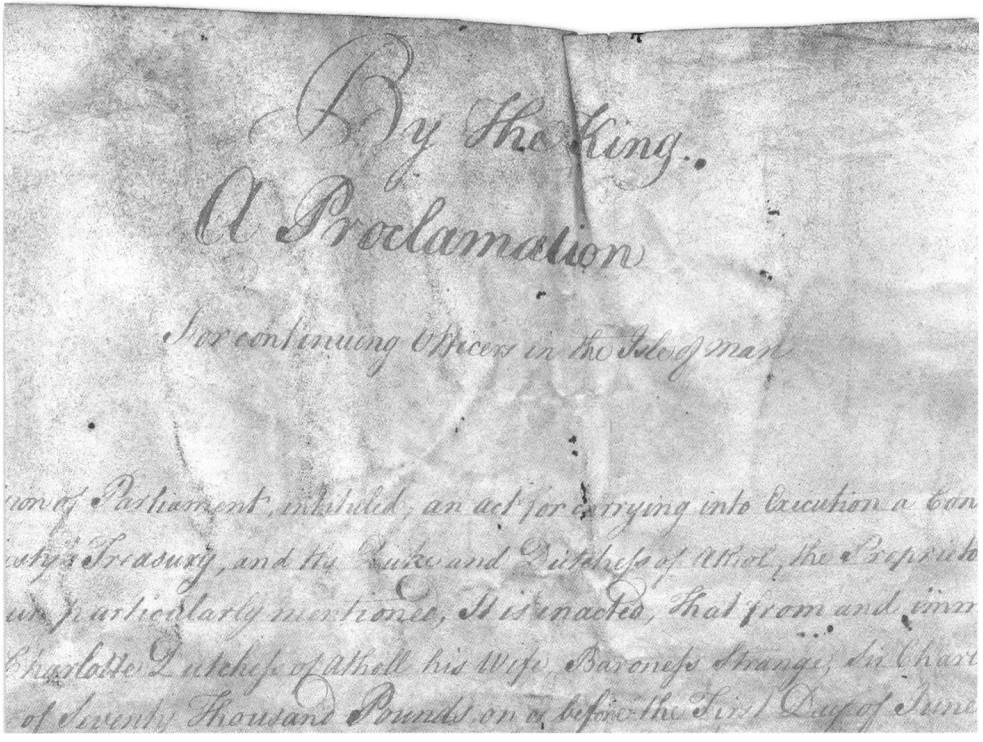

Details of the Royal Proclamation of the Revestment Act, 1765.

The procession passed by the line of troops, through the crowd of onlookers and finally gathered in front of the Castletown cross. No one in Britain had thought to have the proclamation written in Manx, the principal language of the people to whom it was to be addressed, so it had been speedily translated and roughly drawn up and was now read out by John Quillin, the Attorney General. The proclamation decreed that it should also be 'publickly read in all the principal Towns in the said Island, between the Hours of Eleven in the morning & Two in the afternoon, & printed Copies thereof to be affixed in the most Publick Places'.[156] The clergy were informed that it should also be read out at every church and chapel 'on the next Lord's Day after they shall receive the same'. When Quillin finished the declaration, 'three loud huzzars' were called for and given.[157] The Manx flag was struck, the Union flag was hoisted in its place and three celebratory volleys were fired by the troops. The procession then went indoors to the court room for the Attorney General to read the Governor's commission and the Governor himself to take his oath of office on the Bible:

> I John Wood, Esquire, do swear, that I will truly and uprightly deal between our Sovereign

Lord the King and his subjects within this isle, and as indifferently between party and party as this staff now standeth, so far as in me lyeth; and when I think it necessary, will call together the Council of this isle, or so many of them as shall be present within the same, and advise with them in any matter that may concern the State and Government thereof; and that I will do and perform, as far as in me lyeth, these and all other things appertaining to the Government of this isle, and the post and office of Governor in Chief and Captain General, according to the purpose and extent of my commission.[158]

Another volley was fired. The Governor then administered the taking of the oaths of the officials. The Deemsters' oath ended with the pledge to execute the laws justly and 'indifferently as the herring back-bone doth lie in the midst of the fish'. Unsurprisingly the Duke of Atholl was not present, but his representatives officially surrendered the Island to the Crown by delivering the Sword of State and the Public Seal.[159] Finally, Governor Wood gave a speech in which he said, 'Gentlemen I need not engage your time with recounting the many incidents that have brought about this revolution amongst you, let it suffice to say that you are now become the immediate care of a prince as distinguished for his goodness as he is renowned for his power'. He went on to promise that every encouragement would be given to the fair trader and that any complaints and grievances would be listened to. He warned against the continuation of the smuggling trade, 'hazardous and uncertain as it has been', and assured those assembled, many of whom had been active in 'the trade', that the troops of the 42nd Regiment of Foot of Lord John Murray's Black Watch (*Freiceadan Dubh*), who had been brought to the Island recently, were there 'not to oppose, but to protect you in your properties and to circulate their money amongst you'. Governor Wood had taken care of the interests of the Duke of Atholl for the past four years, making the most of the smuggling trade for his Lord's revenue, but with revestment came a change in policy, and throughout the next twelve years Wood would act on behalf of the Crown to suppress the very trade he had previously promoted. Feelings of suspicion and foreboding would have been felt by many who heard Wood's final statements, and those who had prospered from smuggling must have despaired for their financial future. However, that would be then, and this was now, so for the moment everything was focused on the celebrations and pageantry. With the formal ceremony completed, the procession returned to the Governor's house where the dignitaries were entertained, feasted well and toasted George III's health from glasses filled with fine claret whilst the troops did the same from overflowing mugs poured from a hogshead of beer. The eventful day concluded with further festivities, the highlight being a great bonfire which lit up the summer evening sky.

The suzerainty of the hereditary Lords of Man now came to an end. The sovereignty of the Island was vested inalienably in George III and his successors to the British Crown.[160] The two main parties to the agreement, the British Parliament and the Atholl family, carefully restricted themselves to safeguard their own immediate interests and ignored those of the Manx altogether. It is immediately striking that neither in the negotiations leading up to the Revestment and Mischief Acts nor in the drafting of the Acts themselves were the rights of the people taken into account. Little of the Island's surplus customs revenue was intended to come back for its benefit.

The action of Britain and the consequences on the Isle of Man have raised much comment since. Some thirty years after revestment John Feltham recorded part of a popular contemporary refrain:

> All the babes unborn will rue the day
> That the Isle of Man was sold away;
> For there's ne'er an old wife that loves a dram,
> But what will lament for the Isle of Man.[161]

Future commentators, with the benefit of hindsight, considered the situation. Spencer Walpole, Governor of the Isle of Man from 1882 to 1893, put it simply that the British Parliament technically had 'the right to legislate for any portion of the British Empire, and its exercise of this right does not depend upon questions of supremacy, but on questions of expediency'.[162] A. W. Moore considered that, whilst the laws and tenures of the Isle of Man were not altered as a result of the Revestment and Mischief Acts, the:

> Imperial Parliament legislated with respect to customs, harbours and merchant shipping, and, in measure of a general character having reference to the Empire at large, it occasionally inserted clauses, without the consent of Tynwald, by which penalties in contravention of those Acts might be enforced in the Island. It also assumed the control of the insular customs duties. These actions could only be justified on the ground that Parliament is supreme in all the Crown's dominions, a principle which it had proved impossible to enforce with regard to the American colonies, but which the Isle of Man was powerless to contest.[163]

Thomas Grindley considered that the Revestment Act gave Britain no new rights in addition to those of the ancient Lords:

> It merely transferred the existing rights and prerogatives of the Lord of Man from the Duke of Atholl to the King of England. Just that, nothing more. Everything else - the independence of the legislature, the liberties of the people, the details of the administration - was left untouched, and, of right, was as before. But that one event - the passing of the sovereign authority to the Crown of England - was enough [to allow Britain to act with supreme authority].[164]

Even the 1911 committee of enquiry, appointed directly by the Home Secretary, Winston

Churchill, and under the chairmanship of Lord MacDonnell, in its important *Report of the Departmental Committee on the Constitution, etc., of the Isle of Man*, had an opinion. It considered that revestment had subjected the Island to 'the harassing commercial restrictions which the short-sighted policy of that time imposed on English dependencies'.[165]

Immediate repercussions

There is little doubt that, on the basis of contemporary private and official documents, the Island was adversely affected directly after the Revestment and Mischief Acts, with a significant proportion of the population of the principal towns, who had grown used to the smuggling way of life, having to quickly adjust to the consequences of change or, in some cases, having to leave the Island.

Initially the Acts dealt a blow not only to smuggling but to legitimate trade in general. Merchants, manufacturers and agriculturists, who had been blatantly misled by the assurance that there was no intention to sell the Island, were all affected. The direct importation of all foreign goods was prohibited and the exportation of goods likely to compete with British products was not allowed, causing Manx trade to be burdened 'with all the restrictions and regulations usually imposed upon foreign countries'.[166] The bustle of commerce ceased, and 'the merchants, imagining that the treasures of their warehouses would be immediately confiscated, disposed of them greatly beneath their original value, and retired to other countries'.[167] The restrictive measures certainly temporarily curtailed the Island's fortunes. The businessmen of Douglas were devastated. 'The sale of the Island', one of the trustees of St George's chapel wrote later, 'which put a period to our opulence, put a period to everything that depended upon it'.[168] Indeed, an example of the parlous situation of the main trading town of Douglas was the cessation of the building of St George's which had commenced in 1761. Concern about their businesses resulted in many of the people who had pledged financial support for the new chapel withdrawing their offers. The building work was brought to a stop in 1765 with outstanding debts and was not recommenced until ten years later.

The situation caused much worry and hardship amongst the poorer inhabitants. The loss of the opportunity to earn a decent living and, indeed, prosper from the smuggling trade was devastating to a good part of a generation which had become accustomed to using it to supplement the meagre and uncertain income available from farming and fishing. The House of Keys claimed that many young Manx people, 'destitute of employment, are abandoning their Homes and seeking a Livelihood in foreign Parts'.[169] Bishop Mark Hildesley wrote in an 'Address to the Publick' about the consequences revestment had on those involved in the fishing industry, 'above a thousand of whom have been obliged to leave this island . . . for want of employment, to the distress and irreparable loss of the country'.[170] This is an incredible figure, given that the total population was only about 20,000.[171] Others who stayed became poverty stricken.

The residents were immediately subjected to the authority of Britain whose dictum was put into practice by appointed officials. A few weeks after the Revestment and Mischief Acts had been imposed the Reverend Philip Moore, Bishop Hildesley's colleague and friend, wrote to Hildesley, who was staying with friends in England, to inform him that:

> Nothing now but Anarchy & Confusion, ruled by Custom house officers, tide waiters & vinegar men. . . . Bands of armed men go about the Country, terrifying the people & entering their Houses in search of teas, &c, even the Homes of Deemster Lace & Capt Curphy, have been searched. . . . Mr Lutwidge, the Gen[era]l Surveyor has no less than 50 coast officers & tide waiters along with him, planted in the sev[era]l ports, besides the crews of 2 or 3 cutt[e]rs at a call. All this must naturally occasion riotous & tumultuous Doings. One side, in pursuit of & chastising, with great severity, those they suspect to be inform[e]rs, & the other side protecting & Defending them. 'Tis a very melancholly situation that we are in at pres[en]t, for want of a regular form of Civil Gov[ernmen]t amongst us. The Grievance complained of w[ould]d ha[ve] dyed away of it self, without these violent & unconstitutional proceedings, and truly if some redress cant be had and that soon, we shall be of all subjects the most miserable. All our people of property are making up their matters as fast as they can & preparing to Quit a place, governed by martial law & the violence of arms. . . . This is the Wisdom & Council of Gothomic men, w[i]th a Sledge Hammer to break an Egg. . . . I pray God, y[ou]r Lordship's endeav[ou]rs to remedy these Cruel Evils of our unsettled state may be attended with success. I have almost wrote myself sick.[172]

A. W. Moore, the historian, later claimed that the whole direction of the Island's affairs 'was handed over to officials, for the most part connected with the Treasury, who regarded the island as a pestilent nest of smugglers, from which it was their duty to extract as much revenue as possible, but for which they were under no obligation to do anything'.[173] This forthright opinion appears to somewhat overstate the situation. Certainly, Charles Lutwidge, onetime British Surveyor General, had been appointed directly after revestment as Receiver General and Collector of Revenue along with sufficient replacement officers to oversee the collection of customs duties.[174] Nevertheless, the other existing resident officials (many of whom were Manxmen) appointed by the Duke of Atholl had retained their posts, including John Wood who had been re-appointed Governor.

It seems unlikely that the Manx domestic economy of 1765 can be viewed as being healthy unless the important economic indicators of mortgage lending and property transaction activity were themselves healthy. They were not. During that year not one mortgage or property transaction was recorded.[175] Improvements would only come during the summer months of 1766 when land and property were again bought and sold, albeit at prices below those of the early 1760s. The trading towns became almost deserted, and the rents of houses and lands fell to one-third of their former value.[176]

The public economy also suffered a major decline. Indeed, the total annual revenue from customs duties during the thirty years after revestment was less than that for the previous thirty years under the Dukes of Atholl.[177] This extended dip would have been affected by the lost volume of duties previously paid by the merchants involved in smuggling. Any continuation of smuggling after revestment, with some smugglers now bringing goods surreptitiously into the Island for local use only and paying no duties at all (much the same practice as was happening throughout Britain and Ireland), would also have contributed to the situation. Britain accepted low returns from the Manx customs revenue for many years in order to protect its own Exchequer.

In April 1766 George Moore, the Chairman of the House of Keys, and Thomas Moore MHK were accompanied to London by the Reverend James Wilks to put to those of influence the case for improving the dire situation the Isle of Man now found itself in.[178] This was followed up in December when George Moore again went to London to present further proposals and arguments. Not in the best of health, he went alone to speak with officials at the Treasury and the Customs as well as certain individuals, including the Chancellor of the Exchequer, the President of the Board of Trade, the Duke of Atholl, Charles Lutwidge and the Speaker of the House of Commons. The Speaker, Sir John Cust, was most sympathetic, and met with Moore on several occasions. One early morning in the New Year, Moore arrived at Cust's residence to discuss with him some documents he had previously left. Cust was not expecting Moore, who recorded that 'the porter told me he was not yet up, but on telling him my name, he said he w[oul]d go & see; He immediately returned & telling me his mas[te]r was in the parlour'. Cust warmly welcomed Moore, asked him to be seated and took the documents out of a drawer in his bureau. The Speaker sat back in his chair and carefully reread Moore's papers. He was most sympathetic, expressing his opinion that 'the Government thro[ugh] an Exercise of Power had deprived the inhabitants of the Isle of Man of their privileges'. Later, Moore presented his documents and a memorial from the House of Keys to the Treasury. Both sets of papers claimed that the rights of the people of the Island should not have been bartered away. Moore was looking for concessions on trade and customs. For week after week he sat kicking his heels in the cold antechambers of the Treasury without any outcome.[179] He returned to the Island in March uncertain what, if anything, he had achieved.

Aftermath

Despite the sudden setback caused by revestment and the uncertainty of the future, it appears that the Island soon came to terms with the financial consequences. It was not permanently damaged. Internal trade was now the primary source of income generation. Hannah Bullock commented later

Douglas Harbour and South Quay seen from the Duke of Atholl's residence on North Quay showing a trading vessel, shipbuilding area, herring houses, dwelling house and brewery, 1789.

that 'the sums brought in by strangers, increased the circulation, and gave the necessary stimulus to commerce and agriculture'.[180] Douglas recovered rapidly due to the arrival of a variety of these 'strangers', including lawyers, doctors, shopkeepers, artisans, impoverished gentlefolk escaping their creditors and, later, retired half-pay officers. All of these new residents flocked to the Island because of its few local district taxes, cheap cost of living and less stringent laws on debtors, as well as its still comparatively low customs duties. The popularity and prosperity of the town was also assisted by it being served by an ideal bay, harbour and quayside to receive many large ships. It was increasingly becoming the Island's principal commercial and population centre:

> To the society of English, Douglas is considerably indebted. They have given life and gaiety to the town, and have contributed to polish the manners of the natives. Convivial societies, assemblies and card parties are now frequent among the higher circles of Douglas. Whist is their favourite game and they seldom play high. Cards are introduced on every occasion, and generally accompanied with a plentitude of excellent wines. . . . Among the inferior classes gaming is far more pernicious. Inebriation is here its constant attendant.[181]

The other major trading towns took somewhat longer to revive:

> Castletown, though dignified with the residence of the Governor of the Isle, is in wealth and mercantile importance greatly inferior to Douglas. . . . Previous to 1765, Peel had a considerable traffick with the Irish and Scotch smugglers, but since then, its trade has almost disappeared. The town is at present inert and solitary, and the houses in general have a poor and miserable aspect. . . . What I observed of Peel may with little variation be extended to this town [Ramsey]. Both places before the sale of the Island flourished by the gains of illicit commerce.[182]

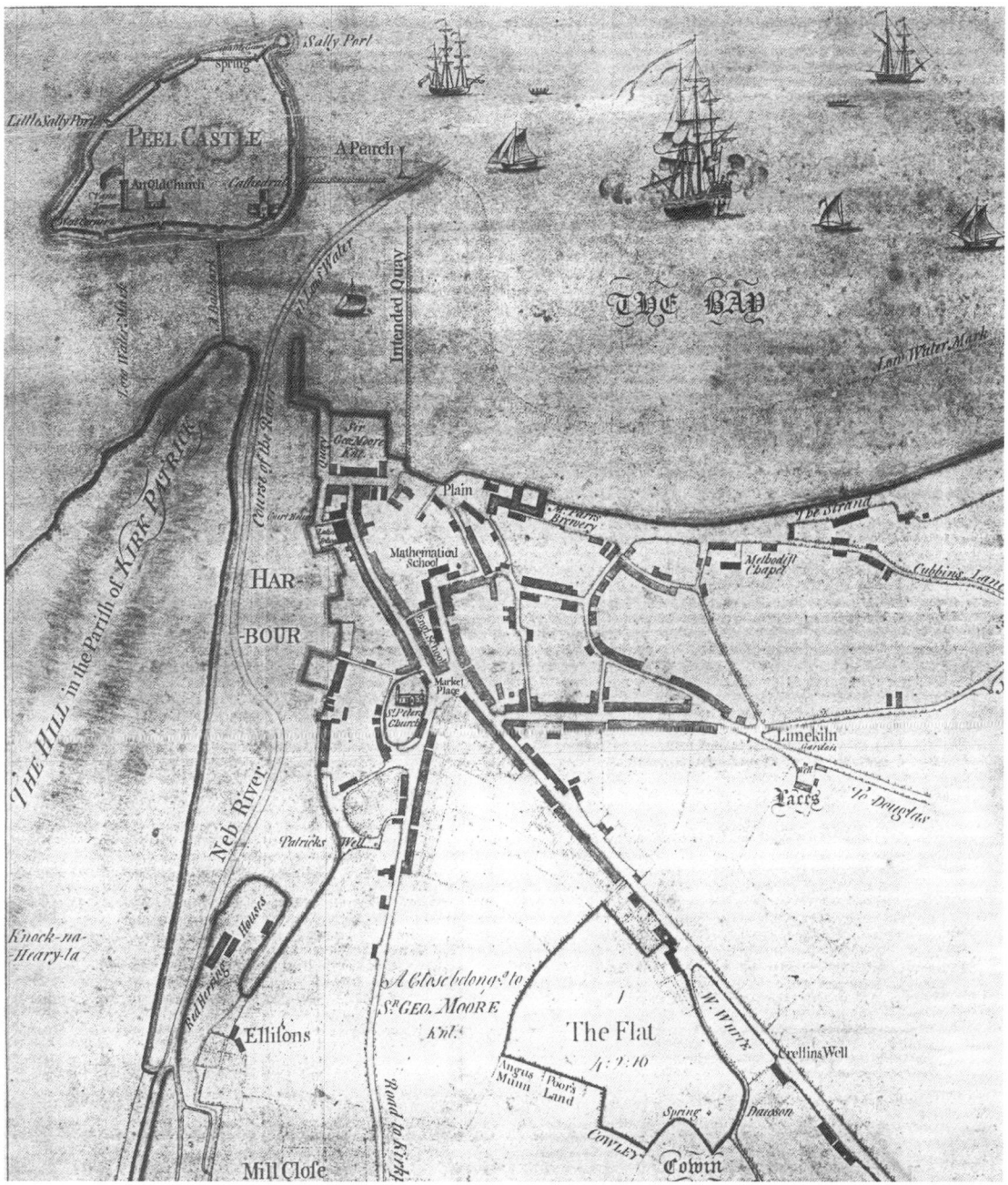

Peel, its Castle, Harbour, Bay and surrounding area, 1784

Life outside the trading towns appears not to have suffered to the same extent through the closing down of 'the trade', indeed some of it prospered in part as a direct result:

> The far greater number of people who inhabited villages, the mountains and the valleys, were strangers to the trade and its advantages. . . . The merchants who have enriched themselves by trade are now purchasing large tracts of uncultivated land and improving them at great expence.[183]

Despite the adversities caused by revestment, many prominent entrepreneurs remained in the Island and prospered, developing their local estates and carrying on their businesses by concentrating on the legal side of the world-wide trading networks they had established over many years.[184] Others still continued to illegally supply the smuggling trade, which had been curtailed but certainly not stopped. Yet others left the Island to carry on their business elsewhere. The great smuggling storehouse of the Isle of Man was now succeeded by other places, including the Faeroe Islands, Guernsey and certain Dutch and French ports.[185]

Whilst the Isle of Man did not become part of the realm of Britain as a result of revestment, it was subjected to its general authority. In its role as the imperial parliament, Westminster legislated for the Manx customs, harbours and shipping, and, with reference to the British Empire at large and without the consent of Tynwald, it now set about introducing Parliamentary Acts directly affecting the Island. Whilst the manner of control varied widely throughout its empire, Britain considered that the will of Parliament was supreme in all the Crown's territories. It assumed complete responsibility for the government of the Island, exercised through the offices of the Governor. The Island's surplus customs revenue accrued in the British Exchequer. Britain ignored the fact that it did not have the lawful right to assume any greater power than the previous feudal Lords of Man to levy any form of taxation without the consent of the Manx people through Tynwald.

What was certain was that for the first time ever Manx customs duties were to be imposed by Acts of the British Parliament, and they were set with little reference to Tynwald, whose previously supposed share of control of the principal insular finances was now ignored. The first of these Acts, 'An Act for encouraging and regulating the trade and manufactures of the Isle of Man', was passed in 1767.[186] It allowed the British Parliament to repeal the duties previously set by Tynwald Court and assume the power to impose taxes on the people of the Island by enacting new customs duties. In order to assist stamping out smuggling, the Act levied heavier customs duties on imported goods, a limit was placed on the amounts of certain goods allowed to be imported by licence and such goods were only to be brought by British ships into Douglas. These restrictions were meant to limit the availability of cheap goods, such as spirits, tea, coffee and tobacco, for

Brig Caesar, a Douglas trading vessel, in the Bay of Naples, 1788.

smuggling out of the Island. The duties were in future to be set and collected under the authority of the Treasury. The first clause of the Act stated that 'it is expedient that provision be made for encouraging, improving and regulating the trade and manufactures of the said Island and the fisheries on the coasts thereof; and whereas it is necessary that a revenue should be raised'. The revenue was to pay bounties to encourage, improve and regulate the local herring fishery and linen manufactories and to defray the expenses of government and the administration of justice. Another clause stated that any surplus remaining after this was to be paid directly into the British Exchequer, 'distinctly and apart from all other branches of the public revenue'. The House of Keys maintained that these clauses meant that the surplus should form the basis of a definite insular income which would then be spent in the Island. But the Treasury did not view the matter in that light and claimed the right to use it in any way it pleased as the surplus was 'reserved for the disposition of Parliament'.

For quite a number of years following the Act there were occasions when the annual surplus was very small or the income was less than the expenditure, resulting in the Island being run at a loss.[187] This was the price Britain was prepared to pay in order to do away with smuggling and protect its own revenue. Any proposals for general or capital schemes needed to be put by the Governor to the Treasury for consideration, but there is little recorded evidence to show that the Island's wellbeing was being budgeted for or that much in the way of benefits, other than those referred to above, ever returned to the Island. As a consequence, harbours and public buildings were neglected and fell into disrepair.[188]

The British Government, no doubt, considered its policy as justifiable as its recent disastrous treatment of the American colonies, when, to meet the cost of military defence in North America, it had asserted its right to place direct taxes against the colonists, without their consent, by introducing George Grenville's disastrous Act in 1765 which applied stamp duties on official transactions and another in 1767 which imposed customs duties on certain colonial merchandise.[189] The cry of 'no taxation without representation' was understandably raised against this policy. No greater, and probably a lesser, right existed for Britain to tax the people of the Isle of Man who were members of a country with an ancient parliament.[190] However, in this respect, size and distance were very important. The policies of Britain were unlikely to offer much in the way of sympathy for the small and near Isle of Man. Whilst an adjacent island could quite easily be controlled, the distant American colonies presented a more formidable problem. Edmund Burke, the political philosopher and Whig Member of Parliament, referred to the matter in a lengthy speech during a parliamentary debate on the 'granting certain duties in the British Colonies and Plantations in America' in April 1774:

> The American Revenue Act is the forty-fifth chapter [in the Statute Book of 1767]; the other to which I refer is the forty-fourth of the same session. These two Acts are both to the same purpose, both Revenue Acts; both taxing out of the Kingdom; and both taxing British manufactures exported. As the 45th is an Act for raising a revenue in America, the 44th is an Act for raising a revenue in the Isle of Man. . . . Now will the noble Lord [Grenville] condescend to tell me why he repealed the taxes on manufactures sent out to America and not the taxes on manufactures exported to the Isle of Man? The principle was exactly the same, the objects charged infinitely more extensive, the duties without comparison higher. Why? Why, notwithstanding all his childish pretexts, because the taxes were quietly submitted to in the Isle of Man, and because they raised a flame in America.[191]

Chapter 4

DETERMINED DUKE

Significance of the new relationship

The third Duke of Atholl died in tragic circumstances on 5 November 1774 aged only forty-five. Having suffered an apoplectic fit, he was being taken care of at his Dunkeld residence in the Scottish Highlands when he swallowed hartshorn (sulphate of ammonia) which was being used to bathe his forehead.[192] He immediately began to bleed from his nose and mouth. Although a careful watch was kept on him, he managed to slip away, and, delirious and in great pain, he threw himself into the river Tay near to his ducal seat and drowned. The Duchess Charlotte relinquished all her rights in the Island by deed to their nineteen-year-old son, John Murray, the fourth Duke of Atholl.[193] He blamed his father's mental state at the time of his unfortunate death directly on the pressure put on him by the British Government, George Grenville in particular, to sell the family's regalities and customs in the Isle of Man, writing that 'while I live I shall ever consider a noble heart was broken by that lamentable transaction'.[194]

There is much evidence that smuggling was still active both into and out of the Island for some time after revestment. One example is shown in a letter written by John Crosse, a merchant of Islay in Scotland, to John Taubman, who was Speaker of the House of Keys from 1780 to 1799, offering to sell Highland whisky to him, stating that 'I could send a boat from here with little risque from the revenue officers and land the goods I want in a corner with a little risque'.[195] Another example, referring to the seizure in England of a vessel ostensibly carrying Manx red herrings, features in a letter from Thomas Quayle, a member of one of the most politically influential and wealthy trading families, to his father in the Isle of Man informing him that 'This ev[enin]g so great a disaster has happened that the Custom House officers have discov[ere]d either one or two tuns of claret on board her. . . . The officer went to the place at once where the wine was concealed so must have had an informant'.[196]

In 1780 'An Act for granting to His Majesty several additional duties upon certain goods imported into the Isle of Man; and for the better regulating the trade and securing the revenue of the said Island' had been introduced by the British Parliament in an attempt to deal with these continuing problems.[197] Certain goods had their duties and allowances revised. Seizing on an opportunity these changes presented, the fourth Duke petitioned the British Parliament in 1780 and again in 1781, asking leave to introduce Bills to protect his land and property in the Island

John Murray, fourth Duke of Atholl, and family.

and to amend the Revestment Act.[198] He alleged that the customs revenue had not been properly or fairly collected and that the annual amount of customs revenue used in calculating the figures for the purchase of the Island had consequently been too small. The Duke's petitions were opposed by the House of Keys, whose retiring Chairman (the position from then on would become termed as 'Speaker') George Moore and John Cosnahan MHK gave evidence against them at the House of Lords, fearing that any increased payment to the Duke would be at the expense of the Island and claiming that it should have the surplus revenue for its own purposes. The petitions were also opposed by Charles Lutwidge, the Manx Receiver General, and Wadsworth Busk, the Manx Attorney General. The 'rather improbable alliance' of Keys members and Manx officials argued the case for the Island.[199] The Duke's petitions were considered and reported on by the British Attorney General and the Solicitor General, and his claims eventually passed the House of Commons, but were opposed in the House of Lords.[200]

The two Manx officials were heavily involved in the whole situation at this time. It appears that Receiver General Lutwidge was not averse to using his status for his own profit. A letter to the Marquis of Rockingham, the First Lord of the Treasury, accused Lutwidge of conniving with the smugglers, being 'an egregious smuggler' himself, bringing in ships with his own contraband on board and being 'in too violent a hurry to amass a fortune' since taking up his position in the Island.[201] Wadsworth Busk, the Attorney General, had been a long term critic of the Atholls and did not get on with the Duke, and the feeling was mutual; the Duke described Busk as 'that rascal'.[202] When the Duke became the Island's Governor in 1793, Busk would retire to England. Wadsworth Busk and George Moore were both knighted later in 1781 which suggests that Britain considered that it also had benefited from their efforts. As was often the case, those who had acquired almost anything that money could buy, then claimed one last reward - the social status that came from an honour.[203] That status, however, came at a price for the recipient, from hundreds of pounds for a knighthood to many thousand for a hereditary peerage. George Moore's grandson, Thomas Quayle, wrote to his father, 'I have heard it said a Knighthood costs ab[ou]t £100, my G[ran]df[athe]r has not p[ai]d his Fees yet'.[204]

In 1789 the Duke renewed his claims. He argued that his parents had not had the power to 'make the settlements or invest the trustees, under the authority of which or by the concurrence of whom the sale of the Island was made and the lawful heirs of entail became disinherited'.[205] This point is an important and contentious legal factor when considering the history of the revestment of the Island. Each Lord stood in possession of the Isle of Man for his lifetime, during which he was not able to sell or dispose of it in any manner and after which it had to pass on to his heir as laid down by the 1406 settlement which had granted it to Sir John Stanley, 'his heirs and assigns in perpetuity'. The Duke's relative, General James Murray, a Member of Parliament, sought to bring in a Bill to appoint a commission to enquire into the extent and value of certain rights, revenues and possessions in the Isle of Man. This use of family members to bring their powerful influences to protect and further his personal ambitions was a ploy that the Duke would use on many occasions: both self-interest and nepotism to the highest degree. The British Government supported the request to appoint an investigating commission. Amongst those opposing it was John Christian Curwen, a Whig Member of Parliament and, later, a Member of the House of Keys.[206] The Keys themselves opposed it, and three of their members, Speaker John Taubman, Richard Stevenson and Daniel Callow, met with Curwen in London in April 1790 to oppose the Duke's Bill which their colleagues in the Island considered 'does not go to any thing specifically and therefore the more dangerous and the more difficult to guard against' and prophetically foretold that it could be 'a Ten Years Business before the Enquiry may be closed'.[207] But, for the time being and with a weight of opinion against the Duke's claims, the British Government withdrew the Bill. William Pitt the Younger, the First Lord of the Treasury and Chancellor of the Exchequer, was reported as saying that:

> notwithstanding his full conviction of the propriety, and even necessity of proceeding

with such a measure, yet, after the unfavourable impression which had gained ground upon the subject, he should think it in no degree prudent to attempt to push the Bill further at present.[208]

'Cursed crew of Taubmans and Quayles'

The fourth Duke of Atholl continued to believe that the situation his family was in as a result of the Revestment and Mischief Acts was unfair and unjust. He considered that a contributory factor which had led to his family's loss of the suzerainty, regalities and customs had been as a result of the 'reports of dishonest servants'.[209] A great number of the officials who had served his father were part of the Manx establishment. They and their families had made fortunes through their dealings in the smuggling trade and had built on this success by establishing worldwide legal trading businesses. Other than the Duke himself, they were amongst the Island's principal land and property owners and would have had their keen eyes on the Atholls' remaining rights. The Duke considered that these men, many of whom were also Members of the House of Keys, made up the hard core of an opposition party which was working against him. Many Members of the House of Keys took on their positions to protect their own vested interests, and the principal members around this period came from a few prosperous local families.

Amongst the Duke's most notable antagonists were the influential Taubman and Quayle families, 'scoundrels and smugglers' who 'will not leave the Duke a bird's nest in the Island by the time they have done with him'.[210] They were joined by others, including John Lace, a Member of the House of Keys, a future Deemster and 'a noisy bully'. These adversaries were seemingly led by Richard Dawson, Lieutenant Governor from 1775 to 1790, 'an adulterous rascal who connived at the prostitution of his own wife', and who held together the various antagonists, 'though they all hate each other'. The Duke even fell out with his own mother who he once wrote was at work with the 'cursed crew of Taubmans and Quayles'.[211] Bishop Claudius Crigan sent a letter to Mrs Calcraft, who had been one of his parishioners and had once worked for the Duke's mother, claiming that 'This Island still continues in the flames of Party rage, kindled and kept in full blaze by your good old friend Quayle's Arts & Malignity against the Master who enriched him and his family, aided by the Purse & by the Pride & Passion of the New House of Taubman'.[212] Whether the Bishop considered his letter was confidential or not, Mrs Calcraft thought its reference to the Taubmans, the Quayles and the opposition party was of sufficient importance to be passed on to the Duke. The Atholl Papers contain a document which includes a list of names of Members of the House of Keys, of whom twelve were relatives of John Taubman and another four were directly linked with him through business.[213] All of these members were in the Keys towards the end of the time when Taubman was Speaker (1780-99) or shortly afterwards when his son was elected as his direct successor (1799-1823):

Satirical print of the House of Keys in session at Bishop Wilson's library, Castletown, 1790.

John Taubman
John Taubman, son
John Christian Curwen, brother-in-law
Thomas Gawne, first cousin
Edward Gawne, first cousin
Norris Moore, first cousin
Frederick Stevenson, cousin
James Oates, cousin
Thomas Harrison, cousin
John Cosnahan, cousin
Thomas Kerwin, married to first cousin
Daniel Tellett, married to first cousin
Robert Quayle, married to cousin
John Quayle, partner with first cousin
George Quayle, partner in bank
James Kelly, partner in bank
John Harrison, former clerk to Taubman's father

A great deal of important original documents still survive, and they contain a fascinating range of information which gives a remarkable insight into the extensive business transactions of a number of merchants operating out of the Island during this period. The important Taubman,

*John Taubman (senior),
Speaker of the House of Keys, 1780-99.*

*John Taubman (junior),
Speaker of the House of Keys, 1799-1823.*

John Quayle, Clerk of the Rolls.

George Quayle, Member of the House of Keys.

Quayle and Moore manuscripts (Goldie-Taubman papers, Bridge House papers and George Moore letter books) show the vast extent of the trading and business interests, including smuggling and slavery, of many notable Manx families before and after revestment. Members of many of these families intermarried, thereby creating an elite establishment, a 'clique', which dominated the Isle of Man in terms of trade and politics for many generations.

Commissioners' Report

With the British Government on his side but Parliament against him, the fourth Duke, still unwilling to relinquish his objective, took a course of action in 1791 similar to that attempted two years earlier. He consulted with Henry Dundas, later Lord Melville, a neighbour of his in Scotland and Home Secretary in Pitt's administration. As a result, the influential Dundas recommended that the Crown should appoint commissioners to visit the Island to make a thorough investigation into the general state of its revenue and commerce.[214] Consequently, in September John Spranger and William Osgoode (English barristers), William Roe (commissioner of the English Board of Customs), David Reid (commissioner of the Scottish Board of Customs) and William Grant (Member of Parliament) were appointed as commissioners to examine matters. They were to be assisted in the Island by a committee of the House of Keys. The commissioners took evidence from many witnesses, including the Duke of Atholl, the Governor in Chief and Captain General, the Lieutenant Governor, Members of the House of Keys, civil officials, revenue officers, traders, merchants and many other local people. The commissioners collected a mass of details before closing their investigations at the end of November.

On 21 April 1792 *The Report of the Commissioners of Inquiry for the Isle of Man* (a mine of historical information) was produced for the Home Office.[215] The Home Office, founded ten years earlier in order to reorganise the duties previously undertaken by two Secretaries of State who shared domestic business, had amongst its responsibilities the requirement to take account of the interests of the Isle of Man. The commissioners reported that the Duke's allegations had been that:

- The ducal revenues had not been fairly collected prior to revestment.
- The Dukes of Atholl had had the power to increase the customs duties, with the consent of Tynwald, which would not have been refused.
- Some rights had been incorrectly vested in the Crown.

The commissioners considered these three points.[216] They agreed that the Lords' revenues had not been fairly paid or collected prior to revestment owing to the mismanagement of the system. The fourth Duke had pointed out in his evidence that the key revenue officials in the employ of his father had been earning small salaries: the Receiver General £40 a year, the Collector and

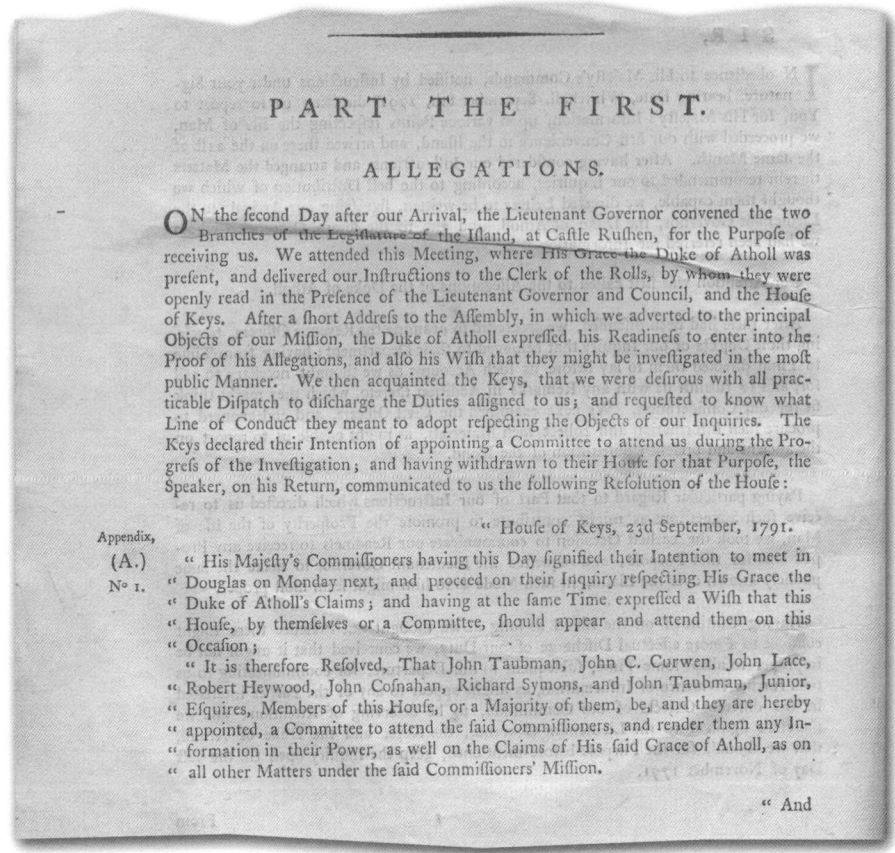

Duke of Atholl's allegations, Report of the Commissioners of Inquiry, 1792.

Controller £32, the searchers £3 or £5 and their assistants £1 or £3.[217] He had gone on to state that 'When I hear of people on such salaries as these, living splendidly, bringing up numerous families, or dying opulent, I cannot but doubt the fair collection [of the customs duties]'. Given that his father must have been fully aware of these salary levels and any additional legal perquisites and certainly must have known that the officials had been supplementing their incomes by siphoning off some of the revenues as well as involving themselves in smuggling for their own and his family's benefits, the Duke's follow-up statement, true as it most certainly was, comes across as at best naive, at worst hypocritical. Whilst the commissioners agreed that there was no doubt that the Lord had had the power of increasing customs duties with the consent of Tynwald Court, they pointed out that it was improbable that Tynwald would have consented to this 'without an equivalent'. They agreed with the Duke's claim that certain rights had been unnecessarily vested in the Crown, and they declared that the continuation of these rights with the Atholls would not have encouraged smuggling.

From the testimony of the officials, the commissioners found that the weakness of the present system supported 'the truth of the representation alluded to in our instructions, "that illicit practices do still prevail in the Isle of Man"'.[218] But, in contrast to pre-revestment when entrepreneurs openly brought goods into the Island and paid the legal duties, certain goods were now being smuggled in and, consequently, no duties were paid at all. The smugglers used:

> Luggers, Cutters and Wherries, which continually hover upon the Coasts and sometimes come into the Bays of the Island, for the Purpose of running the Whole, or Part of their Cargoes; and the Manks Boats, which, upon Signals, go off to these Smuggling Vessels from the Harbours, Bays, or Creeks, in order to convey on Shore the Goods meant to be so landed; or which take on board, and tranship at Sea, or transport across the Channel, the Articles intended for illegal Adventure.

The commissioners found that the principal 'illicit practices' involved French brandy, Geneva (gin), tea, tobacco, silks and salt. Large amounts of brandy and gin, which were only allowed to be imported on payment of British duties, were being smuggled into and out of the Island. At the same time, British spirits and rum, which were allowed in by licence but none had been legally imported since 1784, were in open use in the Island, further proof of the continued existence of smuggling.[219] The commissioners considered that the existing allowance for licensed rum should be increased and that a limited amount of brandy and gin should be imported on payment of Manx duties.

But it was not only the commissioners who were aware of the continuation of smuggling. David Robertson, who previously had been a customs official in the Island and returned to tour it in the summer of 1791, recorded that he sailed over from Whitehaven in a revenue cutter which came upon a small boat anchored beneath Maughold Head.[220] The customs officials boarded the boat and discovered that it was laden with wine, rum and tobacco ready to be smuggled over to England. The smugglers were arrested, and Robertson recorded that the owner of the boat 'retired to a corner of the vessel, wringing his hands', exclaiming, '"Now am I ruined indeed! How shall I return to my wife and family?"'. Richard Townley, whilst resident in the Isle of Man in the same year, wrote in his journal:

> The *Swift*, of Port Glasgow, a fine cutter-built rig, is come into the harbour, in her return from Scotland to the French coast, for another cargo of brandy, and other articles, in the illicit trade. We were taught to expect a total suppression of the smuggling business; but, I fear, the shameful traffick is reviving very much upon the coasts of Scotland and Ireland, as well as upon the east coast of England.[221]

The commissioners' report revealed that the total customs receipts at the four trading ports during 1790 had been £3,016 (Douglas £2,793, Castletown £104, Ramsey £87 and Peel £32), whilst the total expenditure of £3,322 had been for herring bounties (£781), salaries of the revenue (£919) and civil (£1,474) officers and incidental expenses (£148).[222] Other smaller receipts used for harbour improvements came from harbour dues and herring customs. The figures featured in this and other reports again confirm that Britain was prepared to run the Island at an occasional loss for a number of years in order to protect its own revenue. The commissioners came to the conclusion that, whilst there were nearly forty local staff employed to look after the customs' operation (including a Receiver General earning £300 a year, a collector, a comptroller, a warehouse keeper, a gauger, searchers, riding officers and boatmen), the management system of the customs revenue in the Island was 'ill digested, incomplete and unfit' and that 'nothing short of a radical change can reach the evil and communicate order, regularity and energy'. They considered that the best method of producing such change was to transfer the administration of the Manx customs system from the Treasury to the direct management of the Commissioners of Customs for England or even Scotland.

The commissioners were very concerned about the licence system which allowed the importation of limited quantities of spirits, tea, coffee and tobacco by certain select people. Shortly after revestment a number of English merchants had gained control of this new system to the detriment of the Manx merchants.[223] Some of these merchant strangers had used fictitious names to obtain further licences:

> A Mr Richardson of Whitehaven by making use of a number of names along with his own, obtained Licences for twenty Hogsheads [of tobacco], which he imported into the Island . . . at the rate of 3d per lb [pound weight], and insisted upon the Dealers giving his own price, 5d per lb, ready money.

The abuse of the system had resulted in merchant strangers having the monopoly of the licences and, as a result, the ability to charge exorbitant retail prices to the public. The commissioners agreed with the Governor, the Members of the House of Keys and the majority of the inhabitants of the principal towns that, as the merchant strangers were applying for and being given licences ahead of local merchants, 'a heavy and needless Grievance arises out of the present System of these licensed Importations. It is alleged, that a Monopoly is thereby introduced, to the prejudice of the Island'.[224] The commissioners considered that the licence system should be tightened up and the law should be changed to give the locals priority over merchant strangers.

The report offered a wide variety of suggestions to deal with the multitude of other problems. These included altering various duties, tightening up the valuation method for obtaining duties raised on the ad valorem basis, additionally rewarding the members of the resident military force for their efforts in preventing smuggling and stationing armed revenue cruisers off the Island's coast.[225] The report also dealt with the Isle of Man's revenues, trading situation, constitution and possible future benefits, and the commissioners reckoned that if the trade of the Island was opened up with Britain then, 'Where the constant and solid Returns of legal and avowed Commerce are understood and enjoyed, the perilous, irregular, and dishonest Gains of illicit Traffic must decline'. But the Manx people would have to wait more than fifty years before their trade with Britain was changed from 'beyond the seas' to be placed on the terms of the 'coasting trade'.

Further compensation

Directly after the commissioners' report was made known, determined and dissatisfied as ever with events, John Murray, the fourth Duke of Atholl, defined in a memorandum the 'Preliminaries which will satisfy me and render an arrangement and final settlement under the authority of the British Parliament much more simply and easy'.[226] The principal requirement he made was to be appointed as the next Governor in Chief and Captain General of the Isle of Man. He had recently been informed by Lieutenant Governor Alexander Shaw that the opposition party was plotting that John Christian Curwen, who continued to oppose the Duke in the British Parliament, should be appointed the next Governor in Chief and Captain General.[227] Shaw had been approached by the plotters to assist in this scheme with the promise that he would remain as Lieutenant Governor. The Duke met with Henry Dundas and William Pitt early in 1793 when he reiterated his requirements.[228] These were agreed with in part, but he would only accept the terms with the caveat that they were simply 'primary steps to that final arrangement which is intended to follow'. When the Governor, Major General Edward Smith, died later that year, the Duke was appointed in his place, a position which gave him the advantage of being able to deal with his opponents whilst continuing to promote and protect his remaining family interests in the Island.[229] He was generally an absentee Governor, so he appointed various relatives to offices in the Island to keep an eye on his rights, and he relied on his Lieutenant Governor to administer the government. Even with these arrangements, the Duke continued to be in disagreement with a variety of opponents. If the British Government had hoped that appointing him as Governor would result in the conclusion to his petitions and also heal the bad feelings that had arisen between him and a variety of people - a problem which had existed throughout his long association with the Island and would continue up until his death - then it was mistaken.

It was not until 1798 that some of the recommendations of the report prepared by the commissioners were eventually carried out through 'An Act for the further encouragement of the

John Christian Curwen, appointed a Member of Parliament in 1786 and a Member of the House of Keys in 1791.

trade and manufactures of the Isle of Man; for improving the revenue thereof; and for the more effectual prevention of smuggling to and from the said Island'.[230] By this Act the licence system was amended, limiting the importation of certain goods to specific merchants and further restricting the amounts imported. The importation of British spirits was prohibited, but foreign spirits were allowed in instead, revenue cutters were again stationed off the Island, all boats in the Manx herring fleet were to be registered and certain tariffs were increased. As a consequence of the changes, the Island's annual gross customs revenue almost trebled in the short time from 1790 to 1800, and would now generally continue on an upward trend.[231]

The substantial increase in revenue motivated the Duke to present another petition to the King in Council in 1801 seeking additional compensation and claiming that his parents had been forced to submit to revestment 'by dread of a greater calamity which they had too much reason to apprehend might take place if they did not'.[232] The petition was prepared whilst William Pitt was still in office but reached the King in Council during the crisis which led to Pitt's resignation from power. It was referred to a committee of the Privy Council in June 1801 during the early part of the administration of Henry Addington, Viscount Sidmouth. A counterpetition was presented by the House of Keys which was also referred to the committee in March 1802.[233] The committee passed matters on once again to the Attorney General and the Solicitor General to investigate and report on the relevant evidence laid before the House of Commons and the Treasury at the time of the Revestment Act.[234] The two law officers made their report in November 1802. They found that there were no grounds for claiming that the previous compensation had been inadequate. The report was referred back to the committee, but it was nearly two years before a decision was made. In March 1804 the committee rejected the Duke's petition. Before the report could be confirmed, the Duke asked that it should be suspended until he had prepared a supplementary petition.[235] This was probably a delaying tactic, knowing that political change was in the offing:

> The Duke had by now maintained the struggle for the best part of twenty-five years. He had been defeated in the House of Lords, he had been defeated in the House of Commons, and he had been defeated, it might have been thought, finally, in the Privy Council; yet he was on the very eve of securing a long deferred victory. The whirligig of politics, which had disappointed his expectations by replacing Pitt with Addington in 1801, now replaced Addington with Pitt in 1804.[236]

In June 1804 the Duke presented yet another of his many petitions to the House of Commons for relief in respect of what he considered had been inadequate compensation paid to his family in 1765.[237] The Keys promptly resolved to send three or even more of their members to London to yet again attempt to protect the interests of the Manx people - and their own.[238] Pitt allowed the petition to go before another committee of the Privy Council, but this time, without taking the opinion of the Attorney General and the Solicitor General, it reversed the previous decision and recommended that further compensation should be given, reporting that it appeared to be reasonable that a proportion of the increased customs revenue should be allowed to the Atholl family and that a suitable Bill should be introduced.[239] This report was approved by the King in Council in August 1804. The Duke consequently presented a petition to the House of Commons in March 1805 requesting that provision should be made in a Bill which was before the House for the improvement of the revenues of the Island to also give him this extra compensation. He was supported by some of the principal merchants in the Island who backed his claims, 'deeply connected as they are with the advancement of the prosperity of the Island'.[240] The merchants referred to the Duke as 'the warm, the active and the only powerful friend of the Island' whose claims should not be opposed. Another petition from the 'landholders, merchants and other inhabitants' of the Island also supported him. This praise from the various commercial classes was, no doubt, fuelled by self-interest. A counterpetition was presented by the House of Keys.[241] All these petitions were referred to a select committee which reported that the Duke had fully established the claims in his petition, that he should be granted further compensation and that such compensation should be charged on the customs revenue of the Island.[242] The report explained that the surplus customs revenue of the Isle of Man under the 1767 Act had been £23,000 and that £20,000 of this amount had been placed with the Island's Receiver General. The adoption of this report was opposed in both Houses of Parliament, led by John Christian Curwen in the Commons and his cousin Lord Ellenborough in the Lords, but was supported by the government. In the face of all-round opposition, 'An Act for settling and securing a certain Annuity on John, now Duke of Atholl, and the heirs general of the seventh Earl of Derby' was forcibly passed on 12 July 1805, providing that the Duke and his heirs should be paid an annuity of 'one-fourth part of the gross annual revenue arising from the duties of Customs now payable and arising within the said Island'.[243] By this time, with the customs system operating more efficiently, the gross customs revenue of the Island for the previous five years had increased to an average in excess of £10,000 a year. The one-fourth annuity granted to the Duke of Atholl would be assigned by indenture to a definitive sum of £3,000 a year in May 1810.[244]

The Lord Chief Justice, Lord Ellenborough, declared that the transaction was 'one of the most corrupt jobs ever witnessed in Parliament' and that the manner in which the claim was pressed was 'a proceeding which would only be sanctioned by Parliament in the worst and most corrupt times'.[245] Spencer Walpole, writing many years later, considered that the influence of Pitt on the outcome of the issue was all-important:

> Whether private friendship or the desire to secure political support, may have actuated his conduct, there seems no justification for the Act itself or for the manner in which it was done. . . . It was the influence of Pitt which secured the Duke the compensation he sought; it was Pitt's authority which persuaded a reluctant Legislature; and Pitt, and Pitt alone, must be held responsible for what was done, and for the manner of doing it.[246]

At the same time as the Act for settling the one-fourth annuity was reaching completion, 'An Act for regulating and encouraging the trade, for the improvement of the revenue, and prevention of smuggling to and from the Isle of Man' was introduced by the British Parliament on 10 July 1805.[247] The major change brought about by this Act affected the placement of the Manx customs revenue. By the Act of 1767 the surplus Manx customs revenue had to be kept 'distinctly and apart from all other branches of the public revenue'. This provision had been omitted from the Act of 1798, but the Act of 1805 took a much more formidable and worrying step and directed that the surplus 'shall go to and make part of the Consolidated Fund of Great Britain'.[248] The Consolidated Fund had been set up in 1787 to gather together the various taxes and other branches of the revenue into one central fund, 'a fund into which shall flow every stream of the revenue, and from which shall issue the supply for every public service'.[249] The Manx customs revenue was no longer to be set aside specifically. It was taken further away from its source, the Manx people. This would cause further long-standing problems in the relationship between the two countries.

Bitter end

The foreign debt law of 1737, which had encouraged debtors to come and settle in the Island, was eventually repealed in 1814 by 'An Act for affording Relief to Insolvent Debtors in the Isle of Man', which was a more stringent Act and resulted in the Island no longer being the safe sanctuary it once was for debtors, so, many people moved elsewhere.[250] This was at first a great loss to the Island generally and Douglas in particular. But within a few years the population was considerably swelled, due in no small part to the immigration of numerous half-pay officers who had been retired from service due to the cessation of the Napoleonic wars and the American and Canadian frontier conflicts and who were attracted by the comparatively low cost of living and freedom from taxation the Island offered. The influx of these new residents would give an important impetus to the prosperity of the country. A growing number of summer visitors, principally from the thriving cotton mills and wool producing counties of Lancashire and Yorkshire, were also beginning to come over on holiday. Douglas, with its harbour 'accounted the best dry one in the Irish Sea', was fast becoming a popular seaside destination due to its healthy environment and extensive entertainment amenities:

> The goodness of the sands and the unmixed purity of the water, render it one of the most agreeable bathing places in this part of the world. Bathing machines are provided by Mr Thomas Dixon of the British Hotel and others, and hot and cold and shower and vapour baths are fitted in a neat and comfortable manner by Mr Geneste. The inns are good and sufficiently numerous for the accommodation of their various visitors. Douglas contains public libraries, news-rooms and billiards-rooms; dancing assemblies, card assemblies and other convivial meetings are not infrequent. Boats for aquatic excursions, horses, gigs and post-chaises may be had at several inns at the shortest notice.[251]

Despite the upturn in the economy, the financial position of the general inhabitants was put at risk by the needs of the Murray family. In 1817 landowners and tenant farmers were outraged when the Bishop of Sodor and Man, George Murray, with the support of his uncle, Governor John Murray, the fourth Duke of Atholl, attempted to collect certain green crop tithes which had not been demanded since revestment:

> Dear Uncle, he cried, I have found out a way,
> Whereby I can make more of corn tithe and hay;
> To the field we must go, with our spade and shovel,
> And there find potatoes and turnips without trouble.[252]

Bishop Murray's appointment in 1814 had been yet another example of the Duke's use of placing members of his family in important positions to try to control the Island for his own purposes.

The land-owning interest, 'which was all powerful in the Legislature', was also aggrieved during this time over the allowance for the free importation of foreign corn.[253] There had been a series of poor harvests in the three years 1814-16 which had required corn to be shipped in. Some members of the Keys were alarmed by this, fearing a break-up of their monopoly and control of Manx corn prices, and eventually they convinced the British Government to introduce 'An Act to repeal certain Acts regulating the importation and exportation of corn, grain, meal and flour' in July 1821 which immediately stopped any importations.[254] This resulted in an increase in the cost of local flour and bread to the general public which led to protests and riots throughout the land that October and November. In Peel rioters marched on the shops of the flour dealers and bakers and forced them to reduce their prices.[255] They also attacked the properties of those who had signed a petition to exclude imported corn.[256] Several of the rioters were arrested but were quickly released on bail when a stone throwing mob surrounded the court house where the prisoners were being held. Thomas Shimmin, who was put on trial as one of the ringleaders of the rioters, attacked a witness giving evidence at a court convened by Deemster Thomas Gawne. The Deemster, 'laying aside his dignity', leapt from the bench and assisted the constables in restraining the defendant. In Douglas several hundred people attacked shops and houses, breaking windows and destroying the contents.[257] The rioters moved out of town to the Nunnery estate where they intended to attack its mill but were beaten off by three constables and an armed party led by General Thomas Goldie, the occupier of the Nunnery House. Throughout the disturbances the Manx Yeoman Cavalry and the constables had struggled to maintain order, so much so that Lieutenant Governor Colonel Cornelius Smelt arranged with the Home Secretary, Viscount Sidmouth, for two companies of infantry to be sent over to assist in the matter, but only forty men arrived.[258] Sidmouth firmly refused to send any further reinforcements.[259] The angry protests and the lack of further support from the Home Office forced Tynwald to quickly petition the Crown to lift the embargo, and the price of corn accordingly came down.

As the flour riots and protests were going on, the rights of the Bishop's green crop tithes proposal were brought before the local exchequer court and, to the dismay of the landowners and farmers, they were adjudged to be lawful.[260] Support for this unpopular decision was eventually given by the Privy Council four years later in 1825. The Bishop promptly announced that a tithe of 12/- an acre would be levied on potatoes, an excessive rate as in Ireland it was 3/- and in the north of England it was 2/6.[261] As potatoes and herring were the staple diet of the poor, and crops and fishing had both failed that summer, such a high tithe was likely to add to the plight of the poor and cause desperate people to react. In October attempts were made by the Bishop's agents

George Murray, Bishop of Sodor and Man.

to collect the tithe, but riots broke out across the Island. The Duke and Bishop's chief agent, James McCrone, reported that 'the entire of the law of the Island and liberty of the subjects are in the hands of the mob'.[262] The Bishop's stores were ransacked, potatoes thrown into the sea, carts destroyed, horses driven away and houses of two of the tithe agents demolished. Thousands of protestors assembled at St Marks in Malew, brought together 'by the blowing of horns and ringing of church bells', and they elected a deputation to dictate their terms to McCrone at Castle Rushen. Meanwhile, in the north a mob was marching to confront the Bishop at his palace at Bishopscourt. Sixteen soldiers in two coaches drawn by four horses each were quickly dispatched, but the mob dispersed without doing any damage. Bishop Murray arranged for himself and his family to be escorted by armed troops to shelter at his uncle's private house in Douglas. On a cold November morning a crowd of protestors marched on Castle Rushen to bring their concerns directly to Tynwald Court. A deputation met with Lieutenant Governor Smelt and Bishop Murray and was told that the green crop tithe would not be collected that year. The Bishop reported to the Duke that 'the mob have prevailed'.[263] There would be no further attempts to collect the tithe. But all was not over yet in relation to recent events. Troops and constables were dispatched to search out the leaders of the riots. Only two, John Kermode and William Hudgeon, were brought to trial that December for their part in an arson attack, an offence punishable by death, but the jury refused to send either of them to the gallows, instead Deemster Christian sentenced them to transportation to Botany Bay for life.[264] James McCrone believed that 'the Keys are at the bottom of the mischief', and Bishop Murray believed that the real instigators should have been punished, not merely 'a set of deluded wretches'.[265]

In his role as Governor, the fourth Duke was constantly at odds with the House of Keys. He had no respect for the members. He dismissed a memorial from fifteen of them sent to the Home Secretary, Robert Peel, in September 1821 which complained about the Duke appointing officials to the Legislative (previously, Lord's) Council and it requested that officials 'should be fixed by proper authority'.[266] Their memorial also claimed that the Duke's 'interests as a subject are often in opposition to those of the Crown, and generally at variance with those of the people of the Island'. The Duke counterclaimed 'that each of the Keys who had signed the memorial . . . should be prosecuted for the offence'. In 1822 he derisively referred to them as being 'no more representative of the people of Man, than of the people of Peru'.[267] Consequently, the Keys sent another memorial of complaint about the Duke to the Home Secretary.[268] Early in 1823 the Duke, in turn, informed Robert Peel that the Keys were having secret meetings and should not have increased powers and privileges because, 'if the Keys desire that they should have the same powers as similar assemblies elsewhere in the Kingdom, they should not be a self-elected body, but one which really represents the people and is elected by them'.[269] Indeed, the Duke was even considering dissolving the House.[270] However, Peel was not supportive. He thought that the Duke's behaviour towards the Keys had added to the ill feeling between the parties.[271]

The Duke was also having difficulties with certain of the Crown appointed officials. During February and March 1823 he presided over a secret Court of Inquiry which had been established by the Home Secretary in order to consider the conduct of Deemster Thomas Gawne.[272] The Deemster had been accused of attempting to pervert the course of justice by encouraging Catherine McBride to bring a law suit against Captain Thomas Fell for recompense of one year's wages for her dismissal from his household. The case had then been heard by Deemster Gawne. Throughout the secret inquiry graphic detail was gone into regarding the personal relationship between Gawne and McBride. Thomas Garrett told the inquiry that McBride 'was one of Deemster Gawne's ladies'. The Reverend James Hutchins produced records from St George's Church which showed that 'John, illegitimate son of Thomas Gawne and Catherine McBride, privately baptised 4 Dec[embe]r 1821'. Catherine McBride was accused of 'having conducted herself improperly with different Gent[leme]n', running up credit, being drunk, dressing in men's clothes, staying out late at night and using indecent language. Her fellow servant, Elizabeth Kewin, told of McBride talking lewdly through their windows with a man lodging in a house opposite who 'was sometimes undressed'. Fell's advocate, William Roper, a supporter of the Duke, later claimed that the Deemster 'connected himself with a prostitute, and instead of paying her himself, led her, unjustly, to commence a suit against an innocent tradesman'. After hearing the evidence, with many witnesses giving contrary accounts of the various issues, a copy of the proceedings was sent to the Home Secretary who consequently instructed the Duke to 'inform Mr Deemster Gawne that his Majesty has no further occasion for his Services'. This resulted in the Keys complaining yet again, this time to the King in Council.

Towards the end of winter in 1824 the Duke was in London, once more meeting with Robert Peel to discuss his family rights but still not getting the support he hoped for. He recorded that 'Mr Peel's reception of me at this interview was formal and constrained, in my opinion. He scarcely deigned to rise from his chair'.[273] At the same time, Thomas Gawne, supposedly ill in bed, was also in the city opposing the Duke.[274] Whilst at his London home, the Duke received a letter from his relative Captain Mungo Murray which began with an account of his recent sea crossing from Liverpool to Douglas on board the ship the *Duchess of Atholl*, a journey which had begun at seven o'clock in the evening and was only completed the next day at one o'clock in the afternoon when the ship arrived at the snow-covered Isle of Man.[275] 'A very disagreeable night, the sea extreamly rough, the old swell meeting the wind boarded us on all quarters in a most terrific manner splitt our jibb and mainsail. Made the Calf light at 4am'. Later on in the letter Mungo made a number of acerbic remarks about Lieutenant Governor Cornelius Smelt, 'the old fox'. Mungo claimed that Smelt had put off a Tynwald meeting because 'old Corney has fained sick having seen something to bogal at'. But Smelt, aged seventy-five, was in fact quite ill with a feverish cold and had been visited by Dr Oswald 'who has taken a pint of blood from him, I wish he had drained him, I do not think there is a sound drop in his whole body. . . . he is but in a bad way, that is but speeking as we could wish perhapes'.

Cornelius Smelt had been appointed Lieutenant Governor in 1805 and continued in that role until he died aged eighty-three in 1832. With the Duke spending a great deal of time at his home in London or at his Scottish estates, it was left to Smelt to take on the responsibilities for the government and other affairs of the Island. In this respect he was a popular figure with both the people and the Keys. His relationship with the Duke was quite different; it had always been extremely strained. Smelt knew that he was 'disliked in very high degree by the Duke'.[276] The various disputes went back to Cornelius Smelt's original appointment, as is revealed in a draft memorandum from the Duke to the Home Secretary, Viscount Sidmouth, in which he stated, 'I shall be immediately relieved from the difficulties, not to say insults, I have experienced in my official situation as Governor in Chief of the Isle of Man, since the appointment of the present

Governor Cornelius Smelt.

Lieutenant Governor to the situation'.[277] Over many years the Duke sent numerous complaints about him to Sidmouth and his successor, Robert Peel, using a multitude of reasons in attempting to have Smelt removed from office in order to have a member of his own family installed as Lieutenant Governor, thereby ensuring a strong Atholl grip on Manx affairs.[278] He claimed that Smelt was insubordinate, colluded with others against him, was duplicitous, did not cooperate, was not keeping proper records, had refused to hand over official correspondence and, instead of supporting the Royal prerogative as embodied in the Governor and Council, had upheld the Keys in their attack on it. A feud over Smelt and his family living in the Governor's official residence had run on and on, with the Duke again demanding the Home Office to support his demands. At one stage in this disagreement the Duke had visited the Island, and whilst in Castletown carrying out his duties as Governor he had to hire a room to stay in at The George Inn, just yards from his official house in Castle Rushen.[279] From The George he wrote to Smelt stating that 'it is impossible for me again to be exposed to the disagreeable necessity of feeling all the inconveniences of an Inn, separated so far from the Courts where my public duty demands my attendance' and claiming that the 'inconveniences . . . might affect my health'. The Home Office steadfastly refused to remove the Crown appointed Lieutenant Governor Smelt from either his position or his residence. His presence was a restraint on the machinations of the disgruntled fourth Duke.

Late in 1824 the Duke and Duchess, together with their party, arrived in the Island on board the steam ship the *Majestic*.[280] Over Christmas and New Year they stayed at their private residence the Castle Mona which was situated near the shore at Douglas. The building of the Castle Mona had been completed twenty years earlier, and in order to mark the occasion at that time many local and visiting dignitaries had been invited by the Duke to a sumptuous dinner.[281] On a summer evening the guests had made their way across the lawned approach to the Duke and Duchess' magnificent new mansion from where they were able to admire its square form, with a wing on the south side and a circular tower rising from the centre. The exterior was made of freestone brought in from the Isle of Arran. The guests made their entrance through a stately portico which opened into a long and spacious hall supported by pillars. They proceeded into a magnificent salon with a ceiling the height of two floors, and from there they were invited to dine in the banqueting hall, after which they had graciously applauded the architect, George Steuart, who attended the latter stages of the proceedings although very ill. But no such large turn out, grand occasion or grateful applause marked the leaving of the Isle of Man by the Duke and Duchess in early February 1825 on board the *James Watt*.[282] They were bound for Liverpool and from there on to their London home. This, as it happened, was their last visit to the Isle of Man.[283]

All the disagreements had caused great discontent, which finally came to a head in the spring of 1825 when the House of Commons was considering a Bill which would enable the Treasury to negotiate with the Duke for the outright purchase of the one-fourth annuity.[284] The House of Keys presented a petition to the Commons supporting this sale of the Duke's remaining rights in the Island to the Crown, which the Keys considered would result in 'the comfort and happiness of the people of the said Island'.[285] The Duke found himself more and more isolated. Bishop Murray informed him that 'From the moment it was known that you intended to dispose of your rights, every Manksman turned against us'.[286] Any lingering support was now to be lost. 'An Act to empower the Commissioners of His Majesty's Treasury to purchase a certain Annuity in respect of Duties of Customs levied in the Isle of Man, and any reserved Sovereign Rights in the said Island, belonging to John, Duke of Atholl' was passed on 10 June 1825 authorising the purchase to be financed from the Consolidated Fund (where the proceeds from the Manx customs revenue were placed) and allowing the Treasury and the Duke to appoint arbitrators.[287] With the majority of the people and the local legislature against him, and with little support from the British Government, which was now eager to purchase his remaining rights, the Duke expressed his readiness to sell.[288]

Castle Mona, residence of the fourth Duke of Atholl, c.1810.

William Courtenay, a Master of the Court of Chancery, on behalf of the Treasury, and William Harrison, King's Counsel, on behalf of the Duke, were appointed as arbitrators to ascertain and determine the value of the annuity granted in 1805 (the customs revenue had more than doubled from £9,516 in 1805 to £22,275 in 1825), any reserved suzerain rights which the Duke still claimed and possessed, and all his real property, manorial and other rights, ecclesiastical patronage and other hereditaments reserved by the Revestment Act of 1765.[289] In case the arbitrators were unable to come to an agreement within six calendar months, the two parties appointed John Bernard Bosanquet, a Sergeant-at-Law (senior barrister), as umpire.

On 5 July 1825 'An Act for regulating the trade of the Isle of Man' was introduced.[290] The customs duties were now to be set and collected under the authority of the Customs Department. The recording of the income and expenditure was to be more organised. Though part of the revenue continued to be used to pay bounties to the herring fishery, the costs of government and administration of justice were the principal items of expenditure. The budgeted surplus continued to be paid directly into the Exchequer to become part of Britain's Consolidated Fund. Indeed, in the years since revestment, other than £24,000 spent on the Red Pier at Douglas, £10,000 on fortifications and minor amounts on other harbour works (expenditure which not only helped the Island but benefited Britain in its control there), little of the surplus returned to the Island.[291] The Act increased certain duties and annual allowances - the added cost the Manx people were expected to pay yet again to assist Britain with the expense of buying out the Atholls.

Throughout the long time of his involvement with the Island, the fourth Duke of Atholl had put unstinting efforts into ensuring that his family was rewarded for its losses as a consequence of the Revestment Act. The dogged determination of the Duke would certainly have been motivated in order to raise funds to support the lifestyle of an important noble family which had many extensive estates in Scotland, two ducal properties at Blair Atholl and Dunkeld, a home in the Isle of Man and a lavish property in London, all requiring expensive upkeep. Most certainly his efforts would additionally have been fuelled by the circumstances which he claimed contributed in a large way to the unfortunate death of his father. Towards the end of 1825 he recorded in his journal:

> It is now fifty years since, on my father's death, I succeeded to the family honours and such estates as remained, after losing the Isle of Man. I have every reason to think that the illiberality and injustice with which he considered this princely inheritance was taken from him, without due comprehension, or sufficient knowledge on his part of the great value of an inheritance of which he knew nothing, save from the reports of dishonest servants, preyed severely on his spirits, and ultimately produced a brain fever.[292]

On 9 January 1826 the fourth Duke attended the Treasury to sign a contract to progress the sale of his remaining rights.[293] In his journal he described it as 'the most memorable day of my life', clear evidence of the financial importance of the Isle of Man to his family, immense satisfaction with the compensation for the Atholl's lost rights and heartfelt relief that his demands were at last to be resolved. After an extended and deliberate inquiry, involving much bitter bargaining, the arbitrators arrived at the following valuation:

Customs revenue annuity under Act of 1805	150,000	(paid in 1826)
Lord's or quit rents and alienation fines	34,200	(paid in 1827)
Ecclesiastical patronage, possessions of the religious houses, demesne lands, glebe lands, wastes, mines, quarries, services or works of tenants, rectories, tithes, commons, forests and all other rights reserved by the Act of 1765	232,944	(paid in 1828)
	£417,144[294]	

Britain's purchase of these rights for a total of £417,144 (now equivalent to £27.7 million) was finally completed in 1828. A 'Bill for confirming the Sales and Conveyances made to His Majesty, of the Isle, Castle, Peel, and Lordship of Man, and other Estates in the said Island of Man, lately belonging to John, Duke of Atholl' was introduced into the Commons on 19 May 1829.[295] However, the Bill was never proceeded with, 'the British Government probably considering that it had power to complete the purchase without fresh legislation'.[296]

From first to last - 1765 to 1828 - the British Government awarded the Atholls a total of £317,315 (now equivalent to £24.5 million) in recompense for their lost revenue from Manx customs duties:

1765	Revestment, customs	£24,000	(£2.7 million)
1765-1804	£2,000 a year from the Irish revenue	£80,000	(£8.6 million)
1805-09	One-fourth of customs duties	£15,315	(£0.8 million)
1810-25	£3,000 a year in lieu of the one-fourth annuity	£48,000	(£3.0 million)
1826	Final settlement in lieu of annuity	£150,000	(£9.4 million)

and £313,144 (£23.4 million) for their other rights:

1765	Revestment, regalities	£46,000	(£5.1 million)
1827	Rents etc.	£34,200	(£2.3 million)
1828	Patronage, properties, tithes etc.	£232,944	(£16.0 million)

Unsurprisingly, what were most certainly very generous settlements caused much resentment in the Isle of Man for many years. The hard facts were that the Lords of Man had already received vast sums of money from all their feudal rights in the Island from 1405 to 1765, and even after revestment they continued to receive revenue from their remaining rights. In addition, the Atholl family had received the equivalent of almost £48 million compensation from the British Government from 1765 to 1828. The Manx people were then made to pay for this compensation by having to accept the imposition of higher customs duties from which the resultant increased revenue was then placed in the coffers of the British Exchequer with little of it ever meant to return to the Island.

John Murray, the fourth Duke of Atholl, directly associated with the Island for over fifty-five years, died at his ducal seat in Dunkeld on 29 September 1830.

Chapter 5

Financial Threat

Calls for reforms

With the death of John Murray, the fourth Duke of Atholl and Governor in Chief and Captain General of the Isle of Man, came the end of a feudal link which had lasted for four hundred and twenty-five years. No sooner had the focus moved from the Duke of Atholl than it centred on two other issues: the need to reform the self-elected House of Keys and, principally, the struggle to fight off attempts to revise the Manx customs duties by bringing them more in line with those of Britain. The efforts of the constitutional modernisers and the opposers to fiscal changes - at times unusual and reluctant allies - would have important influences on the Island's destiny. Through the well co-ordinated work of both sets of activists there was now the beginning of a radical determination to introduce constitutional reform taking place alongside a conservative determination to retain the financial status quo.

In Britain Lord John Russell was playing a leading role in the passage of the 1832 Reform Bill which totally changed the House of Commons by disenfranchising many of the so-called rotten and pocket boroughs.[297] The development of reform politics was followed by the ending of the old colonial system, overwhelmed by the beginnings of Britain's policy regarding the principles of free trade. But changes in Britain's imperial policies did not as yet extend to the Isle of Man. Russell's future involvement as Home Secretary in calls for a more elementary extension of parliamentary reform in the Island would not be as liberal as his part in bringing about the recent changes in Britain. Whilst transformation was happening to the Commons, the continuation of an almost feudal House of Keys left the Island's constitutional position open to major criticism. Constitutional problems inevitably went hand-in-hand with fiscal issues, and Britain was concerned that any change to the establishment of the Keys would lead to demands for local control of all public finances. Britain was additionally concerned that there still existed remnants of smuggling and set about attempting to bring it to an end through the assimilation of the Island's customs duties to those of its own, 'thus at one stroke prejudicing the economic fortunes of the Island by raising the cost of living and threatening all cherished pretensions to national identity and sovereignty and possibly pointing the way towards annexation and incorporation into Britain'.[298]

Possible threats to their democracy and definite injury to their pockets galvanised the activists into action. They would now raise their voices in protest. The demand for constitutional reform

Robert Fargher, owner and editor of the Mona's Herald newspaper.

in the Island did not come directly as a result of Lord Russell's Reform Bill. Instead it came about by the need to solve a much more basic anomaly: that of the people of the Island having no elected representatives in Tynwald. The 'Castletown clique', the disparaging contemporary term used to describe the Keys and their supporters, had ignored the progress of reform in Britain and had resisted demands to change their own establishment. The preponderantly land-owning members of the Keys were part of a self-perpetuating oligarchy and a very powerful force, mainly concerned with furthering their own interests. Although there was some passive opposition to the continuation of an unrepresentative House of Keys, the population as a whole was generally inactive in calling for reform.[299] That 'the clique, the landowners and a few rich merchants exercised a powerful, if indirect, influence over many people' appears to have been enough to ensure that no organised movement for reform was undertaken. And the ultimate threat of annexation was always there to silence protest. So, the impetus for constitutional change did not come from a popular uprising. The agitation now emerging was the work of a minority, and that minority was led by Robert Fargher, a local printer with experience of London life and progressive political ideas.[300] In 1833 Fargher launched the reforming and dissenting newspaper, the *Mona's Herald*, which would become involved in a persistent and vigorous campaign to bring about the establishment of a democratically elected House of Keys to represent the interest of the people, an ambition which contrasted with the self-interest of the members of the Manx establishment. Through the liberal *Mona's Herald* the political reformers now had a vehicle to express their concerns.

Other much different reforms were also being considered at this time. The British Government was concerned that smuggling, though substantially reduced, was still active. To bring an end to this remnant of the Island's past, the eventual assimilation of the customs duties of the two countries was seen to be the answer. There was another related matter which brought the Island's fiscal status to the attention of the British authorities. Petitions were being raised complaining of the unfairness of the licence system, claiming it was being misused to the benefit of a minority of residents who had taken over from the merchant strangers in using the quota system to control the supply and inflate the prices of a variety of goods to their personal benefit. The Isle of Man had become the refuge of new residents who came there to enjoy an enhanced lifestyle as a consequence of the comparatively low cost of living. So, the consequences of possible customs duties assimilation and problems with the licence system instilled in many the fear that they would be unable to maintain their living standards. There was further concern that, whilst customs duties had been increased over the years, very little of the surplus revenue, which went directly into the British Exchequer, came back to the Island for new public works schemes and social improvements. Amongst the resident strangers who had made the Isle of Man their home were John Courtney Bluett and Sir William Hillary, both of whom would feature prominently in forthcoming events.[301]

'A Stranger'

John Welch, an architect, civil engineer and surveyor, is credited with writing *A Six Day's Tour through the Isle of Man* by 'A Stranger' which was published in 1836. Welch, who was certainly no stranger to the Island where he had lived and worked from time to time, provided an interesting perspective on the Island's situation during this period of uncertain change, commenting on its attraction to both the summer visitors and 'men of retiring domestic habits, averse from public broils, people of limited incomes, half-pay officers, and, indeed, of all such as are desirous of having a shilling's worth for sixpence'.[302]

Welch described how he sailed that summer from Liverpool on board the paddle-steamer the *Queen of the Isle*, 'cheered from time to time by music, a tolerable batch of drummers and fiddlers, who gave us their merriest airs in succession, compensating for the want of harmony by double vigour in scraping and beating'.[303] The ship was crowded with passengers whiling away their time either on deck or in her saloon with 'cheese and porter, playing backgammon, reading what spare volumes could be picked up about the cabins, or such books and papers as they might have brought with them'. On arrival at Douglas, Welch made his way to stay at the recently opened Castle Mona Hotel, onetime residence of the Duke of Atholl. The hotel's owner, George Heron, invited him to take dinner, but he had just had a meal on board the *Queen of the Isle* and therefore declined as 'I was fortunate enough to bring my dinner ashore' unlike some passengers who had been seasick! The hotel's weekly tariff for someone staying on full board and lodging was two guineas, children were charged half price and the hire of a private sitting room was from one guinea to £2. 5. 0.[304] The Castle Mona was surrounded by about thirty-five acres of beautiful gardens and pleasure grounds, and, in order to get a proper view of it and the bay, the next day Welch climbed the wooded slopes behind the hotel which led up to the Falcon's Cliff, the property of his friend Sir William Hillary and so named after the ancient homage exacted from the Lords of Man as the tenure for their possession of the Island.[305]

Welch was positive about the Island's future:

> there can be little uncertainty as to the future prospects of this lovely little isle. She has just risen from her long night of obscurity, fresh, vigorous, and beautiful as the ocean wave, and is preparing for a lengthened march of flourishing greatness. If she proceeds as she seems to promise, with what pleasure might we not be allowed to anticipate her state and condition fifty years hence. What changes must she not have seen! What improvements must she not have undergone![306]

Whilst heaping praise, he was not oblivious to the sorry state of certain parts of the Island. Possibly seeing a chance to benefit through his business, he expressed concern over the southern end of Douglas and considered that improvements should be carried out by:

> making a communication and splendid drive by way of the Parade, from the Pier to the Crescent, without passing through the wretched outskirts which now form the only direct avenue to the Castle. It were to be wished the whole of the line of mouldering hovels which constitute Sand-street and part of Fort-street were totally demolished, and in their place substituted some good houses fronting the sea and the proposed road.... The town itself (that is to say, the Old Town) is a wretched collection of disjointed lanes and alleys,

which seem to have been thrown together like dice upon a backgammon board, without the slightest reference to order or regularity, being built, I believe, for the convenience of smuggling, every lane end and corner assisting your imagination in conceiving of the zig-zag race of the pursuer and pursued, the smuggler and the custom-house officer.[307]

Possible assimilation

In 1833 'An Act for regulating the trade of the Isle of Man' had been passed by the British Parliament, but there was little change in the customs arrangements.[308] The exportation of any of the articles was strictly prohibited, and anyone who attempted to abuse the licence system could be fined £500 for every such event. The rates of the customs duties of the two countries make an interesting comparison:

	Manx[309]			British[310]		
	£	s	d	£	s	d
Brandy, a gallon		4.	6	1.	10.	0
Gin, a gallon		4.	6	1.	10.	0
Rum, a gallon		3.	0		9.	0
Coffee, a pound		0.	4		1.	3
Tobacco, a pound		1.	6		3.	0
Muscovado sugar, a cwt.		1.	0	3.	3.	0
Refined sugar, a cwt.		-		8.	8.	0
French wine, a tun	16.	0.	0	69.	6.	0
Other wine, a tun	12.	0.	0	34.	13.	0

At the annual Tynwald Day ceremony and proceedings held on 5 July 1836 at Castle Rushen the Governor, Lieutenant-Colonel John Ready, informed Tynwald Court that he had learnt unofficially that the British Government was about to introduce a Bill into Parliament to further regulate the trade of the Island.[311] Sir George Drinkwater, onetime mayor of Liverpool and who had a country house and estate in the Isle of Man, had received a letter on behalf of Lord Sandon, Member of Parliament for Tiverton, Cheshire:

> for the information of such of his constituents who may be interested in the Isle of Man, that Mr Poulett Thomson, the President of the Board of Trade, told him last night that it is his intention to bring into the House of Commons, this session, a Bill having in view the gradual assimilation of the fiscal and commercial laws of England and that Island.[312]

Governor John Ready.

Governor Ready advised Tynwald that it was his intention to address Lord John Russell, the Home Secretary, on the matter, and he would request that a copy of any proposed Bill should be sent to the Island for consideration before it was finalised. Four days later Ready again called together Tynwald Court to consider an official communication he had received on the matter.[313] Subsequently, a memorial of concern signed by all the members of Tynwald was sent to Lord Russell and to Charles Poulett Thomson, President of the Board of Trade.[314]

Joseph Train, who was staying in the Island preparing his *Historical and Statistical Account of the Isle of Man* when the news of the proposed assimilation of customs duties first reached it, witnessed that 'every class of the community seemed to indulge in the most gloomy forebodings of the disasters which would inevitably result from such a radical change in their fiscal regulations'.[315] John Welch commented that 'Should the general government ever assimilate the condition of this country to that of the surrounding shores, it will deal a blow, under the effects of which the place must reel and stagger for many long years'.[316] The *Manx Sun* - the conservative organ of those, including Members of the House of Keys, favouring the preservation of the fiscal benefits brought about by low taxation and the continuation of the constitutional status quo - claimed that 'petitions for reform, and libels on the local government and House of Keys have at length produced a political cloud from which it will require the utmost ingenuity to escape'.[317]

The *Manx Sun* unleashed a tirade against those who had complained to the British Government about the Island's laws and the licence system. It went on to remind its readers of the hue and cry made by some of the Members of the House of Commons when 'rats and other vermin were defrauded of their spoil' due to provisions in the 1765 Revestment Act and the 1767 Customs Act which had allowed Liverpool traders to remove poor quality grain from their warehouses and send it to the Island where it was crushed and returned to Liverpool as meal. 'An Act to amend laws relating to the importation of corn' had been introduced in 1828 to rectify the problem.[318] In 1835 more legislation had been brought into being by 'An Act to regulate the importation of corn into the Isle of Man' which laid down that 'it shall not be lawful to import into the Isle of Man any foreign corn, grain, meal or flour, except upon payment of the same duties as are by the said Act made payable on the importation into the United Kingdom of corn, grain, meal or flour'.[319] The *Manx Sun* considered that the Bill now in question derived from the same 'scarecrow' source as these two Acts. It also reported that a number of Liverpool traders had taken advantage of another Act - which permitted the timberless Island to import balk timber virtually duty free for its own use - to establish shipbuilding yards in the Island which had caused much concern to the shipbuilders of Liverpool and Cumberland. The *Manx Sun* claimed that the only possible article that could pay for smuggling was brandy, of which 10,000 gallons were allowed to be imported annually for the supply of the 40,000 inhabitants of the Island. 'Why', it stated in astonishment, 'it is scarcely a bottle per annum per head, and yet reports have been made of our smuggling it into England, because two or three females in the course of a year have been detected with a bottle concealed in their bustles'. The *Manx Sun* considered that the prime cause of the proposed Bill could probably be traced to the protests and jealousies of the contending licensed importers in the Island. The *Mona's Herald* was equally alarmed, but for a very different reason. It blamed the House of Keys for the situation, relating the possible assimilation of customs duties to the lack of reform by the Keys in becoming a democratically elected body:

Charles Poulett Thomson, President of the Board of Trade.

For many years past have we been strenuous in recommending every class of society to open their eyes to the fact that the first duty they owed themselves and their country was to put their *House* in such order that it might manfully, justly and successfully resist the innovation [customs duties assimilation]. We have over and over again entreated the House of Keys to assume the natural position of a House of Representatives.[320]

Resistance

The inhabitants of Douglas and its neighbourhood were called to a public meeting in July 1836.[321] The respected and influential Sir William Hillary, who had lived in the Island for many years, acted as chairman. He read out a petition he had addressed to the House of Commons which pointed out that there was no necessity for any increase in customs duties as a surplus of more than £16,000 of the Manx customs revenue was already handed over annually to the British Exchequer, little of which was subsequently returned for improving the local situation. Hillary claimed that any additional duty on imported timber would cause ruinous consequences to the present and future prosperity of the Island as it did not produce any suitable local timber for boat building and housing. John Courtney Bluett attributed the cause of the contemplated changes 'to the vexatious memorials under which the table of the Home Secretary has groaned'.

The controversial Bill was never progressed as parliamentary time ran out, and many months passed without further news of it or any strategies to deal with its threat. The *Mona's Herald* lamented that nothing had been heard from the House of Keys or the public committee. 'From the House we expected nothing, and are not, therefore, disappointed; but that gentlemen so honourably nominated, and from whom so much was hoped - we feel our pride a little taxed in holding them up as examples of patriotism'.[322]

In early 1837 Fox Maule of the Home Office sent to Governor Ready a copy of a letter from Poulett Thomson which stated that the Privy Council for Trade had recently considered again 'the inconveniences' which arose from the commercial and fiscal regulations relative to Britain and the Isle of Man, and that it was intended in the ensuing session of Parliament to submit certain alterations in the existing laws of customs and navigation.[323] The Governor and Tynwald were asked for their opinions upon the following possibilities:

- The Laws of Navigation would now bring the Island under the operation of those regulations which applied to Britain.
- The commerce between the Isle of Man and all parts of Britain should be placed on the terms of the coasting trade.
- In lieu of the present customs duties on imported goods paid in the Island, the duties in force in Britain, with certain exceptions, should be equally in force in the Island.
- The exceptions would be spirits, sugar, tea, tobacco and wine. They would not be subjected to the full amount of the British duties until after the expiration of a term of about ten years, during which time the Manx tariffs would be increased by stated additions until the duties of the two countries were equal.
- The amount of allowance of duty on refined sugar exported from Britain into the Island would alter in relation to the increase in its tariff, this being the only article upon which any such allowance was due at present.
- The set levels on the quantities of imported articles may need to continue until full assimilation of the customs duties was completed.

*Sir William Hillary, financial protectionist and founder of the
National Institution for the Preservation of Life from Shipwreck.*

On hearing of the above, the public committee appointed the previous year moved into action and called a meeting.[324] It was agreed that a deputation made up of advocates, George William Dumbell, Samuel Harris and John Courtney Bluett, and merchants, John Duff and Francis Matthews, should meet with the Governor, Council and Keys to point out that the unanimous opinion of the meeting was that every legal and constitutional means should be made to induce the British Government to abandon any intention of assimilation of customs duties, which, if introduced, would bring great financial hardship to all classes of people. The meeting proposed that a deputation of the Legislative Council, the House of Keys and representatives of the mercantile and trading interests of the Island should be appointed to go to London to communicate with the authorities there. The High Bailiffs and the Captains of the parishes were to be requested to convene public meetings in the various districts of the Island for the purposes of ascertaining the opinion of the general public and the election of local representatives.

Bluett wrote to the Governor requesting detailed information on the proposed alterations, and Ready lost no time in forwarding copies of the above correspondence to him.[325] Bluett then wrote to a recently appointed Tynwald select committee, advocating that the Island should resist the proposed increase of customs duties.[326] The Tynwald committee acted swiftly. It produced a report which considered with alarm the outcome to the Island should the proposed customs regulations be adopted.[327] It pointed out that the present healthy state of the public finances was shown by the gross customs revenue for the previous year approaching £25,000, which, after deduction of the expenses of the collection of the revenue and administration of justice, left a surplus of £16,000 which went to the Consolidated Fund of Britain. Despite an accumulating surplus, the Island received little benefit in return to deal with its public works and social issues. The report went on to state that, whilst the herring fishery formed the largest part of the trade of the Island, not one herring fishing boat could be built of locally grown timber. The lack of local timber also limited the building of houses for the increasing number of new residents. The committee considered that the assimilation of the customs duties would compel these residents to move to foreign countries, withdrawing an estimated annual income of £100,000. The people's deputation was then called upon to address Tynwald Court.[328] The Governor said he was happy to hear that the people were taking action on their own behalf. He handed the Tynwald committee's report to them to study. This they did and informed the Court that it reflected the people's wishes and sentiments.

Ready forwarded the report to Fox Maule, and in his accompanying letter he pointed out that 'it is not saying too much that the greatest alarm is felt by all classes in this Island'.[329] Ready could not see how the Island would benefit by the proposed changes. He reminded Maule that, as the residents had little local trade other than farming and fishing, it was necessary to import other essential items. This meant that there were many complaints locally of the 2½% ad valorem duty payable on the importation of British manufactured goods into the Island. The amount received from this duty was about £2,000 a year, which he argued could be raised instead by an additional duty on brandy, gin, wine and tobacco. He did not want the low duties on ordinary tea and raw sugar amending as these commodities were essential to the poorer classes. He considered that any possible change to the timber duty would most certainly deeply affect the interests and prosperity of the Island.

The *Manx Sun* again referred to its contention that Britain's interest in the Isle of Man had been precipitated by 'the incessant and galling petitions to the Treasury'.[330] These petitions, it claimed, had arisen partly as a result of insular Customs House seizures:

> Every trifling article of the most common mill work has been seized by the Customs House. The ordinary articles of dress from the modists, tailors and hatters of Liverpool, even the monthly magazines and periodicals have all undergone the same ordeal. . . . We will give an example: A young English lad, at an insular academy, had a parcel sent to him from his friends containing a pair or two of worn, mended pantaloons and other trifles, including a schoolboy's plum cake from his indulgent mother. This formidable bagatelle was seized. The master interfered and was told that he must memorialise the Treasury!!! This he declined, stating that the youth's father was a solicitor at Liverpool, and that the seizure should be referred to him, and he might employ the formidable state remedy to redeem the plum loaf. After this intimation the parcel was delivered from bondage.

A letter to the editor of the *Manx Liberal* from 'E. D.' also gave an opinion on the situation:

> The truth is that the ruling authorities are not the only parties to whom blame attaches for the culpable so unhappily evinced towards the public welfare. Equal censure is due to the principal inhabitants, and particularly the tradesmen, for their apathy and supineness in suffering, without a single preventive endeavour, a disastrous measure to ripen into maturity, in which their own interests, and those of the Island generally, are so deeply involved.[331]

The *Mona's Herald* prophetically looked at the issue from another angle by considering the possible advantages of the proposed changes:

> If we pay a higher duty for our brandy and gin we shall doubtless be allowed the use of British, Scotch and Irish spirits at the same prices as in respective countries of production; we shall have the abolition of our 2½ and 15 per cent duties, and eventually, no doubt, all the advantages of the free trade and bonding system of England. We are not among those, therefore, who view the change with all the gloom of despair.[332]

An all-Island public meeting took place in Douglas towards the end of January.[333] Dumbell and Bluett gave a full account of their interview with the members of Tynwald Court. George Dumbell, whilst referring to the House of Keys, was pointing out one of his favourite claims regarding the 'evils' likely to result to the public from popular election and the enjoyment of the elective franchise, which he designated as a curse, when he was assailed by hisses from various parts of the hall.[334] But the *Manx Sun* agreed with him and claimed that the possibility of a popular election of the House of Keys was 'scarcely worth noticing' and queried as to 'where could twenty-four persons be found with more integrity, respectability or desire for the country's good than those now composing that House'.³³⁵ However, it went on to point out the shortcomings of the existing system of a self-elected House of Keys which could not impose customs duties to raise revenue or even have any voice in the expenditure of the current revenue raised by duties imposed by Britain, also claiming that 'They cannot even impose rates for the keeping of the roads or for any municipal charges, trifling as they are, without first having the sanction of the Governor in Council'. Various districts now took further action, raising petitions and giving support to the measures being taken by the public committee and its delegates.³³⁶ Another successfully attended all-Island meeting took place when about forty delegates from the various towns and parishes were present.³³⁷ James Holmes, a banker, John McHutchin, Clerk of the Rolls, and Robert McGuffog, Comptroller of Customs, were chosen by the delegates as a people's deputation to proceed to London to fight the Island's corner. A general petition was approved at the meeting, and, after receiving the signatures of 3,783 of the most prominent inhabitants of the Isle of Man over the next few weeks, it was forwarded by the Governor to Lord Russell at the Home Office.³³⁸ The following other petitions were also sent:

- The Isle of Man Building Society and proprietors of houses in the town and neighbourhood of Douglas. They claimed that additional customs duties on imported timber and the exodus of new residents would result in a decrease in the demand for housing which would lead to 'multitudes of mechanics and labourers now enjoying the blessing of abundant work and comfortable support for their families will be entirely thrown out of employ'.
- Tradesmen, including joiners, house carpenters, cabinet makers, masons, stone cutters, plasterers, painters and glaziers and others employed in house building in the town and neighbourhood of Douglas.
- Residents of various towns and parishes, including Castletown, Onchan, Ramsey and Patrick.
- The Isle of Man Steam Packet Company. It was the principal carrier of summer visitors to the Island from the adjacent populous areas of mainland Britain and Ireland.
- Retired half-pay officers sent their petition to the King in which they claimed the measures would 'drive from the Island all who have come to dwell in it on account of the few remaining privileges'.

Various merchants in the Island had sent letters to secretary Bluett expressing their concerns, principally regarding the 2½% ad valorem duty.³³⁹ Thomas and John Wilson, linen and woollen drapers, stated that the removal of the duty would benefit locals by making British goods that much cheaper to buy. William Quiggin & Company, timber merchants, pointed out that the value of timber imported into the Island in the previous year for house and fishing boat building was about £11,000 and the quantity of timber grown on the Island to be used for farm purposes during the year was only about £300. J. Quiggin, on behalf of booksellers, pointed out that, whilst they were able to claim drawback on the British customs duty paid on imported books, they seldom did as the quantity imported at one time was too small. George Jefferson also wrote on the potential detrimental effect on the book trade. From ironmongers, shoemakers, stationers, tobacco merchants, wines merchants and spirits merchants came opposition to the proposed assimilation. Gavin Torrance, a Douglas wines and spirits merchant, was a lone voice in fully supporting the benefit of assimilation, pointing out the disadvantages of the present system to the Island, which 'amounts to prohibiting against all manufactories'.

The House of Keys unanimously appointed two of their members, John Thomas Moore of the Hills estate in Douglas and Captain John Goldie Taubman of the Nunnery estate in Braddan, as delegates to represent them in any discussions on the contemplated alterations.[340]

At another public meeting the three people's delegates previously elected stood down.[341] Holmes resigned, McHutchin thought that because of his official capacity he should not form part of the people's deputation and McGuffog could not stand as the Commissioners of Customs had refused him leave of absence to go to London. Consequently, John Courtney Bluett and Thomas Arthur Corlett, the Vicar General, were appointed in their stead.[342] At the next meeting it was revealed that there were rifts in the relationships between the main protestors and that petty jealousies were endangering progress - it was a wonder that anything got done. Thomas Arthur Corlett did not attend the meeting, and Hillary claimed that a recent letter to the press from Corlett was tantamount to his resignation from the people's deputation.[343] Major David Stewart said Corlett's objection arose from 'some expression made by Bluett', but Corlett had said he would stay in office if there were other delegates appointed. As a result, John James Moore and Thomas Kneale were then elected as additional delegates to Bluett and Corlett.[344]

London

In March 1837 Bluett was the first of the delegates to proceed to London, not knowing whether any of the others would follow him.[345] Hillary, who could not travel himself because of ill-health, had given Bluett a letter of introduction to the various departments of the British Government. He warned Bluett that 'if you wish to show your face with credit in the Island, put an end to the licence system, root and branch, it is the source of monopoly, it robs many, enriches a few and is ruinous to the poor'. As previously arranged, Bluett reported to Governor Ready on his various interviews. In his first letter he explained that, in discussing the details of the proposed measures,

Isle of Man Steam Packet Company's paddle steamer Mona's Isle leaving Douglas on a stormy day, c.1837.

the questions of the lack of democratic representation in Tynwald and the responsibility of the Manx revenue were raised.[346] He expressed his concern over these conjoined issues, a concern which highlighted the differences between those people involved with the fiscal matters and those involved with the constitutional ones. He stated that:

> the spirit of the times would never allow so large a sum to be extracted from the pockets of the people without representation. If we are to have Members, the Reform Bill must be altered - the Elective Franchise of some kind suited to the Island - and trouble of various kinds start forward.

Bluett informed Hillary that he had learnt from a friend that James Hume, formerly commissioner and secretary of the Commissioners of Customs but now joint secretary of the Board of Trade, was 'the managing man in all matters of detail'.[347] He had obtained an introduction to him and they had had an informal discussion, but Bluett was anxious that this contact should not be made public. He thought that the whole measure rested solely with Hume and by private negotiations with him they could expect to succeed in their aims. Between 1822 and 1825 Hume had worked as an officer in the long-room of the London Custom House on consolidating and simplifying the laws of the Customs Department, which resulted in the arrangement of the laws under ten different headings, including one for the Isle of Man.[348] Hume had been paid £6,000 plus £450 expenses for his efforts at this time. In an accompanying letter to Hillary, Bluett told him that he regretted that he had to 'write with a spice of concealment as to the manner of my having obtained my information and the persons from whom and through whom it is derived'.[349] He went on to say that both the Tory and Whig governments had long been resolved to do away with the anomalies respecting the relationship between the Isle of Man and Britain, and it was considered that the Island was 'perfectly blind to her own interests, and that keeping her eyes steadfastly fixed upon the trifling advantage of cheap luxuries they lose sight of the incalculably great benefit they might derive'. Bluett explained that it was 'freely admitted however that in grappling with the question, variously difficulties arise, and amongst the rest, the very important one of "taxation *quere* representation"!!!'. Bluett wrote that, with every successive government and every change in the heads of departments, the same negative views had been handed down as a result of the various occurrences which brought the Island again and again to the notice of Britain.[350] He went on to explain that the government was therefore determined to put an end to this situation. It believed that assimilation of tariffs would bring great benefits to the Island, a 'new field that would be opened for embarking capital instead of the narrow boundary to which it is now confined' and 'merchants would speedily flock to its shores, and a way be opened to everyone to attain the same degree of opulence'.

Hillary, in turn, wrote to Bluett on the recent controversial public meeting, which 'was from many causes - hail, snow and apathy - most unfortunate'.[351] Hillary had some additional disagreeable news to tell. Thomas Arthur Corlett would only go to London on his own conditions. Hillary had consequently had a requisition signed by eleven deputies to call a new meeting and 'T. A. Corlett's *yes* and *no* is referred to them to say *delegate* or *not*'. Corlett had insisted that 'an extraordinary voucher of his own manufactory, suitable to his own extraordinary mission' should be signed by Hillary, but Hillary had refused.[352] Hillary expected that the difficulty of the delegates should be resolved at the next meeting, including the problem with Corlett who 'will not allow he has resigned'.[353] Hillary, writing from his home overlooking Douglas bay and harbour, went on to argue for safer havens around the Island's coast, particularly his favourite plan of a refuge harbour in Douglas. He was also tempering his demands with the acceptance of the inevitability of change. 'Give us free trade and good harbours, then there might be some compensation for additional taxes. Release us also from that wretched narrow policy of the licence system'.

Letter from Sir William Hillary to John Courtney Bluett informing him that the 'Deputation are coming', 18 April 1837.

Bluett continued with his busy round of interviews.[354] He met with Poulett Thomson at the offices of the Board of Trade and then with Robert Wallace, a Whig Member of Parliament, who had been informed by Poulett Thomson that he was determined to carry out the gradual assimilation of the Manx customs duties. Bluett also spoke to Lord Lowther, the previous president of the Board of Trade, who confirmed that there had been plans to assimilate the Island's customs duties during the previous eight years, and only his sudden retirement from office had prevented him putting them and other more substantial measures into practice.[355] Bluett had now seen persons of all parties and politics and they all were of the opinion that the anomalous situation of the Isle of Man must be done away with. His anxiety that he alone of the people's deputation was active in London led him to complain that 'I am constrained to say that unless the deputation arrives in a few days I must leave London and return to the Island'.

At the next public meeting in the Isle of Man there was a long discussion on the legality of the last meeting, with arguments between the Douglas and other delegates, so a re-election took place.[356] Thomas Arthur Corlett and J. J. Moore now became the additional delegates and they were authorised to go to London and join Bluett. There were still underlying problems concerning the egos of and the relationships between the various protestors. Writing to Bluett, Lawrence Craigie, correspondence secretary, considered one of delegates: 'Notwithstanding his [Moore's] second election, there exists in the minds of all respectable persons a strong prejudice against him. Subscriptions are even refused for his support', and 'From what escaped Mr Moore's cautious lips, I could see that he greatly disapproved of your having had any interview with persons in office'.[357] Craigie went on to report that 'Poor Mrs B[luett] is against the ingratitude of the Manx people, and will never again allow you to leave her on such a mission'. At last, Corlett and J. J. Moore set sail for Liverpool on 18 April and arrived in London three days later.[358] Meanwhile, the official Tynwald delegations were in turmoil. The Legislative Council had appointed Deemster John Christian and John McHutchin, Clerk of the Rolls, as its deputation to go to London, but no one from the Council ever went.[359] The House of Keys replaced Captain Goldie Taubman with Dr Philip Garrett. Eventually he and John Thomas Moore made their way to meet up with the people's delegates.

The combined Manx deputation of Bluett, Corlett, J. J. Moore, Garrett and John Thomas Moore met in London, put aside their personal disagreements and became united.[360] John Meadows White, a solicitor of Lincoln's Inn Field, was employed as the deputation's agent to prepare statements and evidence. Hillary informed Bluett that it was 'very satisfactory that all our insular delegates are in town acting harmoniously and zealously together in the public cause'.[361] Bluett met with William Blamire MP, a Manx sympathiser, who arranged for the deputation to meet with Poulett Thomson.[362] Hillary had issued the Manx deputation with supporting papers and a pamphlet he had had published to summarise the Island's case.[363] In these documents he stressed that it was most important that, whilst the 'inconveniences' caused by the Manx customs duties may need to be removed by the British Government, any resultant burden placed on the Island should not injure the rising prosperity of the country. He called for the removal of the partial and oppressive monopoly of the licence system. He also addressed the necessity for protecting the Island's shipbuilding industry by not increasing the rate of duty on imported timber, except possibly that required for larger vessels. He expressed similar concern over increasing duties on timber for house building. He pointed out that the introduction of more temperate habits amongst the inhabitants of the Island should be supported by not increasing the duty on tea, coffee and Muscovado sugar. He called for all the ad valorem duties to be abolished and the coasting trade to be thrown open Island-wide. He considered that overall duties somewhat less than half the British duties, together with his other suggestions, would protect the British revenue. He went on to propose that if any increase in duties should come into operation then they should be moderate and immediate. Importantly, he considered that the British Government should be reminded that the Isle of Man had its own government and laws. Equally importantly, he called for part of the Manx surplus revenue to be used to improve the Island's bays, harbours and ports in order to 'induce the wealthy merchant or shipowner of England to transfer his capital to her rugged coasts'.

With their arguments prepared and acting in concert, the Manx deputation met with Poulett Thomson and other ministers on 8 May as arranged.[364] The following proposals and concerns were put forward by the deputation:

- The 'inconveniences' caused by the Manx customs arose from the licence system and the ad valorem duties. Both these should be abolished and the Island should be placed on the coasting trade.
- Total assimilation of duties would lead to the loss of capital investment in the Island, the departure of many resident strangers, a decrease in the Manx commercial revenue of £200,000 and few advantages resulting at all to the Island.
- A scale of duties was submitted which should address the objectives of the British Government. However, these proposed changes were made upon the understanding that the additional revenue should in the future be placed at the control and disposal of Tynwald for local improvements and purposes.
- If the Isle of Man was in the relation to Britain as 'a colony to its mother country', the deputation argued that the Island's right to the control and disposal of any surplus revenue would be 'undoubted', and they would in that case content themselves with claiming the benefit of the principle laid down in the Act of Parliament, 18 George III, chapter 12, of 1778 by which the revenues of the North American colonies were declared as a matter of principle to be at the disposal of the colonies themselves. But the deputation claimed that the Isle of Man stood on a higher footing, being 'an ancient and independent kingdom with peculiar laws and a constitution which it had enjoyed from its earliest period'.
- If the British Government's claim depended on the constitution of the Isle of Man, no tax or customs duty could be imposed without the joint agreement of the Crown and Tynwald Court.
- If the claim depended on the constitution of Britain, it was a vital part of Britain's constitution that no tax could be imposed without the consent of the tax payers. The Isle of Man was not part of Britain, and hence consent would need be obtained from Tynwald.
- The deputation accepted the undoubted right of the British Government, 'as standing in the position of the paramount or protecting state', to subject the Isle of Man to such laws and duties as the protection of the British revenue may require. But any such fiscal laws should constitutionally be limited to the object for which they

were imposed and that all profit arising from those laws belonged to the Island.

Poulett Thomson replied that the British government's objective was to ultimately assimilate the Island's customs duties to those of Britain, and with that principle in view he was happy to receive any suggestions. He would not increase the quantities of licensed goods as that would only perpetuate smuggling, the 'evil' he wanted to remove. The British Government considered that it was anomalous to have one part of the 'kingdom' so different to the rest, and it contended that the Isle of Man would benefit from the changes. After the meeting, a comprehensive letter was sent by the members of the deputation to Thomson in which they reiterated their arguments. As they anticipated meeting soon with Russell, the deputation sent a copy of the letter to him.

The deputation did not want details of their delicate negotiations to become public until matters were at a more advanced stage.[365] But Hillary was pressing and anxious that the deputation should make available any information which was not of a confidential nature. The *Mona's Herald*, as acerbic as ever, was also concerned over secrecy and lack of news:

IMPORTANT NEWS FROM LONDON

A   Well, Mr B., what news this morning - anything from the Deputies?

B   W . . h . . y - there is some news (pulling a long face), but I assure you, Sir, it is dangerous these times to talk of what we hear.

A   Anything particular? If so, you may depend on my keeping it secret.

B   There is something very *mysterious* about what I have heard, yet I believe it is of great moment to the *best* interests of this Island; but should it get into the Manx papers it is all over with us - therefore I would entreat you to keep it particularly secret - for should the King, or any of his Ministers hear of it, the Island will be ruined to a dead certainty - in fact, I consider the information I have heard very little short of treason - *treason*, Sir!

A   My God! What can it be? I beg you will not keep me any longer in suspense.

B   Well here it is - now mind and keep it secret. (Here a dead silence for about a minute takes place). Information has been sent down, by one of the Deputies, that - that - I really can scarcely give it utterance . . .

A   Do not be so alarmed, my dear Sir. Why, you turn quite pale! What the devil can it be?

B   The Deputy states in his letter, that *there is more CABBAGE growing in the HILLS GARDEN, near Douglas, than there is in COVENT GARDEN in the great City of London!!* Now, Sir, what do you think of that? Is it not awful? (Shaking his head). Is it not a *libel* on the first City in the world?

A   CABBAGE! CABBAGE!! CABBAGE!!! Really there is something very mysterious - *very mysterious, indeed!*[366]

It had been arranged that the Manx deputation would have a meeting with Lord John Russell, Poulett Thomson and other ministers after some further information had been supplied and a report of the Commissioners of Customs upon the proposals submitted by the deputation had been studied.[367] The delegates were in daily expectation of an interview, after which they intended to immediately return to the Island. But events were put into turmoil. Shortly after two o'clock in the morning of Tuesday 20 June 1837, the very day the deputation was due to meet Russell, King William IV, who had been ill for some time, died at Windsor aged seventy-one. Consequently, the parliamentary session was brought to a close as soon as the most important Bills were dealt with, whilst all others were allowed to stand over for the consideration of the first parliament in the reign of the new monarch, Queen Victoria.[368] The people's deputies remained several more days in London but returned to the Island without any satisfactory information as to the future intentions of the British Government.

Although neither changes to the customs regulations nor concessions to the trade regulations happened at this time, the events which surrounded the situation present an interesting insight into the various processes employed. Tynwald, with the support of the Governor, had put the Island's concern to the Home Office. Tynwald and the Governor had kept in close touch with the principal members of the protest movement. Public meetings had been organised all over the Island. The combined delegation had worked well together to put forward the Island's case and some alternative proposals to the sympathetic but resolute British personnel. These mechanisms would be a useful rehearsal for when the customs issue would be raised again in the near future.

The 'clique', the 'squib' and the 'bogey'

Whilst all the meetings and discussions were going on, the import licence system was still very much a bone of contention, and the Governor and the Legislative Council were set to meet to approve the applications for the controversial allotment of licensed goods.[369] The *Mona's Herald* claimed that 'if ever any act of the administrative government of this Island has created heart burning and discontent among the community, which justice in every other case cannot excuse, the way in which the allotments have hitherto been made has been that act'. It reported that certain merchants were selling brandy at 16/- and 17/- a gallon which would leave them a profit of 9/- and tea at 5/- a pound which only cost the merchants 2/-. One person's licence had been advertised to be sold by public tender for upwards of £200. Again the *Mona's Herald* castigated the Keys, calling them 'a knot of upstart men banded together for their own selfish purposes what we wish to get rid of'. It claimed that Tynwald was 'possessing no representative character and owning no responsible power. In fact the deputies negotiate for a portion of the public monies to be put into the hands of men who may employ them without control, and expend them without giving an account'.

The considerable disaffection that now prevailed throughout the Island against its fiscal and constitutional situations, and particularly against the House of Keys and the mode of their election, was encouraged by a series of articles which from time to time appeared in the *Mona's Herald*. At this juncture, 'Hunt the Keys', an adaptation of an old and favourite Manx folk song called 'Hunt the Wren', was published.[370] The lines, a mix of contemporary reference and personal attack on both conservatives and radicals alike, were printed and freely circulated throughout the Island. The 'squib' was published anonymously, but the author was well-known to be a man of wit, John Kelly, High Bailiff of Castletown and himself a Member of the House of Keys. The pungent comments on particular persons or incidents produced a great effect:

HUNT THE KEYS

1 Let us hunt the Keys, says Jack Meary Vooar;[371]
   Let us hunt the Keys, says Juan Jem Moore;[372]
   Let us hunt the Keys, says Davy St. Ann;[373]
   Let us hunt the Keys, says the Union Mill man.[374]

2 They bridges won't build, says Jack Meary Vooar;
   Granane is untill'd, says Juan Jem Moore;[375]
   The chiels are no skill'd, says Davy St. Ann;[376]
   And the churches are fill'd, says the Union Mill man.

3 How can we capsize them, says Jack Meary Vooar;
   By telling big lies man, says Juan Jem Moore;
   But don't make a noise mon, says Davy St. Ann;
   The Game Bill will suffice, says the Union Mill man.

4 Their house is too old, says Jack Meary Vooar;[377]
   They'll be easily sold, says Juan Jem Moore;
   The *Herald* shall scold, says Davy St. Ann;
   We'll all be enroll'd, says the Union Mill man.[378]

5 They'll have a lease of it still, says Jack Meary Vooar;[379]
   But we'll sell the goodwill, says Juan Jem Moore;
   Who'll swallow the pill, says Davy St. Ann;
   We'll demur to the Bill, says the Union Mill man.[380]

6   The petitions get on, says Jack Meary Vooar;[381]
    I'll wait on Lord John, says Juan Jem Moore;[382]
    You're a delegate mon, says Davy St. Ann;[383]
    And I've seen No. 1, says the Union Mill man.[384]

7   We've 'Billy Ballure', says Jack Meary Vooar;[385]
    As butter milk pure, says Juan Jem Moore;
    I'm no varra sure, says Davy St. Ann;
    No radical truer, says the Union Mill man.

The constitutional reformers, fully aware of the much more advanced parliamentary representation and electoral systems which had been operating in Britain for a long time, continued to call upon the Keys to 'amend themselves, to lead a new political life, and become de facto, what they now unjustly and falsely assume themselves to be, the true and just representation of the insular state'.[386] Petitions demanding constitutional amendment were raised in all the towns, parishes and sheadings, and a combined one containing in excess of 3,000 signatures was presented to Governor Ready in February 1838.[387] Unlike his response to the financial petitioners, Ready did not accept the demands of the constitutional petitioners with any enthusiasm, being of the opinion that 'a great number of the respectable and wealthy inhabitants are favourable to the existing constitution and desire no change'.[388] Indeed, one of these 'respectable and wealthy inhabitants', John Welch, dismissed the establishment of a representative House of Keys as 'a revolution of piddling importance'.[389] Members of the establishment were anxious to maintain the constitutional status quo, and Governor Ready sought support from Lord John Russell to 'silence the persons who are agitating the question'.[390] This was at a time when Britain was in the process of suspending the constitutions of Canada and Jamaica and was having problems with certain of its other territories, so it would not be sympathetic to the suggestion to change the status of a much smaller and closer dependency.[391] In the early spring of 1838, after receiving advice from Lord John Russell, Ready slightly modified the Home Secretary's words to defend the retention of the status quo and to threaten the Island with possible annexation to Britain:

> I have had under consideration a letter presented by Messrs Moore and Clucas as a deputation from the petitioners praying that a constituency of the inhabitants of the Isle of Man may be formed for electing the House of Keys; and it is my duty to inform you that such a change in the constitution cannot be agreed to; and I have further to inform you that a representation for the Island in [the British] Parliament may be the measure of reform adopted.[392]

Thus, the bogey of parliamentary annexation was used to fight off reform. 'A self-elected House of Keys was better than no House of Keys at all, as even the reformers had to admit'.[393] Whilst the constitutional reform movement had failed, it was now well established as a body of protest, initially as a reactive force but now paving the way for proactive innovation. However, the strengthening Manx demands for Tynwald's control of all the primary public finances and a publicly elected legislature would produce further resistance from Britain. The threatened loss of the Isle of Man's limited autonomy would be used yet again by Britain as a weapon for keeping economic and political control ultimately in its hands.

Chapter 6

FREE TRADE

Discontent

The spectre of customs duties assimilation and the threat of constitutional annexation hung over the Isle of Man on into the 1840s. The Island's main means of taxation and the detested licence import system for certain goods proved to be continuing problems:

> The rich paid no taxes, but levied contributions from the poor; the yachts of the opulent entered the ports scatheless, while the boats of the poor fishermen paid taxes to the state; the well-to-do had licences for the introduction of foreign commodities, and sold to shopkeepers and consumers the excess not required for themselves, their families, and friends.[394]

There was an awareness that changes were required and, indeed, were being contemplated by the British Government, and it is worthwhile briefly placing these considerations in the context of wider issues. Throughout the 1840s resistance in the Isle of Man to customs assimilation and demands for reforms, especially of the ad valorem duties and the licence system, were taking place against the backdrop of major events in Britain which included the advancement of free trade, concerns over the Corn Laws, the influence of liberal politics and the eventual coming to power of the Liberal party. The Conservative Prime Minister and First Lord of the Treasury, Sir Robert Peel, was able to persuade Parliament to institute the economic policy of free trade (unrestricted trade between countries of each others' products) in place of protectionism (restricted trade which favoured local at the expense of foreign products). Britain's commitment to unilateral free trade and the lowering of duties for the benefit of all nations certainly best suited Britain itself and was 'a rational choice of the most appropriate economic policy for the "First Industrial Nation"'.[395] The main purposes of the Corn Laws had been the securing of an adequate supply of grain to meet domestic requirements, maintaining prices at profitable levels and giving local growers a monopoly of the market by excluding all foreign grain. As Britain became increasingly industrialised, dependence on foreign food sources rose, and mercantile interests demanded that Parliament repeal the Corn Laws, a measure for which the classical economists had been pressing since the early part of the century. Their eventual repeal in 1846, urged on by Peel, certainly informed the views of the British Government on the benefits of free trade. Free trade was one of the prime causes of the

Douglas Customs House, previous residence of the Duke of Atholl, next to the Market Place with St Matthew's and St Barnabas' churches nearby, 1841.

Liberal political party which had been formed a decade earlier by the coalition of the Whigs and the Radicals with a policy for advocating reform on constitutional lines.

The alterations to the commercial and political systems in Britain and the progression of the Manx fishing, mining and, most importantly, tourism sectors contributed to the improvements which were taking place in the Island's general economy. But not everyone was benefiting. Farm workers were feeling the consequences of crop failures and changes in agricultural methods.[396] Indeed, many rural families fell on hard times and either moved into the towns or emigrated. The *Mona's Herald* put it that, whilst any positive reforms affecting Manx trade and public funds would be generally acceptable, any increased taxation without an equivalent return would not. It was concerned about the dire consequences if any such change was introduced without protest: 'Allow the principle of taxation to be quietly acquiesced in, and the next step might be quietly to saddle us with the full amount of English duties'.[397]

The licences to import goods were issued locally by the Collector of Customs in Douglas. Each application had to specify the date, name, residence and occupation of the applicant. Copies of the licences had to be sent to the Governor who allocated what he thought were fair and equitable proportions. A report of such allocations was sent by the Governor to the Lord Commissioners of the Treasury and a duplicate to the Commissioners of Customs. The Governor was assisted by the Legislative Council in ensuring impartial allocations. The persons to whom licences were granted were required by law to give bond for the due importation of the goods. Early on in its application, the licence system had mainly confined goods to merchants and dealers, but in more recent years the quantities usually granted to them had been reduced in order to accommodate a greater number of private individuals who required the goods for their own household consumption. Allocations were first distributed amongst householders, according to their 'circumstances, rank and establishment', and then the remaining allowances were distributed to merchants, innkeepers, dealers and shopkeepers, by whom the bulk of the population was supplied.

The expressions of discontent which were being voiced in the Island over the licence system, ad valorem duties and detrimental amendments to the customs arrangements continued to be led by the *Mona's Herald*, whose owner and editor was still the campaigner Robert Fargher. The *Herald* had been scathing in its criticism of the inaction of the local population in demanding reforms:

> the proverbial apathy of Manxmen, who are said to be 'a day after the fair' or 'just in time to be too late', was never more forcibly illustrated than by the indifference with which the changes contemplated by the British Government, in regard to the interests of this Island, are viewed at the present moment, by the people in general.[398]

But there were concerned members of the public. A partiality complaint regarding the licence system had been made in April 1842 by a Mr Fowler who had recently come to the Island and had been refused a private licence.[399] He wanted the Governor to place an even larger proportion of the licensed goods into the hands of private individuals and increase their allocation, but Ready considered this would result in fictitious applications, the sale of licences, injure the honest dealer and enhance the price of basic necessities to the community at large. Under the nom de plume of 'Espionage', a correspondent with the *Manx Liberal* claimed that the licence system was corrupt and that Francis Matthews, a merchant and a Member of the House Keys, was granted a licence of the value of £800 (now the equivalent of £57,000) per annum and was boasting that 'he could live without business on the produce of his licences'.[400] 'Espionage' concluded, 'The days of the licence system are numbered'. In late 1842 and early 1843 a number of scathing letters to Governor Ready from 'One of the Proscribed' were published in the *Mona's Herald*.[401] They criticised the licence system, again claiming privilege and corruption. These letters were published not only in the local press but also in *The Times*, bringing matters to the attention of the British Government. The correspondence included details of the quantities of licensed goods that had been allowed into each of the four trading ports for the dealers and for others in the year 1835, the latest year of published figures.[402] 'One of the Proscribed' claimed that these figures showed that more than half of the quantities were allowed to thirty-seven dealers in Douglas, one-eighth to eleven individuals in Castletown, one-twentieth to thirteen individuals in Peel, one-seventh to fourteen individuals in Ramsey, about one-fortieth to lawyers, clergymen and officials, and about one-twelfth to the remaining members of the general public:

> If a rigid analysis of the rank and station of these individuals were gone into, it would be found that nearly all belong to what is called our Island aristocracy - all of that station which permitted them to claim acquaintance, if not with your Excellency, at least with such gentlemen of undoubted respectability as their Honours the Clerk of the Rolls and the Southern Deemster, and their Worships the Water Bailiff and the High Bailiff of Douglas. About ten or twelve fortunate individuals having yearly incomes of from £300 to £1,200 out of the pockets of the poorer classes; these ladies and gentlemen are, of course, all your Excellency's most humble admirers, and of course, they are also *very sincere* in maintaining that the present system is the best of all possible systems.[403]

It was also the manner of distribution which was the subject of complaint by the Island's merchants and dealers. They claimed that their allocation should also be increased as the present quantities of goods were insufficient and inadequate for their trade and were limited due to first preference being given to private individuals. Throughout 1842 they issued many letters and petitions.[404] John Winram and William Quiggin of Douglas wrote to the Board of Trade complaining about having to pay British import duty on cordage and then having to pay duty again in the Island. John Winram and five other manufacturers of hemp objected that hemp was not exempt from duty as cotton and flax were. Henry, Thomas and Richard Cubbin of Castletown and Douglas, importers and retailers of cotton and woollen goods, reminded the Board of Trade of their memorial to Sir Robert Peel regarding grievances in having to pay ad valorem duties which were normally exempt. Ellis, Everington & Company of London also complained to the Board of Trade about the situation of their 'correspondents' in the Island who imported cotton, woollen and other British manufactured goods.[405] The reply from the Board of Trade to all these complaints was that it was understood that some of the merchants were not complying with the customs regulations, including filling in customs documents and bringing in articles by goods boats. The Board concluded that there was insufficient reason at present to alter the system. The complaints again brought the general dissatisfaction with the system to the attention of the British authorities.

The willing Dr Bowring and the unwilling House of Keys

Towards the end of 1842 the Cubbin brothers, the importers and retailers of Castletown and

Dr John Bowring MP.

Douglas, decided to take matters further and wrote to Dr John Bowring, the recently elected Member of Parliament for Bolton, expressing their concerns.[406] Bowring, a staunch advocate of free trade, offered to take up the cause and lobby Parliament, agreeing that all taxes that impeded trade were pernicious and the ad valorem import duties seemed particularly unjustifiable. In March 1843 he presented a petition to the House of Commons from 'the merchants, tradesmen and other inhabitants of the Isle of Man'.[407] The petition, reputed to be twenty yards in length, requested the removal of all impediments to free trade between Britain and the Isle of Man. As a consequence of his interest, Bowring was asked by the British Government to consult with the Board of Trade to give an unbiased opinion on the subject of certain new customs duties being considered for the Island which would increase the revenue from in the region of £22,000 a year to £30,000.[408] Bowring opposed such an increase and raised related questions with William Gladstone, the President of the Board of Trade.[409] Gladstone, ignoring the recent letters from the Manx merchants, declared that he did not believe that any complaint on the subject had been raised in the Island. Unsurprisingly, Bowring was not satisfied with this response and successfully asked for copies of recent returns for Manx customs revenue to be produced for scrutiny by Parliament.[410] In May and June 1843 Bowring reported to William Kelly (a local land owner, soap boiler, director of the Isle of Man Commercial Banking Company and 'the Union Mill man' of 'Hunt the Keys' fame who was raising support both on and off the Island for fiscal and constitutional reform) that he had now obtained a promise from the British Government that the whole subject of customs regulations in the Island would undergo revision.[411] In August Bowring came to the Island to discuss the issue, and when he returned to London he reported to the Board of Trade that if there was to be any increase in the customs duties then the Island should have the resultant extra revenue.[412]

The initial reaction of the House of Keys to the calls for reforms of the licence system and the customs duties was negative - they wanted no change. They told Governor Ready that they felt that most of the people in the Island were perfectly satisfied with the present fiscal laws and regulations.[413] The Keys, as ever, were supported by the conservative *Manx Sun* in fighting off calls for change. In early 1844, whilst advocating the retention of the status quo and fearing the loss of spending of the resident strangers, it claimed that:

> It only requires a plausible tongued person, more especially if he can address his countrymen in Manx, which is sacred to a Manxman in the remote parishes; and we know of no one more ready or more fit to entice his countrymen to sign these extravagant memorials than our old correspondent, Mr W. Kelly. With a petition in his hand, and with the vernacular on his tongue, he is irresistible to the people of the far north.[414]

Reform, however, was fast approaching. In early 1844 Gladstone indicated that changes to the customs system were now being firmly contemplated and the 2½% duty on British manufactured goods would be done away with.[415] Cautious optimism was accompanied by guarded wariness from the *Mona's Herald*, which stated that 'the measure proposed by the Government is much more liberal than we could have expected. But we think it would be well for the gentlemen who were appointed delegates some years since, to resume their functions at the present crisis'.[416] On the defensive as ever, the *Manx Sun* still stuck to its arguments for the retention of the present system, whilst also taking the opportunity to fire a broadside at its arch rival the *Mona's Herald*, referring to it as a 'pothouse journal'. A contrary opinion dealing with the origins and operation of the licence system was put forward by Bowring:

> Monopoly and privilege thus assumed a strange form in the legislation of the Isle of Man. They were represented by the word *Licence* - the most important articles of consumption being imported under licence alone - and licences being granted under the authority of the ruling powers only, none but those in favour with the ruling powers could obtain them.

Licences were given solely to the opulent and influential. The rich man revelled in cheap tea, cheap sugar, cheap spirits, cheap tobacco; while the poor man paid double price for all the articles that he consumed, either to the privileged party who possessed a licence, or to the party who purchased licences of others. The trade in licences was an important one. They were sold by auction - they were made the instrument of extorting higher rents - they were employed in all ways for purposes of oppression and corruption. The unprotected consumer paid a high price for what he wanted, that high price being caused by the licence monopoly; but not one farthing of the augmented price went into the public treasury.[417]

Clearly the defenders of the status quo were those with vested interests who could exploit the import licence system. Bowring's arguments against this monopolistic and corrupt system were unassailable.

In March 1844 John Henry Thomas Manners-Sutton, Under Secretary of State of the Home Office, wrote to Governor Ready enclosing a package of measures put together by John Shaw-Lefevre, Joint-Assistant Secretary to the Board of Trade, and asking the Governor for his and Tynwald's opinion on it.[418] Shaw-Lefevre had learnt from 'respectable and independent testimony' that the licence system did not produce moderate prices on goods sold to the inhabitants of the Island, and it considered that the system constituted a monopoly, the benefits of which most of the community did not share. He considered that certain changes might be made which would relieve the general consumer whilst at the same time increase the revenue:

- A new scale of duties should be implemented.
- All duties on goods of British manufacture should be abolished.
- Duties on certain foreign goods should be increased, some remain unchanged and others lowered.
- The existing 15% ad valorem on foreign goods should be suspended, subject to an express power granted to the Lords of the Treasury to re-impose it again if it was deemed fit. The intention of this backstop provision was that the Treasury could withdraw the suspension if there was any evidence of illicit trafficking.
- Full assimilation of customs duties of the Isle of Man to those of Britain was no longer intended.
- The limitation of the quantities of goods now allowed should be amended.
- The trade of Britain with the Isle of Man should be placed upon the footing of British coasting trade. The Island should be given practically the entire freedom to trade.
- There should be no risk of converting the Isle of Man into a depot for the smuggling and contraband trade.

*John Henry Thomas Manners-Sutton,
Under Secretary of State of the Home Office.*

- Any measure which would have the effect of materially increasing the pressure of taxation in the form of import duties upon the general inhabitants of the Island should be avoided.

The *Mona's Herald*, elated that some of its calls for reform were now imminent, triumphantly declared that 'Now's the day and now's the hour. Resist taxation. Demand free trade. The utter abolition of the detested licence system and the entire surplus revenues for insular purposes'.[419]

Banners of the Manx Sun and Mona's Herald newspapers, 1844.

Outspoken rival newspapers

Throughout the period during which the historical relationship between the Isle of Man and Britain was being questioned by internal and external institutions and individuals, the local newspaper publishing industry was dominated by four titles: the conservative *Manks Advertiser* and *Manx Sun* and the radical *Mona's Herald* and *Manx Liberal*. These newspapers were based in Douglas and all forcefully expressed their opinions on the disputed fiscal and constitutional affairs. They would frequently attack one another on these and more personal issues in the most outspoken and defamatory ways.

The *Manks Advertiser* was first produced in 1801 by its owner and editor George Jefferson from an office in Duke Street.[420] In its early form the *Advertiser* recorded very little insular news and reported for the most part on British and foreign affairs, particularly the stirring military events in Europe and America, but this news was reliant on the sailings of the supply ships:

> As some of our readers may not have been acquainted with the cause of our having delayed this Paper two days later than the day of publication - it may be necessary to observe that in consequence of the want of London and Foreign Intelligence, of a recent and interesting nature, it was considered most eligible to wait the arrival of the Packet.

George Jefferson was involved in a number of lawsuits. One in 1826 had involved a libel directed against the chaplain of St George's church in which the jury returned a verdict of guilty and Jefferson was called upon to pay £50 damages. Jefferson had run-ins with other newspaper proprietors, and one particular spat in 1840, which involved much baiting by Joseph Ritson Wallace, the owner of the *Manx Liberal*, resulted in the *Advertiser* referring to Wallace as 'Satan's representative in the Isle of Man'. Wallace continued in his attacks, and eventually a staff member of the *Advertiser* waylaid him in the street and publicly horsewhipped him. The *Advertiser* took the *Mona's Herald* to account in 1841 when it complained that the *Herald* had printed on the very morning of the *Advertiser*'s publication 'a little paltry slip containing a short account of the late Transactions in China, and to engage a running stationer to hawk the same through the town at the price of one penny'. Jefferson sold the newspaper in 1842 and it ceased to issue in 1845.

The *Rising Sun*, the newspaper of the establishment, was launched in 1821, renamed the *Manx Rising Sun* in 1824 and eventually became the *Manx Sun* in 1826.[421] Its most famous proprietor and editor, 1824 to 1845, was James Grellier, an ex-army surgeon who had served in India under Sir Arthur Wellesley and lived at the Hills House in Douglas. Grellier and members of the Quiggin family were its co-owners for a number of years and published it from the North Quay.

The *Mona's Herald* was the longest running Manx newspaper, lasting almost one hundred and fifty years from its foundation in 1833.[422] William Walls published the *Mona's Herald and General Advertiser* in offices in New Bond Street Lane. He was soon joined in partnership by Robert Fargher who acted as editor, having learnt his trade with his relative, George Jefferson, at the *Manks Advertiser*. Fargher took over sole responsibility for the newspaper in 1839. Before its first edition appeared, the total subscribers to the *Mona's Herald* exceeded those of both its rivals put together. The intrusion of the radical *Herald* on the scene was bitterly resented by the conservative *Sun*, and a rivalry was set up which lasted for many years. Fargher was an outspoken and determined man who was intent on reform:

> Whatever else was said of Robert Fargher (and his press rivals and political opponents heaped plenty of abuse on him) he was never charged with timidity or servility. He lashed out with tremendous gusto at bureaucratic ineptitude, absentee officials, abuses of public rights and liberties, and unceasingly at the self-elected Keys and their practice of sitting in private to deal with matters affecting the whole community.[423]

Fargher's inflammatory 'letters to the editor' resulted in a series of acrimonious libel actions being brought against him by George William Dumbell, one of the ablest and bitterest opponents of political reform, who exercised immense power as a banker, lawyer and Member and Secretary of the House of Keys. The first prosecution arose out of a letter in the *Herald* in 1844 accusing Dumbell of giving misleading information on the Isle of Man Joint Stock Bank of which he was a director. During his release on bail, Fargher attacked his enemy again, claiming that 'such measures as Dumbell has resorted to in this case will hasten the day of reckoning when bank swindlers and petty tyrants who now infest Mona will meet their signal overthrow'. Nearly a year later Fargher was tried, found guilty and sentenced to ten days imprisonment and a fine of £10 which he refused to pay. He was gaoled in Castle Rushen and that was the address he attached to articles he sent to the *Herald*. His eventual release was marked by an extraordinary demonstration:

> On 15 December 1845, fifteen carriages assembled on Douglas Market Place to convey one hundred and thirty well-wishers to Castletown. With the procession went a brass band which struck up as the cavalcade approached Castle Rushen. Crowds of people poured into the Market Square and the jailer, fearing disorder, hastily sent for the High Bailiff to read the Riot Act if things got out of hand. But this proved unnecessary. A deputation entered the Castle and paid the fine - the money having been subscribed by sympathisers.

On his release Fargher set off in a triumphal procession to Douglas. The *Herald* reported that 'Flags were displayed on public houses, shawls and handkerchiefs were hung out at the farm houses, and, in the absence of these, at thatched cottages patriotic old matrons hung out their wearing garments'.

The first edition of the *Manx Liberal* was published in 1836 by John Penrice and Joseph Ritson Wallace in Great George Street.[424] Its banner showed Britannia standing with a raised shield beside the Horn of Plenty against which was another shield emblazoned with the Three Legs of Man emblem. Its motto beneath the subtitle was 'This is not the cause of faction, or of party, or of any individual, but the common interest of every man'. In keeping with the other newspapers, the *Liberal* was not reticent in attacking its rivals in the most shocking ways.[425] A salacious report in 1844 alleged that Charles Johnson (dubbed the 'Long Yankee Colonel' and 'Colonel Slick'), the American editor of the *Advertiser*, was patronising a brothel and 'investigating the womanly qualities of Sally Innett'.[426] The *Liberal* went on to state that 'a married man and father of a family is in a more fitting sphere when by his own domestic hearth, than when he is occupying a cubicle in 66 Strand-street'. The 1841 census returns show that a Margaret Ennett, aged twenty-four and of independent means, was living at premises in Sand/Strand Street in Douglas.[427]

A new Act

A special meeting of Tynwald Court held in March 1844 received the Board of Trade's proposals to begin the reform of the Manx customs system.[428] The House of Keys decided to adjourn the matter for further consideration whilst they ascertained the general feeling of the inhabitants of the Island. The Legislative Council accepted the need for the protection of the British revenue and trade by preventing goods being smuggled from the Island into British ports, the importation of limited but adequate supplies of such goods at rates of duty still lower than those of Britain and any surplus revenue created by alterations in the duties to be applied to the benefit of the Island. Tynwald agreed to inform the public of the substance of the British government's proposals by having them published in the local press and asking the Captains of the parishes to inform their communities of the changes. The House of Keys met on 10 April to hear the arguments of several area deputations and receive public petitions.[429] Animated discussion consequently took place between the members for almost five hours. With the abolition of the 2½% duties and virtually doing away of the 15% duties, the Keys were prepared to consent to the imposition of some additional duties to make up the subsequent loss, but they also considered that the increased surplus should be able to be used by Tynwald. They were concerned that, as the main public and private incomes were supplied by British people coming to live in the Island and summer visitors spending their money, any alteration in duties could drive these people away.

A public meeting was held in Douglas courthouse in April with the veteran campaigner Sir William Hillary in the chair.[430] Principal speakers were those who had long been involved in demanding customs reform for the Island, some of whom would later turn their attention to constitutional reform. Many of the campaigners of 1837, including Sir William Hillary and John James Moore, called for a united Manx front in dealing with any form of imposition of financial change on the Isle of Man by the British Parliament. Robert Fargher, as ever, stuck with his more radical views and unsuccessfully called for support in proposing that any surplus revenue should not be placed under the control of Tynwald, 'a self-elected irresponsible body', but entrusted to parish commissioners. Speaker after speaker called for free trade and the abolition of the ad valorem duties and the licence system. The meeting concluded by claiming the right of the Manx people to be able to impose through their own legislature all taxes and duties. It was resolved that resolutions should be forwarded to the Governor, Legislative Council, Keys, Board of Trade, Home Office, Dr Bowring and other Members of Parliament. A people's deputation, consisting of Samuel Rogers, Thomas Garrett and Robert Duff, was appointed to proceed to London to meet Dr Bowring to assist him with details on the matter.[431] They also met with members of the Board of Trade who went through the entire Bill with them word by word, accepting many of their suggested alterations. Another deputation, consisting of George Dumbell, Secretary to the House of Keys, and some of his colleagues, also visited London to further their own arguments and submissions.

A draft Bill 'To amend the Laws relating to the Customs in the Isle of Man' was brought in by the House of Commons in May 1844.[432] The changes from the earlier package of measures put together by Shaw-Lefevre were remarkable in that, although some customs duties were firmly set at the scheduled tariffs, others stayed at the existing tariffs, others were set somewhere between the scheduled and existing tariffs, whilst others were even reduced below the existing tariffs. Whilst the Bill was progressing, the Home Office wanted to know Governor Ready's further thoughts on doing away with the licence system for the importation of certain goods of foreign growth or manufacture.[433] Ready went into the history of the system and pointed out that its present form had been recommended in the report drawn up by the Commissioners of Inquiry in 1792. In order to take away the temptation to smuggle and to establish a legal trade and ensure a supply of foreign and other goods at a moderate cost, certain limited quantities of goods were allowed to be imported by licence on the payment of moderate duties. The allotment to private persons was limited to enable the Governor to distribute to the merchants and dealers such quantities as would induce them to sell articles at a moderate cost. Ready accepted that this mode of allotment had not 'given satisfaction or attained the object', but he thought that an increase in quotas, the continuation of the licence system and the setting of customs duties at moderate rates would be best for the Island. The reasons for Ready advocating the general retention of the status quo, with minor adjustments, are unclear. He undoubtedly had confidence in the principles of the system, claiming they had beneficially 'produced a large amount of revenue and illicit trade is extinguished'. Concerns that any increases in tariffs could adversely affect future revenue and bring about the return of smuggling would most certainly have played a part in his thinking. He could also possibly have seen the continuation of the system as a means of rewarding and maintaining political support by protecting the welfare of the Manx establishment.

An amended Bill went through the House of Commons.[434] By it the trade of the Island with Britain was to be freed and changed from 'beyond the seas' to be placed on the 'coasting trade'. The harbour dues were abolished. The licence system was to remain, probably a result of Ready's qualms, but in a limited form. Wine, tea, coffee and sugar had their restrictions removed. The quantities of spirits and tobacco allowed to be imported were increased. The 2½% duties were done away with and the 15% duties suspended. The major tariff changes were decreases on coffee, French wines, gin, and rum and increases on refined sugar, black tea, cigars, Eau de Cologne and liqueurs. Tariffs on Muscovado sugar, green tea, tobacco and brandy stayed the same. Foreign timber above 8 inches was to be charged at 8/- a load and timber from the British possessions was to be duty free. Up to the very last moment, Bowring was still talking with Gladstone and eliciting further beneficial changes for the Island through modifications to the Bill.[435] Refined sugar, originally to be increased from 1/- a hundredweight to 14/-, was altered to 9/4 and yet again to 9/-. The tariff on all wine was agreed to be £12 a tun. Brandy and gin had an additional 6d a gallon added to the revised duties to replace the lost income from harbour dues. Very importantly, £2,300 from the customs revenue was to be given annually to the Harbour Commissioners in lieu of the harbour dues for improvements to the Island's ports. 'An Act to amend the Laws relating to the Customs in the Isle of Man' was passed on 19 July 1844.[436]

The financial changes were celebrated in the Island. The liberal *Mona's Herald* reported that the measures would prove to be a vast boon to the Island and enhance its prosperity.[437] There was a complete about-turn by the conservative *Manx Sun* when a poem, a mixture of praise and satire, appeared on its front page in August 1844.[438] 'The Heroes of the Fiscal Bill' commended Dr Bowring and the local reformers and slated the House of Keys:

> What did the Keys, who heroes were of yore?
> They heard with terror their great master roar!
> They gaz'd astounded, paralyz'd with fright,
> Forsook their colours, and they turned to *White!*[439]
> Quick to their kennel slunk the twenty-four,
> They cried *peccavi*, and they closed their door.

The positive action of the petitioners contrasts vividly with the procrastination of the Members of the House of Keys.

Sir William Hillary received congratulatory letters from Dr Bowring, William Gladstone and Sir Robert Peel.[440] Bowring stated that 'The strength of *my* case and of *my* position was in *your* grievance. There existed a state of things which truth and justice could not defend'. Gladstone wrote that 'It is to me of great satisfaction, that in the discharge of my public duty, I should have been instrumental in framing a measure which is acceptable to so loyal and respectable a portion of my fellow-subjects'. Peel was 'gratified by learning that the inhabitants of the Isle of Man do such ample justice to the motives and intentions of Her Majesty's Government in aiding in passing the law to which this resolution refers', and he hoped 'that the practical operation of that law will greatly conduce to the welfare of the Island'. A dinner was given at the Victoria Hotel in Douglas by forty of his admirers to their veteran leader, Sir William Hillary.[441] In his introduction, the chairman of the event wittily said that he had begun to think he saw Dr Bowring at the bottom of every cup of tea he drank and 'it was made sweeter by the sugar he had secured for us'. A further letter from Bowring was read out, including his argument that:

> the state of things would not bear investigation - it was indefensible - and the wonder is, *how* it could have so long remained unreformed! Harbours *repelling* by heavy dues, instead of

Douglas Market Place with the Customs House on the right and St Matthew's church behind, 1846.

inviting and *welcoming* the tempest-tost mariner; licences *lowering* prices to the *rich*, *rising* them to the *poor*; the Isle of Man a *foreign land* in the eyes of our fiscal laws - taxing British manufactures, and making exports from Great Britain subject to numberless vexations.

Dr and Mrs Bowring were invited to the Island to celebrate the satisfactory resolution of the many years of efforts to obtain for the Island a fair share of its own customs revenue and the opening up of its trade with Britain.[442] The couple arrived in Douglas harbour one evening in late September on board the Isle of Man Steam Packet Company's vessel *King Orry*, on which the Steam Packet had given them free passage. The shipping in the harbour displayed flags, bonfires were lit and cannons were fired. Thousands of spectators crowded on and near to the pier. The guests disembarked, with Mrs Bowring on the arm of Sir William Hillary and Dr Bowring on the arm of the campaigner William Kelly. They took a horse-drawn carriage along Customs House Quay, through the market place and on through the town. Triumphal arches were erected along the line of the procession, which was upwards of one-and-a-half miles long and led on to the shore road where bands were playing. During their stay in the Island the Bowrings were given a suite of rooms at the Castle Mona Hotel, onetime residence of the Duke of Atholl. The next day the guests headed west and visited Peel. An Odd Fellows dinner was held that evening in Douglas where Bowring spoke on his efforts to have the Island's customs system revised. He also spoke on the need for constitutional reform, 'My own opinion is that you need to reform your House of Keys, and not overturn them. I should be sorry to see the House of Keys abolished. Your insular affairs require a local legislature. If the Keys will look around them and judge wisely, they will reform themselves'. Bowring then went to the northern town of Ramsey, with more processioning, jubilation, dining and speeches. He again criticised the House of Keys, claiming that they should have redressed the fiscal grievances and not left it to 'the mere chance of accident'. The next day he went south to Castletown to once again speak and dine.

The changes the customs arrangements brought to the Isle of Man were considered by Bowring to be 'one of the earliest experiments in favour of free trade'.[443] The most obvious beneficial repercussion was the stimulation of the Island's economy. Trade was now opened up, no longer considered as 'beyond the seas' but placed on the 'coasting trade' with Britain. The licence system was tightened up and made fairer. The Isle of Man Harbour Commissioners had authority to use a definite annual amount out of the customs revenue to finance harbour works. The amount, £2,300, was well covered by the £4,200 gross increase. This was the first time that a fixed sum of money had been allowed back to the Island to be managed there. When comparing the last financial year under the old Act with the first year under the new one, the quantities of goods consumed went up on almost everything, even those items on which customs duties had been substantially raised.[444] The 1841 and 1851 censuses show an average increase in population of between four and five hundred people each year: rising from a total of 47,975 to 52,387.[445] There was an added boost in spending from the new working residents and the increasing number of summer visitors, who were all coming to the Island as a result of the rising tourist trade. It was estimated that some 20,000 to 30,000 visitors arrived each year.[446] Any concerns and fears that the customs changes would bring about a substantial return of the smuggling trade or even a decline in the population did not happen. Joseph Train summed up events when writing in his 1845 *Historical and Statistical Account of the Isle of Man*:

> Their trade with the United Kingdom is no longer liable to the formalities of foreign voyages, it being now upon the same footing as the coasting trade of Great Britain, with the privilege of carrying bonded goods in smaller vessels. Though the license system is not wholly swept

away, a check is put to huxtering in surplusages. . . . The harbours of the Isle of Man will henceforth be 'harbours of refuge', open to every tempest-tossed vessel free of entrance tolls.[447]

Demands for constitutional reform

Calls for Manx fiscal reform were generally associated with demands for constitutional reform, and in 1844, immediately following Dr Bowring's visit, reformers were able to concentrate on the outstanding constitutional grievance, that of the self-elected House of Keys. The movement was at its most progressive in Ramsey and the north, the area most geographically isolated from the 'Castletown clique'. Throughout the latter part of the year committees were formed and delegates appointed.[448] A petition containing thousands of signatures was raised across the Island, and in January 1845 a delegation of representatives presented the petition to Governor Ready for forwarding to the Home Secretary. Further petitions were raised throughout the early part of 1845.[449] An unenthusiastic Governor Ready claimed that the petitioners 'represented a small portion of the real property and intelligence of the Island'.[450] Unsurprisingly, the Keys themselves did not support the call for their reform, claiming that 'this system of agitation appears to have originated with a few shopkeepers, to have been adopted by some stranger residents'.[451] But the local reformers certainly found quite a volume of support from the new residents and in 'the commercial centres where the growth of a wealthy and politically conscious trading class bred resentment of a self-elect, land-dominated legislature'.[452]

There was now a new Governor, the Honourable Charles Hope, who, aged thirty-seven, succeeded Ready in very tragic circumstances.[453] Ready had been ill for many months and had been taking both internal and external medicines. In July 1845 he died after accidentally drinking a solution of sulphate of atropine in mistake for a draught of morphine. Shortly before his death, Ready had received a query from the Home Office regarding the failure of the Isle of Man Joint Stock Bank two years previously and the delay in resolving the matter. Concerns had been raised by disgruntled shareholders.[454] Only a few weeks into his new appointment, Hope was contacted by Manners-Sutton with a letter following up this query and containing information, advice and caution on constitutional and fiscal matters.[455] Manners-Sutton pointed out to the new Governor that public meetings had been held around the Island calling for constitutional reform and memorials of complaint against the House of Keys had been received by the Home Secretary which made reference to the collapse of the Joint Stock Bank, an event which had caught out persons of all persuasions, conservatives and liberals alike. Manners-Sutton went on to remind Hope that the customs revenue of the Isle of Man ultimately belonged to Britain and 'that a proposition for the surrender of these revenues, or of any part of them, the Government is not prepared to accede'; the surplus revenue must continue to go into the British Exchequer. He urged

Governor Charles Hope.

Hope not to lose sight of this point, for, if the House of Keys was ever to become a democratically elected body, it would scarcely be inclined to continue to comply with the current arrangement by which the surplus was merged into the general funds of Britain.

Before replying to Manners-Sutton, Hope met with representatives of the people in December 1845 to hear their grievances and receive a further petition for electoral reform. He reported back to Manners-Sutton in great length, referring to general complaints regarding the Keys still being a self-elected body, not representing the people, levying certain minor taxes without giving any account of the expenditure of the money and sitting in government behind closed doors.[456] He referred to claims of the lack of opportunity for the people of the Isle of Man to know what laws were being considered by the legislature until they were actually passed and the reluctance of the Keys to amend the existing laws. Hope also remarked on the failure of the Joint Stock Bank and the fact that several of its directors were Members of the House of Keys. Having referred to all these faults and problems, he then remarkably went on to state that he could not say that there was any material ground for complaint against the Keys in the performance of their functions. He doubted whether so small a community as that of the Isle of Man would be better governed under a representative assembly than it had been under a self-elected one. He informed Manners-Sutton that he could not recommend any change to the constitution of the Keys:

> I do not say this because I consider the present constitution of that House perfect, but because I think it is well adapted for its purpose. It has no great power and even if so disposed could do very little harm; and if the present constitution were to be altered I do not see how it could be replaced in such a manner as to be satisfactory to the inhabitants of the Island or to meet the wishes of those who desire a change, without interfering with the present interests of the Empire in such a manner as I should think would not be agreed to.

Hope echoed Manners-Sutton's fear that a popularly elected assembly would never be satisfied with the small share of power which the House of Keys currently possessed, and he agreed that a reformed Keys would endeavour to regain control over the customs revenue of the Island, and that such a claim would come with much more force if made by an elected assembly which possessed the confidence of the people. The *Manx Liberal*, reporting on the attitude of Governor Hope to constitutional reform, would later write that 'Clique influence has been his law, opposition to reform his motto, and contented degradation his text and his mandate; and all, forsooth, because he was a Tory'.[457]

Early in 1846 and again in 1847 further petitions calling for reform of the constitution of the Keys were raised throughout the Island and sent to the Home Secretary.[458] The eventual reaction from the new Home Secretary, Sir George Grey, was important and interesting, if somewhat predictable:

> I am not prepared to deny that an anomaly is presented by the existence in an Island almost within sight of England, and forming part of Her Majesty's dominions, of institutions very dissimilar from those of this country. I cannot, however, consider the Isle of Man in the light of a British colony, entitled as such to a separate Legislature, based on a representative system. I regard it rather as a portion of the mother country, possessing, indeed, from accidental circumstances, peculiar customs and institutions.[459]

Grey went on to threaten that the situation could be addressed by the Isle of Man being incorporated with Britain and 'of being admitted, by such incorporation, to a participation in those free institutions of which the memorialists speak in terms of just admiration'. The *Isle of*

Man Times, despairing at the lack of effort by the House of Keys ('the antiquated humbug') to reform, also deliberated on the possibility of incorporation, urging its readers to consider calling for a 'Union with England, free Municipal Institutions in the Isle of Man, coupled with the continuance of our present Fiscal privileges'.[460] The owner and editor of the *Isle of Man Times* was William Shirrefs, who came to the Island to take advantage of the exemption from stamp duty on newspapers published in the Isle of Man. Grey repeated his stand in 1848 when Dr Bowring again raised the issue of parliamentary reform. Grey stated that 'a complete remedy for the evils complained of was to be found, not in a separate legislature for a small island within a few hours' sail of the British coast, but, on the contrary, in the complete incorporation of the Isle of Man with the United Kingdom'.[461]

The threat of annexation again temporarily subdued the constitutional reformers, and, whilst Britain's policy was that its free trading territories did not necessarily require detailed regulation, the continuing presence in the Isle of Man of a British appointed Governor with comprehensive powers reinforced the point and ensured the maintenance of imperial authority. Whilst significant changes had been made to the Island's trade and licence systems and some regulation in the use of the increased surplus customs revenue had been allowed, the fiscal and constitutional situations were matters of concern which would continue to be raised by the progressive radicals and the members of the new commercial middle classes, none of whom was allied to the establishment, the House of Keys or the Governor. The emphasis was slowly changing.

Chapter 7

Britain's Continuing Authority

Isle of Man and the Treasury

In the early 1850s the Isle of Man was busy and prospering.[462] Shipbuilding was booming, with the construction of barques in Douglas, schooners in Peel, fishing boats in Castletown and Port St Mary and wooden and iron ships of up to 2,000 tons burdened weight in Ramsey. Shipbuilding, fishing, net making and other associated trades financially supported about a quarter of the Island's population. The extraction of lead, silver, copper and zinc were also major industries. The mines at Foxdale were being brought under the Joint Stock Companies Act and those at Laxey were having a giant water wheel constructed to pump them dry of water. Agriculture had improved through the introduction of subsoil ploughing, artificial manuring, draining tiles and the Tithe Commutation Act. The Isle of Man Steam Packet Company was ferrying 50,000 passengers a year to the Island in its fleet of paddle-steamers. Plans were being drawn up for a breakwater to protect Douglas harbour from the south-easterly gales, and further breakwaters for Ramsey, Peel, Port Erin and Castletown were being considered. The improvements to the Island's ports and harbours, thereby making the Island much more accessible, would be of immense benefit to all aspects of Manx trade and commerce.

All of these ongoing developments required the support of suitable public works, so additional money managing schemes were needed to provide the necessary extra funds. But the British Treasury was reluctant to return any more of the Manx surplus revenue than it had to. An example of this took place in 1850 when the inhabitants of Castletown and the Harbour Commissioners requested finances to remove the bar and other impediments in the harbour and were starkly informed by the Treasury that there were no funds available.[463] The Island required financial security and stability. Any attempt at revised national economic strategies, however, would again bring into question the control and disposition of the Manx customs revenue, which in turn would raise concerns about the constitutional position of the House of Keys and result in queries regarding the nature of the relationship which existed between the Isle of Man and Britain. With more changes in the offing and fiscal and constitutional protestors becoming of one mind, the idea that 'if financial reorganisation was achieved, constitutional reform would inevitably follow, had taken firm root'.[464] The new commercial classes of Manx residents were pressuring for economic transformation. Even the Members of the House of Keys were becoming reconciled to accepting

Shipbuilders working on the foreshore at Castletown. Bowling Green House (onetime residence of the Heywood family) to the right of centre and the Governor's residence (Lorne House) and Castle Rushen behind, c.1850.

that their own reform and their input into controlling the Island's customs revenue were irrevocably linked. In spite of the general recognition of the need for these changes, the reformers, the protestors, the Keys and even the cautious Governor were all unprepared for the dubious dealings from within the British Treasury, dealings which very much reflected the ideals of the commercial and imperial state with its hegemonic culture.

The main objectives of the Treasury during this period were to accurately assess Britain's revenue, ensure it was efficiently collected and punctually paid and have its expenditure carefully regulated.[465] Whilst its control of the economy was at the heart of its very being, the Treasury did not have the authority to fix the expenditure levels of the independent departments. Though its influence was expanding, there were important practical limitations to its authority. Its principal control, however, lay early on in the process, largely through the requirement for its prior approval for the funding of departmental schemes. The Treasury's involvement in the public finances of the

Opening ceremony of the 'Lady Isabella' waterwheel at Laxey mines, 27 September 1854.

Isle of Man, however, was more comprehensive, enabling it to directly supervise and approve the Manx customs revenue. It was this authority, exercised by an increasingly powerful department, which was on occasions exceeded by the deliberate discounting of the constitutional rights of Tynwald Court.

In the late summer of 1852 Governor Charles Hope contacted the Assistant Secretary of the Treasury, Sir Charles Edward Trevelyan, regarding the import licence system.[466] Hope thought that the whole subject should be reconsidered with a view to modification, if not total abolition. He was having problems in allotting licences, made all the more difficult by the vast increase in quantities being applied for by some people - although the maximum total quantities allowed for the whole of the Island were not being exceeded. Hope could not see any advantage to the Island as a whole by retaining a system which hampered trade and was no longer required to prevent smuggling out of the Isle of Man.

With this opinion from the Island's Governor, the Treasury went into immediate action. The

Commissioners of Customs were asked for their opinion on Hope's suggestion. Their resultant report, issued in late 1852, cautioned against abolishing the licence system without at the same time increasing the duties on Manx imports which, if left at the present low rates, they feared might incite the return of smuggling.[467] Consequently, the Financial Secretary of the Treasury, James Wilson, asked Hope for his thoughts on a Treasury report issued early in 1853.[468] Wilson's position of Financial Secretary was next in seniority to the Chancellor of the Exchequer, and all important Treasury business was submitted to the post holder, who had the power to decide a great part of it.[469] In the Treasury report it was proposed that any changes should be included in an Act which would be introduced in the next session of Parliament. At this early juncture the report showed that the Treasury had mixed feelings on the matter of restructuring the licence system, recognising the 'serious evils' which arose out of the existing system whereby a monopoly of supply was created which deprived consumers of the advantages of the lower Manx customs duties, whilst at the same time reasoning that the current system of limiting the quantities of certain articles was the only means by which extensive smuggling could be prevented. In spite of their initial misgivings, the Treasury had come to the conclusion that a moderate increase in the existing duties on brandy, gin, rum, tobacco, Eau de Cologne and liqueurs would have the effect of preventing any smuggling and should not cause any major increase in the price of goods to the consumer, provided that the licence system was entirely abolished and open competition established.

Hope agreed in the main with the proposals in the Treasury report.[470] He thought that smuggling goods out of the Island was no longer an issue, as proved by the amounts of licensed goods being legally imported never reaching the full amounts calculated sufficient for local consumption, thereby indicating that there was no surplus to smuggle out. Brandy, probably the article most likely to be smuggled, was limited to 20,000 gallons a year, but only just over 14,000 had been imported in 1851. Hope feared, however, that any major increases in tariffs would inevitably lead to more costly imports which, in turn, could lead to temptations and the return of smuggling into the Island. With this in mind, he believed that the increases proposed in the Treasury report were too great and that smaller ones should be applied, which would create more demand for goods and thereby produce higher overall revenue. Hope suggested that, if there was a concern that lower rates might encourage smuggling, power could be reserved in the new Act to enable the Treasury to re-establish the licensing system, similar to the power given in the 1844 Act with regard to the 15% ad valorem duty. An important point he raised was that the £2,300 allocated annually to the Harbour Commissioners for port improvements had been fixed at this figure in 1844 with no allowance made for an increasing revenue. Since then, the population of the Island had grown considerably and, along with it, demand for all commodities had risen, increasing the Island's trade and its customs revenue. Any such rise in trade would have proportionally

James Wilson, Financial Secretary of the Treasury.

increased the income from the now defunct harbour dues. The Island was not benefiting from either scheme, so was suffering financially in both respects. Hope therefore considered that any new revenue should be used to provide an additional sum for harbour improvements. These proposals from Hope were generally accepted by the Commissioners of Customs.[471]

In April 1853 part of the British Government's annual budget featured the reformation of its Customs Department.[472] James Wilson laid the full plans before the House of Commons, and at the conclusion of his explanations he pointed out that there was a 'small matter' which the Government meant to change which was of 'considerable importance'. He explained the situation in the Isle of Man, and described the historical position the Island was in when under the lordship of the Dukes of Atholl. He said that its low customs duties had caused difficulties to the British Exchequer through smuggling. To help obviate these difficulties, after revestment it was arranged that licences should be granted to particular persons to import limited quantities of articles into the Island. This had worked well early on but was no longer satisfactory. Wilson went on to explain that, after obtaining suggestions from the Governor, the Commissioners of Customs had come to the conclusion that it would now be wise to entirely abolish the licensing system, permit unlimited imports and raise the rates of duty. Such measures, it was reasoned, would see off any vestiges of smuggling and, at the same time, they were in accordance with the idea of free trade, which, by the 1850s, was official British policy and an enduring ideology.

Further resistance

Whilst the two politically opposed Island newspapers continued to lambast each other, there was general agreement on the proposed changes. The *Mona's Herald* queried where the Governor derived the constitutional authority to seek to change the Island's fiscal situation.[473] It accused the British Government of violating its own parliamentary constitution by seeking to alter the Manx customs duties without the consent of the Island's population, 'ay, behind their backs and over their heads, by the act of a body wherein a Manxman's voice cannot be heard'. It bluntly claimed that 'we are fleeced every year'. The *Manx Sun* reported in a similar way, claiming the British Government 'coolly ignored the rights and privileges of the Isle of Man' and was 'predetermined on increasing our taxation whilst relaxing their own'.[474]

People of all persuasions who were concerned about the proposed changes to the duties, the inadequacy of the Manx customs system and the Island's deprivation of the balance of the surplus revenue were galvanised into action. A public meeting was held at the end of April 1853 in Douglas to consider the Treasury proposals.[475] Robert Fargher was elected secretary. It was resolved that, yet again, a people's deputation should go to London to fight the Island's cause and to try to prevent any clause which could injure the Island being included in a Bill to reform the Customs Department.

A meeting of Tynwald Court was convened in early May to discuss matters. Charles Hope claimed that he had always intended to summon Tynwald when he was in a position to lay before them something definite on the subject, but he had held off as he had had nothing official to report.[476] However, he was now able to detail some of the possible alterations to duties, but that was all. The Members of the House of Keys considered they were not being sufficiently briefed and requested the Governor to produce copies of any relevant correspondence between himself and the British Government.[477] Hope's reply was much the same, that he had no correspondence at present which he felt justified in laying before the Keys, but he expected he would shortly be in possession of such information. The Keys were not satisfied with this reply either and asked him to forward a letter of theirs to the Treasury requesting full information and with the observation that the members could not imagine that the British Government would introduce any measure directly affecting the Isle of Man without first submitting the same to Tynwald and the people.

The Keys contacted British politicians sympathetic to the Isle of Man's situation. They sent a request to Sir Robert Inglis for him to ask for copies of all recent pertinent correspondence.[478] In May Wilson was questioned in the House of Commons by William Ewart, who twice asked whether the proposed customs changes affecting the Island were ready yet.[479] Wilson replied they were still being prepared and he could not provide any details yet other than the tariff increases would be small. The Keys continued with their pressure on Wilson and the Treasury, and one of their members, George Dumbell, was able to report that John Meadows White, who the Keys had again appointed as their representative in London, had met with Inglis and Wilson and had sent papers to the Board of Trade.[480] The Keys wrote again to the Treasury, claiming that it would be unjust and unconstitutional to impose any form of taxation upon the people of the Isle of Man without first seeking their opinions and those of the House of Keys, 'the *only* representatives of the Island'. This reference was a thinly veiled criticism of the Douglas deputation.

Meanwhile, the Douglas deputation of Samuel Harris, Thomas Garrett and Robert Fargher arrived in London where they met with the committee chairman, John James Moore, who was based there.[481] The deputation sent extensive documentation to the Home Secretary, Viscount Palmerston, who referred them on to the Treasury.[482] They met with James Wilson, and he explained that the Bill dealing with the Isle of Man customs had been delayed due to his indisposition - this 'indisposition' was possibly to enable him to rethink the situation and seek legal opinion from the Treasury's solicitors. The deputation also met with Sir Joshua Walmsley, another Manx sympathiser, in the lobby of the House of Commons and requested his assistance.[483] Walmsley had been one of those involved in bringing grain into Liverpool and claiming it had been grown in the Isle of Man when in fact it had been imported from abroad. He informed the members of the deputation that 'I ought to assist the Isle of Man, as I made £30,000 by it; but you must expect my assistance contrary to my opinion, and my opinion is that you will do no good in the Island until you are assimilated in all the fiscal and legislative measures that we have in England'.[484] The members of the deputation were surprised and alarmed by his response, and J. J. Moore recalled later that, 'upon consultation of the danger of his influence, we avoided him'. However, Walmsley successfully applied for copies of the Manx surplus customs revenue returns to be made available and sent them to the Douglas deputation.[485] The *Mona's Herald* claimed the figures within these returns showed that the British Government had 'plundered' and 'fleeced' the 'poverty stricken' Island.[486] The *Mona's Herald* not only criticised the British Government but also took a swipe at the lack of effort by the Keys over the years to obtain the surplus revenue for the exclusive use of the Island and to become a democratically elected body:

> They have seen the fat hand of old John Bull pounced into Mona's [ancient name for the Isle of Man] little pocket, lo! . . . There is something inexplicable and mysterious in this

matter, to those who cannot peep behind the scenes. Let us lift the veil a little and look in. These twenty-four men feel that they are tenants at sufferance, and if not very gracious to the landlord, they will be ejected. The implied compact between them and the Home Government is this. They say to John Bull, 'Just allow us to elect ourselves as of yore, and perpetuate this irresponsible farce, and we'll be mum about the surplus, and let our simple ones, for whom we are guardians, be robbed of it to right and left'.

Controversial inclusion in a General Bill

At the beginning of June 1853 Wilson informed Hope that the long awaited Bill would soon be forwarded to him for consideration prior to its introduction into the British Parliament.[487] However, nine days later Wilson wrote again, saying that the new regulations affecting the Island were now to be included in a British Customs Consolidation Bill (a utilitarian measure encompassing Britain and its possessions), and it would not be possible to send a copy of the same for consideration by Tynwald and the people prior to its being presented to the House of Commons. The surprising decision that the Island would be included in a general British Bill, with little opportunity for input from Tynwald or the people, came as a bombshell. The Council and the Keys agreed to unite against this imposition and claimed that such a course was contrary to the precedent set by the Revestment Act of 1765 which had determined that any such changes affecting the Island had to be enacted by distinct Acts of Parliament.[488] Separate resolutions from the both bodies were drawn up in protest.[489] The Keys also organised a public protest petition to be sent to the British Government.[490] Governor Hope forwarded copies of all these resolutions to the Treasury and the Home Office.[491] In his covering letter to the Treasury an aggrieved Hope wrote, 'I am not aware of the reasons which have induced their Lordships to adopt this course, but it is one which I fear will cause considerable dissatisfaction to the inhabitants'. In his letter to the Home Office he wrote, 'It is contrary to the former practice in any Legislation in the Customs Regulations of the Isle of Man, which have always been contained in separate and distinct Acts'.

At the end of the month Sir Robert Inglis addressed Wilson in the House of Commons, asking him why the promised separate Bill for the Island had now been combined with the General Customs Consolidation Bill.[492] Wilson replied that it had been decided to put the issues relating to the Island into the British Bill as they were simple and short. He said that he had sent notice to the Island of the plans three weeks previously and believed the proposed changes had met with the approval of the people. Walmsley and Ewart challenged him to produce evidence for both these remarkable statements. In the Isle of Man the Members of the House of Keys were equally appalled by these false claims. Wilson had only recently informed the Island that it was to be included in the Consolidation Bill and he had totally disregarded the parliamentary and public protests. To address this controversy, Tynwald agreed on 6 July that a further petition should be

George Dumbell and William Callister, Members of the House of Keys and the deputation which went to London in July 1853 to oppose the Isle of Man being included in 'A Bill to amend and consolidate the Laws relating to the Customs, Trade and Navigation'.

sent to the British Government and that two of their members, George Dumbell and William Callister, should go to London to try to remove any 'false impressions'.[493] The Keys deputation left the Island the next day, taking with them the petition. Soon after they arrived in London they had interviews with the Chancellor of the Exchequer, William Gladstone, and the Home Secretary, Viscount Palmerston.[494] The status of Dumbell and Callister as representatives of the people of the Island was brought into question by the Douglas committee, who informed Palmerston that 'these two gentlemen do represent their own House . . . but they do not represent the inhabitants of the Isle of Man' - a counter-swipe at the Keys.[495]

An embittered Matthew Henry Fielde, who had tried to get an import licence whilst residing in the Island and was now living in Dublin, wrote to Palmerston complaining about the House of Keys, which 'does not work well, does not give satisfaction to any but the few who profit by its corrupt administration'.[496] It was also his opinion that the 'intelligent portion of the community are rejoiced that the monopoly is doomed'. He also criticised the *Manx Sun* and the *Mona's*

Herald. Fielde additionally wrote a number of letters to Wilson, using much the same points and encouraging the British Government to treat the Island as part and parcel of Britain, 'What have they done that they should not be annexed to an English county? Why should not they bear their part in a general scheme of taxation? Why should the English artisan pay more than double duty for his brandy and tobacco than the Manxman?'.

In early July a draft of 'A Bill to amend and consolidate the Laws relating to the Customs, Trade and Navigation', with six clauses relating to the Island, was received by Governor Hope, who referred it to Tynwald.[497] The Keys were still dissatisfied and forwarded a further resolution to the Home Office and the Treasury, again protesting against the Island being included in the Bill, complaining that it was unconstitutional and contrary to every principle of legislation and denying the right of Britain to legislate for the Island other than for the protection of the revenue of Britain. Hope, on the other hand, seemingly accepted the fait accompli. In his covering letter enclosing the resolution, he brought a couple of practical points relating to the Bill to Wilson's attention. The first referred to clause 160 which declared that 'The Isle of Man shall be deemed and taken to be part of the United Kingdom for all purposes of this or any other Act relating to the Customs'. Hope considered that this clause should be amended to make clear that it was confined solely to the new Act. Worded as it was, it could be deemed that any other Customs Act without any special reference to the Island would apply to it, having been passed by the British Parliament without any opinions being sought from the Island. The other point which Hope thought would cause problems was the omission of a provision which had featured in certain previous Acts whereby the customs revenue of the Isle of Man, subject to certain deductions, should be paid 'into the receipt of Her Majesty's Exchequer distinctly and apart from all other branches of the public revenue'.

Meanwhile, the Treasury produced a minute in reply to the main concerns expressed in the earlier Tynwald resolutions.[498] It was admitted that it had been originally intended to embody the Manx customs duties regulations in a separate Act, but the Treasury was of the opinion that the new British Customs Act would be incomplete if it excluded 'so near a possession' as the Isle of Man. With regard to the claim that there was an intention on the part of the British Government to interfere with the separate privileges enjoyed by the Island, the Treasury wished the Island to be assured that there was no such intention and there were no motives other than a desire to benefit as much as possible the trade of the Island. The Treasury was prepared to insert a clause expressing in the most explicit terms that nothing in the Act should be construed in any way to affect the rights of the Isle of Man. The Treasury addressed the objection regarding the disposal of the surplus revenue after defraying the cost of its collection and the government of the Island. This had been raised in two forms: one in a wider form regarding the disposal of any surplus revenue after defraying these costs and expenses, and the other in a limited form regarding the disposal of any additional revenue which may arise from the increase of duties now proposed. With regard to the first, the Treasury was adamant that it was expressly enacted that all such surplus revenue should be paid into the British Exchequer and made part of the Consolidated Fund. With regard to the second, the Treasury was prepared to add to the £2,300 reserved under the 1844 Act a further sum likely to be received under the changes now proposed to the tariffs.

After Tynwald had considered this Treasury minute, the Governor and Council presented a draft resolution expressing their further opinions to the Keys.[499] It was hoped that this draft would form a joint resolution of the two branches of the legislature to be laid before the British Government. The Governor and Council considered that they could now lift the objections which they had previously held, and they believed that, whilst there may be differences of opinion as to the exact amount of duties which should be imposed, the Treasury and Customs had probably gone as low as they could. There was relief that the increase of revenue expected to be derived from the proposed increases was to be applied for the benefit of the Island and not for the increase of the British revenue. It was not thought wise at this time to enter into discussions on the question of the general revenue of the Island, but the Governor and the Council again wished to call the attention of the Treasury to the omission in the proposed Bill that the customs revenue of the Island should be paid into the Exchequer 'distinctly and apart from all other branches of the public revenue'. The House of Keys, meanwhile, wanted to defer expressing their opinion on the Treasury minute until they had communicated with their deputation in London, which they quickly did and agreed on yet another resolution protesting against the Isle of Man being incorporated into the Bill, expressing their particular concern that:

> any misapprehension should have arisen in the minds of the Lords of the Treasury as to an acquiescence on their part in the proposed alterations being included in the General Customs Consolidation Act for the United Kingdom. The Keys are at a loss to conceive how so erroneous impression could have been formed.[500]

'If the House of Keys had been a representative body'

Britain's attitude to the fiscal and constitutional situations in the Isle of Man was reflected in two influential periodicals. *The Economist*, seeming to show a lack of appreciation of the situation of the Isle of Man, reported that:

> It is hardly credible that at our period of history, after Scotland has been united to England for a century and a half, and Ireland has been united with it for more than half a century, and all are placed under one code of laws so far as the commerce of the Empire is concerned, that there should exist, nearly midway between these three principal parts, an

WHAT IS THE HOUSE OF KEYS?

THE *Court Circular* tells us that a deputation from "the House of Keys" had an interview with one of the official somebodies or nobodies at Downing Street the other day, and MR. WILSON, M.P., told the House of Commons the other evening that he had a series of resolutions by "the House of Keys" in his possession. After some research we find that "the House of Keys" is something or other in the Isle of Man, answering probably to the vestry of a parish, the beadledom of an arcade, or some other small local authority.

We should like to be present at a debate among "the Keys," for we are curious to know whether they allude to each other as the "Honourable Member for Street Door," "the Honourable and Learned Member for Padlock," or "the Gallant and Distinguished representative of Tea-caddy." We do not quite understand the principle of election that can prevail in the Isle of Man, if its council consists of nothing but a bunch of keys; and we are rather puzzled to guess whether the franchise attaches to persons or things, and whether it would be the door or the owner of the door, the watch or the owner of the watch, that would send "a Key" to Parliament. There is one peculiarity of result in having a House of Keys instead of a House of Commons; for, of course, in an assembly where the members are all keys they would be unable to deal with any open question. Perhaps, however, we may have mistaken the sort of "Keys" of which the "House" in the Isle of Man is composed, and the members may be mere musical "keys"—a set of sharps and flats, playing any tune, just like any other ordinary house of representatives. We cannot conclude without remarking that a very long debate in "the House of Keys" would remind one of "a lock jaw," though the association is not agreeable.

Punch magazine, 'What is the House of Keys?', 1853.

island about thirty miles long and twelve broad, with a Legislature and separate government of its own, with peculiar taxes imposed by its own Legislature, and with a system and commercial and revenue laws totally distinct from those of the rest of the Empire.[501]

Considering that *The Economist* had been founded ten years earlier by James Wilson, such comment may not be totally unexpected. *Punch*, under the heading 'What is the House of Keys?', satirically considered that:

> After some research we find that 'the House of Keys' is something or other in the Isle of Man, answering probably to the vestry of a parish, the beadledom of an arcade, or some other small local authority.... There is one peculiarity of result in having a House of Keys instead of a House of Commons; for, of course, in an assembly where the members are all keys they would be unable to deal with any open question.[502]

Dumbell and Callister had meetings with Wilson and Gladstone later in July to discuss the most recent Treasury minute.[503] The two delegates suggested that the title of the Bill should be changed to include the name of the Isle of Man, all enactments relating to it should be put at the end of the Bill and a clause should be inserted expressing in the most explicit terms that nothing in the course taken should be construed in any way to affect any of the privileges or rights already enjoyed by the Island. Dumbell and Callister agreed to certain increased duties. They wanted any surplus customs revenue to be placed in a separate account and paid, as directed by Tynwald, for harbour and other improvements. James Wilson now took control of matters. He explained to the two delegates that the proposal to allow Tynwald to have control of the surplus could not be allowed as it was impossible to permit the House of Keys, a self-elected body, to have any say in the distribution of public money. However, he said that the British Government would be prepared to treat any future claim in a very different spirit if the Members of the House of Keys were to be elected by the people. In Britain itself, the electoral Reform Act of 1832 had extended the vote to all men owning property worth £10 or more. This had virtually tripled the number of eligible voters. The Keys deputation replied to Wilson, pointing out that the establishment of the Keys was part of the constitution of the Isle of Man, members had always been self-elected, and, indeed, they protested, it was hardly fair to find fault with this method of election when the British Government had previously refused to allow it to be altered. Dumbell pointed out that he was one of a party which a few years previously had applied to the British Government to permit the Keys to be elected by the people (a complete about turn from his personal opinion expressed so forcibly not so many years previously), but then, as on former occasions, the British Government had refused the request. However, if the British Government now wanted the House of Keys to be so elected, the deputation requested from Wilson a minute of their meetings which would include this seeming change of heart and policy which was a sudden, unexpected and total reversal of Britain's long-standing reluctance to allow the House of Keys to become a properly elected and responsible assembly. This encouragement for a major change to take place to the Island's constitution was no doubt brought about by Britain's maturing and progressive imperialistic attitude.

Wilson issued such a minute.[504] In it he agreed that he would alter the title of the Act to 'Consolidation of the Customs Acts of the United Kingdom and the Isle of Man'. Instead of the clauses affecting the Isle of Man being placed in the middle of the Bill, they would be put at the end. He further agreed that clause 160 should be modified to apply only to the present Act, leaving out the words 'or any other Act relating to Customs'. He agreed to introduce the same words as were in the 1844 Act, whereby the balance of the revenue would 'be brought and paid into the receipt of Her Majesty's Exchequer distinctly and apart from all other branches of public revenue'. He also agreed to a suggestion made by the Governor and Council that the average consumption of the next three years should be used to determine the likely increase of revenue under the tariff changes and to devote this increase in addition to the £2,300 already appropriated to improve public works in the Island. With regard to the method of applying this surplus, the Keys deputation had proposed that it should be placed in a separate account to be administered by

Tynwald, with the Governor having a veto as to its application. As this proposal involved an entirely new principle and practice, Wilson reserved a definitive reply until he had conferred with the Lords of the Treasury upon it. With regard to Tynwald having the whole of its customs revenue and control of the excess, Wilson stated that the Treasury was unable to discuss this as it was a constitutional question which should be conducted through the Home Secretary. However, Wilson did reiterate his unexpected statement made at the meeting:

> I was authorised to say that if the House of Keys had been a representative body, elected by the people of the Island, the Lords of the Treasury would have been disposed to have taken a much more favourable view of your proposal to intrust to it the administration of these funds, and the control of the improvements and works to be effected thereby. And I am further authorised to say, that in the event of the present proposals of the Government being carried into effect, in the only way in which under present circumstances the Government can consent that they should, and that if at any future time the House of Keys shall become a representative body, the Lords of the Treasury will be prepared to reconsider the question of placing the administration of the surplus revenue, determined as the excess caused by the present readjustment of duties, at their disposal, as proposed by you.

Dumbell returned to the Island to confer with his colleagues on Wilson's statement regarding their constitution. The Members of the House of Keys accepted, with some reluctance, the need for this historic change. Dumbell went back to London bearing a signed resolution agreeing that the House of Keys was prepared to become a popularly elected body.[505] Referring to Wilson's statement, the *Mona's Herald* wrote that it was 'a thunderbolt that has fallen on the heads of the Manx oligarchy'.[506] It claimed that, because the Keys were not popularly elected, Britain had not been prepared to hand over the surplus customs revenue which had been 'swamped in the consolidated vortex - ay, to the tune of £600,000, besides more than a million pounds of interest!'. It revelled in the situation that the Keys and, in particular, Dumbell found themselves:

> This terrible blow had its immediate effect - it struck the Keys' Secretary stark mad, and sent him bolt from London to this Island. This Secretary bolts back again to London with a document in his pocket, signed by a large majority of the Keys, consenting to popular election, if the gear can be forthcoming. What have we here? Who is the leading bellwether of this converted flock? Is he not the very man who in 1845 stood up in the House of Keys, and thus addressed its members? 'Let me see the man in this House who shall dare to consent to be elected by the people. You have all sworn "to use your best endeavours to maintain the ancient laws and customs of this Isle", but to consent to popular election is to overturn the ancient customs of the Island, and thus commit perjury'. . . . Now hang yourselves, gentlemen, on which horn of the dilemma is most agreeable to you.

Despite the proposals from Wilson, it was obvious that he had no powers to discuss the constitution of the House of Keys. Whilst his position as Financial Secretary of the Treasury was one of the most important posts in the government not held by a member of the cabinet, and the Treasury had financial control over the other departments of the state through the power of prior approval and influence, neither Wilson's nor the Treasury's responsibilities extended as far as constitutional issues. The two members of the Keys deputation were aware that the matter could not be dealt with by the Treasury, so they now brought the Home Secretary's attention to it.[507] They wanted to know whether he would be prepared to recommend the Royal Assent if an Act of Tynwald was passed to provide for the election of the Keys. Home Secretary Palmerston asked Hope for a report on the matter. Hope explained the nature of Tynwald, including the legislative and judicial functions of the Keys.[508] He then considered the question as to whether the constitution should be altered so as Members of the House of Keys would in future be elected by the people. He stated that in 1845, when a number of petitions for such a change had been before the British Government, his opinion on the subject was sought by the Home Secretary, Sir James Graham. Hope had expressed grave reservations then and saw no reason to alter them now. Whilst he considered that there could be no difference of opinion upon the correctness of the general principle of a representative system of government, he felt it was necessary to consider the peculiar position of the Island. His understanding was that the Isle of Man, though possessing a separate legislature and privileges of its own which had existed unchanged for several centuries, was directly under the 'superintendence' of the Home Office and liable to the 'supervision' of the British Parliament. The surplus of the Manx customs revenue had been claimed in the past for local purposes, and most certainly that claim would be urged more strongly by an assembly which had the additional claim of being elected by the people. If the manner of election was amended, Hope considered it would enable an assembly elected by a small community to have control of very large funds. He had no doubt that in a very short time this would place an elected House of Keys in Tynwald at issue with the British Parliament. Whilst Hope held to his long term belief that an alteration in the constitution of the House was not desirable, he was somewhat perplexed by Wilson's surprise statement, which he considered could now change matters. He pointed out that, when his opinion had previously been sought by Sir James Graham, he had been directed not to lose sight of the question of the customs revenue and had been informed that the British Government was not prepared to surrender any part of it. But the recent letter from Wilson to Dumbell and Callister had totally altered the situation. Hope put it to Palmerston that the control of public money could only be given to Tynwald if at least a portion of the Keys was elected by the people, so that the representatives of the public would have a voice in the disposal of the public money. If such a change was desired by the people it would then be a very different question as to whether it would be right for the British Government to resist such a wish.

End of the licence system

At the same time as the related constitutional situation was being discussed, the fiscal considerations and negotiations were moving on. Hope responded to Wilson's request for his and the Legislative Council's thoughts on the outcome of the meetings in London between the various parties.[509] The Governor and Council were of the opinion that the proposals of the British Government, with certain alterations, would be advantageous to the Island. They considered that the differences remaining between all parties were very few. However, they emphasised again that all future increases in customs revenue should be applied to the purposes of the Island, and they proposed that a method of arriving at such a figure would be to calculate the extra revenue as a fraction of the total customs revenue and apply that fraction for funding public improvements. With regard to the questions of the general revenue of the Island and the constitution of the House of Keys, the Governor and Council agreed that it would be better not to enter into discussion on these at present as they were not relevant to the measures under consideration.

In early August Dumbell and Callister met with Wilson on a number of further occasions.[510] After more haggling and claims of errors and misunderstandings over the computation of the extra revenue from the new scale of duties, agreement was finally reached on the details of the Manx aspects of the new Bill. Duties would be increased on spirits, manufactured tobacco and cigars, reduced on tea and refined sugar and ended on timber. Wilson explained that these changes would result in an overall net increase of £3,240, calculated to be approximately one-ninth of the new gross revenue, and this fraction should be used in the future to determine an extra annual amount for the Island above the £2,300 already allocated for public improvements. The one-ninth would be primarily devoted to harbour works, with Tynwald deciding what improvements should be undertaken, subject to the veto of the Governor.

The 'Consolidated Customs Bill of the United Kingdom and the Isle of Man' was produced on 5 August 1853.[511] The main clauses which affected the Isle of Man were under section 12:

346 The Island would be deemed to be part of Britain for the purposes of this Act, but nothing would prejudice or affect any of its rights or privileges.

347 No foreign goods of a higher import duty in Britain or Ireland than in the Island should be shipped from the Island into Britain or Ireland.

348 Goods grown or manufactured in the Island could be exported from the Island into Britain or Ireland without payment of any customs duties.

349 Before any goods could be shipped from the Isle of Man into Britain, proof of produce would be provided to the Collector of Customs.

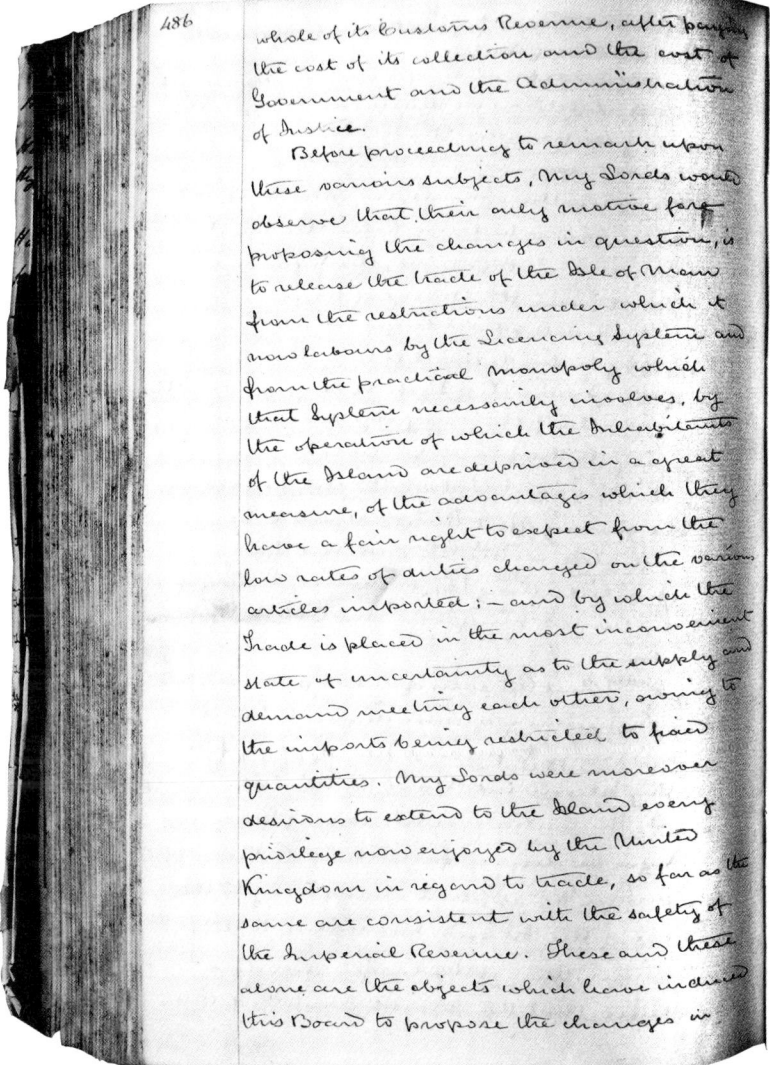

*Government Office Correspondence Book,
recording the ending of the licence system, 8 July 1853.*

352 The Treasury could re-impose the restriction on any foreign goods imported into the Island at any time.

353 The customs duties on imported goods should be collected, paid, recovered and accounted for under the control of the Customs Department. After deducting the necessary charges for this control, the duties should continue to be paid into the Exchequer distinctly and apart from all other branches of the public revenue to become part of the Consolidated Fund of Britain.

354 The necessary expenses of government, the administration of justice and other local charges, along with the current annual sum of £2,300 for use by the Harbour Commissioners, would continue to be retained and paid by the Collector of Customs of the Island before the remaining revenue balance was passed on.

355 In addition, a sum equal to one-ninth of the revenue should be applied by the British Treasury to assist with further improvements in the harbours and other public works; the repairs and improvements in the harbours taking priority. Tynwald, with the Governor's veto, would determine these improvements.

In addition and of great importance, the licence system would be finally done away with and restrictions would no longer be placed on the quantities of goods allowed to be imported. The resultant two new Acts, 'An Act for Consolidating Customs Duties Acts' and 'An Act to amend and consolidate the Laws relating to the Customs of the United Kingdom and of the Isle of Man, and certain Laws relating to Trade and Navigation and the British Possessions', were finalised on 20 August 1853.[512] When considering the changes some fifty years later, A. W. Moore, the historian and Speaker of the House of Keys, claimed that these Acts 'practically ensured the freedom of Manx trade'.[513]

'A palpable breach of faith'

The outcome of the fiscal negotiations did not please all the protestors. At a series of public meetings held in the parishes in early 1854 campaigners yet again raised the issue of the right of the Island to the whole of its surplus customs revenue.[514] J. J. Moore again took the lead, travelling around the Island addressing meetings and acting as the people's agent in London (he would later tour the principal ports of the north-west of England, seeking support for the Island to have control of the whole of its revenue to enable it to fund a 'Harbour of Refuge'). Even John Courtney Bluett put in an appearance, convening a meeting in his capacity as High Bailiff of Douglas. Numerous committees were formed, made up of many prominent officials, local figures and seasoned reformers, whose initial remit was to obtain signatures to an all-Island petition demanding that the surplus revenue should be appropriated by Tynwald for improvements to utilities, especially the harbours.

With all this activity, it came as a surprise when Britain sought to introduce another controversial Act affecting the Isle of Man - probably more controversial in perception than in effect, but certainly authoritarian in complexion and seen once again as an affront to the Manx. In April 1854 Sir Charles Trevelyan, the Assistant Secretary of the Treasury, advised Governor Hope that the British Government wished that in future the gross customs revenue of the Island should be paid into the British Exchequer before, instead of after, the deduction of the expenses of government.[515] Tynwald considered the proposition and unanimously signed a resolution in response, expressing the opinion that the proposition was entirely at variance with the rights and interests of the inhabitants of the Island. But the British Government was set on a course, and James Wilson sent Hope a draft of the Bill at the beginning of June for Tynwald to consider and make any observations.[516] Wilson explained that the main object of the Bill was to establish a new system applicable to Britain without exception, namely, that the gross revenues of the Customs, Inland Revenue and Post Office should be paid into the Exchequer without any deduction whatever. Ignoring the fact that the Isle of Man was not part of Britain, Wilson was making manoeuvres yet again. He informed Hope that the Treasury had delayed going into committee on the Bill until 12 June to give Tynwald the opportunity to respond. Hope arranged a meeting of Tynwald, but before this could happen he read in *The Times* of 3 June that the Bill had passed through its first stages in the House of Commons on the very day that Wilson had sent his letter telling of the delay. Hope thought some mistake might have taken place.[517] He pointed out to Wilson the very awkward position in which he was now placed, with a meeting of Tynwald arranged to discuss the very Bill which Britain was seemingly moving on without any regard to the Isle of Man's opinion. He said he had grave doubts whether the proposals would have been accepted by Tynwald anyway, but the situation now created would 'give great dissatisfaction unless some explanation is made which I have not at present the means of giving'. Whilst Hope was writing his letter of protest, Wilson was writing to him to explain that the 'Public Revenue Bill' had passed through committee early, as it was 'for the convenience of the Government that it should do so'.

Tynwald met to discuss matters, and the Governor and Legislative Council issued a resolution to the Prime Minister, the Earl of Aberdeen, and copied it to the Treasury, expressing regret that the Bill had been passed without Tynwald having had the opportunity to make observations.[518] The Council claimed it was clearly contrary to the rights of the people of the Island that a Bill of the British Parliament, which materially affected the interests and privileges of the Isle of Man, should be brought into the British Parliament and passed without first giving Tynwald an opportunity of expressing an opinion on the subject. The Council also wished to call the attention of the Treasury to the fact that the gross customs revenue of the Island was not part of the revenue of Britain, and claimed that, after deducting the necessary expenses attending the collection of it and the government of the Island, it should be solely applicable to the purposes of the Island. The Keys agreed to send a resolution of their own on the subject to the Prime Minister and the Home Secretary in which they pointed out that Wilson had reneged on his promise. They considered his action was 'a palpable breach of faith' and a 'positive insult to the Legislature of the Isle of Man', and they asked Aberdeen and Palmerston to consider whether Wilson's actions were 'consistent with the dignity of Her Majesty's Government'. Aberdeen's response was to inform Hope that he had directed that the relevant correspondence should be laid before the Commissioners of the Treasury. In fact it was referred to the subject of the complaint, Wilson. Wilson replied, writing that the Treasury was not prepared to accept that the balance of the customs revenue of the Island should be reserved for solely local purposes, as, since revestment, Britain had the right of controlling and regulating the customs of the Island, and the balance of the customs revenue was to be used for the general purposes of the British Government, including the protection and security of the Island. The Treasury also thought that Tynwald misunderstood the parliamentary process, as the third stage of the reading of the Bill would afford Tynwald the means to have an input. With this in view, the Chancellor of the Exchequer, William Gladstone, had agreed to postpone the third reading to a later date.

Tynwald's two chambers reacted to this news in very differing ways. The Legislative Council did not feel justified in assenting to a measure which could so materially affect the interests of the Island. The House of Keys resolved that the Bill should be amended. The preamble should be altered by adding after the words 'United Kingdom' in the eighth line the words 'and the Isle of Man'. Because the Isle of Man was not part of Britain, this was a distinction always called for by Tynwald. An additional clause should be added to the Bill, stating that 'nothing herein contained shall be deemed to prejudice or affect the consideration of any claim that may be made by the inhabitants of the Isle of Man to the Customs Revenue arising from that Island'. Wilson replied that the Lords of the Treasury did not object to the Keys' first resolution, and would insert the words 'and the Isle of Man', but were unable to comply with the views of the Keys on the second resolution, as they could not, 'even inferentially', recognise the claim of the Isle of Man to the entire customs revenue.[519] Wilson ended simply with the note that 'My Lords must adhere to their former decision'. J. J. Moore, again deputed to act on behalf of the people, wrote to Wilson and the Lord President of the Council, Earl Granville, informing them that the inhabitants of the Island were adverse to the Bill including reference to the Island in any manner whatever.[520] He also presented the all-Island petition to the Home Secretary, Viscount Palmerston. All the protests were to no avail. On 7 August 1854 Wilson advised Hope that a revised Bill was about to be passed and enclosed a copy of it.[521] Hope hastily replied, calling Wilson's attention once again to the short notice given, thereby debarring the matter being laid before Tynwald. But, with no time for the Island to protest, the Bill was passed on 12 August, to become 'An Act for the further Alteration and Amendment of the Laws and Duties of Customs'.[522] The Treasury had effectively steamrollered its financial policy right through the constitutional rights of the Island:

> My Lords are unable to recognise the proportion of the public revenue derived from the Isle in any other light than that in which they regard the revenue derived from any locality of the United Kingdom or otherwise than as applicable in the same way to Imperial purposes. With regard to the improvements of the Island, my Lords are of opinion that they can only be considered upon the same principle as is applicable to all other places. Those which are of a purely local character must be undertaken from local sources and those which are of a public and Imperial character must be provided for by votes of the Imperial Parliament in relation to their urgency as compared with other works of a like nature in other parts of the Kingdom as Parliament may decide.[523]

The Keys forlornly protested to the Earl of Aberdeen, again denying the right of the British Parliament to pass any Act altering the laws of the Island without the sanction of Tynwald, and claiming that 'it is manifest that the notice given by Mr Wilson to the Lieutenant Governor by letter of the 8 August could not be made use of by the Authorities of the Isle of Man, of which fact Mr Wilson must have been perfectly aware at the time'.[524] The Keys demanded that Aberdeen should give directions to prevent any similar situation happening again. The Earl of Aberdeen, however, had other things on his mind. He was trying to find effective solutions to fund the Crimean War and relieve the national debt. He was also about to be succeeded by Viscount Palmerston as Britain's Prime Minister. Wilson, meanwhile, seemingly unhindered by his 'palpable breach of faith', now went on to reorganise the Treasury.

James Wilson had included the Isle of Man in Parliamentary Acts without the approval of Tynwald or the Governor. In this great age of the supremacy of the British Empire, he was seemingly allowed to act on his own initiative and without proper consultation in his determined handling of the Isle of Man situation. But Wilson had also pointed the way for a possible change. Tynwald had been given some additional financial authority, including its gain of part of the functions of the Harbour Commissioners. Wilson had then tantalisingly raised the prospect of the whole of Tynwald being even more fully involved in the finances should the House of Keys become a democratic assembly. Seemingly the British Government had authorised the Financial Secretary to encourage the House to reform itself. Although they were unprepared for this unexpected offer, the attitude of the Members of the House of Keys was changing, albeit very slowly and reluctantly. They were coming round to the unpalatable idea that financial and constitutional reforms were inextricably linked. They had also demonstrated positive responsibilities in Tynwald - which undoubtedly would have been recognised in Westminster and Whitehall - by again sending resolutions to the Home Office and the Treasury, instigating public petitions and appointing Keys delegates to meet with influential Members of Parliament and senior ministers. However, it would be more than ten years before any crucial alterations would take place - a delay which was undoubtedly the result of Governor Hope's cautious resistance to change, the Keys' tardy acceptance of the need to become a less self-interested 'clique' and Britain's continuing imperial subjugation of the Isle of Man. The Home Office, through its continuing appointment of the Governor and the majority of the Legislative Council, retained control of the decision making in Tynwald. The Treasury, whilst releasing some funds to Tynwald for harbour works, still retained control of the primary public finances.

Chapter 8

Fiscal and Constitutional Reform

Governor Loch and the state of the Island

Francis Stainsby-Conant-Pigott served only three years, 1860 to 1863, as Governor of the Isle of Man. His arrival was marked by a tremendous celebratory procession in Douglas, of which possibly the most controversial feature was a decorative arch erected outside the home of Robert Fargher in Mona Terrace.[525] Hanging from the arch were twenty-four rust-coloured pasteboard keys, a jar of oil, some sandpaper and a placard which declared 'A New Hand to Scour a Rusty Bunch'. Pigott's governorship was hindered by illness, and he died in office leaving the public business in a great deal of arrears.[526]

Henry Brougham Loch, aged only thirty-five and just recently married, was appointed to succeed Pigott.[527] Loch had previously served in the army for seventeen years, and during his early career he had proved himself to be outstanding in military, diplomatic and administrative affairs. He had resigned from the army in 1861 and had become Private Secretary to the British Home Secretary, Sir George Grey.[528] This close association with Grey would serve Loch well in the opening years of his governorship. Each Governor received a commission appointing him to the position and a set of detailed instructions specifying the nature of the particular tasks which he was expected to perform.[529] Amongst Loch's eight instructions were the following:

> That you endeavour to make the People of the said Island thoroughly sensible of Our Royal inclination to promote their happiness in common with all our other good subjects, and you will particularly explain to them the advantages to be derived from the protection of Our Government, and from their ready and cheerful obedience to the Laws of this realm as far as they concern them, which are so much calculated to their interest and prosperity. And for the better preventing all illicit and clandestine Trade which may be carried on to the prejudice of the Revenues of Our United Kingdom of Great Britain and Ireland, and to the detriment of the fair and industrious Trader, you are hereby required to carry into strict and steady executions the provisions and regulations made or which hereafter may be made, for that purpose from time to time, by the legislature of Our said United Kingdom.

So, Britain, seeking to assure the Island of the 'advantages to be derived' from its 'protection', was still anxious that elements of smuggling could still be surviving. However, there was no

Dumbell banknote.

evidence of any illegal trading activities. Indeed, the economy of the private sector in the Island was very buoyant due to the success of its legitimate trades.[530] These trades were principally reliant on the fishing and tourism industries. Rents and duties from Crown properties totalled £10,645. Rents of land varied from £1 to £3 an acre in the country and £5 an acre near the towns. There were two local banks, the Bank of Mona and Dumbell, Son & Howard, both of which issued £1 notes which were secured by guarantees on land. No stamps were required for bills or receipts. The total population in 1861 was 52,469 and would rise to 54,042 over the next ten years. People were moving in great numbers from the country to the towns. The number of houses in the Island was 9,540, with 8,948 occupied, 502 unoccupied and 90 being erected. The gross customs revenue for 1863 amounted to £28,337. Trade restrictions had been lifted, and exports included 20,000 quarters of wheat, barley and oats and 12,000-15,000 tons of potatoes. Other major exports were iron and lead ores, corn, cattle, horses, poultry, eggs, butter, rope, twine, soap, starch and linen. The fishing industry's season lasted from June to October, with 1,100 boats and 7,500 hands (over half being Manx based) operating out of its ports. Boats used for fishing ranged from 15 to 30 cwt. in size and cost about £250 each to build. Thirty-two million herrings were caught each year and were packed into over 40,000 barrels for export, sold at £1 12s 0d a barrel and realised an annual income

Governor Henry Loch.

of almost £70,000. The burgeoning tourist industry was bringing in an increasing number of summer visitors each year: approximately 50,000 in 1852, 60,000 in 1866 and 90,000 in 1873. This new trade would do most to secure the Island's economy for the next one hundred years.

Upon taking up his appointment in February 1863, Governor Loch found that, at a time when major parliamentary reform had been achieved in Britain over the previous thirty years, the constitution of Tynwald remained unaltered. Although Tynwald Court could enact, abolish or revive all insular laws, the real government in the Island still consisted of the Governor in whom legislative, judicial and executive powers were largely concentrated. He was generally supported in the Legislative Council by the officials appointed by the Crown and the Lord Bishop. He was ultimately responsible for appointing the Members of the House of Keys who served for as long as they wished and were not answerable to the people they represented. The Governor presided over Tynwald and was effectively Chancellor of the Exchequer. Given all this, even his powers were ultimately subject to the direction of the Home Office on matters of policy and the Treasury on matters of finance. People in the Island had been seeking greater financial autonomy and constitutional amendment for a long time, and circumstances which occurred fairly early on in Loch's governship - the need for improved port facilities and controversies concerning the House of Keys - convinced him that he must speedily, determinedly and single-mindedly bring about further improvements to the public finances and comprehensive changes to the constitution.

> Of all the holders of place in our great Colonial Hierarchy, Sir Henry Brougham Loch is unquestionably the strongest. He is an autocrat, his autocracy scarcely leavened by a respect for tradition. It is purely a personal despotism, born of a desire to have his own way; and this love of personal rule came into existence in the Isle of Man.[531]

Breakwater and harbour works

Regular Isle of Man Steam Packet sailings had continued to increase to cater for the growing resident population of the Island and its increasing number of visitors. Because of the lack of proper berthing facilities at Douglas, steamers had to anchor in the bay and the passengers were then rowed ashore. The amount of cargo traffic was also increasing, adding to the problems of the busy but inadequate harbour. 'The town, and especially the pier and quay, generally present a scene of bustle and activity. The vessels belonging to the port at present time, are numerous and of considerable tonnage'.[532] There was, therefore, an urgent need for a deep-water berth for safer shelter and easier movement of people and goods. In a report in January 1856 engineer James Walker of Messrs Walker, Burgess & Cooper, acting on behalf of the Isle of Man Harbour Commissioners, had recommended that, as an initial measure, a breakwater built of stone should be constructed from the two-gun battery on Douglas Head to protect the town's harbour from the damaging south-easterly winds.[533] But Walker's stone-built breakwater proposal was not acted upon. Whilst Tynwald preferred his more solid design, the estimated cost had been increased to £50,000 due to the additional requirements of the Admiralty.[534] So, a slightly cheaper option, costing £48,000 and consisting of a creosoted wooden framework built on a sloping foundation of rubble designed by James Abernethy, was forced on Tynwald by the Admiralty for seemingly minor economic reasons. The development was to be financed by borrowings raised against the one-ninth gross revenue allocated by the Consolidated Customs Act of 1853.

When Governor Henry Loch assumed office it was clear to him that the Abernethy design (lampooned as 'Abernethy's bird-cage') would be unable to withstand stormy weather. Loch set up an enquiry into the condition of the breakwater, which had been commenced in 1862 and had almost reached half its intended length of 1,100 feet. In August 1863 John Clarke Hawkshaw, a civil engineer acting on behalf of the Public Works Loan Commissioners and who had a long knowledge of the Island's harbours, inspected Abernethy's new works at Douglas and also those at Ramsey and Peel.[535] He sent in his report some two months later in which he stated that the three harbours were 'wholly inadequate for the trade of those places'. The stability of the ongoing structures gave him serious concern. During 1864 repeated disasters befell the construction of the Douglas breakwater.[536] Heavy waves washed away the loose rubble foundation, and the superstructure of the poorly creosoted timber was too weak to resist the pressure of the rubble-filled wooden frames which were placed upon it. On several occasions from late winter until early summer the piles gave way and the frames broke. Various attempts were made to strengthen the work but with little real benefit. 'Abernethy's bird-cage' was collapsing. Loch announced at Tynwald Court that, in his opinion, the work in its present form must stop. In October Hawkshaw again visited the Island and recommended further strengthening of the works.[537] Before anything could be done, the situation got worse. Ordinary, by no means violent, winds beat into the harbour and tore up large portions of the works.[538] That November saw a heavy gale pass over the Island, doing more damage to the framework of the breakwater.[539] On the last few days of January 1865 another great storm from the south-east swept over the Island, one of the worst storms to hit the eastern and southern coasts for some twenty years. It destroyed £30,000 worth of private property at Douglas, damaged the promenade and washed away the 'bird-cage'. Tynwald now stood to lose a large proportion of the £45,000 which had been borrowed from the Public Works Loan Commissioners on the security of the one-ninth of the gross customs revenue.

Loch told Tynwald Court that he considered that a permanent stone structure was what was needed for the breakwater, and he would obtain suitable plans and estimates.[540] He wrote to the Treasury informing them that the bay was now dangerous for vessels entering or leaving the harbour because the storm debris had formed a mound of rubble rising directly in the channel which vessels used.[541] Loch considered that the incident had proved the impossibility of a wooden breakwater being constructed of sufficient strength to resist the heavy seas on the Island's east coast, and it would be a waste of money to attempt the reconstruction according to the original plans. The only alternative was to have any future work constructed of stone. He was anxious to confer directly with the Board of Trade on the subject, and he also wanted to lay personally before William Gladstone, the British Chancellor of the Exchequer, a suggestion by which the revenue of the Island could be materially increased in order to fund a robust and permanent breakwater.

In the meantime, legal proceedings had been instituted by the British Treasury's solicitors against Thomas Jackson, the contractor for Douglas breakwater. But Jackson and his two sureties

Abernethy breakwater, irreparably damaged by storm, January 1865.

were insolvent.[542] Jackson's solicitors threw the blame on to Abernethy, claiming that his design had been disapproved by the majority of engineers and was not the preferred choice of the Isle of Man Harbour Commissioners. It was the Admiralty, with the practical responsibility for the Isle of Man's harbours, which had wanted the cheaper wooden frame and rubble stone method, and Jackson had been 'induced to tender for and enter into a contract to do the work of course knowing nothing of the inherent defects of the design'. The contract sum was £48,822 in total, and part of it (approximately £20,000) had already been paid to Jackson as the work had progressed, subject to a reduction of 25% which had been retained by the Harbour Commissioners as a material guarantee for the fulfilment of the contract. Abernethy vehemently denied any responsibility for the problems.[543] He deflected the blame back on to Jackson, claiming that the design of the breakwater was not new and that the problems were caused mainly by the defect in the physical construction of the rubble mound forming the base of the work. He attributed the failure to the way in which the contractor had carried out the work. As Jackson was insolvent, a decision was made for Tynwald to take possession of and future responsibility for the remaining harbours works.[544]

Self-elected Keys

In March 1863 John James Moore, the veteran Manx reformer, who was once again acting as agent for the inhabitants of the Isle of Man, requested Governor Loch to forward to Queen Victoria a petition containing 3,373 signatures complaining about the constitution of the House of Keys and claiming that Tynwald was enacting laws without the consent but at the expense of the people.[545] The matters which J. J. Moore specifically referred to included taxation imposed for the building of a lunatic asylum, expenditure of public funds on inappropriate harbour structures, effects of highway rates on the poor and enclosure of unappropriated lands and forests by the Crown. Moore demanded that Royal Assent to a Bill to amend the Isle of Man Disafforestation Act - whereby land was able to be compulsorily taken from proprietors in order to increase the Crown revenue but with little compensation in return - should be withheld. With no response, nearly a year later Moore presented to Loch another petition complaining about the Keys and signed by elected delegates representing fifteen of the Island's parishes. In June 1864 Moore queried with Home Secretary Grey why there had been no response to the two petitions and informed the Home Secretary that 'it is considered advisable to apply to the House of Commons for the appointment of a Select Committee to investigate the grievances of the inhabitants of the Isle of Man' with particular reference to the Manx people having 'no voice whatever in the appropriation of any public monies'. The pressure was on once again for constitutional change.

Calls for reforms were also being raised from a familiar quarter, that of yet another forceful owner and editor of a Manx newspaper. James Brown of the *Isle of Man Times* used his newspaper to enlarge the mantle of political criticisms and demands for social progress previously taken by the radical *Mona's Herald*.[546] Early in 1864 the recently created Douglas Town Commissioners had introduced into Tynwald a Bill to extend and consolidate the Commissioners' powers.[547] This Bill came before the House of Keys in February, and, after lengthy and acrimonious discussions, it was thrown out. Amongst the many pejorative remarks made in the Keys about the Commissioners was one from a member to the effect that the most they could be given was control over the donkeys on the shore. In reporting the proceedings of the House of Keys, the *Isle of Man Times* declared that 'this elicited marks of approval of the donkeys around him'. The *Isle of Man Times*, the self-styled 'leading Liberal journal', commented in very severe terms on the undemocratic nature of the Keys, referring to 'the struggle between the people and their despotic rulers'. The *Mona's Herald* also condemned the proceedings of the House in a very outspoken article. It commented on the state of Douglas which the Town Commissioners wanted additional powers to improve:

> There was the shore wasted and despoiled by nightly robbery - there were the cars, the carriages, the porters, practising daily imposition on strangers and sometimes endangering their safety and their lives - there were the pleasure boats grown into a nuisance by extortions, and the putting of the lives of excursionists to hazard - there were the market and fairs disgraceful to the civilisation of the nineteenth century - there were the slaughter houses teeming with stench and malaria, exposing the citizens to fever and death, and disgusting our visitors as they passed along the streets.[548]

The newspaper went on to castigate the Keys in their handling of the Town Commissioners Bill:

> Such wretched and contemptible work of the matter, as was never witnessed either in Bedlam, or among a pack of drunken Indians. We have known the status and idiosyncrasies of this posse of imbeciles for very many years; but in all the absurd and foolish things we ever knew them to do (and we have known them to do many such) we never knew them so thoroughly to disgrace themselves before the public as they have done in this instance.

It went on to refer to the members of the Keys as 'bunglers', 'Tory obstructives', 'spoonies, putting the fool's cap on their heads' and 'boobies'. It then informed its readers that 'Douglas Commissioners are not self-elect, and for life, like the rotten Keys'.

At a sitting of the House of Keys, which was still meeting in its Castletown chambers, John Moore Jeffcott raised a matter which he felt was his duty to bring before the House.[549] He said that he had no doubt that every member had read 'certain libellous and slanderous articles' which had appeared in the two newspapers. He claimed that the articles were a contempt of the House and a breach of its privileges. The two newspaper owners were summoned to attend the bar of the House the next day. James Brown defended his own case. Speaker Edward Moore Gawne informed Brown that the House had already resolved that he was guilty of contempt and breach of privilege and now considered that the manner of his defence was further aggravation of contempt and had resolved that he should be imprisoned in Castle Rushen gaol for six months. An ill John Christian Fargher, the new owner of his recently deceased father's *Mona's Herald*, expressed regret over the article in his newspaper and offered to publish an apology in the next edition. The Keys accepted this and dismissed him. James Brown, however, would not be silenced, and from his cell he continued to attack the Keys, proclaiming that he had been imprisoned for:

> questioning the correctness of statements recklessly put forth, and devoid of all truth, by some members of the House of Keys whose sole delight appears to be to oppress and insult the people of this Island; and for casting back into the very teeth of these insolent braggarts and sneerers against respectable tradesmen, their ribald jests, their coarseness buffooneries and their illiberal and dogmatic assertions.[550]

James Brown, owner and editor of the Isle of Man Times newspaper, writing whilst in Castle Rushen gaol, 1864.

That April saw counsel acting on behalf of Brown in the Queen's Bench in London move for a writ of habeas corpus.[551] Lord Chief Justice Cockburn and three other judges agreed that the writ could be made absolute, ruling that the House of Keys had no powers while sitting as a legislature to judicially try and sentence for contempt and that a British court was able to overrule a Manx one for such purposes, as 'An Act respecting the Issue of Writs of Habeas Corpus out of England into Her Majesty's Possessions Abroad' of 1862, which forbade the issue of a writ of habeas corpus to 'a *foreign* dominion', did not restrict the issue of such a writ to the Island which, whilst it was not part of the realm, was deemed to be 'a dominion' of the Crown.[552] The order imprisoning Brown was withdrawn, and after more than seven weeks in gaol he was released amidst fervent public demonstrations of support. He then filed an action of common law in the Manx courts, placing damages at £2,000 against all the Members of the House of Keys who had signed the warrant which had resulted in his imprisonment. The resultant trial before Deemster William Drinkwater and a special jury lasted for four days in June 1865. In his address, Brown's lawyer pointed out the anomalous position held by the House of Keys as a self-elected legislature which 'presumed to constitute themselves into judge and jury to try and adjudicate upon their own complaint'.[553] Brown won his court claim and was awarded £519 damages and £33 costs for wrongful imprisonment.[554] Twenty of the twenty-one Members of the House of Keys who had been present on the day when the House unanimously condemned Brown to gaol were now forced personally to pay the price for their action. The twenty-first member, Frederick John LaMothe, who had recently died, was pursued beyond the grave by his ex-colleagues who attempted to claim his portion of the fine from his estate, but their claim was steadfastly rejected by his son.

Proposals and negotiations

The gravity of the above situations - the need to have sufficient public money to complete the harbour works, the continued calls for reform of the House of Keys and the involvement of the Keys in the acrimonious incident with the two newspaper owners - helped to convince Governor Loch that changes to the fiscal situation and the constitution of the House of Keys were matters requiring urgent action. He was also aware that, with rates fixed and levied under the authority of Tynwald for the repairs of highways and bridges and plans to set a new rate to pay for a pauper lunatic asylum, there was a strong feeling amongst the inhabitants of the Island that they should be represented in a democratically elected House of Keys in order 'to have some voice in matters of taxation'.[555] Loch set about negotiations to improve matters, negotiations which would be conducted by him alone, without any reference to Tynwald until arrangements were well advanced and agreed with the British Government. There followed a year of private, careful and complicated negotiations.

In a letter dated 21 March 1865 Loch made a proposal to the Home Secretary, Sir George Grey, and the Commissioners of the Treasury regarding the need for alterations to the present customs duties to allow for a larger expenditure on public works in the Island than the one-ninth of revenue allocated under the Consolidated Customs Act of 1853 could supply.[556] The expenditure to which he referred was required for building extensive new breakwaters throughout the Island. He explained that he had carefully considered how the revenue could be increased without imposing a burden on the majority of residents of the Island. He had studied the differences between the duties levied in the Isle of Man and those in Britain on similar imported articles. He wondered whether the people benefited to the full extent that might be expected from the differences which existed between the two tariffs or whether the benefit contributed principally to 'swell the profits of the dealer'. His plan was to equalise duties on certain articles, which would

Sir George Grey, Home Secretary.

improve the insular revenue and enable the important public works to be carried out. Loch asserted that the principle that duties levied in the Isle of Man should not be increased except with the consent of the people had been conceded previously by the British Government.

Loch considered that tea, coffee and sugar should not have their tariffs increased. He pointed out that the consumption of tea in the Island was prevalent amongst a large number of the poor who lived outside the towns and villages. The extra cost of carriage to and in the Island increased the current retail price to these remote consumers to about the same as that in Britain. Any additional increases would hit the poor the most. He felt the same applied to sugar, which he did not think the consumers currently benefited to the extent they should when considering the low level of duty that was levied on it. Hewn and sawn timber was imported duty-free, and, as there was a scarcity of locally grown timber in the Island, he thought it unwise to place a duty on its import as this would have severe consequences on the building and other associated works which he was attempting to encourage. The articles Loch considered should be assimilated were the luxury ones of spirits, tobacco, Eau de Cologne, liqueurs and wine. He knew that a great proportion of the quantity of spirits imported was consumed by the visitors during the summer months (59,000 had arrived between the months of June and September in the previous year). Of all the articles imported into the Island, Loch believed tobacco was the only one on which the consumer derived any important benefit from the difference in duty. High quality cigars were manufactured locally in large quantities, and there could be some opposition to the assimilation of the two tariffs, but it appeared to him that there was not sufficient reason to exempt tobacco from being treated in a similar manner to spirits, and he considered that the alteration in tariff would cause little reduction in the quantity consumed.

Loch proposed that the extra annual revenue raised from the goods which would have their customs duties assimilated to those of Britain should be mortgaged and applied to the construction of a stone built replacement breakwater with a landing stage and wharves at Douglas and for harbours and public works in other parts of the Island.

In another letter, again dated 21 March 1865 and again addressed to the Home Secretary, Loch made a second proposal.[557] He explained that the House of Keys was not an elected body, and when any vacancy occurred, the House selected two prospective members whose names were submitted to the Governor who then appointed one of them. Members retained their seats for life. Without interfering with the working of the constitution of the Island, Loch thought a change might be effected that would be agreeable to the feelings of the people and remove a not altogether unfounded grievance. He suggested that the life members of the House of Keys should be gradually replaced by elected members to serve for a period of six years, with four of the present members to retire by ballot in the first year, six the second, seven the third and seven the fourth. He did not believe that the current members of the House of Keys would be averse to this proposal (he was wrong, they were, and it did not happen gradually but all at once in 1867). If Grey approved the principle of his suggestion, Loch said he would submit the matter to Tynwald for its opinion, after which he could enter more fully into the details necessary for carrying the proposal into effect. A reply from the office of the Home Secretary less than a week later stated 'that Her Majesty's Government see no objection to you taking the course which you propose in the matter'.[558] This ready acceptance of the need for constitutional amendment highlights the changing attitude of the British Government and the different thinking and policies of closely successive Governors.

In May Loch raised his concern with the Chancellor of the Exchequer, William Gladstone, regarding the possible knock-on effect some recent Budget changes to the British customs arrangements might have on the Manx revenue.[559] Gladstone had reduced direct and indirect taxation for the last three years, and, with the British public's consumption of tea having more than doubled in the last twenty years, he was now able to lower its customs duty from 1/- to 6d a pound.[560] This reduction made the British duty equal to that applying in the Isle of Man. Loch's carefully laid plans were placed in turmoil. The arrangement in 1853 between the Treasury and Tynwald never contemplated the effect any assimilation of duties might produce, and therefore the

*Hugh Culling Eardley Childers,
Financial Secretary of the Treasury.*

present difficulty was never considered. The situation was that, unless it was somehow secured specifically for the Island, the increase which would arise from an assimilation in the duties would result in a loss to the Island. Loch put a number of possible resolutions to the Board of Customs and the Treasury in order to overcome the problem, but the Treasury had doubts regarding these.[561] The material point that the Treasury made was that the Island should certainly have full credit of the whole of its one-ninth customs revenue, and it seemed to the Treasury that this would only be attained if the customs duty for tea imported into the Isle of Man was to yield as much in the future as it had yielded in the last three years. It was therefore thought preferable, pending a decision on the general question, not to lower the duty on tea just yet.

In November 1865 Hugh Childers, Financial Secretary of the Treasury, was involved in putting together the beginnings of a very important strategy to incorporate certain of the suggestions of Governor Loch and those of the Customs and Treasury for the revision of the

Manx customs revenue.[562] But first Childers asked for Loch's opinion on some possibilities. One involved all the Island's customs duties being totally assimilated to those of Britain. Loch could not agree to this extreme proposal, and he was certain that Tynwald would not agree either, 'nor would it be advisable to make so great and so sudden an alteration in the duties, as it might possibly for a time paralyse trade and ruin the dealers'. He was also concerned about the second proposal, that part of the revised allocation of the surplus revenue should include a fixed payment of £10,000 by the Island to Britain to compensate the British Exchequer for its losses. Whilst he agreed that all expenses of government in the Island should be paid out of the duties, he did not agree that so great an amount could or should be borne by the Manx revenue. Childers, however, considered that anything less than £10,000 for the fixed contribution was unacceptable and this was final.[563] Loch, unhappy with this response, reminded Childers that the Island 'was not purchased as a land investment, but to stop smuggling; the result was a saving of £350,000 a year'.

Loch arranged to meet Childers in London in early December to discuss matters, and it was probably at this meeting that the two men devised the basis for a very crucial Treasury minute on the revised strategy for the Manx customs revenue, a document which would result in great consequence and benefit to the Isle of Man. This minute was drafted on 21 December and sent by Childers to Loch for his further opinion.[564] In response to Loch's continuing anxiety to speedily resolve the matter, Childers apologised, but explained that he had 'spent more hours over the question than over others involving very far more important considerations', and 'you must remember that twice after it was entirely settled you reopened it on questions of figures involving careful inquiry'.[565] Loch agreed in principle with Childer's proposals. With certain alterations made to the minute, the following important recommendations would dramatically change the responsibility for the operation and use of the Manx public finances:

- Deductions were to be made to cover the cost of the collection of duties, the government of the Island, the administration of justice and other charges incurred.
- The sum of £2,300 payable to the Harbour Commissioners under the Act of 1844 was to continue.
- One-ninth of the gross customs duties payable under the Act of 1853 was to continue to be set aside for harbours and other public works, subject to the control of Tynwald.
- On security of a further two-ninths of the gross customs duties, the Harbour Commissioners were empowered to borrow money for harbour improvements with the approval of Tynwald and the Treasury.
- A fixed contribution of £10,000 was to be paid into the British Consolidated Fund.
- Finally and most importantly, it was further provided that any clear surplus not

expended should then form part of the Isle of Man's own Accumulated Fund. Tynwald Court was to have control of it for public purposes, subject to the supervision of the Treasury and the veto of the Governor and all at the risk of the Island.

The Treasury admitted that the £10,000 fixed contribution was directly linked with the capital sums of £70,000 and £150,000 paid by the British Government to the Dukes of Atholl in 1765 and 1825. The Treasury considered that the Imperial Contribution (still in existence today under the title of the Annual Contribution and currently standing at £2.5 million a year) was not excessive, considering that 'the inhabitants enjoy all the privileges of British citizenship and the protection of the army and navy' and that 'a contribution at the rate of £10,000 an annum, 4.5% on the capital invested [£70,000 + £150,000 = £220,000], will be a very moderate return to ask from the Island'. The minute also admitted that the £10,000 was additionally intended by the Treasury to take the place of the Manx surplus reserves presently paid into the British Exchequer. Whilst there is reference in the minute to the need for military and naval defence, this would appear to be incidental to the real reason for the Imperial Contribution. It was now the desire of the Treasury to continue to get an equivalent of what they were about to lose.

In March 1866 Loch was able to go to Tynwald to disclose the results of his year long negotiations for amending the control of the Island's customs and reforming the election of the House of Keys.

First of all he presented the Legislative Council with the two proposals.[566] He explained that he had negotiated with the British Government and was now able to report that if Tynwald agreed to an increase in the amount of customs duties payable on certain articles imported into the Island then the British Government would be prepared to sanction the application of the additional revenue towards the improvement of the harbours and for other public works in the Island. A condition, one resulting from Loch's own initiative, of the acceptance of the above fiscal changes was to be that the representatives in the House of Keys should in future be elected by the people. The Council agreed that it would be advantageous to the Island to accept both proposals.

The next day Governor Loch requested a conference with the Keys and informed the full gathering that he had two very important proposals to lay before them[567]. He explained that the first proposal affected the fact that the existing funds available for public works, including breakwaters and harbours, were altogether inadequate. No additional amount to any great extent could be borrowed on security of the one-ninth of the customs revenue. He considered that an increase in some customs duties might be made without causing any great burden to fall upon the residents and that such an increase would generate considerable extra revenue. The British Government had consented to such an increase of duties and to the Island having the full benefit of the surplus customs revenue, although it would be all at the risk of the Island. Instead of the British Government continuing to receive the surplus, it would be replaced by a fixed sum of £10,000 a year. Loch informed the Keys that the Island's present gross customs revenue was about £34,000, and he calculated that the proposed increase would, after a time, bring the revenue up to £56,000 (this optimistic figure would not be realised for another twenty-two years). From this amount would be deducted the expenses connected with the government of the Island, repairs of courthouses, payment for harbours, education, coast-guard, etc., together with the fixed sum of £10,000 (£10,000 represented an incredibly high amount out of the forthcoming year's customs income of £44,356). Making an allowance for a falling off in the consumption of certain articles, he calculated that there should be a sum of about £19,000 to £20,000 a year available for public works. In the event of a loan being required to be raised upon this surplus, the British Government had consented that two-ninths of the gross customs revenue should be added to the one-ninth presently assigned, so that three-ninths could be made available as an absolute security for any advance that might be needed to commission necessary public works. The remaining balance would then be available totally for Island purposes. Loch went on to explain that the British Government, in consenting to make the large financial concessions to the Island, had attached an important proposal, which was in fact a firm condition - although he did not mention that this condition was made on his advice. This second proposal affected the constitution of the Keys and was to be contingent upon acceptance of the first proposal. Loch understood that in 1853 the question of the constitution of the Keys was raised as an issue, and the majority of the Keys had consequently passed a resolution to become a democratically elected body. Loch was aware that the British Government had avoided giving a decision on the proposal then. However, times had moved on and it was now prepared to accede, but the two proposals for the revision of the customs duties and a popularly elected House of Keys must stand or fall together.

The Keys returned to their own House where the two proposals were discussed at some length. It was resolved, as the changes were 'of too great importance to be determined by the Keys on their exclusive responsibility, that the proposals be laid before the country'. Loch could not agree. He considered that it was not a matter to put to the people, it was strictly for Tynwald to determine, and it needed quick action. The Keys were asked to accept or reject the proposals as a whole, reserving questions of detail. He reiterated what he had said previously, that the two proposals were dependent on each other, and although he had referred them to the Keys as one general measure, he wished separate answers to be given as he had to communicate with the Treasury on the finances and the Home Office on the constitution. The question was discussed further by the members of the Keys, who, after a long deliberation, eventually agreed to endorse both proposals.

Five days later Tynwald Court was called together to collectively consider the two proposals. Deemster Drinkwater read a report by a committee recently appointed to meet with Loch.[568] The committee had sat with him at Government House three days previously to look at the various documents connected with the proposed changes to customs duties. The committee pointed out that the increases would only marginally affect prices: foreign spirits less than ½d a glass, British spirits slightly more than ½d a glass, Muscovado sugar less than ¼d a pound and refined sugar less than ½d a pound. It was not intended that any article should be imported duty paid, but all would be imported into the Island in bond. The committee considered that the three-ninths would total at least £16,000 a year. They recommended the adoption of the proposals for increased duties as submitted by the Governor the previous week. Loch then explained to Tynwald that on his return from London he would introduce a Manx Bill to progress the other proposal to amend the present mode of electing the House of Keys. Tynwald agreed to both these historic changes.[569] Loch then arranged to go to London for three weeks, to liaise there with the members of the Tynwald committee and for them all to confer with the Treasury on the details of a British Bill to amend the customs duties.[570]

The *Manx Sun* considered the possible consequences of the increase in customs duties on the visitors and the locals:

> Another evil anticipated from the new tariff is that our visitors will desert us. But what class of visitors? Those who seek "cheap grog"? If so, we can perhaps bid them adieu with advantage to ourselves, and shall probably get better in their place. Change will affect the working classes, persons most affected by sugar and tobacco - 2d a week sugar for a family, and 2¼d a week average smoker. In return for this the industrious classes will receive double profit by the increased demand for labour consequent upon the construction of public works; and secondly, they will share in the increased prosperity of the Island.[571]

Double dilemma resolved

Governor Henry Loch's successes in dealing with the British authorities, regaining the bulk of the surplus customs revenue for local use and overcoming the resistance to change in the House of Keys reveal a man of great negotiating skills. His handling of the matter as to who suggested the fiscal changes and the reform of the House of Keys was a nice sleight of hand to get what he wanted, and the leverage he was able to exert was very impressive. The struggle between Loch and the House of Keys is a fascinating account, revealing the perseverance of a man well used to action and the not unnatural resistance to change of a body steeped in history and self-interest.

Two Acts, one British and one Manx and both of great importance in the Island's history, would now be introduced to move on Loch's ambitions for the Isle of Man.

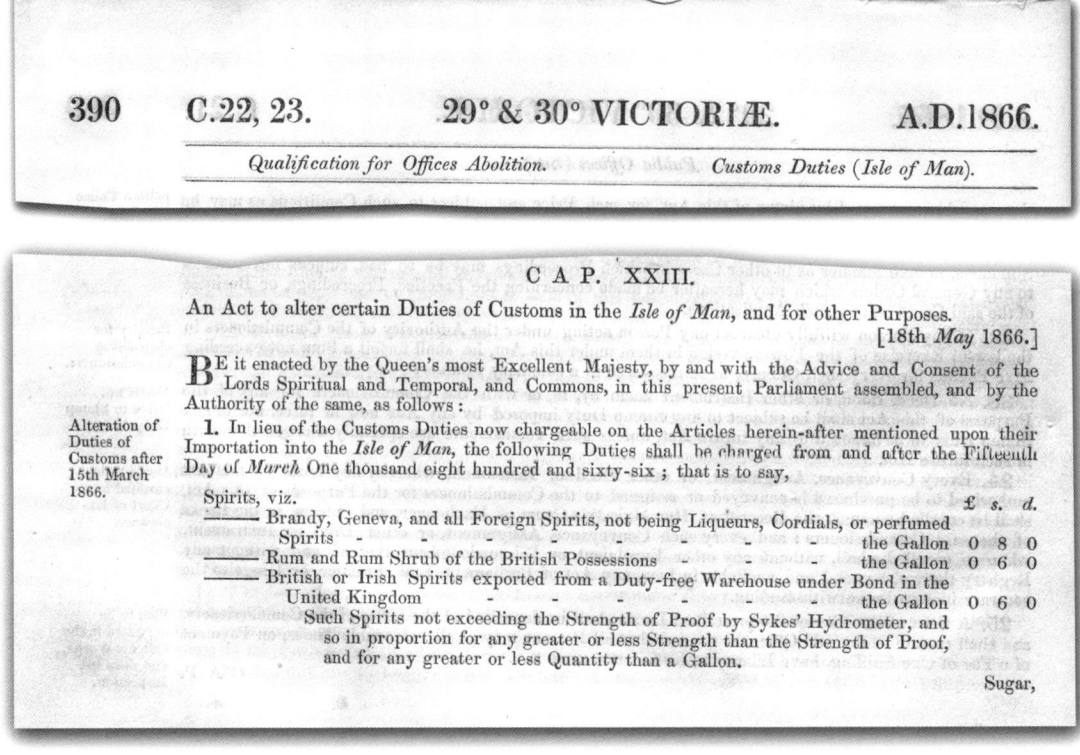

Isle of Man Customs, Harbours and Public Purposes Act, 1866.

1 Isle of Man Customs, Harbours and Public Purposes Act, 1866[572]

From London, J. J. Moore wrote to the *Mona's Herald* enclosing a copy of the Bill to amend the Manx customs.[573] The Bill had obviously been prepared well in advance, as it was ordered by the House of Commons to be printed on 23 March 1866, just three days after Loch had informed Sir George Grey of Tynwald's acceptance of the proposed increases. 'An Act to alter certain duties of customs in the Isle of Man, and for other purposes', cited as the 'Isle of Man Customs, Harbours and Public Purposes Act, 1866', was consequently passed in the British Parliament on 18 May 1866. The new duties incorporated those previously proposed by Loch. The Act would serve to fund the economic strategy agreed by Loch and Childers in the important 21 December 1865 minute.

In July Loch received regulations from the Treasury for giving effect to the new Act.[574] The Treasury admitted that the British Exchequer had previously 'profited by surplus of income over expenditure', but in future such surplus would be handed over to Tynwald. This acknowledgement by Britain that it had gained at the expense of the Isle of Man was a very important admission when considering the historical relationship between the two countries. The Treasury went on to claim that, under the new agreement, strict economy would be in the interest of both countries - for Britain in order to ensure due payment of the fixed contribution and for the Island in order to realise as much as possible for local improvements. It was, therefore, most desirable that both the Treasury and the Governor should have every opportunity of ascertaining and controlling the details of public expenditure, and, with this end in view, the Treasury required the Governor to have an estimate of expenditure drawn up before the commencement of each financial year. This estimate should also be laid before Tynwald. In order that the Governor would have full knowledge of expenditure incurred within the limits of his governance, the Treasury would request the different departments of the British Government dealing with the Island to furnish him with all the information he required. In order to properly administer the new situation, the Home Office and the Treasury considered that the Island now needed a Treasurer.[575] John Thomas Clucas had been Clerk of the Council and Secretary since March 1864, and he was now appointed to hold the additional position of Government Treasurer on an increased salary.[576] In the first full year under the new Act, the general revenue totalled £46,090, of which £45,235 was accounted for by the customs revenue, an incredible 35% more than the last year under the old Act.[577]

2 House of Keys Election Act, 1866[578]

Back in May the Governor and the Council had met with a deputation from the Keys to progress the new constitutional scheme. Loch handed to them the 'House of Keys Election Bill', a most formidable document, consisting of 141 sections of conditions.[579] The initial acceptance of the need for their political reform was now tempered by suspicion by some members. William Callister asked for a copy of any correspondence that had taken place between the Governor and the Home Secretary to be laid before the House. John Senhouse Goldie-Taubman stated that he understood it was contemplated that the salaries of certain officials of the Island were to be increased and would be funded out of the additional revenue expected to be derived from the new customs duties. He also understood, from the statement made by the Governor when he first introduced the contemplated changes, that the net surplus revenue would be at the disposal of Tynwald. Goldie-Taubman, therefore, made a resolution in the House of Keys that no increase should be made in the salaries as the proposal had not received the approval of Tynwald. Robert John Moore, Secretary to the Keys, opposed this resolution, claiming it was an attempt to override an Act of the British Parliament. He pointed out that in the new Isle of Man Customs, Harbours and Public Purposes Act it was provided that the expenses of government should in the first instance be paid by order of the Treasury and that the surplus should be at the disposal of the Tynwald Court only after payment of these expenses. He thought it was not likely that the Crown, which appointed the officials, would consent to give up the power to fix their salaries. The majority of the Keys, however, were adamant that their understanding was that, after deducting the charges referred to in the Treasury minute, Tynwald would have control over the whole of the surplus, including the increased salaries of the officials. After considerable discussion, Goldie-Taubman's motion that no increase of salaries to officials should be made without first having the consent of the Keys was carried by a majority of thirteen to six.

In June Loch addressed the Keys on both issues.[580] He assured the Keys that he had no wish to withhold any information from them which it was in his power to give. On the issue of the salaries, he directed the attention of the Keys to the third clause in the Customs Act whereby the 'expenses attending the government of the Isle of Man' were made a first charge on the revenue. Loch said that no one could possibly have been misled over this because when the question had been raised previously he had distinctly stated that the British Government reserved to themselves the entire control over these expenses. As a means to overcome any concerns, Loch now proposed that before any permanent increase in the Island's expenditure was made in the future the matter should be laid before Tynwald. Despite these explanations, there continued to be an element of doubt in the minds of some members of the Keys regarding the outcome of Loch's determination to reform the House and change the customs duties. Some of them claimed they had not fully understood the implications of the changes, in particular the limited financial control of the Keys. They had been under the impression that if they agreed to be elected by popular franchise then they would have greater control over the Island's finances:

> It was represented that, in a moment of unprecedented and extraordinary generosity, the British Government were prepared to grant what they have always refused and what we have always claimed as a right - the surplus revenue - the only condition being that we were to dissolve our constitution. We did not at that time thoroughly understand the bearing of the scheme. We felt we were driven into a corner. To use the luminous expression of one member of the deputation, the whole control of the Tynwald Court over the revenue is reduced to the consistency of 'moonshine'.[581]

At the next meeting of Tynwald Court, William Callister raised his concern over the scheme for the present Members of the House of Keys to vacate their seats over the next three years. He claimed that 'abolishing the Oligarchy by piecemeal' was unsatisfactory:

> such a piebald House - consisting partly of self-elect and partly of representatives of the people - would not only be an anomaly, but an absurdity, which could never be harmonised. The one party would represent the people, while the other would represent

themselves; the one would labour for progress, while the other would cling to the old system of their forefathers.[582]

Callister called for the old Keys to resign their seats en masse, and the Keys agreed, resolving that the House should be dissolved in a body within three years after the promulgation of the Act and that a new House should be elected within twenty-one days thereafter. The Election Bill was passed for the first time by the Keys by 17 votes to 3 (Speaker Gawne, Edward Curphey Farrant and Patrick Taubman Cunningham voted against). Amendments introduced into the Bill by the Keys were discussed between them and the Council, and compromises were adopted.[583] The revised Bill allowed for the towns of Peel, Ramsey and Castletown to have one member each, the town of Douglas and the sheadings of Ayre, Michael, Garff, Glenfaba, Middle and Rushen to have three each. Those entitled to be Members of the House of Keys were males of full age (21) who were owners of real estate of the net value of £100, over and above all rents, charges, mortgages and other encumbrances, or who were owners of real estate of the net annual value of £50 and a yearly income of £100 from personal estate or effects of any nature or kind. The qualifications for voters were that they must be males of full age (21) and not subject to any legal incapacity. They had to be owners of real estate of a net annual value of not less than £8. Tenants had to occupy land, tenements or other real estate of a net annual rent of not less than £12. The records indicate that out of a male population of approximately 25,500, 13,200 were aged 21 and over and 5,500 of these were eligible to vote.[584]

The Town Commissioners of Douglas passed a unanimous vote of thanks to Governor Loch for his services in bringing about the reform of the House of Keys.[585] The liberal press of the Island congratulated the people upon the restoration to their ancient privileges. These praises, however, would later be tempered with expressions of concern and criticism. James Brown's *Isle of Man Directory* of 1881 claimed that, soon after the successful progress of the Bill, rumours had circulated that powerful cabals had procured the highly restricted franchise and imposed the property qualification for a seat in the House of Keys, which was tantamount to closing its doors to all except the propertied families who had hitherto monopolised the House.[586] The *Directory* considered that the reform of the House of Keys had been:

> conceived in an eminently conservative spirit, and that, while providing that the members should have the sanction of popular election, and thus, to that extent, possess the authority conferred by the representative principle, the franchise was carefully limited to the narrowest circle possible, and included only a very small proportion of the population.

The reformers criticised the distribution of seats, and 'the townsfolk claimed that their interests had been totally ignored and, despite having over two-fifths of the population, they only

> 372 *House of Keys, Election.* A.D. 1866.
>
> Promulgation. At a Tynwald Court, holden at Saint John's Chapel, the 16th day of August, 1866.
>
> ISLE OF MAN, TO WIT.
>
> At a Tynwald Court holden, at Saint John's Chapel, the sixteenth day of August, in the thirtieth year of the reign of our Sovereign Lady Victoria, by the grace of God of the United Kingdom of Great Britain and Ireland, Queen, Defender of the Faith, and in the year of our Lord one thousand eight hundred and sixty-six, before his Excellency Henry Brougham Loch, Esquire, Companion of the most Honourable Order of the Bath, Lieutenant-Governor, the Council, Deemsters, and Keys.
>
> "The House of Keys Election Act, 1866," being an Act to render the House of Keys elective; and for other Purposes. [1]
>
> Preamble. Whereas it is expedient that the present system of selecting persons to serve as members in the House of Keys should cease, and to provide for the election by people of property and intelligence in this Isle of members to serve in such House, and to abolish the judicial powers of the said House of Keys: We, therefore, your Majesty's most dutiful and loyal subjects, the Lieutenant-Governor, Council, Deemsters, and Keys of the said Isle, do humbly beseech your Majesty that it may be enacted, and be it enacted, by the Queen's most Excellent Majesty, by and with the advice and consent of the Lieutenant-Governor, Council, Deemsters, and Keys of the said Isle, in Tynwald assembled, and by the authority of the same, as follows (that is to say):—
>
> Construction of Act.
> I. With respect to the construction of this Act:
>
> Interpretation.
> 1. The following words and expressions shall have the several meanings hereby assigned to them:
>
> The expression "Justice" shall mean Justice of the Peace, and shall include High-Bailiff:
>
> The expression "Revising Advocate" shall mean any advocate appointed to revise any list of voters under this Act:
>
> The expression "Returning-Officer" shall mean any person or persons to whom by virtue of this Act the execution of any writ or precept doth or shall belong for the election of
>
> [1] Amended by the Tynwald Proceedings Act, 1876; the House of Keys Election Act, 1881; the House of Keys Election Act, 1883 (temporary); the House of Keys Election Act, 1886. See the Appellate Jurisdiction Act, 1867.

House of Keys Election Act, 1866.

had one-quarter of the seats'.[587] The northern inhabitants objected that their representatives were unfairly outnumbered by those of the south. However, everything was brought to a conclusion on 16 August when the House of Keys passed the Bill which allowed for the Island's first popular election to take place in April 1867. The 'banner of reaction was nevertheless upheld to the last'

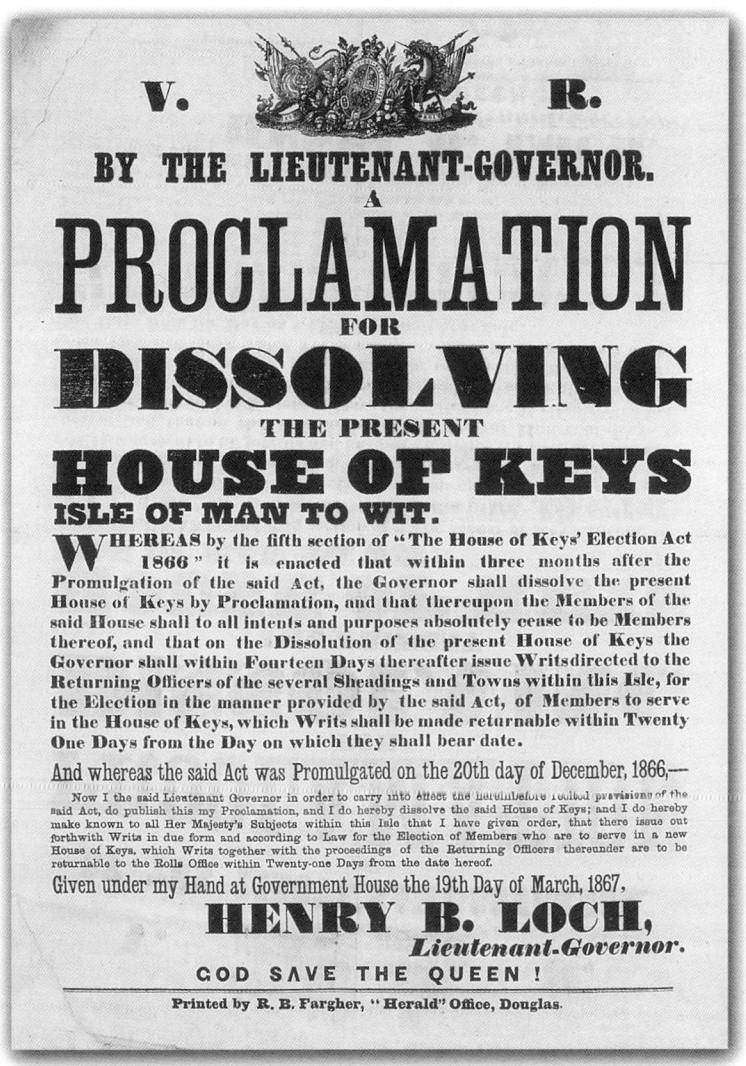

Royal Proclamation issued by Governor Loch dissolving the self-elected House of Keys, 1867.

by Edward Moore Gawne, Edward Curphey Farrant and Patrick Taubman Cunningham, who all again voted against the Bill. Each of these members would suffer different fates as a result of the forthcoming elections: Gawne resigned, Farrant was elected and Cunningham was rejected.

Loch sent the 'House of Keys Election Act, 1866' to the Home Office for Royal Assent in

August, and the Act was promulgated by Tynwald Court in December.[588] It was at the same Court that Edward Moore Gawne, the long-time Speaker, resigned. As an act of courtesy to the old House, the British Government offered him a knighthood, but he declined.

The prospect of a popularly elected House of Keys was slow to capture the imagination of the people, not altogether surprising as the electorate was made up of a very narrow franchise. The *Mona's Herald* forlornly reported that 'Manx people in general are showing very little interest in the forthcoming election'.[589] But in early 1867 the campaign began to gather momentum, and meetings were arranged for prospective candidates to declare their policies and get their nominations confirmed.[590] One meeting which took place in February at the Lord Street assembly room in Douglas saw scarcely a dozen members of the public in attendance at its outset, although before it closed there were close on sixty. But another meeting at the Victoria Hotel saw 800 to 1,000 people come to hear the views of the candidates. Crowds gathered, mainly at local school houses, all over the Island to hear the thoughts of the prospective Members of the House of Keys. Thomas Fargher, who would have the lowest number of votes of all at the forthcoming general election, receiving only four, addressed a meeting at Maughold with a long, noisy and declamatory harangue which resulted in such a general clamour that the chairman had to adjourn the meeting. An uncertain John Edward Christian issued two manifestos, one for the constituency of Ramsey and another for the constituency of Garff. John Caesar Tobin Harrison, a candidate for the rural constituency of Middle, had his nomination objected to as he was a lawyer who was employed at times by Douglas Town Commissioners, and 'he has promised the town everything, he has promised the country everything'. The objector went on to claim that Harrison was changeable, 'just like a weathercock', and was 'the person who treats the electors in the public-house to rum, or gin, or whiskey, or anything they will drink, if they will only vote for him'.

The all-island elections were scheduled to take place on 3 and 4 April. In five constituencies, Ayre, Michael, Castletown, Peel and Ramsey, there were no contests, so the nominated candidates were all declared to be Members of the House of Keys.

In Douglas there were four nominees for just three seats.[591] William Fine Moore and John Senhouse Goldie-Taubman, the sitting members, together with George William Dumbell were the establishment's choice and offered themselves en-bloc. But the lawyer Richard Sherwood came forward as a surprise liberal opponent who added an element of interest to the forthcoming hustings. On nomination day the weather was fine, which was fortunate as most of the proceedings took place in the open air. People gathered early outside the court house in Athol Street to watch the arrival of the candidates. The first to arrive was Sherwood who earlier in the day had met with his committee, all of whom sported blue rosettes, at the Wellington Hotel. Next to arrive was Major Goldie-Taubman, followed by Dumbell and Moore who both came by carriage. Moore's

Crowds outside Douglas court house awaiting the results of the first publicly elected House of Keys, 3 April 1867.

supporters included ladies dressed in red outfits and gentlemen on horses decorated with red ribbons, and Moore himself wore a scarlet camellia in his buttonhole. Polling day in Douglas was on Wednesday 3 April, and glorious sunshine ensured that the flags and banners hanging outside the houses and shops were displayed to their best. Voting took place from eight o'clock in the morning. Carriages decked out in blue or red ribbons and covered in placards conveyed the voters to the two polling stations, one at the court house in Athol Street and the other at St Matthew's church in Market Place. The atmosphere was made more electric by the progress of the vote being announced every hour to the excited crowd. One of the red supporters got so carried away that he seized a blue flag and broke its staff. A drunken carriage driver drove into the crowd, but his horse was forced back by a dozen sturdy men, causing the driver to fall out of his seat. Accusations of intimidation and partiality were made because votes were not made in secret but were openly recorded in ballot books by tellers, some of whom were members of Dumbell's banking staff. The result was declared from the court house at four o'clock that afternoon. Moore received 471 votes, Dumbell 461, Goldie-Taubman 457 and Sherwood 317. The three successful candidates were paraded around the town in carriages pulled by their supporters before they all adjourned to their committee room at the British Hotel on the North Quay. A barrel of ale was 'gratuitously distributed to all-comers', photographs were taken and church bells were rung.

Similar scenes celebrating the historic elections were held all over the Island, even in uncontested constituencies. In Ramsey the principal shops were closed on nomination day, and a great number of people assembled outside the court house which was decorated with flags, bunting and an arch of evergreens surmounted by a flag bearing the legend 'Representation and Progress'. The crowd then marched to the beat of a band to Milntown, the residence of the unopposed candidate, William Bell Christian. The Reverend Christian was asked to step into a carriage drawn by four light-coloured horses, and the whole procession returned to Ramsey for speeches, celebrations and parades. The only place which did not enter into the spirit of the occasion was Michael sheading. A great number of jubilant people, who had come from Ballaugh and included in their ranks thirty filled carriages, found no more than six electors awaiting their arrival.

This first public election of the House of Keys saw thirteen of the previous twenty-four members elected.[592] The eleven new members were mainly of a similar political persuasion as the previous members. John Senhouse Goldie-Taubman was chosen to serve as Speaker, thwarting the ambitions of George Dumbell who, 'ceasing to take the open field, skulks under a political hedge'.[593] Although the election processes had been novel and exciting, the reality was that only a small minority of the population had the right to vote, an even smaller number had the property qualification to stand for Parliament and the conservative character of the new House had hardly altered from that of the old. Despite the disappointments, Governor Loch's reforms were significant and ensured the implementation of the most important element of the Isle of Man's democratic needs: properly elected political representation. This right was linked directly with a significant advancement in Tynwald's control of public finances. The reforms brought about by the Election and Customs Acts of 1866, although by no means fully complete, were major steps towards more competent and mature self-government.

Chapter 9

Common Purse

Ambitions

The separation of the Manx customs revenue from Britain's was a major landmark in the Island's economic redevelopment and ensured that the surplus was now able to be fully utilised for local purposes. The finances were significantly freed up and greatly increased, although Britain retained the right to legislate for and regulate the customs duties, and, whilst the expenditure was applied and disposed of as Tynwald approved, the Governor had the veto on the decision and the Treasury had ultimate control. The Customs Act allowed the Governor and the Treasury to budget for the public finances. Before the commencement of each financial year the Governor drew up an estimate of expenditure. He took into account the current and capital schemes he considered were necessary, as well as the cost of administering the government and the justice system. Part of the expenditure was used to defray any borrowings and other expenses. The Customs Department drew up an estimate of its own for the cost of collecting the duties. An estimate of income needed to cover all the above expenditure was then taken into consideration. The Governor put the estimates to the Treasury and laid them before Tynwald. The remaining calculated balance of income over expenditure was placed in the Manx Accumulated Fund for future use. Whilst the customs tariffs were only changed when necessary, they were constantly considered by reference to all the above estimates and were set by the Treasury with the consent of Tynwald. The duties continued to be collected, paid out and accounted for under the control of the Customs Department. The Governor continued to be the authority from whom all executive decisions emanated, and this authority enabled him to be the sole negotiator with the Treasury in the sanctioning and financing of schemes.

With an impressive record behind him, Governor Henry Loch now set about bringing further major improvements in the affairs of the Isle of Man. He introduced a major programme of progress for the Island, financed by enhanced public funds and made easier to ratify in Tynwald by the establishment of a democratically elected House of Keys. Further Tynwald authority was put in place during this period through the gradual establishment of a Board system to carry out the various governmental responsibilities.

An extensive development of Douglas harbour was planned.[594] A breakwater at Peel, piers at Port St Mary and Ramsey, and improvements at Castletown harbour followed. In 1872 a daily mail

*Opening ceremony of the Douglas to Peel railway
with the engine Sutherland at the head of the train, 1 July 1873.*

service throughout the year was started. A railway line was laid between Douglas and Peel in less than a year and was opened in 1873. Lines to Port Erin and Ramsey followed. The redesign of lower Douglas was a major priority for Loch. He inaugurated the building of Loch Promenade on land reclaimed from the foreshore. The initial work on a sea wall started in 1874, and the promenade, including a horse-tramline, was completed by 1877. Over the next few years terraces of hotels were built, with the sale of the plots paying for the construction of the promenade. The new Villiers Hotel, so called after the family name of Loch's wife, was the first hotel on Loch Promenade and made an immediate impression on the arriving visitors. Associated with the promenade work, the construction of Victoria Street - the new main thoroughfare leading from Loch Promenade and connecting with Prospect Hill - provided a link between old Douglas and its new uptown suburbs.

There was a dramatic increase in legislation during Loch's term of office, including the modernisation of law and the revision of the criminal code. In 1872 Tynwald undertook direct

Tynwald Court and Government Offices.

responsibility for compulsory education through the Public Elementary Education Act. Tynwald granted parliamentary suffrage to women by the Election Act of 1881 whereby spinsters and widows aged over 21 who owned property were given the vote, well ahead of their sisters in Britain. The seat of government in Castletown had been appropriate when the official residence of the Governor, the offices of government and the law courts had been centred in and around Castle Rushen. However, with Castletown's position in the south being unsuitable geographically to serve the expanding development of the Island and the increasing prominence of Douglas as the trading, tourism and political centre, there now came about inevitable changes. Loch was responsible for the gradual removal of government and the law courts from Castletown to Douglas. Douglas became the Island's capital in 1869 and Tynwald Court moved into the former Bank of Mona building on Prospect Hill in 1879.

During the years of unprecedented change, Loch set about tidying up the official records and building upon the good relationships he had developed with the Home Office, the Treasury and the Customs Department. He issued a number of reports to Whitehall on the Island's situation, including one in 1873 which stated:

> When I arrived in the Isle of Man, in the beginning of 1863, I found that the official correspondence in the Governor's office had not been kept with great exactness, and that the recorded correspondence upon general questions with the Home Office, Treasury, etc., was very meagre, while there appeared to be little, if any, record preserved of the correspondence that must have passed on local questions between former Governors and the various subordinate officers, and there was much difficulty in tracing and ascertaining the position of many questions affecting the interests of the Island.[595]

In a report in 1879 Loch expressed his disappointment that the responsibilities of Tynwald had not progressed as much as he had hoped:

> The members of the Council disclaim any obligation to support the Lieut.-Governor, even if he is acting under express instruction from the Imperial Government. . . . This position is, in my opinion, untenable. . . . In the House of Keys there is no representative of the Government to take charge of bills passing from the Council.[596]

Throughout the term of his administration, 1863 to 1882, Loch had detailed and lengthy negotiations with the various departments of Whitehall. Analysis of the correspondence he had with them reveals a relationship which started well and got even better as the years progressed.[597] The early confidence his patron, Sir George Grey, and the authorities had placed in Loch's judgement enabled him to progressively have wide discretion with respect to the policies he wished to carry out and the manner in which he developed and financed them. From matters as diverse as increasing the salary of the matron at Castle Rushen gaol from £20 to £30 a year and settling the expenses of the upkeep of the Chief Constable's horse, to obtaining sanction for a guarantee to be given by Tynwald to promote the construction of a new railway line and arranging a £224,000 loan with the Crown Agents, Loch was the responsible executive, responsible not to Tynwald but to the British Crown.[598] He possessed extensive powers, greater in many respects than those exercised by his equivalents in the Crown colonies. However, Loch's financial dealings with Whitehall were not without occasional controversy. The most serious example involved the wrangle which took place between 1870 and 1879 relating to a long running argument as to whether the expenditure on the continuing repairs to the ill-fated breakwater at Port Erin was the responsibility of the Isle of Man or Britain.[599] The outcome was that the cost of the original 1864 loan, which was still being met by Britain, was liquidated by a one-off payment by the Island. Loch, ever the keen negotiator, ensured that there were trade-offs in the settlement, including the Island receiving an annual allowance for certain imported goods on which customs duties had already been paid in Britain. An example of the British Government withholding its sanction to certain improvements took place in 1871.[600] Tynwald had voted work to be carried out on piers, harbours, breakwaters and approach roads and the construction of a legislative building and law courts, but, despite Loch putting forward the arguments in favour and asking the Home Office to intervene, the Treasury was not prepared to approve the funding as it was not satisfied that the Island's revenue could bear the charges.

By the early 1880s Governor Loch had more authority than any previous holder of the post since revestment was imposed almost one hundred and twenty years previously. He had by statute the direct veto on all public expenditure and no motion involving finances could be made in Tynwald without his sanction. Additionally and importantly, he had the confidence of Westminster and Whitehall. Loch's authority was tempered by a sympathetic Governor who had been fully responsible for bringing about a positive and more relaxed relationship with the British authorities, a secure public revenue and the opportunity for a responsible House of Keys to become more involved in the national decision making. The way ahead was prepared for greater economic development.

Towards further financial freedom

After nineteen years of service, Henry Loch's aim to secure even higher office was to take him away from the Isle of Man. In 1882 he was briefly appointed Commissioner of Woods and Forests at an annual salary less than the £1,200 he had been earning as Governor. But this new appointment was based in London and calculated to provide him with the opportunity to be close again to those who could influence his future career ambitions. One month before his resignation as Governor, Loch pointed out to the Home Secretary, Sir William Vernon Harcourt, that the Island had 'acquired a revenue rather by the amendment of its financial system, than by the imposition of additional burdens'.[601] Loch's many reforms had made possible a period of accelerated development. The Island's gross annual customs revenue had increased from £28,337 in 1863 to £48,536 in 1882. With the country's infrastructure improved and its economy more robust and broadly based than ever, his beneficial legacy to the Island is unquestionable. But his departure coincided with varying changes in the fortunes of a number of sectors of the economy. Fishing, mining and manufacturing would all soon see recession due to competition from Britain and the influence of tourism on the availability and cost of labour.[602] Tourism and agriculture, the latter riding on the back of the former, were very successful, with the increasing number of summer visitors making tourism the Island's principal industry. The number of visitors more than doubled from 90,000 in 1873 to 183,000 in 1884 and would further increase to 312,000 by 1895. The increasing amount of holidaymakers would be crucial in the calculation of the soon to be established Common Purse Arrangement, the important customs sharing scheme between the Isle of Man and Britain. With limited options other than to put most of its eggs into the tourism industry basket, the Island had to take this opportunity to provide its citizens with an enduring means of income.

Governor Spencer Walpole.

Spencer Walpole was appointed as successor to Loch in 1882.⁶⁰³ Aged forty-three, Walpole was another relatively young Governor, and during the eleven years he held office he would continue at a similar pace the financial restructuring, public works, liberal reforms and revised legislation instigated by Loch.⁶⁰⁴ Walpole was a descendant of Sir Robert Walpole, Britain's first Prime Minister. His father had been Home Secretary on three occasions under the premiership of the Earl of Derby, and Spencer had served as his father's private secretary. Spencer Walpole was also an historian, whose study of the Isle of Man, *Land of Home Rule*, was published directly after his governorship ended and is an invaluable reference work, in particular coming from the perspective of his direct involvement in forming the Island's history. With a Governor steeped in politics and proven administrative expertise leading the way, the Island was set to be well-served. The tough bargaining by Walpole with the determined officials of the various departments of the British Government, including the Home Office and, in particular, the Treasury and the Customs, ultimately resulted in a financial agreement which would greatly benefit the Island.

Although it would take some time for Walpole to set about introducing major changes in the Island's economy and the systems which administered it, when he did they produced a much more secure fiscal base. He continued Loch's progressive financial reforms and also argued the case for minimal interference from the Home Office and the Treasury in his and Tynwald's running of the Island's finances.[605] Indeed, the tight Treasury control was fast relaxing. Walpole commented on the situation, 'The revenue, partly from a natural expansion, partly from increased taxation, has grown very rapidly, while the cost of government has not sensibly increased. In consequence the Treasury has no longer a direct interest in interfering with the wishes of Tynwald'.[606]

Tynwald's part in determining the Island's economy was also gradually improving. In 1886, as Loch had twenty years earlier, Walpole gave a personal undertaking that he would not make any addition to the cost of government without first acquainting the Court and giving the members opportunity to object.[607] Acceptance of the need for greater Manx autonomy was also evidenced by the introduction of 'An Act to amend the law respecting the Customs Duties of the Isle of Man' in 1887 by which the British Parliament allowed Tynwald to once again impose, abolish or vary tariffs, to take effect within six months from the date of the resolution and to renew the arrangement by way of annual resolution, all subject to the approval of the Treasury.[608] Tynwald was now able to set its own customs duties for the first time since revestment, a significant restoration of its authority. Nonetheless, it was only able to carry out such changes with the support of the Governor and the British authorities. Walpole later put it that 'this provision has maintained the supremacy of the Imperial Parliament, while, as Parliament now merely registers what Tynwald proposes, it has maintained it without exciting heartburning or jealousy'.[609] With freedom, though limited freedom, to impose domestic customs duties once more and keep them at a level somewhat lower than those of Britain, the Island then generally followed any subsequent increases in the British tariffs, thereby dealing with any lingering concerns over the possible return of smuggling.

Walpole realised that the Island's returns from customs revenue needed to become more certain in order to pay for the much needed betterment of public works and services. Since 1879/80 there had been an arrangement for making a beneficial allowance to the Island on some goods brought in which had already paid the British duties, but the inefficiency of this arrangement meant that not all of the allowance was being passed on to the Island. Walpole considered that there needed to be a fairer and more reliable method of compensation. He also considered that, as people consumed taxed goods at a greater rate when on holiday than at home, this increased consumption was not being properly reflected in the Manx customs returns either. The Isle of Man was at an economic disadvantage as a result of these circumstances, and it was this situation which concerned Walpole.

Tea duty - Britain: 4.88 pounds, Isle of Man: 6 pounds

At a meeting of Tynwald Court in April 1890 Walpole was to present his annual statement on the Island's financial situation.[610] With no income tax, the Island depended to a very large extent on its customs duties to finance central government operations. Before Walpole explained the revenue and expenditure for the year, he addressed the Court on two changes in customs duties in Britain which had been made the previous week and which he considered would affect the Island. He wished to deal with the possible expectation of certain members of Tynwald and businessmen for similar changes to take place in the Isle of Man. Then he wanted to explain his proposals to revise the insular customs duties. George Goschen, Chancellor of the Exchequer in Lord Salisbury's Conservative government, had reduced Britain's customs duty on tea from 6d to 4d a pound, the same as it had been in the Island since 1867.[611] Whilst it had been the principle of the Island to keep its customs duties somewhat lower than those of Britain, Walpole explained that after careful consideration he was inclined not to adopt this principle with respect to tea this time. Walpole elaborated on his reasoning. He had researched the question of tea consumption in the Island. Even with the differential duty of 2d in favour of the Manx trade, the statistics showed that there was a tendency on the part of the Island consumers to buy tea directly from large tea merchants in Britain (presumably at a better price for the quality and quantity required). In 1885 25,000 pounds in weight of tea had been recorded as imported into the Island having paid duty in Britain. In 1889 that amount had risen to 48,000 pounds. He argued that a small reduction in tea duty would be of no benefit to the richer classes. Equally, such a reduction would be of no benefit to the poorer classes either, as they bought their tea in such very small quantities that a small reduction would never find its way into their pockets. If Walpole could neither help the rich nor the poor, he argued that he had better protect the position of the Manx revenue and not decrease the duty but leave it at 4d. Walpole went on to remind Tynwald that, by an arrangement with the British Government, tea imported into the Island which had been recorded as having paid duty in Britain had the difference subsequently transferred to the Island. He believed that, whilst most of the tea which came into the Island duty-paid was detected, it was the undetected imports which resulted in the Island being out of pocket. Walpole then turned his attention from tea to brandy. He remarked that the previous day he had been told that there had been some anticipation in the Island that he intended to make an alteration in the duty on spirits, following the example which had been set in Britain, by adding an extra 6d to the duty. However, he was not intending to do this. To the amusement of most members, he recounted an experience he had had whilst crossing on the boat from England to Douglas the previous Saturday. A slow passage of five and half hours in an 'inconveniently small boat', which he claimed might easily have been accomplished in an hour less in a 'larger and more commodious one', afforded him the opportunity for protracted conversations with the other passengers:

> There happened to be on board one of the leading hotel-keepers of Douglas, and before I reached Douglas he entered into conversation with me. I believe we talked on a great many subjects of local politics together, which I should be sorry to betray his confidence by repeating. But he also did say to me, 'I observe that the Chancellor of the Exchequer has imposed an additional sixpence on spirits in England'. I confess I thought that that was an awkward remark, because I was not anxious to rehearse on board the boat on Saturday the statement I was likely to make in the Court today. Consequently, I turned the remark by a question and said, 'How would you like that addition here?' I confess I thought it was a harmless remark to make, but I am told it was immediately inferred I was meditating such an increase, and that, at any rate, a very large amount of whisky was taken out of bond yesterday, and the collector of customs had a very busy day.

John Robert Cowell MHK responded to the Governor's statement. He remarked that it was common talk that many people were in the habit of persistently ignoring local tradesmen and going to England with the object of buying goods cheaply in Civil Service stores or other large corporations. Also, a system had emerged recently whereby salesmen came to the Island and went from door to door to take orders for tea which had paid duty in Britain. Subsequently, the Island did not get any allowance on this tea as it was not declared. The inspector of customs went round the Island annually to find out from retailers how much they imported a year, but Cowell queried how tea brought into the Island by hawkers was recorded. He claimed that anyone could import it in packages, brown paper parcels or barrels 'marked as starch, mustard or anything', and there was no means of checking. He went on to caution Tynwald that the British traders would say that the Isle of Man was 'free ground' if the Manx tariff was the same as the British. Cowell proposed that it was desirable that the duty on tea should be reduced from 4d to 2d. After further discussion the motion was withdrawn, to be left until the next week's meeting of Tynwald.

Walpole was determined that a robust and equitable system needed to be established to ensure that the Isle of Man received its fair share of the customs revenue from goods imported and consumed there. He was leading the Island to the gradual assimilation of its duties to those of Britain, and, importantly, linking this major step with a system which would use a 'fiscal population' figure to ensure the Island got the full benefit of its customs revenue. The calculation

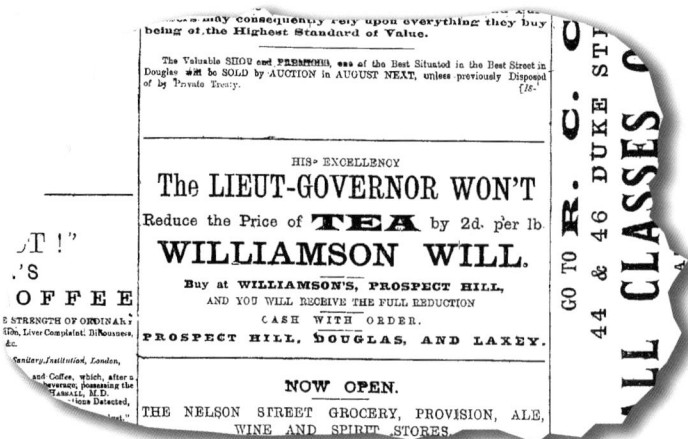

Tea merchant's cheeky advertisement, Isle of Man Examiner, 31 May 1890.

and use of this fiscal population figure and its formulaic development would become the important and essential basis in establishing the future Common Purse Arrangement. But before Walpole could develop his plans, which were only at an embryonic stage, he had to deal with the continuing call in Tynwald for the reduction in tea duty.

At the next week's meeting of Tynwald Court, Walpole detailed the consumption of tea per person in Britain and per person in the Island.[612] According to the latest returns, Britain's tea consumption was calculated to be 4.88 pounds per person of the population and the Island's was 6 pounds. This 6 pounds figure had been calculated by the following method. The population of the Isle of Man was approximately 56,000. This figure was increased in the summer by approximately 260,000 visitors arriving at Douglas. It had been estimated that each of these summer visitors remained in the Island for one week, and therefore the 260,000 visitors when divided by 52 weeks in a year was equivalent to a permanent addition to the population of 5,000 in the year, thereby raising the figure of 56,000 to 61,000. The Island's total consumption of 366,000 pounds of tea, divided by the fiscal population figure of 61,000, equated to 6 pounds per person. These crucial calculations would become the means for Walpole to develop a very important strategy to improve public finances. Meanwhile, he detailed to Tynwald various urgently needed capital schemes. These included harbour works at Ramsey, Peel and Port St Mary, a new poor asylum, alterations to the Tynwald Court building and a new courthouse at Peel. These capital schemes, totalling more than £50,000, could be met by an assured surplus of £8,600 a year. But it would be a totally different matter if that surplus was cut at one blow by the loss of £3,000 to the Manx revenue by the reduction in tea duty from 4d to 2d. Of the £62,000 general revenue of the Island, £59,000 was raised by customs duties, and £50,000 of this was raised from three sources: tea and coffee ('the liquors which cheer and do not inebriate'), spirits ('the liquors which cheer and do inebriate') and tobacco.

Walpole thought it was absolutely necessary to devise some fresh form of direct taxation which would fall on the community as a whole, but he admitted that he did not know whether Tynwald was prepared for such a radical step. Cowell continued to argue the case for a reduction in tea duty. He claimed that the surplus customs revenue was 'the life' of the Isle of Man and that it was the duty of the members of Tynwald to conserve the surplus by every means in their power. Walpole replied to Cowell, saying that, whilst they both agreed on the importance of the surplus revenue, the member was then asking Tynwald to throw away £3,000 a year of that surplus. Cowell responded to this by pointing out once again that there was a vast loss to the Island's revenue by the importation of non-recovered duty-paid tea. Walpole counterclaimed by asking why it should be assumed that if the duty was lowered to 2d in the Isle of Man as compared to 4d in Britain then the leakage would not continue. If there was an inducement to leakage between the British rate of 6d and the Manx of 4d, there would be precisely the same inducement between 4d and 2d. When put to the vote in Tynwald, Cowell's proposal for a reduction in tea duty was lost. It was a tight call in the Keys, whose members voted nine to eight for the 2d reduction, but the Legislative Council voted unanimously against. With the two branches of Tynwald at variance, the motion fell by the rules of the Court. This rule and the general, though not guaranteed, support for the Governor by the Council ensured that his power and control in Tynwald was virtually absolute. The defeat of the wish of the Keys was commented on by the *Mona's Herald*:

> Here, we have not merely taxation *without representation*, but taxation contrary to, and in *defiance of representation*; while at the same time, an established principle of our financial policy is contravened. The power which imposes burdens on the people for the public service - which spends their money and makes requisitions to which they must, perforce, consent - that is the ultimate governing power; and if it is not the representative power, then what is it? Well, we see what it is not, it is not the House of Keys.[613]

Establishment of Common Purse Arrangement

In July 1890 the Treasury and the Customs departments enquired of Walpole if it was the intention of Tynwald to make any alteration to the 4d tea duty as a consequence of the lowering to the same amount which had been made in Britain three months earlier.[614] Walpole replied that he had been watching carefully for any effect the alteration of the British duties might have on the revenue of the Island over the last few months, and he requested a few more months before replying. It was almost three months before he contacted the Treasury with any firm information

Reginald Earle Welby, Permanent Secretary of the Treasury.

on the matter.[615] He claimed that circumstances had changed in the Island. With the assimilation of the Manx tea duties to those of Britain there had been a falling off in recorded imports, indicating that a considerable amount of tea was being imported, having paid duty in Britain but escaping the notice of the customs officers in the Island. The previous incentive created by the lower duty was now lost. Instead of an improvement in the Island's public revenue as a result of the assimilation arrangement, there was a consequential major loss. This possibility had been predicted by John Robert Cowell and others. Walpole reluctantly submitted that it might be necessary to restore the differential by making a reduction in the duty to encourage the local trader to pay duty in the Island, but, if the duty on tea was to be reduced and the revenue consequently decreased, some corresponding addition would have to be made to the general revenue. Walpole had discussed the possibility of introducing stamp duties on cheques and property with Reginald Welby, Permanent Secretary of the Treasury, whilst recently in London.[616] Welby had no objection to the proposal, but Walpole was concerned as to whether he would be able to carry this change through Tynwald as, not unsurprisingly, the members would probably object to the introduction of a new form of tax burden on the people. This dilemma would continue to play on his mind.

Walpole gave the matter a great deal of further thought. He wrote again to the Treasury explaining that he had proposed the possible stamp duties scheme because at the time he saw no other alternative except the loss of a considerable annual income.[617] It had since occurred to him that the difficulty might be obviated by a unique arrangement, a development of his calculations used to compare the levels of consumption of tea in the Isle of Man and Britain which he had brought to the attention of Tynwald six months earlier. He had settled on a means of resolving the Manx customs revenue problem by devising a system to calculate accurate figures to be used for the equitable sharing of the two countries' assimilated customs duties - the nucleus of what would become the Common Purse Arrangement:

- In the case of any articles incurring customs duties in the Island the same as in Britain, then the total duties of both countries should be paid into the British Exchequer and subsequently apportioned between the two governments. The only article presently falling under this category was tea.
- Such apportionment was to be based on the average consumption of the Island and Britain respectively for the three years ended 31 March 1889.
- The apportionment was to be settled in succeeding years by ascertaining the average consumption per person in the Isle of Man and Britain respectively in the three years selected for the basis and correcting it each actual year.
- The average consumption in the Island would be larger per person than the average consumption in Britain, mainly due to an annual addition of 250,000 to 300,000 visitors to the Island's normal population.
- In the case of the Island, where there were no means of accurately estimating the growth of the population between the decennial censuses, the population of the preceding census would be assumed to be the population of the succeeding ten years.
- The apportioned sum for the Isle of Man was then to be paid into its own Consolidated Fund.

Walpole had spoken with Welby again in London at the end of September, and Welby thought that the new proposal was worthy of consideration.[618] It had been accepted that, if the Treasury agreed with the suggested arrangement, Walpole would withdraw his initial scheme for the imposition of stamp duties. He offered to go to London once more to discuss matters to help move on the new proposal - he was looking for a speedy reply from the Treasury as the Island's revenue from tea duty was declining rapidly and something needed to be done soon.[619] After much concern and many reminders, just before Christmas 1890 came the response which Walpole had wanted and waited for.[620] The Treasury officials saw no objection in principle to his proposals, nor were they aware of any difficulties in carrying out the details. Whilst assenting to it, they thought it advisable to limit the arrangement at first as an experiment over three years, reserving the right to end it in case of unforeseen objections arising.

After receiving this reply, Walpole immediately approached the Island's Attorney General, Sir James Gell, telling him of his proposals and seeking advice.[621] Walpole considered his solution to the matter was very favourable to the Isle of Man, 'how favourable I hardly like to say'. He now wanted to know from Gell whether he agreed that the alteration did not require legislation, but the reply was not what he had hoped for. Gell thought that legislation was necessary to introduce such a change. Walpole was disappointed with this information, but pressed his argument again. First of all, Walpole thanked Gell for his approval of the proposal, 'I am glad you like my revenue plan, I am rather proud of it myself'. He went on to consider that the Isle of Man Customs, Harbours and Public Purposes Act of 1866, section 3, directed the Customs to apply the customs duties collected in the Island to certain specified items. Section 4 and 7 did the same. Section 8 placed the surplus at the disposal of Tynwald. Section 9 directed its payment into the Consolidated Fund. Walpole asked Gell to consider what had been the practice previously under this law. The Customs had retained the whole amount of the customs duties collected in the Island and paid out the charges incurred, balancing the two amounts at the end of the financial year and paying the Island the difference. He queried how this differed from the principle suggested by him now with regard to the tea duties. The amount collected in the Island would be paid into the Customs Account in the Bank of England precisely as before. Walpole wished Gell to also consider another aspect of the present arrangement. Since 1879/80 the Treasury had made an allowance to the Island of the amount of duty on goods imported into the Island on which duty had been paid in Britain. In other words, the Treasury regularly credited the Island with duty not collected there. The Treasury had done this without legislative authority of any kind, which seemed to stretch the law in the Island's favour much more strongly than Walpole was asking now. Walpole, looking to the interest of the Island, cautioned against raising with the Treasury this lack of authority as 'we benefit too greatly from the arrangement to justify our querying its legality, but it is obvious that if we begin questioning the power of the Treasury in one case, other people, besides myself, may commence to doubt its power in the other'. He said that the Treasury had referred the proposal to the Customs and their legal advisers seemed satisfied. After further careful consideration, Gell agreed that legislation was not required.

At the January 1891 meeting of Tynwald the Governor informed the Court that during the last nine months he had been carefully watching the effect on the insular customs revenue by the reduction of duty on tea in Britain.[622] The figures indicated that a significant quantity of imported tea which was duty-paid in Britain had escaped the detection of the Customs officers. Matters had changed since Walpole's claim of less than a year earlier that there was 'no great leakage of the Island's revenue'. Some major step was now needed to be taken for the protection of the revenue. With this object in mind, Walpole explained to Tynwald that he had been in communication with the British Government and had obtained their concurrence to a Common Purse Arrangement (this appears to be the first official reference to the name of the new customs sharing scheme). The arrangement would be experimental for three years. The whole of the duties received on tea in the Island and Britain would be paid into this Common Purse and subsequently apportioned between

Sir James Gell, Attorney General.

the two governments. The amount of duty payable to Tynwald under the arrangement would be much larger per head of the population than that assigned to the British Government because the proportional consumption of tea in the Island, boosted by the habits of the visitors, exceeded that in Britain. The Island would derive a further advantage from the arrangement because the consumption of tea in Britain had been stimulated by the recent reduction in the duty. Additionally, the local traders and consumers would benefit from the fact that free trade in tea would now be established between the two countries.

There now followed a long period of further formidable negotiations.[623] In February 1891 Walpole was asked by Welby of the Treasury for his observations on a Customs Department report on the apportionment of the tea duties.[624] The report, in the main, concurred with Walpole's aims for a Common Purse Arrangement. The question, however, of accepting as a basis for calculation the rate of consumption of tea in Britain when the duty was at 6d and giving the Island a pro rata benefit of any increase in the total consumption when Britain's duty has been reduced to 4d was one that the Customs thought required further careful consideration. Walpole was concerned that the Island would be disadvantaged if his ideas were not implemented, and he submitted that if any objection was to be raised at all it should have been raised prior to the Treasury's approval of the arrangement.[625] Indeed, Walpole had by now informed Tynwald of his plan, so he pointed out his awkward position if the arrangement had to be modified. Welby responded to Walpole, informing him that the Treasury would not press the objections raised by the Customs, and both departments accepted Walpole's assertion that the advantage to the Island from the reduction of duty in Britain would soon be compensated by the increased consumption of tea in the Island owing to the rapid growth in the number of visitors.[626] However, the Treasury again pointed out that, in agreeing to the trial of the arrangement, the power to put an end to it upon due notice in case of unforeseen objections arising would need to be reserved.

With the confirmation of the adjusted average consumption calculation to be used for the operation of the Common Purse Arrangement, Walpole went to Tynwald in early April to explain his financial statement.[627] He told the Court that there were few matters which he had been able to make since he became Governor which had afforded him more satisfaction than the particular agreement regarding the duty on tea. He said that he was so satisfied with the establishment of the Common Purse Arrangement that he would eventually like to apply it to other dutiable articles.

In July 1891 Walpole set about attempting to fund free education throughout the Island.[628] A Bill to do the same had been introduced recently into the British Parliament, and it was rapidly passing through the House of Commons. Walpole claimed that 'if free education is established in the islands around us, we can hardly avoid extending the same system to this Island'. The Clerk of the Rolls, Alured Dumbell, objected entirely to the whole principle of free education 'as it is utterly inapplicable to the state of this little country and the present law provides everything that is necessary'.[629] The Education Bill was debated later on in 1891 when there was an acrimonious exchange of views, which at times got very personal.[630] Walpole claimed that 'according to the Clerk of the Rolls it is a mistake to educate these people at all', to which Dumbell replied that 'you must not educate them beyond a certain point'. Although there was opposition and delay, Walpole was undeterred and carried on with his plans to fund free education and to do it by assimilating tobacco duties in the Island to those in force in Britain in the same way as had been done with tea. He corresponded and met with officials at the Home Office, Treasury and Customs to agree the details of his plan. More heated debates took place in Tynwald, which eventually came to an end in early 1892 when Walpole convinced the Court that his financial ambitions for the Island should be extended. In summing up his proposals, he finished with the statement:

> Confronted with the difficulty of providing £3,500 for the purpose of free education, I have proposed, if I may use a common and almost vulgar phrase, to put it into our pipes and smoke it (laughter), and I am confident, when we are enjoying our tobacco after

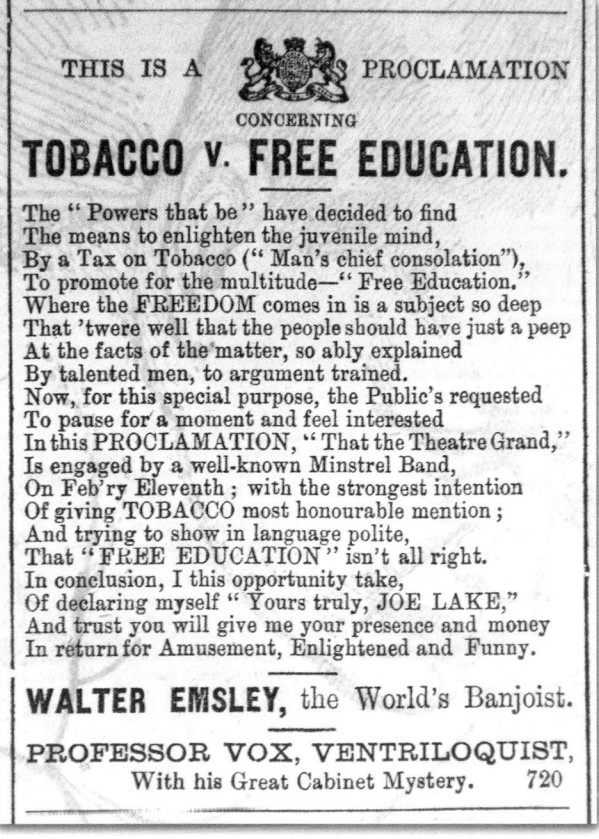

Skit by 'Joe Lake' on tobacco and free education whilst advertising a show at The Grand Theatre, Manx Sun, 6 February 1892.

breakfast, in the morning or in the evening, it will be some satisfaction to us to reflect that we are not merely enjoying indulging in a favourite habit, or as some people say, giving way to an abominable abuse (laughter), but we are providing gratuitous education for over 6,000 children (laughter and applause).[631]

With the financial proposals fully explained, the Tynwald members were won round. There were some delays caused by further negotiations between the Governor and the Whitehall departments, but an agreement was eventually made. On 27 June 1892 'An Act to amend the law respecting the customs duties in the Isle of Man' confirmed the decision.[632] It would be another year before the matter was finalised with the introduction of 'An Act to consolidate and amend the

Laws as to Public Education and Industrial Schools, 1893' which abolished school fees and substituted government grants instead.[633]

Contrasting fortunes

The Manx customs duties were producing more revenue than ever before, principally through the spending of the summer visitors. The 'steamship companies, the banks, the hotel, boarding and lodging-house keepers, the various corporations which provide recreation and amusement, the tradesmen, and, to a lesser extent, the owners and occupiers of land' were enjoying a time of great prosperity.[634] Douglas had over one hundred hotels and boarding houses to cater for the hordes of visitors who came to enjoy it and the rest of the Island throughout the summer season from May to September:

> c/o Mrs Barton's, The Midland, 35 Loch Promenade, Douglas
> Sat[urday] night
>
> My dear Father and Mother,
>   I'll begin by giving you an account of our temporary home and habits and give you a few more details than last time when I was in such a hurry. We have thirty-five boarders in this house and we all sit down at the same table, at the same time, to meals. Breakfast 9.30: fish, turkey, duck, fryed eggs and ham, etc., etc., with butter and bread and jam to finish with and tea or coffee. Dinner 1.30: 4 or 5 courses, specimen: (1) tomato soup, (2) fish, (3) peas, potatoes and game, (4) pudding, (5) stewed fruit and custard. Tea: tea, tongue, eggs, ham, cold meat, butter and bread and jam etc. Supper: grand assortment, I never have any.
>   Thursday night, bed at 11.45, up at 7.00. Will, James and I went for a bathe before breakfast (we three sleep in one bed). We then went to Douglas Head till dinner. After dinner we went to Groudle Glen by Electric railway. After tea we three went round the town. Today we have been to Peel and Glen Maye all day. We hired a conveyance to take us all together. Peel is on exactly the opposite side of the Island. Tonight we have been strolling round the town again. I can't give you particulars of every where. I am enjoying myself immensely. Everything (nearly) is beautiful. The Glens are glorious. We get to places here and there that I feel like stopping at all day. But it has to be seen to be imagined.
>   If I were a millionaire, I should wish for no better holiday resort than the Isle of Man. But one thing puts the damper on all the pleasure! That is the expense. Everything is almost as expensive as it can be, everywhere one goes there is a turnstile at the entrance, where 3d, 4d, 6d or more has to be paid. All the others but 'we three' go somewhere at night that cost 1s or more, in fact if I were to do the same as W. Frith & Co. I should spend all I have got with me, long before the boarding house bill is presented, as it is I can't possibly get through without borrowing, unless I stop about Douglas all the time and it

Thomas Thurman (third from left on back row) and other summer visitors, 1895.

would be a great pity to have come here without making the best I can of it.

Although William and James brought a good bit of money of their own beside £5 cheque their father gave them, they are writing home for more. Will you please send me a little more. I don't know how much I shall require but I am 5s deficient now for the lodging house bill (£2 per week) and then there is next week's 'going about' expenses. It will do any time before next Thursday. I will try and repay sometime. The 'going about' ex[pense]s are 3 or 4s per day and then I walk where the others ride by tram etc.

There is such a lot more to 'put' but I'll save it till I get home as there is no more room and I am going to bed, it is 11.35 now.

Your aff[ectionate] son

Love

T[homas] Thurman[635]

The needs of visitors such as Thomas required the services of boatmen and porters, hotel and restaurant staff, carriage drivers and street cleaners, shop assistants and newspaper sellers, and other such ancillary workers, many of whom came to the Island to seek work although they had

*Alms houses in Alms House Lane which ran between
Bond Street and Stowell Lane, Douglas, c.1898.*

no local family links.[636] But their jobs were only temporary and seasonal, and for a great part of the year many of these people were unemployed. This new class of urban worker, well occupied in the summer but unable to make a living for the rest of the year, was something the Island had not experienced before. Whilst the poor people of the country parishes were able to depend on help from their families, the community and the church at times of need, those of the holiday towns sought assistance from voluntary organisations. With no poor laws in existence, these organisations were the saviours of many individuals and families; but Governor Walpole was concerned that the expenditure of these organisations had been 'reduced to the lowest possible sum consistent, I will not say with humanity, but with the barest decency'.[637] With the backing of the improved public finances, enhanced by the customs revenue, Walpole was able to get support from Tynwald to introduce a Poor Relief Act in 1888 to help deal with the suffering experienced by many people.[638] Where they were not in existence already, the towns and parishes now formed district committees which received government funding to assist with alleviating the problems of poverty. The Douglas Poor Relief Committee met once a month in a room in Fort Street to consider the needs of those in want.[639] It could give financial assistance, create job opportunities, find accommodation, provide furniture, trace missing fathers, fund education, recommend people be sent to the Poor Asylum and grant many other means to assist some very sad circumstances. But at times the committee had to be firm, and an instance of this was recorded in one of the committee's minute books which reveals that an ill and impoverished Susan Wilson, who lived directly behind the grand hotels on Douglas sea front and had been asking for public help for some time, was sent to England to seek assistance from her estranged husband:

> The Inspector reported that he had himself seen this woman, when in Birkenhead last week, and that he was [of the] opinion that she was in a weak state of health and very poor. Resolved that the sum of 4/- per week be sent to this woman by [the] Inspector, for five weeks only, and that she be given finally to understand that after that time has elapsed, she may go into the House of Industry, and that if she decline[s] to take advantage of this offer all relief to her from the Committee must cease.[640]

So, whilst Thomas spent four shillings a day on 'going about' expenses on his exciting holiday, with the certainty of the financial fall-back of his parents if he could not manage, Susan had to live on the same amount a week when trying to sort out her troubled life, with the certainty of the workhouse if she could not manage.

Extension of Arrangement and revised 'fiscal population'

Spencer Walpole presided as Governor over his last Tynwald Court on 15 November 1893. He left the Isle of Man to become Secretary of the British Post Office. During his term of office his dealings with the departments of the British Government had been impressive. The Treasury no longer directly involved itself in Tynwald decisions, and its sanction had become more and more a matter of form.[641] This had resulted in greater financial freedom being accorded to both the Governor and Tynwald. The lessening of the need to interfere in Manx affairs was equally the situation with the Home Office where there was an absence of any major concerns connected with the government of the Island.[642] Whilst the confidence and respect shown by Westminster and Whitehall were in no small way due to Walpole's personal ability, they also reflected on the developing nature of Tynwald. However, it would be almost one hundred years before it could be claimed that Tynwald had a proper and comprehensive responsibility for the Island's governance.

Sir West Ridgeway was appointed as Walpole's successor in November 1893 and installed in office on 13 December at a ceremony in Castle Rushen.[643] Ridgeway, aged forty-nine, was a most experienced and distinguished administrator. He would serve as Governor for a short but fruitful time, during which he further advanced the Common Purse Arrangement through tough negotiations.[644]

After much argument and counterargument between Ridgeway and Whitehall, the existing agreement was allowed to continue, and a Revenue Returns Act was introduced in 1894 which

Governor Sir West Ridgeway.

established a more secure and accurate means of recording all dutiable goods which were being imported under the arrangement.[645] Ridgeway then wanted to encompass wine and other commodities into the scheme in the same way as was allowed for tea and tobacco. He also wanted to establish a revised and fairer fiscal population formula. In order to achieve this he considered that, for calculation purposes, there needed to be an addition made to the Island's resident population figure in order to reflect the growing numbers of visitors benefiting from the lower Manx customs duties.

In 1895 Ridgeway again successfully negotiated with Whitehall.[646] A Customs Department report confirmed that in future the amount payable to Tynwald would be arrived at by a complicated but efficient formula and explanation (see parts 1 and 2 below), both of which are very important in appreciating the means of calculation used in the Common Purse Arrangement.

By this a 'fiscal population' figure was achieved by adding to the total number of local residents a calculated number which allowed for the short-staying but high-spending visitors.

1895 CUSTOMS DEPARTMENT REPORT - Part 1

Combined United Kingdom and Isle of Man Customs Revenue

Tea	3,594,226
Tobacco	10,422,568
Wine	1,143,825
	£15,160,619

Population of the United Kingdom
and Isle of Man = 38,779,031

$$\frac{£15,160,619 \times 20 \text{ shillings}}{38,779,031} = 7.819 \text{ shillings customs duties per person}$$

Isle of Man Customs Revenue

Tea	6,193
Tobacco	18,134
Wine	1,831
	£26,158

$$\frac{£26,158 \times 20 \text{ shillings}}{7.819} = 66,908 \text{ fiscal population of Isle of Man}$$

Fiscal population	66,908
Less resident population	55,608
	11,300 = fiscal addition assumed to be the equivalent in consuming power of 290,474 visitors

1895 CUSTOMS DEPARTMENT REPORT - Part 2

If we take the total population of the United Kingdom [and the Isle of Man] for the year 1894 and the total net duty payments on tea, tobacco and wine in the financial year 1894-

Summer visitors, part of the 'fiscal population', on Loch Promenade, Douglas, c.1895.

95, we shall see that the average net receipt per head is 7.819 shillings. This then represents the average consumption per head of the whole population. If we divide this amount into the £26,158 we arrive at a fiscal population of the Isle of Man for the current year of 66,908. As the native population, as ascertained by the census in 1891, was 55,608, the difference between the two totals, 11,300, may be regarded as the equivalent of any natural increase in the population, and in actual consuming power of the 290,474 visitors who landed in the Island during the year 1894. From this starting point there will be no difficulty whatever in fixing the allowance in future years, so long as the rates of the duties on these three articles of consumption remain the same as they now are in both tariffs. If the consumption per head of the population of the United Kingdom should increase, the allowance would increase in the same proportion. In like manner it would diminish if the consumption per head should show a decrease. Again as regards the population of the Island, the fiscal increase would rise or fall in proportion as the number of visitors should increase or diminish. Thus the allowance to the Island would vary according to the general prosperity of the people of the United Kingdom, as shown by the consumption per head

Local residents buying and selling at the busy Market Place, Douglas, c.1895.

of tea, tobacco and wine. In the event of any alteration of the rates of duty under either tariff, it is of course, understood that a revision of this arrangement will be necessary.

<u>'Fiscal population' x Total revenue assimilated goods United Kingdom and Isle of Man</u>
Population of Britain and Isle of Man

$$\frac{66,908 \ \ \text{x} \ \ £15,160,619}{38,779,031} \quad = \quad \underline{£26,158}$$

The result of this much fairer formula was that the Isle of Man's share of the combined customs duties was automatically adjusted depending on the rise or fall in the number of permanent residents in both countries and the number of summer visitors coming on holiday to the Island.

Ridgeway put the improved fiscal population formula to Tynwald Court on 5 July 1895 and went into its method of calculation.[647] He explained that there were two ways in which the Island would reap an advantage under this revised agreement. If the number of visitors increased, the Island would gain. If the rate of consumption of the assimilated goods increased overall in Britain and the Isle of Man, the Island would also gain. But Ridgeway told the Court that he must be careful in voicing these conclusions:

> On this occasion I am steering my course between Scylla and Charybdis. If I do not point out the advantages which accrue to us from these arrangements, you may not confirm them. On the other hand, if I speak too much of these advantages, my words - if they are reported by the gentlemen who have charge of this duty, and if they have been able to follow me on this occasion - my words will come before the Treasury, and on some future occasion they may be used against me (laughter). I must, therefore, content myself by adopting a middle course, and showing you that this is a fair and equitable arrangement.

Consequently, on 9 July the Revenue Returns Amendment Act was approved by Tynwald which allowed the Island to obtain full beneficial financial recompense with immediate effect for 'wines, spirits, or any other goods, wares or merchandise' whose duties became assimilated in the future.[648]

From uneasy and tough beginnings, the Common Purse Arrangement was finally settled and firmly secured. The long and complicated negotiations which had taken place since 1890 had, by 1895, resulted in an equitable conclusion to the establishment of a method for accurately sharing the combined assimilated customs duties of the Isle of Man and Britain. Governor Walpole had stumbled on it through his early negotiations, and, despite some reservations from within the branches of the British Government, its value had been quickly recognised. The Customs Department had eventually accepted the benefits of the arrangement and had even come up with an improved method for its calculation which recognised the increasing impact of the summer visitors on the consumption of goods. The efforts made by Spencer Walpole and West Ridgeway on behalf of the Isle of Man rank alongside those of the much admired Henry Loch. Walpole's initiative in establishing the arrangement and his and Ridgeway's persuasive powers in seeing it carried through to become the basis of the public revenue were very important to the Island's economic well-being. The two Governors had been able to convince Tynwald, Westminster and Whitehall of the mutual benefits of the scheme to the Isle of Man and Britain. Precedents were set which were eventually followed across almost all dutiable goods. The Common Purse Arrangement was a clever formula which met the needs of both countries, stabilised the Manx public finances and ensured the good fortune of the Isle of Man for years to come. It was very much an idea right for its time.

Chapter 10

CONTROVERSY CONSIDERED

The wheel of fiscal fortune which operated in the Isle of Man during the seventeenth, eighteenth and nineteenth centuries was functioning against the background of the unique constitutional relationship the Island had with Britain. Having been fought over for centuries, the Island had been answerable first to a feudal Lord and then to the might of the Crown. Whilst it was not part of Britain, it was part of its empire, and Britain maintained an unequivocal assertion of its sovereign rights there. Britain saw the Island as something of an anomaly, a curious appendage which it was unsure how to handle. The Island saw itself as a nation with a historically independent identity. Whilst it ostensibly had the parliamentary legitimacy of Tynwald, its constitution was subjugated and the bulk of its customs revenue was appropriated. These two paradoxes were substantially improved, if not fully resolved, during the period this book addresses. Politically the Island progressed from a form of feudalism to the beginnings of proper democratic freedom. Economically it progressed from a basic agricultural and fishing community with an immediate history connected with smuggling and with limited control over and use of its own public revenue to become a successful holiday destination with partial restitution of its fiscal authority. Despite the many adventures and setbacks which took place in between these events, it was undoubtedly a time of significant transition in the history of the Isle of Man.

From 1405 until 1765 the Isle of Man was part of the feudal estates of the Earls of Derby and then the Dukes of Atholl, an asset which produced a useful income from the various suzerain rights, including the customs duties raised as part of the import trade of the Island. From 1692 until 1737 the duties had been illegally set and collected on behalf of the various Lords of Man without the consent of Tynwald. These Lords were generally absentee rulers, represented by Governors who, with the support of the Lord's Council, dominated Tynwald and oversaw the running of the Island. The self-elected Members of the House of Keys represented no one but themselves, the principal landed families.

The financial losses to Britain as a result of smuggling out of the Isle of Man in the early years of the eighteenth century had become something more than mere annoyance. The Island was in a unique position, ideally situated in all respects to provide an opportunity for making a profit at the expense of Britain. Its physical position gave easy access to Britain and Ireland and its political status allowed the Lords of Man and Tynwald to set laws for the Island without any interference by Britain. The Derbys and the Atholls had had the opportunity to ensure that the trade of the Island was run professionally, legitimately, fairly and with the full and proper support of Tynwald. That they saw fit to increase their own fortunes as well as those of others to the detriment of Britain's financial well-being by turning a blind eye to and even involving themselves in the operation of the smuggling 'trade' was solely within their powers to resolve, but they did not. This was the principal reason why Britain set about taking back control of the Island. It was inevitable that Britain would do something to protect its own revenue, and whilst the Island considered itself to be outside its jurisdiction, Britain did not.

During the latter years of the Derby rule and the early years of the Atholl rule there had been a lengthy spell of questionable Manx maritime trading. Britain's involvement in expanding its empire and taking part in a series of worldwide conflicts meant that economies needed making and all possible sources of national revenue needed securing. The financial losses to the Exchequer as a direct result of smuggling out of the Isle of Man were extensive. These were radically placed in check through the Revestment and Mischief Acts of 1765 which led to the purchase back by Britain of the Crown's sovereign rights, the restriction on the importation and exportation of certain goods and the empowerment of customs officers to deal with smuggling. Smuggling was certainly much reduced by the operation of the two Acts. Britain gained much from curtailing 'the trade' and stopping the extensive losses to its own Exchequer. It secured an income producing asset for the Crown and, consequently, a continuing, if reduced, income for the Dukes of Atholl. The Revestment Act ensured that the cost to Britain in recovering its regal rights would be through the appropriation of the Manx customs revenue. There was an inconsistency in the British position regarding this policy which highlighted the unique situation of the Island. It was Treasury's conventional wisdom that specific state incomes were not hypothecated for particular purposes but were made available for general purposes. Contrary to this, the net income from the Manx customs was stated to be set aside 'distinctly and apart from all other branches of the public revenue' and 'reserved for the disposition of Parliament'. Its 'disposition' was used for the particular purpose of redeeming the sums paid to recompense the Dukes of Atholl.

From the Isle of Man's perspective, the changes resulted in the replacement of the Lord with the Crown and subjected the Island to the imperial authority of Britain. Westminster now proceeded to bring in Parliamentary Acts which directly affected the Island, to put in place Governors with almost unrestricted authority to ensure the protection of Britain's interests, to appoint key officials to oversee matters, to regulate and budget the Manx customs system and to impose fresh duties whenever such a course was thought desirable. The authority of Tynwald was subordinated. The self-elected and unrepresentative Members of the House of Keys had few powers, with no responsibility for the major public finances. The power of the Lord and his

Council was replaced by the power of the Governor and the Legislative Council - with the Home Office, Treasury and Customs Department always having the potentiality of the final word. The Isle of Man, small and within easy reach of Britain, could do little more than protest.

It is unclear why Britain initially purchased only part of the Atholl family's suzerain rights and not the full rights or did not go even further by annexing the Isle of Man. There certainly was a good deal of ministerial instability within the British Government at this time which could possibly have affected the circumstances. Most probably the existence of the ancient Manx Parliament of Tynwald would have been very influential in Britain's decision to restrict its claims. Whilst Britain was prepared to disregard Tynwald in matters which it could claim affected the well-being of Britain, there is no evidence to show that it was seriously considering any form of annexation, though the very threat of such would be used at times in the future as a simple and effective restraint. The avoidance of some form of incorporation into Britain importantly meant that the Island's unique political institutions were retained, albeit they were ignored by Britain at times.

The crucial facts that the Isle of Man was neither part of Britain nor represented in the British Parliament had been ignored in imposing the Revestment and Mischief Acts of 1765 and the Customs Act of 1767. A decade earlier, the High Court of Chancery of 1751 under Lord Hardwicke claimed that the Island was held as a feudatory dominion of the Crown of England 'from time immemorial' and 'the laws of England therefore as such extend not to it . . . unless expressly named'. A decade later, the Act of Parliament, 18 George III, chapter 12, of 1778, which dealt with the taxation situation in North America and the West Indies, enacted that 'the King and Parliament of Great Britain will not impose any duty, tax or assessment for the purpose of raising revenue in any of the colonies, provinces or plantations'. The Island had even greater claims to fiscal and constitutional self-determination than any of these other territories, it was an ancient nation. But the close physical proximity of the two countries and the 'immemorial' (a doubtful term in this context) association the Island had with Britain had resulted in its subjection. Britain considered that its imperial and sovereign powers were absolute.

After the dust of revestment had settled down and further controversial financial settlements had later been made to John Murray, the disgruntled fourth Duke of Atholl, Britain stood in firm constitutional and fiscal control of the Isle of Man. For the next thirty years Britain was prepared to run the Manx customs system at an occasional loss in order to safeguard its own revenue. For the next one hundred years it introduced Customs Acts to continue this protection. These Acts clearly set out the purposes of the customs and gave the Governor and the Treasury control of the administration. Manx interests had not been taken into account when Britain secured this control. During the first quarter of the nineteenth century the surplus revenue became more and more substantial. Seemingly the policy of the Treasury was to ensure that the levels of duties, income and expenditure should produce in the future a surplus which related directly to the previous costs to Britain in buying back the rights of the Lords of Man. This policy determined the Manx economy for many years. Conversely, there appears to be very little consideration given in the Treasury's budgetary process to determine a fair monetary return to be used to carry out improvements in the Island. The people's representatives, the Members of the House of Keys, were virtually impotent in matters of public finances. These issues would become long-standing sources of grievance.

Britain set about attempting to bring the Island's customs system more in line with its own. During the 1830s there was deep concern in the Island when it became known that Britain was considering ending the remnants of smuggling by the imposition of a programme of gradual assimilation of the low Manx customs tariffs to those of its own. This concern extended to the fear of erosion of the limited Manx autonomy. Important and influential elements of society - locals and strangers alike - were dissatisfied not only with increased tariffs and the running of the import licence system but also with the lack of insular control and use of the principal source of public income. Public opposition was not led by the 'clique' of old Manx families but by the more informed local radicals and some of the new residents whose main reason for living in the Island was to benefit from its low customs duties. The Island was a place which the rich as well as those of modest means could move to and avoid British taxes whilst leading a comfortable life style. The Island's situation was used then and is still used now by incoming tax avoiders to support their financial interests. The constitutional reformers often found themselves uncomfortably allied with the new social elite who worked for financial protection but did not necessarily agree with the call for electoral reform. Both protest groups brought an element of co-ordinated and well argued claims to these contentious issues.

At the same time as radicals and those with more personal concerns were questioning the Island's situation, the power of the local press was an important aspect in the campaigns for modernisation. The ultimate purpose was to progress the Island's desire for increased legitimate autonomy. The owners and editors of the more liberal newspapers were not only prepared to take on the local establishment and the British authorities but were willing to risk their own freedom in promoting and arguing the causes they supported. Robert Fargher of the *Mona's Herald* led what would become a long and bitter campaign to reform the House of Keys, abolish the licence system and regain control of the ever increasing surplus public revenue. The enlistment of the help of influential and progressive British politicians helped matters. The Members of the House of Keys and the more conservative press were slow to appreciate the situation, and, whilst the Keys eventually allied themselves to the new financial protest movement and were happy to protect their own pockets by retaining low customs duties, they were certainly not going to support the demise of their own status and lose whatever influence and benefits they had by virtue of their position of self-elected patronage.

At a time when Britain was reforming its political system and changing its imperial policy, Parliament was accused of violating its own constitution by imposing customs laws on the Isle of Man and continuing to revise the Island's customs duties without the full authority of Tynwald. During 1836 and 1837 the threat of customs assimilation galvanised the Island into action. There were combined efforts by the financial protectionists, the House of Keys and Governor John Ready in arguing the Island's case. The public delegates were ably led by Sir William Hillary in the Isle of Man and John Courtney Bluett in London. The Keys appointed their own delegates. Important meetings were held by the combined delegation with various Members of Parliament and officials. Governor Ready informed the Home Office that he failed to understand how the Island would benefit by the proposed changes. The dilemma highlights a difficulty which all Governors had when involved in problematic and, at times, futile negotiations with the British Government: balancing the needs of the Island and those of Britain. Before matters could be finalised, however, everything was placed on hold as a result of the death of William IV. Although the proposed system of gradual assimilation of the Isle of Man's customs duties to those of Britain's did not take place, the events which surrounded the situation give a fascinating perspective of the various policy processes.

The situation was somewhat ameliorated by the granting of certain financial concessions in 1844 as a result of protests initiated by the local press and merchants. The commerce of the Isle of Man was placed on the coasting trade with Britain, the licence system was improved and the Harbour Commissioners were allocated £2,300 to finance harbour works. The protests had been supported by the general public and British politicians, including the influential Dr Bowring. It is important to appreciate that the British authorities were prepared to amend their original proposals in order to provide the Island with a definite annual sum for use by the Harbour Commissioners to deal with much needed works, but the concessions were never to be at the expense of Britain. It was the Manx residents who paid increased customs duties which more than covered the amount allowed to come back to the Island. But imports did not suffer as a consequence of the new duties, indeed they increased, due in no small way to the spending of the increasing numbers of summer visitors. The concern over the issue of the duties was being overtaken by the call for the full benefit of the surplus customs revenue to be made available to Tynwald, a development which was firmly resisted by Britain. It would appear that Britain, whilst pandering to the protectionists and the commercial classes, was seeking to control the Isle of Man by the gradual assimilation of its customs duties, assumption of authority over the bulk of its surplus revenue and continued subordination of its Parliament. Britain's view of the Island as a source of revenue is revealed by its stance in not supporting the democratisation of the House of Keys lest it led to the loss to

Britain of the benefits from the proceeds of the surplus Manx customs revenue. Any attempts to progress financial independence and parliamentary democracy were to be discouraged, with the threat of annexation ever present. Britain's control of the Island continued, with the Governor having comprehensive authority in Tynwald. Improvements to the Isle of Man's national situation were not allowed to be negotiated just yet.

By the middle of the nineteenth century the Isle of Man was prospering and the public revenue was increasing. But the restrictive policies imposed by Britain, in direct variance with its own liberal reforms which had changed the constitution of its Parliament some twenty years previously, were still major bones of contention. From 1765 Britain had taken the surplus of the customs revenue of the Isle of Man, keeping a great part of it for its own purposes and returning very little to the Island. The political situation was equally questionable. An unelected House of Keys, with limited effectiveness due to the controlling authority of the Governor and his Legislative Council, was in direct variance to the power of an elected House of Commons. In 1838, when demands for a publicly elected House of Keys had been made, the Governor had been instructed by the Home Office to reply that any change to the constitution might take the form of parliamentary annexation. In 1845 Governor Charles Hope and the Home Office were against any democratic change to the House of Keys because they considered that a popularly elected assembly would most certainly want power to manage the public finances, a situation which they considered would not be in the interests of Britain. In 1847 and 1848 the Home Office, which considered the Island as no more than 'a portion of the mother country', had again used the threat of annexation to deal with calls for political reform.

By 1853 opinions had changed. Although Britain's continuing imperialistic tendencies were still prevalent, as was evidenced when it included the Island in certain of Parliament's own customs laws, it appeared to wish to resolve the fiscal and constitutional anomalies by offering to relax its grip on the Island's public economy on the understanding that the House of Keys became a properly elected assembly. Tynwald had been given responsibility for the £2,300 previously allocated annually to the Harbour Commissioners, plus a further allowance which equated to one-ninth of the gross customs revenue in order to fund further public work schemes. The Keys had reluctantly accepted that further control was dependent on constitutional reform. However, as was seen time and again, the struggle for change was as much against the 'Castletown clique' as against Britain. The status of the 'clique' had been challenged in the Island by the reform delegates who questioned the right of an unelected assembly to represent the people. In face of increasing public opinion which demanded reforms, the conservative House of Keys had for a long time strongly resisted anything which could undermine the political status and financial well-being of its members. The continuing reluctance of the Keys to reform and the caution of Governor Hope prevented an important opportunity to resolve the conjoined anomalies.

These anomalies had caused great concerns but were soon to change. Britain could no longer hold out for the retention of the long-standing restraints. Governor Henry Loch determined to resolve the dichotomy, and he had secret negotiations with the British Government during 1865 and 1866 which resulted in the Island gaining the use of most of its surplus customs revenue through the Customs, Harbours and Public Purposes Act and the House of Keys becoming a popularly elected assembly through the House of Keys Election Act. The changes enabled comprehensive improvements to be carried out to the harbours and other public works in order to benefit both the islanders and the visitors. Tynwald had been given increased responsibility for the necessary expenditure for these schemes, although the need for the approval of the Governor and the Treasury limited its extent. The successful resolution of the double dilemma was no doubt aided by the fact that Britain's imperialistic ambitions were subsiding and its liberal policies were maturing. Loch's close acquaintance with the Home Secretary, Sir George Grey, would have assisted in resolving the long-standing problems associated with Westminster and Whitehall. His clever use of obtaining his own way by implying that his suggested changes came directly from the British Government assisted greatly in his handling of matters with Tynwald Court. Loch was the most powerful and progressive Governor the Island had had since revestment. His reforms made Tynwald Court, in theory, more authoritative. The Members of the House of Keys were now answerable to the people and the function of the House itself was changed by having increased responsibilities.

But Loch's revolutionary actions still left many unrealised reforms. Even after the momentous changes brought about by the Customs, Harbours and Public Purposes Act and the House of Keys Election Act, Tynwald remained weak. The demands for economic improvement fell short of being fully realised, with Tynwald gaining only limited control of the improved allocation of insular funds. Whilst the Island finally had democratically elected representatives in the House of Keys, the narrow franchise gave the vote principally to persons from the same stratum of society as the members of the old House. The continuing strength of the Governor and the Legislative Council saw to it that the new popularly elected Keys did not have the full extent of powers that had been hoped for. The Legislative Council was entirely composed of officials who were appointed by the Crown and the Lord Bishop and were expected to support the Governor. Consequently, the authority of the Island was still firmly in the hands of the Governor, who dealt with most of the legislative, judicial and executive issues, save only for the limited functions of a number of statutory Boards. But even his decisions were liable to be subordinated, which they occasionally were. The reserve powers retained by the Home Office and the Treasury ensured ultimate constitutional and fiscal control, and an Act of Tynwald still remained subject to the Royal Assent. The Island's customs income from 1765 to 1866 had totalled £1,550,000 which, less expenditure of £860,000 (mainly administration charges), left a surplus of £690,000. Only a limited amount of this surplus had ever been returned to the Island for local use. Despite the unfulfilled aspirations, the Isle of Man was in a much improved parliamentary situation and, apart from the Imperial Contribution, it now ceased to be a revenue producing asset for Britain.

The policies of Henry Loch were carried on by Spencer Walpole. The efforts of Walpole brought about a beneficial customs union between the Isle of Man and Britain. The successes of the policies were associated with the changing role of government in society and the growth of the Manx tourism industry. The British authorities showed increasing confidence in the Island's ability to manage itself and they became less directly involved in its affairs. Both the radicals, who had been pressing for financial and political modification earlier in the century, and the conservatives, who had resisted them, had been opposed to assimilation and had argued for keeping Manx customs duties low. But attitudes had changed over the years, and by the time of Walpole the idea of customs assimilation was more readily acceptable in the Island, no doubt helped by the fact that there was no longer an accompanying threat of possible incorporation into Britain. The vast increase in summer visitors meant that there was greater economic activity which automatically generated an increase in government income through a revised taxation system which bore mainly on the visitors and not on the local population. The important tourist industry became the prime source for the Island's private and public revenues.

The impetus for improvements to the Island's fiscal situation and the establishment of the Common Purse Arrangement, which resulted in an increased and steady insular income, came exclusively from the office of Governor Walpole - not from the authorities in Britain, not from local reformers, not from the Legislative Council, not even from the people's representatives, the House of Keys. Indeed, the role of the Keys during the early part of this campaign appears to have been to fight a rearguard action for the retention of the status quo, with a majority of members arguing for the continuation of much lower customs duties and still resentful over the repercussions of political reform, particularly the continuing constraint placed upon their authority by the powerful position of the Governor. In both the House of Keys and the Legislative Council there appears to have been a lack of any financial initiative which, together with a reluctance to change, is rather surprising given the character, financial acumen and clout of some of the members at this time. There was no doubt genuine concern that even a moderate adjustment in the customs duties would affect the pockets and purses of the poorer classes the most, with the possibility that little of the resultant extra revenue would be fully recovered for use in the Island. There might have been a fear that a closer relationship with Britain could undermine the Island's situation or incur further British interference and tighter supervision in some way. There equally might have been a vestige of self-interest in the remnants of the 'clique'. However, the important point here is that, in face of opposition from the British authorities and the exceedingly difficult negotiations, it was the impetus, determination and character of Spencer Walpole which mattered most. Both he and West Ridgeway, his successor, argued skilfully and persuasively with Tynwald and the British authorities in favour of the changes that were introduced. Whilst they were working on behalf of the Island, the two Governors were not, of course, seeking to do anything contrary to Britain's interests. They were pursuing fairness, and the justice of what they were proposing won the day. Success also needed a British Government that was prepared to respond benignly and not simply look after its own narrow financial interest. No doubt the fact that the sums involved were relatively small in terms of Britain's total public revenue would have helped, but credit is due to the British Government for accepting the radical and progressive proposals of the two Governors.

Since its establishment in the late nineteenth century and continuing on throughout the twentieth century, the Common Purse Arrangement (variously known as the Common Purse Agreement, the Customs and Excise Agreement and the Revenue Sharing Arrangement) widened in scope and generally progressed in detail rather than in principle, but, nonetheless, its continuing growth was an important element of the Isle of Man's more recent history. The arrangement provided Tynwald with its principal taxation receipts for funding the country's public services. Its solid, substantial and guaranteed revenue gave Tynwald freedom to lower the rates of direct taxation in the second half of the twentieth century and thus stimulated the development of the financial services industry which eventually replaced tourism as the Island's principal economic activity. During this time, there was major devolution of Britain's authority over the Island and increased confidence shown in each other by the two governments, processes which eventually led to the Island obtaining much greater autonomy.

In 2007 the underlying revenue sharing mechanism was re-negotiated and introduced new criteria which related the proportioning of customs receipts based on the relative growth in the national incomes of the two countries. The worldwide financial crisis which occured in late 2008 included the collapse of Kaupthing Singer and Friedlander (Isle of Man) Ltd. This led to Britain's Chancellor of the Exchequer Alistair Darling describing the Isle of Man as a 'tax haven sitting in the Irish Sea' and announcing, without any consultation with or forewarning to the Manx Government, that there would be a review into Britain's relationship with the Island. It was later revealed that the review would include an investigation into aspects of financial supervision and transparency; fiscal arrangements; financial crisis management and resolution arrangements; and international cooperation; but not the constitutional relationship. In direct contrast to Chancellor Darling's opinion, in April 2009 the influential Organisation for Economic Cooperation and Development included the Isle of Man on a 'white list' of countries which complied with the highest standards for exchanging tax information, thereby placing it in the top tier of the world's best regulated and transparent jurisdictions.

Despite the major advances there have been in the relationship between the two countries, certain of the unique historical connections the Isle of Man continues to have with Britain and the more recent association it has with Europe have a direct bearing on the extent of freedom the Island has in fully controlling the development of its public finances and exercising its parliamentary status. Beneficial as many aspects of the mutual links most certainly are, any risk to the country's ability to determine its own future highlights the fact that, despite the great advances made over the centuries, the Isle of Man continues to live in the shadow of its ancient feudal lords. The progress of and the various changes to the Manx fiscal situation, the maturing of Tynwald and its executive, the transition of the alliance between the Island and Britain, the new connections with Europe and the rest of the world, and the uncertainty of the future are fascinating features of the Isle of Man's modern history. The story continues.

Appendices

APPENDIX I

CUSTOMS STATISTICS, 1736-1900

There had been major consequences on the Island's public finances as a result of Parliament's actions - legal or otherwise - through the Revestment and Mischief Acts of 1765 and the Customs Act of 1767, particularly caused by the imposition of the customs duties and the general retention, control and use of the resultant surpluses. A House of Commons report and various Parliamentary Papers of 1805 had shown that Britain had obtained a beneficial return at a great cost to the Isle of Man.[649] However, complete details of the finances have always been uncertain. During the late 1890s the House of Keys and the *Isle of Man Times* certainly sought to have the statistics revealed, and, around this time, A. W. Moore would be gathering information in order to give an indication of the finances for inclusion in his soon to be published *A History of the Isle of Man*. But no one succeeded then or has succeeded since, until now, in bringing together the actual figures.

This study is able to reveal a much more accurate picture of the Isle of Man's customs revenue, expenditure and surplus statistics for the one hundred and sixty-five year period of crucial change which included the Duke of Atholl becoming Lord of Man in 1736, the Revestment Act of 1765, the various attempts to assimilate the Manx customs duties to those of Britain in the mid-nineteenth century, the granting to Tynwald of a proportion of the surpluses in 1844 and 1853, the Isle of Man Customs, Harbours and Public Purposes Act of 1866, the firm establishment of the Common Purse Arrangement in 1895 and the buoyant customs revenue at the end of the nineteenth century.

Directly after revestment, income from customs duties dropped, with some years showing an overall loss, and it was another thirty years before the income returned to similar levels as at the time of revestment. The expenditure was generally made up of the expenses of running the Island, with a smaller amount used in supporting the herring fishery and minor public works. The surplus amounts which went into the British Consolidated Fund became relatively substantial, and whilst some funds were returned to the Island, these were small by comparison.

The allocation of £2,300 annually from the customs revenue in lieu of the harbour dues for harbour works from 1844, the additional sums for harbour and other public works from 1853 and £10,000 for the Imperial Contribution from 1866 all became part of the expenditure figures.

From 1765 to 1866 the Island's income from customs duties paid into the British

Consolidated Fund totalled approximately £1,550,000. Expenditure of nearly £860,000 left a surplus amounting to £690,000. Throughout this period Britain considered that any contributions to the Isle of Man from the accrued surplus were 'not limited to any fixed proportion of revenue, and to be for all fit and proper charges of government'.[650]

From 1866 the surplus customs revenue was able to be used exclusively for Manx purposes. The Common Purse Arrangement, the important customs sharing scheme between the Isle of Man and Britain, was firmly set in 1895 as an important system to ensure an equitable share of the combined customs revenues to the two countries.

The figures used in the following tables have been obtained from a variety of sources. Those considered to be the most reliable and accurate have been abstracted from the following:

Manx National Heritage Library and Archives
- Abstract of the revenue of the Isle of Man, 1736-62, AP 09707 Book 104
- Abstract of the revenue of the Isle of Man, 1738-1802, AP 09707 X70(2nd)-1
- Amount of Customs on Imports into the Isle of Man, 1804, MB Finances D154/3x/1
- Customs Returns, 1863-66, MB Finances D154/4x/3a
- Isle of Man Statistical Abstract, 1879-1900, MB Finances D154/4
- Financial Statements laid before Tynwald Court, 1869-1900, GOP 09845/Box 39

Parliamentary Papers
- Accounts of duties on Imports and Exports in Isle of Man, 1798-1803, PP 1805 (29)
- Procedures of the Privy Council on the position of the Duke of Atholl, PP 1805 (79)
- Minutes of evidence relating to the House of Keys regarding the petition of the Duke of Atholl, PP 1805 (143)
- Isle of Man Revenues and Payments, 1786-99, PP 1805 (159)
- Isle of Man Revenues and Payments, 1799-1804, PP 1805 (160)
- Returns of the gross Customs Revenue of the Isle of Man, 1804-51, PP 1852 (322)
- Returns of the Revenue of Customs of the Isle of Man, 1805-53, PP 1852-53 (501)
- Surplus Revenue of Isle of Man, PP 1864 (415)

Reports
- *The Report of the Commissioners of Inquiry for the Isle of Man*, 1792
- *Report of the Departmental Committee on the constitution, etc. of the Isle of Man*, (two volumes, Cd. 5950, 1911, and Cd. 6026, 1912)

APPENDIX I

CUSTOMS REVENUE, 1736-1764

	Revenue £Manx	Revenue £Sterling
1736	886	759
1737	568	487
1738	1,849	1,585
1739	1,641	1,407
1740	2,338	2,004
1741	2,350	2,014
1742	2,543	2,180
1743	3,165	2,713
1744	2,622	2,247
1745	2,678	2,295
1746	3,101	2,658
1747	2,925	2,507
1748	2,913	2,497
1749	2,343	2,008
1750	4,537	3,889
1751	3,721	3,189
1752	4,806	4,119
1753	4,871	4,175
1754	5,944	5,095
1755	4,968	4,258
1756	4,749	4,071
1757	5,234	4,486
1758	5,180	4,440
1759	8,083	6,928
1760	7,094	6,081
1761	9,544	8,181
1762	6,391	5,478
1763	7,029	6,025
1764	6,387	5,475
		£103,251

CUSTOMS REVENUE, EXPENDITURE AND SURPLUS, 1765-1866

	Revenue	Expenditure	Surplus
1765	696	407	289
1766	565	1,293	-728
1767	407	495	-88
1768	614	990	-376
1769	1,376	5,182	-3,806
1770	1,535	1,012	523
1771	2,140	3,273	-1,133
1772	2,797	2,012	785
1773	2,810	2,069	741
1774	3,977	2,077	1,900
1775	3,186	2,084	1,102
1776	801	2,065	-1,264
1777	3,251	2,033	1,218
1778	2,986	2,145	841
1779	3,142	2,061	1,081
1780	3,216	2,070	1,146
1781	1,519	2,111	-592
1782	3,735	2,058	1,677
1783	4,051	2,073	1,978
1784	5,195	2,133	3,062
1785	4,112	2,318	1,794
1786	4,803	2,340	2,463
1787	4,094	2,661	1,433
1788	4,582	3,118	1,464
1789	6,968	3,467	3,501
1790	3,016	3,322	-306
1791	3,447	3,552	-105
1792	4,037	3,428	609
1793	4,338	4,583	-245
1794	4,101	3,727	374
1795	6,502	3,514	2,988
1796	4,151	3,736	415

Appendix I

Year				
1797		4,392	7,102	-2,710
1798		5,566	5,503	63
1799		7,113	4,114	2,999
1800		7,973	4,036	3,937
1801		7,417	6,379	1,038
1802		12,580	8,125	4,455
1803		11,683	6,571	5,112
1804		10,473	{	{
1805		9,516	{	{
1806		10,377	{	{
1807		13,257	{	{
1808		13,072	{	{
1809		13,559	{	{
1810		{	{	{
1811		{	{	{
1812	Aggregate for periods	{ 71,669	{ 149,642	{ 76,915
1813		{	{	{
1814		{	{	{
1815		15,109	{	{
1816		12,234	{	{
1817		11,024	{	{
1818		15,502	{	{
1819		15,038	{	{
1820		15,727	{	{
1821		20,570	10,056	10,514
1822		18,451	13,126	5,325
1823		19,431	12,378	7,053
1824		21,266	11,152	10,114
1825		22,275	10,971	11,304
1826		18,833	11,845	6,988
1827		18,338	9,660	8,678
1828		20,302	9,792	10,510
1829		21,143	9,546	11,597
1830		23,613	9,763	13,850
1831		21,862	9,971	11,891
1832		21,655	8,723	12,932

1833		23,878	8,280	15,598
1834		25,904	8,082	17,822
1835		27,279	8,363	18,916
1836		24,429	8,849	15,580
1837		28,606	9,644	18,962
1838		22,458	9,200	13,258
1839		20,772	8,778	11,994
1840		21,870	11,784	10,086
1841		22,501	10,049	12,452
1842		23,661	9,972	13,689
1843		20,864	10,474	10,390
1844		22,516	11,720	10,796
1845		25,086	12,432	12,654
1846		26,662	14,074	12,588
1847		27,417	12,894	14,523
1848		26,849	13,498	13,351
1849		25,624	13,597	12,027
1850		25,653	12,898	12,755
1851		26,286	13,655	12,631
1852		28,077	14,373	13,704
1853		{	{	{
1854		{	{	{
1855		{	{	{
1856		{	{	{
1857		{	{	{
1858	Aggregate for periods	{290,569	{163,269	{127,300
1859		{	{	{
1860		{	{	{
1861		{	{	{
1862		{	{	{
1863	Estimated expenditure	28,337	16,000	12,337
1864	”	33,016	19,000	14,016
1865	”	34,184	19,000	15,184
1866	”	33,546	19,000	14,546
		£1549,214	£856,749	£692,465

CUSTOMS REVENUE, 1867-1900[651]

	Revenue
1867	44,356
1868	45,235
1869	43,603
1870	42,944
1871	43,726
1872	42,787
1873	41,679
1874	43,166
1875	42,346
1876	45,806
1877	47,358
1878	47,629
1879	50,319
1880	47,546
1881	50,160
1882	48,536
1883	49,506
1884	51,271
1885	53,221
1886	52,647
1887	50,529
1888	56,272
1889	57,854
1890	58,910
1891	60,434
1892	65,622
1893	66,063
1894	66,927
1895	65,410
1896	66,363
1897	70,869
1898	70,571
1899	72,226
1900	78,252
	£1,840,143

DETAILED CUSTOMS REVENUE, 1867-1900

	Spirits	Tobacco	Tea	Sugar	Beer	Wine	Misc	Allowance	Total
	£	£	£	£	£	£	£	£	£
1867	22,677	9,679	5,909	4,084		1,528	479		44,356
1868	24,993	9,631	4,249	4,242		1,715	405		45,235
1869	24,567	9,520	3,708	3,905		1,429	474		43,603
1870	23,205	9,283	3,888	4,300		1,382	886		42,944
1871	24,299	9,112	4,274	3,857		1,627	557		43,726
1872	23,542	9,069	3,991	4,060		1,676	449		42,787
1873	22,185	9,440	4,012	4,004		1,771	267		41,679
1874	24,427	9,459	4,409	3,032		1,509	330		43,166
1875	26,182	9,022	4,060	378	1,079	1,415	210		42,346
1876	26,782	9,777	4,459		2,922	1,654	212		45,806
1877	27,635	9,892	4,263		3,704	1,562	302		47,358
1878	27,985	9,528	4,667		3,645	1,536	268		47,629
1879	29,646	10,568	4,532		3,693	1,565	315		50,319
1880	27,254	10,074	4,400		3,363	1,425	356	674*	47,546
1881	28,044	10,338	4,551		3,600	1,282	345	2,000	50,160
1882	26,976	10,324	4,373		3,380	1,303	180	2,000	48,536
1883	27,192	10,209	4,690		3,594	1,068	153	2,600	49,506
1884	28,090	10,412	5,023		3,627	1,173	146	2,800	51,271
1885	28,548	11,447	5,019		3,961	1,273	173	2,800	53,221
1886	27,390	11,692	5,160		3,921	1,154	144	3,186	52,647
1887	25,748	11,340	5,109		3,974	1,024	148	3,186	50,529
1888	29,920	11,880	5,541		4,566	1,012	167	3,186	56,272
1889	30,787	12,281	5,288		4,905	1,035	153	3,405	57,854
1890	31,367	12,674	5,168		5,231	948	117	3,405	58,910
1891	32,507	12,531	6,304*		5,143	984	118	2,847*	60,434
1892	35,707	16,411*	6,607		5,303	1,100	111	383*	65,622
1893	32,707	19,680	6,820		5,288	1,072	113	383	66,063
1894	33,758	19,680	6,792		5,289	919	106	383	66,972
1895	32,729	19,680	6,671		4,930	935	82	383	65,410
1896	34,026	18,134	6,193		5,909	1,755*	84	262	66,363
1897	36,785	18,830	6,563		6,156	2,199	336		70,869
1898	35,906	19,312	6,659		6,088	2,272	334		70,571
1899	37,060	19,201	6,755		6,572	2,314	324		72,226
1900	41,695	18,794	7,991		6,463	2,985	324		78,252

*An arrangement since 1879/80 for the allowance for certain goods imported into the Isle of Man on which duty had been paid in Britain was amended by the Common Purse Arrangement in 1890/91 for tea, 1892/93 for tobacco and 1895/96 for wines.

APPENDIX 2

CUSTOMS DUTIES AND ALLOWANCES

	£	s	d	Quantities allowed
1767				
New				
British spirits, a gallon		1.	0	50,000 gallons a year
Rum, a gallon		1.	6	30,000 ″
Bohea (black) tea, a pound		1.	0	20,000 pounds a year
Green tea, a pound		1.	6	5,000 ″
Coffee, a pound		0.	9	5,000 ″
Tobacco, a pound		0.	2	120,000 ″
French wine, a tun (252 gallons)	4.	0.	0	
Other wine, a tun	2.	0.	0	
Coal, a chaldron (36 bushels)		0.	3	
Corn and grain		10%		Ad valorem
Hemp, iron, deal boards and timber from foreign countries		5%		Ad valorem
All other foreign goods		15%		Ad valorem
All other goods, wares or merchandise entitled to drawback, imported from Britain or Ireland		5%		Ad valorem
All goods, wares or merchandise not previously specified, imported from Britain or Ireland		2½%		Ad valorem
1780				
Revisions				
British spirits, a gallon		1.	0	40,000 gallons a year
Rum, a gallon		2.	0	40,000 ″
Black tea, a pound		0.	6	20,000 pounds a year
Green tea, a pound		1.	0	5,000 ″
Coffee, a pound		0.	4	5,000 ″

Tobacco, a pound		0. 3	120,000 pounds a year
French wine, a tun	8.	0. 0	
Other wine, a tun	4.	0. 0	
Hemp, iron, deal boards and timber from foreign countries		10%	Ad valorem

1798
Revisions

Brandy, a gallon		3. 0	10,000 gallons a year
Gin, a gallon		3. 0	10,000 "
Tobacco, a pound		0. 6	60,000 pounds a year
French wine, a tun	16.	0. 0 }	70 tuns a year
Other wine, a tun	12.	0. 0 }	

1805
Revisions

Rum, a gallon		2. 0	60,000 gallons a year
Black tea, a pound		0. 6	50,000 pounds a year
Coffee, a pound		0. 4	6,000 "
French wine, a tun	16.	0. 0 }	110 tuns a year
Other wine, a tun	12.	0. 0 }	

1825
Revisions

Brandy, a gallon		4. 6	10,000 gallons a year
Gin, a gallon		4. 6	10,000 "
Rum, a gallon		3. 0	60,000 "
Coffee, a pound		0. 4	8,000 pounds a year
Tobacco, a pound		1. 6	60,000 "
Muscovado (raw) sugar, a hundred weight (cwt)		1. 0	6,000 cwts a year
Refined sugar		-	400 "

1833
New

Brandy, a gallon	4. 6	10,000 gallons a year
Gin, a gallon	4. 6	10,000 "
Rum, a gallon	3. 0	60,000 "
Black tea, a pound	0. 6	70,000 pounds a year
Green tea, a pound	1. 0	5,000 "
Coffee, a pound	0. 4	8,000 "
Tobacco, a pound	1. 6	60,000 "
Muscovado sugar, a cwt	1. 0	10,000 cwts a year
Refined sugar, a cwt	-	800 "
French wine, a tun	16. 0. 0}	110 tuns a year
Other wine, a tun	12. 0. 0}	
Iron and timber from foreign countries	10%	Ad valorem
All other foreign goods	15%	Ad valorem
All other goods, wares or merchandise entitled to drawback, imported from Britain or Ireland	5%	Ad valorem
All goods, wares or merchandise not previously specified, imported from Britain or Ireland	2½%	Ad valorem

1844
New

Brandy, a gallon	4. 6	20,000 gallons a year
Gin, a gallon	2. 6	20,000 "
Rum, a gallon	1. 6	70,000 "
Tea, a pound	1. 0	
Coffee, a pound	0. 2	
Tobacco, a pound	1. 6	55,000 pounds a year
Cigars, a pound	3. 0	5,000 "
Wine, a tun	12. 0. 0	
Muscovado sugar, a cwt	1. 0	
Refined sugar, a cwt	9. 0	

Timber from foreign countries, a load	8. 0	
Eau de Cologne, a gallon	10. 0	50 gallons a year
Liqueurs, a gallon	10. 0	50 "
All foreign goods not previously specified	free	
All other goods, wares or merchandise entitled to drawback, imported from Britain or Ireland	free	
All goods, wares or merchandise not previously specified, imported from Britain or Ireland	free	

1853
New

Brandy, gin and foreign spirits, a gallon	6. 0	
Rum, a gallon	3. 8	
British or Irish spirits, a gallon	3. 0	
Tea, a pound	1. 0	(0. 6 from July 1854)
Coffee, a pound	0. 2	
Tobacco, unmanufactured, pound	1. 6	
Tobacco, manufactured and cigars, a pound	4. 9	
Wine, a tun	12. 0. 0	
Muscovado sugar, a cwt	1. 0	
Refined sugar, a cwt	8. 0	(3. 0 from July 1854)
Eau de Cologne, a gallon	10. 0	
Liqueurs, cordials and perfumed spirits, a gallon	10. 0	
Corn, a quarter	1. 0	
Meal, a cwt	0. 4½	

1866
Revisions

Brandy, gin and foreign spirits, a gallon	8.	0
Rum, a gallon	6.	0
British or Irish spirits, a gallon	6.	0
Tobacco, unmanufactured, a pound	2.	6
Wine, a gallon	1.	8
Muscovado sugar, a cwt	3.	0
Refined sugar, a cwt	6.	0

1892
Revisions

Tobacco, unmanufactured containing 10% or more of moisture	3.	2
Tobacco, unmanufactured containing less than 10%	3.	6
Tobacco, manufactured:		
Cigars	5.	0
Cavendish or Negrohead	4.	6
Manufactured in bond	4.	0
Other manufactured tobacco	4.	0
Snuff containing more than 10% of moisture	3.	9
Snuff containing not more than 10% of moisture	4.	6

OTHER CUSTOMS DETAILS

1765
Valuations of the Duke of Atholl's full rights in the Isle of Man

1

Customs duties, landed property and manorial rights		249,373
Bishopric and other ecclesiastical benefices		8,400
Regalities		42,000
		£299,773

2

Present customs duties, per annum		6,387	
Land revenue		1,375	
Tithes		317	
Abbey lands		121	
		8,200	
Less:			
Government expenses	(777)		
Perpetual quit rent	(101)	(878)	
		£7,322	
Customs duties, landed property and manorial rights, £7,322 at 40 years purchase			292,880
Bishopric and other ecclesiastical benefices, £3,000 at 14 years purchase			42,000
Regalities			30,000
Estimate for doubling of customs income in future, £6,387 at 40 years purchase			255,480
			£620,360

1835
Licensed goods imported

	Douglas	Castletown	Peel	Ramsey	Officials	Public
Brandy, gallons	5,000	1,500	700	1,000	100	1,700
Gin, gallons	6,000	1,700	900	1,000	200	200
Rum, gallons	34,100	10,940	5,400	8,300	250	1,010
Black tea, pounds	38,880	9,600	4,200	8,220	2,650	6,550
Green tea, pounds	3,660	680	150	450	30	30
Coffee, pounds	4,220	850	300	350	830	1,430
Tobacco, pounds	30,400	16,600	1,500	11,000	0	500
Wine, tuns	51	19	4	11	10	15
Muscovado sugar, cwts	5,685	1,689	614	1,480	187	345
Refined sugar, cwts	301	63	33	67	80	256

1842
Customs return

Receipts			Expenditure		
Import Duties derived from the following sources:			Payments for services connected with the collection of the revenue:		
British Manufactured Goods	1,571		Customs Establishment	1,824	
Foreign Licence Goods	20,626		Incidental Charges	1,198	3,022
Foreign Ad Valorem Goods	1,023		Superannuation to officers formerly in the service and pensions to widows	940	
			Over-entries and duties returned	43	983
			Salaries to officers on Civil List	4,473	
			Fine Fund	473	
			Constabulary Force	565	
			Attorney General's Prosecution Expenses	57	
			Expenses incurred for census of the Island	172	6,010
			Balance to Receiver General of Her Majesty's Customs		13,205
	£23,220				£23,220

1843 and 1845
Last full year under 1833 Act and first under 1844 Act

	1843		1845	
	£	Quantity	£	Quantity
British Ad Valorem Goods	1,655			
Foreign Goods				
Brandy, gallons	2,318	10,304	4,428	19,681
Gin, gallons	2,205	9,801	2,400	19,195
Rum, gallons	6,164	41,094	4,613	61,510
Tea, pounds	2,518	95,999	5,596	111,926
Coffee, pounds	126	7,435	494	59,205
Tobacco, pounds	3,559	47,451	4,427	56,973
Muscovado sugar, cwt	446	8,925	650	13,002
Refined sugar, cwt	32	842	411	915
Wine, tuns	918	221	1,280	106
Liqueurs, gallons	8	34	5	10
Eau de Cologne, gallons	11	50	34	67
Others			740	
	18,305			
Foreign Ad Valorem Goods	867			
TOTAL	£20,827		£25,078	

Appendix 3

Robert Fargher

Robert Fargher was born in the parish of Maughold in 1803.[652] At the age of fourteen he left the Isle of Man and went to London where he was employed as a private secretary. Three years later he returned to the Island and was apprenticed as a printer in the offices of the *Manks Advertiser*. Soon after starting his apprenticeship, Robert was converted to Christianity at a revivalist meeting, and began at once to seek the salvation of others by conducting impromptu dinner-hour services for his fellow workmen. The *Advertiser* had a very strong conservative, church and state bias.

As Robert Fargher grew older, his views became those of an advanced radical. In 1833, in partnership with William Walls, he launched the progressive newspaper the *Mona's Herald*. They designed it to be the mouthpiece of political reform, nonconformity and temperance. From that moment may be dated the beginnings of the nineteenth century reform movements. There is no doubt that the continuous existence of a reform newspaper, to contend strenuously in debate with the powerful conservative *Manx Sun* was fundamental in supporting and keeping alive the political movement. Fargher persistently and vigorously campaigned in his newspaper for the House of Keys to be open to the press and public, and that its members should be chosen, not by the Governor from nominees of the other members of the House, but by the vote of the people. Fargher soon discovered in the Island men with the same opinions and fervour as himself. They saw the opposition to reform coming from the 'clique': Members of the House of Keys, landowners and a few rich merchants. It is not surprising, therefore, that Fargher made enemies amongst those he denounced. One of the ablest, as well as one of the bitterest, was George William Dumbell.

Robert Fargher did not live to see the fulfilment of his dream of a freely elected House of Keys. Blind and enfeebled, he died in August 1863 at the age of sixty, three years before the self-elected House voted itself out of existence. There is an irony in the fact that his chief antagonist, George William Dumbell, was one of the three members elected to represent Douglas when the first general election was held in April 1867.

Appendix 4

John Courtney Bluett

John Courtney Bluett was born in London in 1793.[653] He entered the Royal Navy as a boy in 1807 and left as a Lieutenant in 1815 on a half-pay pension of £90 per annum. This amount was reduced annually by £30 to pay off debts incurred during his time in the navy. This early problem of living beyond his means was to be a constant anxiety to him throughout his life.

In 1820 Bluett came to the Isle of Man with a friend who had helped to pay off some of his outstanding debts. This move was possibly to escape his creditors and enjoy the Island's low cost of living, but may also have been to escape the consequences of breaking off his engagement to Janetta Caroline Ritchie, a ward. A year later he married Sophia White. Miss Ritchie and her guardian came to the Island to file a suit of breach of promise. Bluett took the unusual step of pleading his own case, and succeeded in clearing his name, though Miss Ritchie obtained £50 damages. Certainly the case provided a shattering beginning to Bluett's early life in the Isle of Man. His court appeal, however, not only put right much of the damage to his purse and character, but also showed him the way to a future career in law.

In 1823 Bluett was articled to John Llewellyn, Secretary to the House of Keys, and was eventually called to the Manx Bar in 1825. He practised as an advocate, first in partnership and then on his own. In 1832 he was appointed Vicar General by the Bishop of Sodor and Man. In 1837 he was admitted to Grays Inn to study for the English Bar. After the death of his first wife in 1839 Bluett married his second wife Mary Wilson in 1843 and had another four children. So, as a twice married man with a large family and ambitions in the legal world, he was constantly worried that bankruptcy would result in great loss both financially and by way of reputation. He held a deep religious conviction about his responsibilities. Bluett's law business increased steadily with a reasonable, if erratic, flow of legal work, but there was often considerable delay between completion of work and receiving payment. In 1851 he was appointed High Bailiff of Douglas and Registrar of Deeds. The condition that he had to give up his private legal practice was perhaps something of a relief, particularly in view of his failing health. He reckoned that the salaries from the two offices of about £250 a year, plus his navy half-pay pension, would be insufficient to maintain his family, so he had to additionally rely on the collection of book debts and fees from the general office business. In May 1852 he was also appointed Seneschal, the collector of the Crown rents. In 1855 he unsuccessfully applied for the vacancy created by Deemster Heywood's resignation. Bluett was greatly disappointed, and did not rise from this low point, dying in August 1855.

Appendix 5

Sir William Hillary

William Hillary came from very humble beginnings.[654] Born into a Quaker family in Birkrigg in Wensleydale in 1771, his talents led him to the diplomatic service in London where he became equerry to Prince Augustus Frederick, sixth son and ninth child of George III. In 1799, shortly after leaving the service of Augustus, Hillary met Frances Elizabeth Disney Ffytche, an heiress from Danbury Place in Essex. Frances' father objected to the resultant romance, so the lovers eloped and were married in London. Family reconciliation was brought about, but Frances' father arranged the family estate in such a way as to protect its wealth from Hillary.

The war with France was at its blackest in the early 1800s, with the invasion of England seemingly imminent. Hillary formed the biggest private army in the country, and for his war efforts, he was made a Baronet in 1805.

In 1808 Hillary and Frances parted, and he moved to the Isle of Man with its many compensations. At this time Manx law provided only for debts contracted within the Island, all others were unenforceable. The low cost of living meant that residents with private incomes could live an enhanced lifestyle. Hillary met Amelia Tobin who he married in Scotland in 1818 after obtaining a divorce from Frances under the Scottish mutual consent divorce law.

During 1822 two incidents off the east coast of the Island involving the rescue of crews from the vessels *Vigilant* and *Racehorse* made an impression on Hillary. The lack of organised volunteer lifeboat crews and the ad hoc award of pensions or financial rewards to the bereaved concerned him. In 1824, due to his efforts, the National Institution for the Preservation of Life from Shipwreck (later the Royal National Lifeboat Institution) was formed.

Hillary slowly prospered, but in order to protect what he had, he arranged for his wealth to be secretly held in trust by Sarah St John, a friend of the family. During the mid-1830s Hillary entered into a number of ventures to fund his high spending lifestyle. He became a shareholder in the new Isle of Man Joint Stock Bank and formed a land development scheme which was funded by a tontine and a lottery. He had interests in mining operations in the Island and England. In 1839 things began to go wrong. Conspiracy and fraud by others involved in the lottery and rising problems with the Joint Stock Bank meant that he had to act. Hillary's mining shares were sold but did not realise enough to satisfy his debts. He lost the presidency of the Laxey and Lonan mines. His estate, including his home the Fort Anne, was arrested and sold. Ill and weak, Sir William Hillary died in January 1847.

Appendix 6

Sir John Bowring

John Bowring was born in Exeter in 1792.[655] After entering his father's wool business as a clerk and then working in a counting house, he set up business on his own, travelling abroad for commercial purposes. He was multilingual, which served him well in his business. His writing skills led him to become the editor of the *Westminster Review* in 1824.

In 1828 Bowring was appointed a commissioner for reforming the system of keeping the public accounts and was consequently appointed to examine the accounts of other countries. Amongst the many awards he received was an honorary doctorate in 1829.

Dr Bowring became a Member of Parliament for Clyde in 1835 and then Bolton in 1841. As well as a traveller, author and politician, he was also a reformer, being a supporter of Richard Cobden, the joint founder of the Anti-Corn Law League. Interestingly, he favoured conversion to decimal coinage and was responsible for the introduction of the florin (a coin worth one tenth of a pound) in 1849.

On resigning from Parliament, Bowring became involved in events in the East, and was appointed Consul in Canton and then Governor of Hong Kong. He was knighted in 1854 and died in 1872.

APPENDIX 7

Henry Brougham Loch, first Baron Loch of Drylaw

Henry Brougham Loch was born in 1827 in Midlothian.[656] As a child, he was for several years an invalid.

Fully recovered, Loch joined the Royal Navy as a midshipman at the age of thirteen in 1840 but left in 1842. After studying at an officers school, he then went into the army in 1844. He joined the 9th Light Cavalry in India and was gazetted to the East India Company's 3rd Bengal Light Cavalry. Though only seventeen, he was chosen by Lord Gough as his aide-de-camp in 1845 and then became Adjutant and second-in-command of the famous Skinner's Irregular Cavalry Regiment in 1849. He was sent to Bulgaria in 1854 to help organise the Turkish Irregular Cavalry to fight the Russians in the Crimean War. Captain Loch became attaché to James Bruce, eighth Earl of Elgin, on a diplomatic and military mission to China in 1857. He was involved in the signing of the Treaty of Tiensin in 1858. After this success, Lord Elgin and Loch moved on to Japan to conclude the Treaty of Yedo. In 1860 the failure to obtain ratification of the Treaty of Tiensin led to another diplomatic and military mission returning to China to re-negotiate. Loch and Harry Parkes, the British Commissioner, rode behind the Chinese lines under a flag of truce, but they were taken prisoner and tortured. They were able to escape their captors just before the arrival of a death warrant signed by the Emperor ordering their beheading. The Treaty of Tiensin was ratified, and Loch was again entrusted to return to England with the new treaty as well as the Convention of Pekin.

Loch resigned from the army in 1861 and became Private Secretary to the British Home Secretary, Sir George Grey. Shortly after his marriage to Elizabeth Villiers, Henry Loch was appointed Governor of the Isle of Man in 1863. He was knighted in 1880.

Loch's aim to secure even higher colonial office was soon to take him away from the Isle of Man. In 1882 he was appointed Commissioner of Woods and Forests. In 1884 he was appointed Governor of Victoria in Australia where he became very popular and well respected in this mainly ceremonial position. In 1889 he was offered the posts of Governor of Cape Colony and High Commissioner for South Africa. His time in Africa was difficult. He had conflicts with both Cecil Rhodes, Prime Minister of the Cape, and President Kruger of the Transvaal.

Loch returned to England in 1895 and was raised to the peerage but took little part in politics, voting with the Liberal Unionists. He died in 1900.

Appendix 8

James Brown

James Brown was born in 1815, the younger son of Cato Brown (previously James Cato, chief boatswain on Nelson's *Victory*, Liverpool foundry worker and possibly of African slave descent).[657] James Brown served an apprenticeship as a printer's compositor with George Woods of Princes Street in Liverpool, and then worked for the *Liverpool Mercury* and other local newspapers. He married Eleanor McKenzie, daughter of Menzie McKenzie, a Scottish master-mason who had worked on the Castle Mona, the family seat in the Island of the Duke of Atholl. Eleanor's mother was a Manx woman named Anne Curphy.

It was in the 1840s that an offshore publishing industry flourished briefly in the Isle of Man, where, apart from the radical press being out of the direct reach of British authorities, there was no stamp duty on newspapers, no duty on the paper on which they were printed and no tax on the advertisements which sustained them. More remarkably, newspapers published and printed in the Island could be sent post-free to Britain and the colonies. In 1846 Brown came to the Island with his Manx wife and five-year old son and worked as a printer on the *National Reformer and Manx Weekly Review of Home and Foreign Affairs*. In 1847 the paper closed, but a Manx relation of Brown's wife raised £30 to set him up in Douglas as a jobbing printer. He also worked for William Shirreffs who was one of the most prolific producers of journals for free-post distribution from the Isle of Man. Shirreffs started a local newspaper, the *Isle of Man Times*, in which he advocated Manx reform. Amongst his targets was the House of Keys, the unelected self-perpetuating oligarchy. Shirreffs' enterprises collapsed following an 1848 Act of Parliament whereby all posted journals which were not genuine local newspapers had to pay the full rate of 4d.

James Brown remained in Douglas and survived precariously, with his son having to leave school and learn the printing trade with him. By 1855 Brown was running a give-away advertising circular which had some editorial content. In 1861 this circular became a newspaper with the revived title of the *Isle of Man Times*, and Brown immediately nailed to his masthead the radicalism which he learnt from his association with Shirreffs and others:

> Many reforms are needed in the . . . legislature and government of this Island and we shall most strenuously urge these reforms upon the highest officials, as well as on the Source of all Power - people themselves.

APPENDIX 9

ELECTION OF THE HOUSE OF KEYS, 1867[658]

	Dates	Constituency
Resigned		
Edward Moore GAWNE	1829-66	
Previous self-elected, not returned by popular election		
Alexander SPITTALL	1846-67	
Richard QUIRK	1847-67	
John George BENNETT	1851-67	
Patrick Taubman CUNNINGHAM	1853-67	
Philip KILLEY	1854-67	
Ridgway HARRISON	1856-67	
William HARRISON	1856-67	
Edward FAULDER	1858-67	
Robert Thomas QUAYLE	1863-67	
Charles Hamilton Edward COWLE	1864-67	
Previous self-elected, returned by popular election		
William CALLISTER	1849-69	Ayre
Edward Curphey FARRANT	1852-74	Ayre
John Frissell CRELLIN	1843-69	Michael
Evan GELL	1844-74	Michael
William HASLAM	1858-71	Garff
John GELL	1854-68	Glenfaba
John Caesar Tobin HARRISON	1865-69	Middle
Thomas MOORE	1864-74	Rushen
William Fine MOORE	1858-74	Douglas
John Senhouse GOLDIE-TAUBMAN	1859-97	Douglas
John Moore JEFFCOTT	1855-67	Castletown
Robert John MOORE	1850-80	Peel
Reverend William Bell CHRISTIAN	1865-83	Ramsey

New members, returned by popular election

John Teare MARTIN	1867-74	Ayre
Thomas CRAINE	1867-78	Michael
John Edward CHRISTIAN	1867-68	Garff
Richard ROWE	1867-86	Garff
William Edward Stevenson MOORE	1867-69	Glenfaba
John Stevenson MOORE	1867-74	Glenfaba
Mark Wilks GOLDIE	1867-72	Middle
William DALRYMPLE	1867-89	Middle
Henry John WATTERSON	1867-91	Rushen
William Baring WOODS	1867-91	Rushen
George William DUMBELL	1867-80	Douglas

Appendix 10

Sir Spencer Walpole

Spencer Walpole came from political stock.[659] On his father's side he was descended from Sir Robert Walpole, Britain's first Prime Minister, and his father, Sir Spencer Walpole, was Home Secretary on three occasions. His mother, Isabella Perceval, was the daughter of Prime Minister Spencer Perceval. Born in 1839, Walpole went to Eton, but did not attend university as his father, a qualified lawyer who had given up a lucrative practice to go into politics, could not afford the fees.

Walpole went to work at the War Office. When his father became Home Secretary, he appointed Spencer as his private secretary. He became an inspector of fisheries for England and Wales in 1867. The same year he married Marion, the daughter of Sir John Digby Murray. Walpole was also a writer and historian, producing a number of scholarly works. In the late 1870s, a Tory sympathiser by birth, he found himself in disagreement with Disraeli's foreign policy, and drifted into the Whig-Liberal camp.

Walpole's appointment as Governor of the Isle of Man gave the Island the benefit of an experienced civil servant, a renowned academic and a liberal in politics and outlook. In 1893 he wrote his history of the Isle of Man, *Land of Home Rule*, the same year he resigned as Governor to take up the appointment as Secretary to the Post Office. He was knighted in 1898. Walpole retired the following year to continue his writing up until his sudden death in 1907.

Appendix II

Sir West Ridgeway

Joseph West Ridgeway was born in 1844, the son of an Essex vicar, and went to school in London.[660] He left school at sixteen and obtained a commission in the Bengal Infantry, spending the next twenty-six years of his life in India. He married Caroline Berwicke in 1881. In 1884 he became involved in the boundary dispute between Britain and Russia over the north-west frontier of Afghanistan. He was knighted in 1886. Ridgeway then accepted the position of Under Secretary for Ireland, and became a member of the Irish Privy Council in 1889.

Ridgeway was appointed Governor of the Isle of Man in 1893. His brief but influential time as Governor of the Island came to an end in 1895 when he was appointed Governor of Ceylon, a position he held until 1903. After a failed attempt to stand as a Liberal Member of Parliament in 1906, he was appointed chairman of a committee which went to Africa to consider the constitutions to be granted to the former Boer republics of Transvaal and the Orange Free State. In 1910, having again stood unsuccessfully for Parliament, Ridgeway became president of the British North Borneo Company. He died in 1930.

Reference Notes

1. Throughout this book, the terms 'Isle of Man' and 'Island' are deemed synonymous. The Manx Gaelic name for the Isle of Man is *Ellan Vannin*.
2. *Isle of Man*, Isle of Man Government Treasury, (Douglas, 1995). *Isle of Man, Sheet 95, Landranger Series*, Ordnance Survey, (Southampton, 2002).
3. *Isle of Man Census 2006*, Isle of Man Government Treasury, (Douglas, 2007).
4. The derivation of the term 'Tynwald' is from the Scandinavian *thing-völlr* (assembly field).
5. The derivation of the term 'Keys' is uncertain, variously thought to be from the Scandinavian *keise* (chosen), part of the Manx Gaelic *kiare-as-feed* (twenty-four) or from the figurative meaning of the English 'key' (providing an explanation or interpretation).
6. The derivation of the term 'Sodor' is from the Scandinavian *Sudreyjar* (the Sudreys or Southern Isles, which included the Hebrides and the Isle of Man). The diocese of Sodor and Man now consists only of the Isle of Man.
7. The derivation of the term 'Deemster' is thought to be from the Scandinavian *dómr* (opinion, judgment).
8. Throughout this book, the terms 'the United Kingdom of Great Britain and Northern Ireland', 'the United Kingdom' and 'Britain' are deemed synonymous. To maintain continuity, 'Britain' and 'British' are used throughout except when other terms are featured in direct quotes.
9. Alan Milner, editor-in-chief, *The Manx Law Reports, 1522-1920*, (Oxford, 2004), 'The Estate of the Earl of Derby, 1522', pp. 1-2, 'The Isle of Man Case (Derby Succession), 1598', pp. 2-4, and 'Bishop of Sodor and Man v Derby, 1751', pp. 11-27.
10. Throughout this book, the term 'Governor' also refers to the positions of the Governor and Commander in Chief (up to 1765), Governor in Chief and Captain General (1765-1830) and Lieutenant Governor (1830 onwards).
11. George Broderick, translator, *Cronica Regum Mannie et Insularum: Chronicles of the Kings of Man and the Isles*, (Douglas, 1979), ff. 32-3. In Manx folklore Godred Crovan is known as King Orry.
12. *Statutes of the Isle of Man*, volume 1, 'Customary Laws', 1422, p. 11.
13. Sir John Stanley (c.1350-1414), Lord of Man 1405-14.
14. *Act of Parliament*, 5 George III, chapter 26. Letters Patent, Latin text with translation, undated but probably 6 April 1406, Manx National Heritage Library and Archives (MNHL), Atholl Papers (AP) 09707/X40-4.
15. James Stanley, seventh Earl of Derby, 'History and Antiquities of the Isle of Man', in Reverend William Mackenzie, editor, *The Manx Society*, volume 3, (Douglas, 1860), p. 20.
16. Thomas Stanley (c.1406-59), Lord of Man 1437-59, first Baron Stanley 1456-59.
17. Thomas Stanley (c.1433-1504), Lord of Man 1459-1504, first Earl of Derby 1485-1504.
18. William Blundell, 'A History of the Isle of Man, (1648-56)', in William Harrison, editor, *The Manx Society*, volume 25, (Douglas, 1876), pp. 56-8.
19. James Chaloner, 'A Short Treatise of the Isle of Man', in Daniel King, *The Vale-Royal of England*, (London, 1656), pp. 6-7.
20. William Sacheverell, 'An Account of the Isle of Man', (c.1692), in Reverend J. G. Cumming, editor, *The Manx Society*, volume 1, (Douglas, 1859), p. 13.

21. Blundell, 'A History of the Isle of Man', p. 52.
22. Sacheverell, 'An Account of the Isle of Man', p. 14.
23. *Statutes of the Isle of Man*, volume 1, 'Customary Laws', 1577, p. 51. Moore, *A History*, pp. 876-7.
24. *Statutes of the Isle of Man*, volume 1, 'Customary Laws', 1582, p. 58.
25. Ferdinando Stanley (c.1559-94), fifth Earl of Derby and Lord of Man 1593-4. *Statutes of the Isle of Man*, volume 1, 'Customary Laws', 1593, p. 62.
26. *Statutes of the Isle of Man*, volume 1, 'Ordinances', 1636, p. 83.
27. *Statutes of the Isle of Man*, volume 1, 'A Book of the Spiritual Lawes and Customes', pp. 41-4.
28. J. R. Oliver, 'A Collection of National Documents Relating to the Isle of Man: Respecting Concessions to the People and Subjects of the Isle of Man', in J. R. Oliver, editor, *Manx Society*, volume 9, (Douglas, 1863), pp. 121-5. *Statutes of the Isle of Man*, volume 1, 'Customary Lands', 1645, p. 100.
29. *Statutes of the Isle of Man*, volume 1, 'Customary Laws', 1609, pp. 70-1.
30. *Statutes of the Isle of Man*, volume 1, 'Customary Laws', 1417, p. 5.
31. *Statutes of the Isle of Man*, volume 1, 'Customs Duties', 1577, p. 38. A 'maze' or 'mease' was a barrel measure of many hundreds.
32. *Statutes of the Isle of Man*, volume 1, 'Herring Fishery', 1610, p. 76. A 'kybbon' (Manx Gaelic: *kishan*) was a basket measure.
33. *Statutes of the Isle of Man*, volume 1, 'A Book of the Spiritual Lawes and Customes', p. 44.
34. Lady Elizabeth, Countess of Derby (1575-1627); William Stanley (1561-1642), sixth Earl of Derby and Lord of Man 1610-27. *Statutes of the Isle of Man*, volume 1, 'Herring Fishery', 1613, p. 79.
35. *Statutes of the Isle of Man*, volume 1, 'Regulations for the Castles, &c, and Ordinances &c', 1561, p. 34.
36. Blundell, 'A History of the Isle of Man', pp. 68-83.
37. *Statutes of the Isle of Man*, volume 1, 'Customary Laws', 1609, pp. 70-1.
38. An 'ob' was a halfpenny (½d) and a 'qs' was a farthing (¼d).
39. *Statutes of the Isle of Man*, volume 1, 'Customary Laws', 1523, pp. 27-8, 'Customs Duties', 1577, pp. 37-9, and 'Statute Laws, Book of Rates of 1692 confirmed by Keys', 1737, pp. 223-32.
40. Chaloner, 'A Short Treatise of the Isle of Man', pp. 52-3.
41. Ann Harrison, 'Economic Opportunities, 1700', in A. M. Cubbon and Ann M. Harrison, editors, *Journal of the Manx Museum (JMM)*, volume 7, number 83, (Douglas, 1967), pp. 81-2.
42. J. R. Dickinson, *The Lordship of Man Under the Stanleys: Government and Economy in the Isle of Man, 1580-1704*, (Preston, 1997), pp. 367-70.
43. James Stanley (1607-51), seventh Earl of Derby and Lord of Man 1627-51. James Stanley, 'History and Antiquities', p. 23.
44. James Chaloner (1603-60), Governor of the Isle of Man 1658-60. Chaloner, 'A Short Treatise of the Isle of Man', p. 30.
45. *Acts of Parliament*, 3 Charles II (1651), chapter 22; 12 Charles II (1660), chapter 18; 15 Charles II (1663), chapter 7; 22 and 23 Charles II (1670), chapter 26; 25 Charles II (1672), chapter 7.
46. J. K. Qualtrough and W. J. Scatchard, *That Island*, (Douglas, 1965), p. 8.
47. H. A. Bullock, *History of the Isle of Man*, (London, 1816), pp. 190-1.
48. Earl of Derby's case, 12 April 1692, MNHL, Derby Papers 01719/3/1-2.
49. William Stanley (1655-1702), ninth Earl of Derby and Lord of Man 1672-1702.
50. Earl of Derby's case, 12 April 1692, MNHL, Derby Papers 01719/3/1-2.

Reference Notes

51. William Sacheverell (c.1665-1715), Governor of the Isle of Man 1693-1696. Order from Governor Sacheverell, retrospectively authorising a Customs Office under Deemster Parr at Castle Rushen, 5 April 1694, MNHL, Civil Records, *Libri Irrotulamentorum* 09864.
52. A. W. Moore, *A History of the Isle of Man*, (two volumes, London, 1900, reprinted Douglas, 1977), p. 816.
53. *Statutes of the Isle of Man*, volume 1, 'Statute Laws, Book of Rates of 1692 confirmed by Keys', 1737, pp. 212-32. *The Report of the Commissioners of Inquiry for the Isle of Man, 1792*, (London, 1805), appendix A, number 3.
54. Colonel Nicholas Sankey, Governor of the Isle of Man 1696-1701. Earl to Governor Sankey, 3 February 1700, MNHL, Civil Records, *Libri Scaccarii* 10071.
55. Moore, *A History*, pp. 431-2.
56. *Statutes of the Isle of Man*, volume 1, 'Customary Laws', 1422, p. 9, 'Customary Laws', 1429, p. 22, and 'An Act Against Non-residence', 1697, pp. 153-5.
57. James Stanley (1664-1736), tenth Earl of Derby and Lord of Man 1702-36. Moore, *A History*, pp. 887-91.
58. Thomas Wilson (1663-1755), Bishop of Sodor and Man 1697-1755. *Statutes of the Isle of Man*, volume 1, 'Act of Settlement', 1704, pp. 161-76.
59. Kenneth Morgan, 'Mercantilism and the British empire, 1688-1815', in Donald Winch and Patrick K. O'Brien, editors, *The Political Economy of British Historical Experience, 1688-1914*, (Oxford, 2002), pp. 165-72.
60. *Act of Parliament*, 6 Anne, chapter 3.
61. Joseph Train, *An Historical and Statistical Account of the Isle of Man*, (two volumes, Douglas, 1845), volume 2, p. 308.
62. *Statutes of the Isle of Man*, volume 1, 'Customs Act, Preventing Frauds in Her Majesty's Customes by the Exportation of forraigne Goods from this Island', 1711, pp. 187-9.
63. *Statutes of the Isle of Man*, volume 1, 'Customs Act', 1714, pp. 196-7.
64. R. C. Jarvis, *Manx Smuggling in the Eighteenth Century*, (Board of Customs, 1955/56), pp. 5-6.
65. Train, *Historical and Statistical Account*, p. 307.
66. Copy lease, 9 February 1721, MNHL, AP 09707/60(2nd)-12. Governor Murray to the second Duke of Atholl, 5 May 1736, MNHL, AP 09707/X9-12.
67. Sir Robert Walpole (1676-1745), first Earl of Orford, Member of Parliament (MP) 1701, Prime Minister 1721-42.
68. *Act of Parliament*, 7 George I, statute 1, chapter 21.
69. *Act of Parliament*, 12 George I, chapter 28.
70. Maurice Wright, *Treasury Control of the Civil Service*, (London, 1969), p. 1.
71. James Murray (1690-1764), second Duke of Atholl 1724-64, Lord of Man 1736-64.
72. William Harrison, 'Records of the Tynwald and St John's Chapel in the Isle of Man', *The Manx Society*, volume 19, (Douglas, 1871), pp. 100-10.
73. 'Sheadings' are the six subdivisions of the Isle of Man: Ayre, Michael, Garff, Glenfaba, Middle and Rushen, and the derivation of the term is thought to be from the Scandinavian *séttungr* (sixth part).
74. James Murray, Governor of the Isle of Man 1736-44.
75. Captain Webber, 'An Impartial Enquiry, c.1760', in G. W. Wood, *An Account of Manx Smuggling*, (Douglas, c.1917), p. 7.
76. Patrick Lindesay, Governor of the Isle of Man 1744-51. The Duke to Governor Lindesay, draft letter, 27 April 1745, MNHL, AP 09707/XII-21.

77. *Statutes of the Isle of Man*, volume 1, 'Statute Laws, Book of Rates of 1692 confirmed by Keys', 1737, pp. 212-32.
78. Train, *Historical and Statistical Account*, p. 239.
79. Webber, 'An Impartial Enquiry', pp. 7-10. Charles Lutwidge to Treasury, 1 July 1764, British National Archives (NA), T 1/434/67.
80. G. Waldron, *The History and Description of the Isle of Man*, (London, 1744), p. 16.
81. Reports, 28 and 30 June and 14 and 18 July 1750, NA, Treasury Papers (T) 1/342/96-8. Deemsters Daniel Mylrea and John Taubman and other officials to the Duke, 7 July 1750, and Deemster Mylrea to Governor Lindesay, 18 August 1750, MNHL, AP 0970/X19-9 and 10.
82. Statement by James Moss to Deemsters Daniel Mylrea and John Taubman, 28 April 1744, and Comptroller John Quayle to the Duke, 30 April 1744, MNHL, AP 09707/X73-19 and 54-18.
83. Customs in Edinburgh to Treasury, 7 June 1764, MNHL, AP 09707/40(B)-6. Malachy Postlethwayt, *The Universal Dictionary of Trade and Commerce*, (two volumes, London, 1751 and 1755), volume 2, p. 126. Malachy Postlethwayt (c.1707-67), economic theorist and writer, is described in the *Dictionary of National Biography*, volume 46, p. 205, as having 'freely plagiarised other writers and presented his results without method or conciseness'.
84. Chris Pickard, 'Eighteenth Century Manx Merchantmen and Privateers', in Joyce Warham, editor, *Proceedings of the Isle of Man Natural History and Antiquarian Society* (*IOMNHAS*), volume 9, number 4, (Douglas, 1980-89), pp. 509-11.
85. Sir George Moore (1709-87), Member of the House of Keys 1755-1780, Chairman 1758-80, Knighted 1781.
86. Frances Wilkins, *George Moore and Friends: Letters from a Manx Merchant (1750-1760)*, (Kidderminster, 1994), introduction.
87. *Commissioners of Inquiry*, appendix B, numbers 89 and 90. Moore, *A History*, p. 646.
88. Sophia Morrison, editor, *Mannin: a Journal of Matters Past and Present relating to Mann*, volume 6 (Douglas, 1914), p. 322.
89. Northside sales, Patrick, 1750 deeds, MNHL, Mortgage and Deeds series 09494. Moore to Pat Lindesay, Edinburgh, 7 October 1751, MNHL, George Moore Letter Books (GML) 00501C.
90. Moore to John Onge, Dublin, 9 October 1750, MNHL, GML 00501C.
91. *Peel City Guardian and Chronicle*, 28 September 1901, 'Manx Annals of Ninety Years Ago', chapter 2.
92. Moore to John Onge, Dublin, 9 October 1750, MNHL, GML 00501C.
93. David Craine, 'A Manx Merchant of the Eighteenth Century', in W. Walter Gill and Ramsey B. Moore, editors, *IOMNHAS*, volume 4, number 4, (Douglas 1945), p. 652.
94. Ibid., pp. 646 and 652.
95. Wilkins, *George Moore and Friends*, p. 3.
96. Moore to Pat Montgomerie, *Lilly*, 22 January and 11 February 1751, and Walter Logan, Boston, 21 March 1751, MNHL, GML 00501C.
97. Moore to Pat Montgomerie, *Peggy*, 12 March 1751, MNHL, GML 00501C.
98. Moore to Messrs Green, Stanton & Ford, Barcelona, 27 December 1751 and 27 January 1752, and John Blundell, Alicante, 27 January 1752, MNHL, GML 00501C.
99. Moore to Henry Atkins, Boston, 21 April 1752, MNHL, GML 00501C.
100. Moore to Robert Montgomerie, *Lilly*, 11 April 1752, and James & George Peirsy, Cork, 20 July 1752, MNHL, GML 00501C.

Reference Notes

101. Moore to William Snell & Co, London, 13 and 29 August 1752, MNHL, GML 00501C.
102. Governor Cochrane to Duke, 23 January 1758, MNHL, AP 09707/X14-18.
103. Basil Cochrane, Governor of the Isle of Man 1751-61.
104. Moore to Collector, 26 January 1759, MNHL, AP 09707/ X46-10
105. Craine, 'A Manx Merchant of the Eighteenth Century', pp. 645 and 650.
106. Wilkins, *George Moore and Friends*, p. 150.
107. Frances Wilkins, *The Isle of Man in Smuggling History*, (Kidderminster, 1992), pp. 60 and 72-4.
108. Moore to Peter Berail, Cette, 29 March and 14 November 1758, MNHL, GML 00501C.
109. Craine, 'A Manx Merchant of the Eighteenth Century', pp. 653-4. A 'letter of marque' (licence) was granted by a state to a citizen to use a 'privateer' (private vessel) to seize merchant vessels from other nations at time of war.
110. Reverend Weeden Butler, *Memoirs of Mark Hildesley, Lord Bishop of Sodor and Man*, (London, 1799), p. 389. C. Roeder, editor, *Manx Notes and Queries: With an Account of François Thurot*, (Douglas, 1904). G. V. C. Young and Caroline Foster, *Captain François Thurot*, (Peel, 1986).
111. A. W. Moore, editor, *Manx Ballads and Music*, (Douglas, 1896), p. xviii.
112. Moore to Sir John Stewart, Grandtully, 17 March 1760, MNHL, GML 00501C.
113. Moore to Pat Montgomerie, *Peggy*, 4 November 1754, MNHL, GML 00501C.
114. William J. Ashworth, *Customs and Excise: Trade, production and consumption in England, 1640-1845*, (Oxford, 2003), p. 319.
115. Exchange of correspondence between the second Duke and Treasury, 22 and 27 November 1754, 23 March 1759, 30 April 1759 and 21 November 1761, MNHL, AP 09707/X73-11, X73-8, X8-18, X8-28 and book 105. The third Duke to Treasury, 20 August 1764, MNHL, AP 09707/book 91.
116. Milner, *The Manx Law Reports*, 'Bishop of Sodor and Man v Derby, 1751', pp. 11-27.
117. *Gentlemen's Magazine*, March 1751, p. 136.
118. Throughout this book, customs statistics are abstracted from appendix I other than when quoted from primary sources. £6 British being £7 Manx.
119. Throughout this book, comparative valuation figures are abstracted from *Composite Price Index, 1750-2003*, Office for National Statistics, (London, 2004).
120. The Duke to Cochrane, 8 February 1752 and 1 February 1755, MNHL, AP 09707/X7-3 and X27-17.
121. *Act of Parliament*, 5 George III, chapter 26.
122. Lady Charlotte (1731-1805), Baroness Strange, third Duchess of Atholl.
123. John Murray (1729-74), third Duke of Atholl 1764-74, Lord of Man 1764-5.
124. Petition from the Duke and Duchess, 8 January 1764, NA, T 1/430/95.
125. Customs reports, 5 July 1758 and February to March 1759, NA, T 1/388/104 and 1/392/16-20. Postlethwayt, *Universal Dictionary*, volume 2, p. 126. Webber, 'An Impartial Enquiry', p. 11.
126. Charles Lutwidge to Treasury, 1 July 1764, NA, T 1/434/67. Attorney General and Surveyor General's report, 6 August 1764, NA, Privy Council Papers (PC) 1/7/105. Customs reports, February to December 1764, MNHL, AP 09707/40(B)-1-25.
127. An 'anker' was a variable measure of wine and spirits.
128. B. R. Mitchell, *Abstract of British Historical Statistics*, (London, 1962), p. 388.
129. *Commissioners of Inquiry*, appendix B, numbers 89 and 90. Moore, *A History*, p. 646. J. Steven Watson, *The Reign of George III, 1760-1815*, (Oxford, 1960), p. 10.

130. Watson, *The Reign of George III*, p. 5.
131. George Grenville (1712-70), MP 1741, Prime Minister 1763-65.
132. Treasury to House of Commons, 18 April 1764, MNHL, AP 09707/42(B)-1.
133. Duke to Comptroller John Quayle for transmission to merchants, papers relating to the sale of the Isle of Man, 18 July and 1 August 1764, MNHL, 00576C.
134. Treasury to the Duke, 25 July 1764, NA, T 1/434/69.
135. Spencer Walpole, *Land of Home Rule: An Essay on the History and Constitution of the Isle of Man*, (London, 1893), p. 215.
136. Order in Council, 17 August 1764, MNHL, AP 09707/book 91.
137. The Duke to Treasury, 20 August 1764, MNHL, AP 09707/32-25, (42B)-11 and book 91.
138. Treasury to the Duke, 12 September 1764, NA, T 1/434/71.
139. Proceedings of Privy Council on petition of the Duke of Atholl, Parliamentary Papers (PP) 1805 (79), p. 16. Report on petition of the Duke of Atholl, PP 1805 (139), pp. 6-7.
140. Ibid.
141. Case of the Duke of Atholl, undated but probably 13 February 1765, MNHL, AP 09707/ 42C.
142. The Duke to Treasury, undated, MNHL, AP 09707/31-9.
143. Valuations of the Island, undated, MNHL, AP 09707/42(B)-24 and 26, see appendix 2.
144. Proceedings of Privy Council on petition of the Duke of Atholl, 19 February 1765, PP 1805 (79), p. 17.
145. Minutes of meetings, 12 to 21 March 1765, MNHL, House of Keys Journals (HKJ) 09191/2/2, ff. 12-17. Case of the Keys, undated, MNHL, AP 09707/44(B)-6 and 27.
146. The Duke to J. Mackenzie, 26 February 1765, MNHL, AP 09707/32(2)-6.
147. Third Duke's memorandum, undated, MNHL, AP 09707/book 91. The Duke to Treasury, 27 February 1765, MNHL, AP 09707/31-10. Case of the Duke of Atholl, 1788, MNHL, Manx Books (MB) Atholl Family F70/2x/2, pp. 12-13. Also in the Atholl Papers is a document, 09707/42(B)-20, again dated 27 February 1765 (though in pencil), which seems to be an optional letter offering a contrary opinion on the sale of the Island and still holding out for the sale of all of the Duke's rights, 'that our treaty may not be for a partial purchase, that, if I must part with my possessions, it may be the entirety'.
148. Statement of estates in Scotland, 24 May 1765, MNHL, AP 09707/book 114: Nairne (£34,982), Blairingone (£6,405), Balquhidder (£3,903), Falkland (£14,399) and Tullibardine (£10,339)
149. Irish Annuity, MNHL, AP 09707/31-1 and 31-3.
150. Walpole, *Land of Home Rule*, pp. 222-3.
151. *Act of Parliament*, 5 George III, chapter 26, 'An Act for carrying into execution a contract made, pursuant to the Act of Parliament of the twelfth of His late Majesty King George the First, between the Commissioners of His Majesty's Treasury and the Duke and Duchess of Atholl, the proprietors of the Isle of Man, and their trustees, for the purchase of the said Island and its dependencies, under certain exceptions therein particularly mentioned'.
152. *Act of Parliament*, 5 George III, chapter 39, 'An Act for more effectually preventing the mischiefs arising to the revenue and commerce of Great Britain and Ireland from the illicit and clandestine trade to and from the Isle of Man'.
153. Royal proclamation and seal, 21 June 1765, MNHL, Castle Rushen Papers 09782 (with Manx translation), and NA, PC 1/7/157.
154. Copies of proceedings and speech, 11 July 1765, MNHL, AP 09707/43(A)-24 and 113-2.

155. John Wood (1721-77), Governor of the Isle of Man 1761-77.
156. Royal proclamation and seal, 21 June 1765, MNHL, Castle Rushen Papers 09782 (with Manx translation), and NA, PC 1/7/157.
157. Copies of proceedings and speech, 11 July 1765, MNHL, AP 09707/43(A)-24 and 113-2.
158. *Commissioners of Inquiry*, appendix C, number 26.
159. Copies of proceedings and speech, 11 July 1765, MNHL, AP 09707/43(A)-24 and 113-2.
160. Attorney General James Gell to Governor Loch, 20 July 1881, MNHL, Government Office Papers (GOP) 09845/5/2.
161. John Feltham, 'A Tour through the Isle of Man in 1797 and 1798', in Reverend Robert Airey, editor, *The Manx Society*, volume 6, (Douglas, 1861), p. 121.
162. Walpole, *Land of Home Rule*, p. 221.
163. Moore, *A History*, p. 804.
164. Thomas Grindley, *The Story of Revestment: A Sketch of Manx History in the eighteenth century*, (Douglas, 1903), p. 25.
165. *Report of the Departmental Committee on the constitution, etc. of the Isle of Man*, Cd. 5950, (London, 1911), p. 4.
166. J. W. Birch, *The Isle of Man: A Study in Economic Geography*, (Cambridge, 1964), pp. 20-1, referring to Moore, *A History*, p. 583.
167. David Robertson, *A Tour through the Isle of Man*, (London, 1794), pp. 139-40.
168. Letter from Richard Betham to Reverend Dr Wilson, undated, MNHL, papers relating to St George's church 01989/26C. Betham was the Collector of Customs in the Isle of Man, father-in-law of William Bligh of *Bounty* fame and trustee of St George's chapel.
169. Petition of the House of Keys, undated, MNHL, AP 09707/33B(2nd)-24.
170. Butler, *Memoirs of Mark Hildesley*, p. 225.
171. Moore, *A History*, p. 616.
172. Philip Moore to Bishop Hildesley, 26 June 1765, MNHL, Records of the Diocese of Sodor and Man 09309.
173. Ibid., pp. 527-8.
174. Instruction issued to Lutwidge, 15 May 1765, NA, T 1/437169-73.
175. 1765-66 mortgages and deeds, MNHL, Mortgage and Deeds series 09494.
176. Case of the inhabitants of the Isle of Man, undated, MNHL, AP 09707/42-26.
177. See appendix 1.
178. George Moore, various letters and notes, 1766-67, MNHL, GML 499C.
179. Craine, 'A Manx Merchant of the Eighteenth Century', p. 660.
180. Bullock, *History*, p. 328.
181. Robertson, *Tour*, p. 22.
182. Ibid., pp. 63, 88 and 115.
183. Charles Searle ('An Impartial Hand'), *A Short View of the Present State of the Isle of Man*, (1767), pp. 5-6. Searle was the Island's Attorney General, 1768-74.
184. Petition of the House of Keys, undated, MNHL, AP 09707/33B(2nd)-24. This includes a list of the names of members, many of whom were wealthy businessmen who had remained in the Island.
185. Frances Wilkins, *The Smuggling Trade Revisited*, (Kidderminster, 2004), pp. 149-68.
186. *Act of Parliament*, 7 George III, chapter 45, see appendix 2.

187. See appendix 1.
188. Moore, *A History*, pp. 602 and 626.
189. *Acts of Parliament*, 5 George III, chapter 12, and 7 George III, chapter 46.
190. John Parr, 'An Abstract of the Laws, Customs and Ordinances of the Isle of Man', in James Gell, editor, *The Manx Society*, volume 12, (Douglas, 1867), p. 142. Deemster John Parr (1651-1713) originally compiled this abstract, but it was substantially edited and expanded by Attorney General Sir James Gell (1823-1905).
191. E. J. Payne, editor, *Select Works of Edmund Burke, and Miscellaneous Writings*, (three volumes, Oxford, 1874-78), pp. 113-14, reproduced at http://www.econlib.org/library/LFBooks/Burke/bkrSWv1c2.html, Library of Economics and Liberty, accessed on 20 July 2004. The American and the Isle of Man Revenue Acts were in fact the forty-sixth and forty-fifth chapters in the Statute Book of 1767.
192. Leah Leneman, *Living in Athol: A Social History of the Estates, 1685-1785*, (Edinburgh, 1986), pp. 7-8.
193. John Murray (1755-1830), fourth Duke of Atholl 1774-1830, Governor of the Isle of Man 1793-1830.
194. John Murray, seventh Duke of Atholl, editor, *Chronicles of the Atholl and Tullibardine Families*, volume 4, (Edinburgh, 1908), p. 364.
195. Crosse to Taubman, 18 July 1780, MNHL, Goldie-Taubman Papers 09591.
196. Thomas Quayle to John Quayle, 6 October 1781, MNHL, Bridge House Papers (BHP) 904/21C.
197. *Act of Parliament*, 20 George III, chapter 42, see appendix 2.
198. Case of the Duke of Atholl, 1780, MNHL, AP 09707/X1-1. Evidence of George Moore, 1780, MNHL, AP 09707/43(3rd)-2. 1780 and 1781 petitions from House of Keys, MNHL, AP 09707/X43(2nd)-19 and 155-13. Minutes and correspondence, MNHL, HKJ 09191/2/2, ff. 79, 82-3, 87-92, and 101-12. Attorney General and Solicitor General's report, 30 April 1781, MNHL, Melville collection of manuscripts 01798/3C.
199. Michael Dolley, 'Procurator Extraordinary - Sir Wadsworth Busk (1730-1811)', in R. A. Curphey, editor, *IOMNHAS*, volume 8, number 3, (Douglas, 1976-78), p. 218.
200. Attorney General and Solicitor General's report, 30 April 1781, MNHL, Melville collection of manuscripts 01798/3C. *Morning Chronicle and London Advertiser*, 19 and 26 May and 19 June 1781. Walpole, *Land of Home Rule*, pp. 223-4.
201. Unknown to the Marquis of Rockingham, undated but probably 1782, MNHL, 05966.
202. Busk to Reverend E. Radcliffe, 23 March 1780, MNHL, Sir Wadsworth Busk's correspondence 10362.
203. John Walker, *The Queen Has Been Pleased: The British Honours System at Work*, (London, 1986), pp. 1 and 31-7.
204. Thomas Quayle to John Quayle, 23 June 1781, MNHL, BHP 904/21C.
205. The Duke's memorial, 1789, and Duke to Treasury, 4 March 1789, MNHL, AP 09707/X70-7. Select Committee's report 1790, MNHL, AP 09707/43-14. *Debrett's Parliamentary Register*, volume 28, March 1789, pp. 307-17, and April 1789, pp. 385-95.
206. John Christian Curwen (1756-1828), MP 1786, MHK 1791, married Margaret Taubman 1776, son became Deemster John Christian, widowed, married first cousin Isabella Curwen 1782, took the additional name of Curwen.
207. John Lace and William Callow to Taubman, Stevenson, Callow and Curwen, 9 April 1790, MNHL, Goldie-Taubman Papers 09591.
208. William Pitt (1759-1806), MP 1781, Chancellor of the Exchequer 1782-83, First Lord of the Treasury and Chancellor of the Exchequer 1783-1801 and 1804-06. *Debrett's Parliamentary Register*, volume 44, May 1790, pp. 561-2.
209. John, seventh Duke of Atholl, editor, *Chronicles*, p. 363.
210. Robert Heywood to his brother Peter Heywood, 16 July 1781, MNHL, AP 09707/122(2nd)-25. Lieutenant

Reference Notes

Governor Shaw to the Duke, 2 March 1792, MNHL, AP 09707/X21-10.

211. The Duke to Henry Dundas, 13 November 1791, MNHL, collection of letters of the Duke of Atholl 01996/7C.
212. Bishop Crigan to Mrs Calcraft, 22 June 1792, MNHL, AP 09707/116(2nd)-3. Canon John Gelling, *A History of the Manx Church, 1698-1911*, (Douglas, 1998), p. 46.
213. *The 24 Keys of the Isle of Man*, undated, MNHL, AP 09707/X43-11. J. Inglis Spicer, 'The Worthiest Men in the Land during Five Centuries', in W. Cubbon, editor, *JMM*, volume 2, number 37, (Douglas, 1933), pp. 143-7.
214. Dundas to the Duke, 16 July 1791, MNHL, AP 09707/X29-3. Dundas to commissioners, 8 September 1791, MNHL, AP 09707/X29-2.
215. *The Report of the Commissioners of Inquiry for the Isle of Man, 1792*, was not formally made public until 1805.
216. Ibid., pp. 7-11 and appendix D, number 34.
217. Ibid., pp. 7-11.
218. Ibid., pp. 44-6.
219. Ibid., pp. 44-6 and 112-20 and appendix B, numbers 77 and 79.
220. Robertson, *Tour*, pp. 3-4.
221. Richard Townley, *A Journal kept in the Isle of Man*, (two volumes, Whitehaven, 1791), volume I, p. 82.
222. *Commissioners of Inquiry*, pp. 23-35 and appendix B, numbers 1, 11 and 14. The total expenditure is at times also shown as £3,272.
223. Ibid., appendix B, numbers 77 and 86.
224. Ibid., pp. 51-5 and 121.
225. Ibid.
226. Memorandum from the Duke, 21 May 1792, MNHL, collection of letters of the Duke of Atholl 01996/11C.
227. Alexander Shaw, Lieutenant Governor of the Isle of Man 1790-1804. Shaw to the Duke, 2 March 1792, MNHL, AP 09707/X21-10.
228. Duke to Dundas, 14 January 1793, MNHL, Duke of Atholl's collection of letters 09979.
229. Major-General Edward Smith, Governor of the Isle of Man 1777-93. Minutes of meeting, 12 March 1793, MNHL, HKJ 09191/2/2, ff. 220-1.
230. *Act of Parliament*, 38 George III, chapter 63, see appendix 2.
231. See appendix 1.
232. The Duke's compensation claim, 27 June 1801, NA, PC 1/3537. Case of the Duke of Atholl, November 1801, MNHL, AP 09707/X43-7. Order from Privy Council, 25 January 1802, MNHL, AP 09707/155-3. Walpole, *Land of Home Rule*, pp. 227-32.
233. Petition of House of Keys, 17 March 1802, NA, PC 1/3537.
234. Report of Attorney General and Surveyor General, 12 November 1802, NA, PC 1/3537.
235. Suspension request from the Duke, 17 April 1804, NA, PC 1/3537.
236. Walpole, *Land of Home Rule*, p. 229.
237. Petition from the Duke, 26 June 1804, NA, PC 1/3537.
238. Minutes of meeting, 26 January 1805, MNHL, HKJ 09191/2/2, f. 46.
239. Report of Privy Council on petition of Duke of Atholl, PP 1805 (64), pp. 1-5. Parr and Gell, 'Laws, Customs

240. Bridson and Stowell opposing Keys' actions, case of the Duke of Atholl, 21 May 1805, MNHL, MB Atholl Family F70/10/1. Landowners' memorial, undated, MNHL, AP 09707/36(A)-13.
241. *Manks Advertiser*, 27 April 1805.
242. Committee report on the petition of the Duke of Atholl, PP 1805 (139), pp. 1-9.
243. *Act of Parliament*, 45 George III, chapter 123.
244. Parr and Gell, 'Laws, Customs and Ordinances', p. 150.
245. Walpole, *Land of Home Rule*, pp. 230-2.
246. Ibid.
247. *Act of Parliament*, 45 George III, chapter 99, see appendix 2.
248. Walpole, *Land of Home Rule*, p. 231.
249. *Act of Parliament*, 27 George III, chapter 13, section 47. The Rt Hon Lord Bridges, *The Treasury*, (London, 1964), p. 25, referring to the thirteenth Report of the Commissioners of Public Accounts, 8 March 1785.
250. *Statutes of the Isle of Man*, volume 1, ' An Act for affording Relief to Insolvent Debtors', 1814, pp. 373-82. Train, *Historical and Statistical Account*, pp. 252-3.
251. *Pigot and Co.'s Directory*, (London, 1824), p. 196.
252. Account by Canon Kissack of his interview with Mr Moore, 22 September 1894, MNHL, Canon Edward William Kissack's diary, historical notes and matters of antiquarian interest 10907/1. Mr Moore, aged 91, of Lhergy Dhoo remembered this amusing contemporary rhyme on the tithe problems.
253. Moore, *A History*, pp. 558-60.
254. *Act of Parliament*, 1 and 2 George IV, chapter 87, section 27.
255. *Rising Sun*, 6 October 1821.
256. John Llewellyn, High Bailiff of Peel, to Duke, 12 November 1821, MNHL, AP 09707/120-7.
257. J. Quirk, High Bailiff of Douglas, to Duke, 12 November 1821, MNHL, AP 09707/120-6.
258. Colonel Cornelius Smelt (1748-1832), Lieutenant Governor of the Isle of Man 1805-1832. Smelt to Sidmouth, 5 October 1821, MNHL, GOP 3/39. Smelt to Sidmouth and reply, 7 and 8 October 1821, MNHL, Government Office Correspondence Books (GOCB) 09845/1/3, ff. 127-9. Duke to Sidmouth, 31 October 1821, MNHL, AP 09707/68-1.
259. Sidmouth to Duke, 17 November 1821, MNHL, AP 09707/68-3.
260. Moore, *A History*, pp. 661-2.
261. David Craine, 'The Potato Riots, 1825', in W. Walter Gill and Ramsey B. Moore, editors, *IOMNHAS*, volume 4, number 4, (Douglas 1945), p. 570.
262. McCrone to Duke, 6 and 30 October and 9 November 1825, MNHL, AP 09707/49-45, 49(2nd)-5 and 49(2nd)-6.
263. Bishop to Duke, 4 November 1825, MNHL, AP 09707/46(2nd)-31.
264. Robert Steuart, Receiver General, to Duke, 10 December 1825, MNHL, AP 09707/46(2nd)-31. Hampton Creer, *Never to Return: The Story of Manx Prisoners Transported to the Penal Colonies*, (Douglas, 2000).
265. McCrone to Duke, 10 November 1825, MNHL, AP 09707/49(2nd)-7. Bishop to Duke, 14 December 1821, MNHL, AP 09707/46(2nd)-46.
266. Memorial of the House of Keys sent to Governor Smelt, 4 September 1821, MNHL, Colonel Mark Wilks Papers, 00332/10. Minutes of meeting, 26 March 1822, relating to meeting of 26 November 1821, MNHL, HKJ 09191/2/2, ff. 102-3.

267. *Rising Sun*, 18 March 1823.
268. Memorial to the Secretary of State at the Home Office, 2 September 1822, MNHL, BHP 2483/1C.
269. Sir Robert Peel, second Baronet (1788-1850), MP 1809, Home Secretary 1822-27 and 1828-30, Prime Minister 1834-35 and 1841-46. The Duke to Peel, 5 February 1823, MNHL, AP 09707/book 98.
270. Various documents belonging to the Speaker, Sir George Moore, 1821-23, MNHL, BHP 4410-23C.
271. Peel to the Duke, 28 February 1823, MNHL, AP 09707/X68-16.
272. Inquiry into the conduct of His Honour Deemster Gawne, 20 February to 13 March 1823, MNHL, Legislative Council Journals (LCJ) 09191/4/1, ff. 455-89. *Manx Advertiser*, 13 March and 3 April 1823. *Rising Sun*, 25 March and 1 April 1823. Keys memorial to the King in Council, 5 July 1823, MNHL, HKJ 09191/2/2, ff. 114-16. William Roper, *A Short History of the Transactions in the Isle of Man on which the House of Keys founded their late Petition to the House of Commons against His Grace the Duke of Atholl*, (Douglas, 1825), pp. 52-7.
273. Account by the Duke of his meetings with Peel, 29 March and 3 April 1824, MNHL, AP 09707/book 93 and 40(A)-5.
274. James Ray to the Duke, 11 March 1824, MNHL, AP 09707/111-23.
275. Mungo Murray to the Duke, 10 March 1824, MNHL, AP 09707/45-34.
276. W. Cubbon, editor, 'Centenary of Erection of Smelt Monument', JMM, volume 3, number 53, (Douglas, 1937), p. 229.
277. Draft memo to Lord Sidmouth, c.1812, MNHL, AP 09707/X29(5th)-18.
278. Exchange of correspondence between all parties, 1812 to 1822, Atholl Papers 09707.
279. Duke to Smelt, 5 December 1812, MNHL, AP 09707/X29(3rd)-9.
280. *Rising Sun*, 19 October 1824. *Manx Advertiser*, 21 October 1824.
281. W. Cubbon, 'The Baptism of the Castle Mona', in W. Cubbon, editor, *JMM*, volume 3, number 45, (Douglas, 1935), p. 75. Leonard Craine, 'The Castle Mona Estate', in R. A. Curphey, editor, *IOMNHAS*, volume 8, number 1, (Douglas, 1976), p. 18.
282. *Manx Advertiser*, 3 February 1825. *Rising Sun*, 5 February 1825.
283. John, seventh Duke of Atholl, editor, *Chronicles*, p. 360. Moore, *A History*, p. 542, states, somewhat ambiguously, that the Duke 'did not visit the island after 1826'. A number of other writers have since incorrectly referred to 1826 as the last time the Duke was in the Island.
284. *Bill of Parliament*, 6 George IV.
285. Petition from Keys to Commons, 3 May 1825, MNHL, AP 09707/18-9.
286. Bishop Murray to the Duke, 28 November 1825, MNHL, AP 09707/46(2nd)-42.
287. *Act of Parliament*, 6 George IV, chapter 34.
288. Treasury to the Duke, 17 June 1825, and reply 18 June 1825, MNHL, AP 09707/book 93.
289. Exchange of correspondence between Treasury and the Duke, 17-25 June 1825, MNHL, AP 09707/book 93. Contracts and agreements between Treasury and Duke of Atholl on the sale and conveyance of Isle of Man, PP 1829 (252), pp. 1-15.
290. *Act of Parliament*, 6 George IV, chapter 115, see appendix 2.
291. Moore, *A History*, pp. 616, 626-7 and 648.
292. John, seventh Duke of Atholl, editor, *Chronicles*, p. 363.
293. Ibid., p. 365.
294. *Bill of Parliament*, 10 George IV.

295. Ibid.,
296. Walpole, *Land of Home Rule*, p. 245.
297. Lord John Russell, first Earl Russell (1792-1878), MP 1813, Home Secretary 1835-39, Prime Minister 1846-52 and 1865-66, Foreign Secretary 1859-65.
298. Ann M. Harrison, 'Reform from the North, 1844-47', in R. A. Curphey, editor, *IOMNHAS*, volume 8, number 4, (Douglas, 1982), p. 403.
299. R. E. Forster, 'A Study of the Constitutional and Financial Movements in the Isle of Man, 1833-1866', (unpublished BA thesis, University of Birmingham, 1951), p. 5. R. E. Forster, 'The Reformist Movements in 1837', in R. E. Forster, editor, *IOMNHAS*, volume 6, number 3, (Kendal, 1964), p. 380.
300. Robert Christian Fargher (1803-63), see appendix 3.
301. John Courtney Bluett (1792-1855), see appendix 4. Sir William Hillary (1771-1847), see appendix 5.
302. John Welch ('A Stranger'), *A Six Day's Tour through the Isle of Man*, (Douglas, 1836), p. 61.
303. Ibid., pp. 11 and 16-17.
304. *Quiggin's Illustrated Guide and Visitor's Companion*, (Douglas, 1841), p. 130.
305. Welch, *A Six Day's Tour*, p. 19.
306. Ibid., pp. 24-5.
307. Ibid., pp. 31 and 44.
308. *Pigot and Slater's Directory*, (London, 1837), p. 823. Ready to Manners-Sutton, 22 April 1842, MNHL, GOCB 09845/1/4, f. 468
309. *Act of Parliament*, 3 and 4 William IV, chapter 60, see appendix 2.
310. *Act of Parliament*, 3 and 4 William IV, chapter 56.
311. John Ready (1772-1845), Governor of Isle of Man 1832-45, rumoured to be illegitimate son of third Earl of Bathurst, army career, member of staff to Lord Lieutenant of Ireland 1807-13, secretary to Governors of Canada 1818-22, Lieutenant Governor of Prince Edward Island 1824-31. Minutes of meeting, 5 July 1836, MNHL, LCJ 09191/4/2, ff. 132-5.
312. *Manx Sun*, 8 July 1836.
313. Minutes of meeting, 8 July 1836, MNHL, LCJ 09191/4/2, f. 136.
314. Charles Edward Poulett Thomson, Baron Sydenham (1799-1841), MP 1826, President of the Board of Trade 1835-39, advocated free trade and financial reform. Ready to Russell and Thompson, 8 July 1836, MNHL, GOCB 09845/1/4, ff. 233-4.
315. Train, *Historical and Statistical Account*, pp. 320-1.
316. Welch, *A Six Day's Tour*, p. 62.
317. *Manx Sun*, 8, 15 and 22 July 1836.
318. *Act of Parliament*, 9 George IV, chapter 60.
319. *Act of Parliament*, 5 and 6 William IV, chapter 13.
320. *Mona's Herald*, 9 July 1836.
321. *Manx Sun*, 15 July 1836. *Mona's Herald*, 16 July 1836.
322. *Mona's Herald*, 27 December 1836.
323. Fox Maule, second Baron Panmure and eleventh Earl of Dalhousie (1801-74), MP 1835, Under Secretary of State of the Home Office 1835-41, Vice-President of the Board of Trade 1841, Secretary of War 1846-52 and 1855-58. Maule to Ready, 6 January 1837, NA, Home Office Papers (HO) 99/18, ff. 255-6.
324. *Mona's Herald*, 17 January 1837.

325. Ready to Bluett, 14 January 1837, MNHL, Bluett Papers (BP) 09566/1/2.
326. Bluett to Tynwald Committee, 16 January 1837, MNHL, BP 09566/2/2. *Manx Sun*, 13 January 1837.
327. Draft report, undated, MNHL, GOCB 09845/4/2, ff. 257-61. *Manx Sun*, 20 January 1837. *Mona's Herald*, 24 January 1837.
328. *Mona's Herald*, 24 January 1837.
329. Ready to Maule, 20 January 1837, MNHL, GOCB 09845/1/4, ff. 255-7.
330. *Manx Sun*, 20 January 1837.
331. *Manx Liberal*, 21 January 1837.
332. *Mona's Herald*, 24 January 1837.
333. Ibid. *Manx Sun*, 27 January 1837.
334. George William Dumbell (1804-87), member of Manx Bar 1826, MHK 1840, partner in Isle of Man Joint Stock Bank, arrested for forgery 1848 but acquitted, chairman of Laxey Mining Company, landowner.
335. *Manx Sun*, 3 February 1837.
336. William Christian to Bluett, 28 January 1837, MNHL, BP 09566/1/3. *Manx Sun*, 27 January 1837.
337. *Mona's Herald*, 31 January 1837. *Manx Liberal*, 4 February 1837.
338. Petitions, MNHL, MB Finance and Customs D154/1x/8248, and BP 09566/4/22 and 5/1-7. Bluett's recording and/or addition of the number of signatories is questionable in accuracy. Maule to Ready, 7 March 1837, MNHL, GOCB 09845/1/4, ff. 275-6.
339. Various petitions to Bluett, March 1837, MNHL, BP 09566/1/9, 11-12 and 17 and 4/6-11 and 14-16.
340. Ready to Maule, 21 March 1837, MNHL, GOCB 09845/1/4, ff. 270-1.
341. *Mona's Herald*, 14 and 28 March 1837. *Manx Sun*, 17 March 1837.
342. Thomas Arthur Corlett (1792-1861), High Bailiff of Ramsey 1815 but removed from position 1828, Vicar General, married Deemster Moore's daughter.
343. *Mona's Herald*, 28 March 1837. *Manx Sun*, 31 March 1837. *Mona's Herald*, 4 April 1837.
344. John James Moore (1794-?), unmarried, landowner and teetotaller from Baljean in Lonan.
345. Hillary to Bluett, 20 and 28 March 1837, MNHL, BP 09566/1/8 and 14.
346. Bluett to Ready, 29 March 1837, MNHL, BP 09566/2/4.
347. James Deacon Hume (1774-1842), Customs 1791-1828, joint Secretary of the Board of Trade 1828-40, advocated free trade, author of many books on commerce, customs and finance. Bluett to Hillary, 31 March 1837, MNHL, BP 09566/2/5.
348. Ashworth, *Customs and Excise*, pp. 369-70.
349. Bluett to Hillary, undated, MNHL, BP 09566/2/6.
350. Bluett to Hillary, 3 April 1837, MNHL, BP 09566/2/7.
351. Hillary to Bluett, 4 April 1837, MNHL, BP 09566/1/18.
352. *Manx Sun*, 7 April 1837.
353. Hillary to Bluett, 7 April 1837, MNHL, BP 09566/1/19.
354. Poulett Thomson to Bluett, 8 April 1837, MNHL, BP 09566/1/21. Bluett to Hillary and Ready, 13 April 1837, MNHL, BP 09566/2/11-12. *Mona's Herald*, 25 April 1837.
355. Lord William Lowther, third Earl of Lonsdale (1787-1872), MP 1808, President of the Board of Trade 1834-35, opponent of reform.
356. Ready to Maule and Poulett Thomson, 13 April 1837, MNHL, GOCB 09845/1/4, ff. 270-1. *Manx Sun*, 14 April 1837. *Manx Liberal*, 15 April 1837.

357. Craigie to Bluett, 17 April 1837, MNHL, BP 09566/1/24.
358. Hillary to Bluett, 18 April 1837, MNHL, BP 09566/1/27. Corlett to Bluett, 21 April 1837, MNHL, BP 09566/1/28.
359. Ready to Maule and reply, 3 and 8 April 1837, MNHL, GOCB 09845/1/4, f. 278.
360. *Manx Sun*, 5 May 1837.
361. Hillary to Bluett, 2 May 1837, MNHL, BP 9566/1/32.
362. William Blamire (1790-1862), MP 1831, defeated Lord Lowther, nephew of John Christian Curwen (MP and MHK). Bluett to Hillary, 5 May 1837, MNHL, BP 09566/2/16.
363. Supporting papers and *Observations on the Proposed Changes in the Fiscal and Navigational Laws of the Isle of Man*, MNHL, BP 09566/4/1 and 6/1.
364. Notes on interview with Poulett Thomson, 8 May 1837, MNHL, BP 09566/4/20. Letter from Manx deputation to Lord John Russell, undated but probably 17 May 1837, MNHL, BP 09566/3.
365. Craigie to Bluett, 12 May 1837, MNHL, BP 09566/1/34.
366. *Mona's Herald*, 30 May 1837.
367. *Mona's Herald*, 13 June 1837 and 18 April 1843.
368. Train, *Historical and Statistical Account*, p. 321.
369. *Mona's Herald*, 18 July and 1 August 1837.
370. William Harrison, 'Mona Miscellany', in William Harrison, editor, *The Manx Society*, volume 16 (Edinburgh, 1869), pp. 112-17.
371. Captain John Clucas was the owner of the estate of Mearyvoar.
372. John James Moore was one of the five delegates who went to London.
373. Major David Stewart, from Ballavale in Santon, spoke broad Scottish.
374. William Kelly was a businessman and fiscal and constitutional reformer.
375. Farmland in Lonan.
376. Young people.
377. The House of Keys.
378. Enrolled in the Reform Association in the Island.
379. The constitutional and fiscal relationship between the Isle of Man and Britain.
380. The threatened Parliamentary Bill to regulate the trade of the Island by assimilating the customs duties payable on the importation of licensed goods into the Island to those of Britain and Ireland.
381. Petitions were organised in all parts of the Island calling for changes to the Island's constitution and its public finances.
382. Lord John Russell, British Secretary of State of the Home Office.
383. The five man deputation that went to London to confer with the British Government on customs duties.
384. Refers to the cell at Castle Rushen in which Kelly was imprisoned as an insolvent debtor.
385. William Christian, from Ballure in Maughold.
386. *Mona's Herald*, 24 October 1837.
387. Forster, *Reformist Movements*, p. 385.
388. Ready to Maule, 9 March 1838, NA, HO 98/80.
389. Welch, *A Six Day's Tour*, p. 97.
390. Ready to Maule, 9 March 1838, NA, HO 98/80.
391. Walpole, *Land of Home Rule*, p. 250.

392. Maule to Ready, 19 March 1838, NA, HO 99/18, ff. 288-9. *Debates of Tynwald*, volume 2, 8-9 February 1888, pp. 203-4 and 252-3.
393. Derek Winterbottom, *Governors of the Isle of Man since 1765*, (Douglas, 1999), p. 40.
394. John Bowring, *Autobiographical Recollections*, (London, 1877), p. 212.
395. Anthony Howe, 'Restoring free trade: the British experience, in Donald Winch and Patrick K. O'Brien, editors, *The Political Economy of British Historical Experience, 1688-1914*, (Oxford, 2002), pp. 194-205.
396. R. E. C. Forster, 'Aspects of Manx Emigration: 1750-1990', in Joyce Warham, editor, *IOMNHAS*, volume 10, number 1, (Kendal, 1992), pp. 23-32.
397. *Mona's Herald*, 20 March 1844.
398. *Mona's Herald*, 9 February 1842.
399. Ready to Manners-Sutton, 22 April 1842, MNHL, GOCB 09845/1/4, f. 468.
400. *Manx Liberal*, 16 July 1842.
401. *Mona's Herald*, 16 November and 21 December 1842 and 11 January 1843.
402. See appendix 2.
403. *Mona's Herald*, 21 December 1842.
404. Merchants' letters, correspondence between Board of Trade and Isle of Man on regulation of import duties, PP 1843 (245), pp. 1-4. *Manx Liberal*, 20 May 1843.
405. Other petitions were sent from England, including Manchester (10), Oldham (1), Huddersfield, (2), London (4), Blackburn (1), Leeds (1) and Stockport (1).
406. Sir John Bowring (1792-1872), see appendix 6. *Manx Liberal*, 6 August 1844.
407. *Manx Sun*, 18 March and 13 May 1843. *Manx Liberal*, 18 March, 1 April and 1 July 1843 and 6 August 1844.
408. *Manx Sun*, 17 August 1844.
409. William Ewart Gladstone (1809-98), MP 1832, President of the Board of Trade 1843-45, Tory Chancellor of the Exchequer 1852-55 and 1859-66, Liberal leader 1867, Prime Minister 1868-74, 1880-85, 1886 and 1892-94.
410. *Mona's Herald*, 18 April 1843. Train, *Historical and Statistical Account*, pp. 328-9. Amount of duties levied on imports into the Isle of Man, 1840-42, PP 1843 (145), p. 3, see appendix 2.
411. *Manx Sun*, 13 May 1843. *Manx Liberal*, 17 June 1843.
412. *Manx Sun*, 17 August 1844.
413. Minutes of meeting, 5 July 1843, MNHL, HKJ 09191/2/2, ff. 402-3.
414. *Manx Sun*, 10 February 1844.
415. *Manx Sun*, 17 February 1844.
416. *Mona's Herald*, 14 February 1844.
417. John Bowring, 'Free Trade Recollections', in *Howitt's Journal*, volume 11, (30 January 1847), pp. 58-61.
418. John Henry Thomas Manners-Sutton, third Viscount Canterbury (1814-77), MP 1839, Under Secretary of State of the Home Office 1841-46. Sir John George Shaw-Lefevre (1797-1879), MP 1833 by one vote but lost seat on petition, civil servant, joint-assistant Secretary to the Board of Trade 1841. Shaw-Lefevre to Manners-Sutton, for the attention of Sir James Graham, 29 February 1844, NA, HO 45/3. Manners-Sutton to Ready, 12 March 1844, MNHL, HKJ 09191/2/2, ff. 404-10.
419. *Mona's Herald*, 10 April 1844.
420. W. Cubbon, *A Bibliographical Account of Works relating to the Isle of Man*, (two volumes, Oxford, 1939),

pp. 1324-5 and 1328-31.
421. Ibid., pp. 1337 and 1342-7.
422. Ibid., pp. 1150-1 and 1354-5.
423. W. T. Kneale, 'The Trials of a Manx Radical: The Life and Times of Robert Fargher, 1803-63', in A. M. Cubbon and W. R. Serjeant, editors, *JMM*, volume 6, number 76, (Douglas, 1960), pp. 89-91.
424. Cubbon, *A Bibliographical Account*, pp. 1362-3.
425. R. C. M. Fyson, 'Bronterre O'Brien: A Chartist in the Isle of Man 1844-1847', in M. J. Critchlow, editor, *IOMNHAS*, volume 10, number 4, (Kendall, 1998), p. 398.
426. *Manx Liberal*, 26 October 1844.
427. *Islands in the British Seas, Enumerator's Schedule, Census 1841*, Douglas, district 8, p. 4, microfilm.
428. Minutes of meeting, 21 March 1844, MNHL, HKJ 09191/2/2, f. 410, and LCJ 09191/4/2, ff. 384-8. Ready to Manners-Sutton, 21 March 1844, MNHL, GOCB 09845/1/4, ff. 515-20.
429. Minutes of meeting, 10 April 1844, MNHL, HKJ 09191/2/2, ff. 411-16. *Manx Sun*, 13 April and 31 August 1844.
430. Samuel Rogers to Graham, 13 April 1844, NA HO/45/31. *Manx Sun*, 13 April 1844. *Mona's Herald*, 17 and 24 April 1844.
431. *Manx Sun*, 17 August 1844. Train, *Historical and Statistical Account*, p. 324.
432. *Mona's Herald*, 4 June 1844.
433. Ready to Manners-Sutton, 6 June 1844, MNHL, GOCB 09845/1/4, ff. 525-9.
434. *Mona's Herald*, 25 June and 9 July 1844. *Manx Sun* (supplement), 29 June, 1 and 6 July 1844. *Manx Liberal*, 29 June and 6 July 1844.
435. *Mona's Herald*, 2 July 1844. *Manx Sun*, 6 July 1844.
436. *Acts of Parliament*, 7 and 8 Victoria, chapter 43, see appendix 2.
437. *Mona's Herald*, 2 July 1844.
438. *Manx Sun*, 3 August 1844.
439. Probably a reference to John Meadows White, the Keys' London agent.
440. *Manx Liberal*, 10 August 1844. *Manx Sun*, 17 August 1844.
441. *Manx Sun*, 17 August 1844.
442. *Manx Sun*, 21 and 28 September 1844. *Mona's Herald*, 24 September and 1 October 1844. *Manx Liberal*, 28 September 1844.
443. Bowring, *Autobiographical Recollections*, p. 213.
444. Official annual returns, 1843-45, PP 1846 (154), pp. 1-3, see appendix 2.
445. *Islands in the British Seas, Isle of Man, Jersey, Guernsey and adjacent Isles, Census 1901*, (London, 1903), p. 1. Throughout this book, the population figures are generally abstracted from the censuses of 1841, 1881, 1891, 1901 and 2006, other than when featured in other primary sources.
446. Moore, *A History*, p. 576.
447. Train, *Historical and Statistical Account*, p. 325. Train's term 'huxtering in surplusages' refers to corrupt dealings in surplus goods imported through the licence system.
448. Minutes of meetings, 14 October 1844 to 20 March 1847, MNHL, Election Association minute book 00290/2. Harrison, 'Reform from the North', pp. 404-5.
449. Various petitions, correspondence on reform of the House of Keys, PP 1846 (88), pp. 1-15.
450. Ready to Manners-Sutton, 24 January and 19 February 1845, MNHL, GOCB 09845/1/4, ff. 533 and 536-42.

451. Keys memorial, memorials on reform of House of Keys, 27 January 1845, PP 1845 (106), p. 5.
452. Forster, 'Constitutional and Financial Movements', p. 19.
453. Honourable Charles Hope (1808-93), son of fourth Earl of Hopetoun, lawyer, MP 1838, Governor of Isle of Man 1845-60, retired to run his Scottish estates.
454. Shareholders to Manners-Sutton, 16 July 1845, and Manners-Sutton to Ready and reply, 18 and 22 July 1845, NA, HO 45/943A.
455. Manners-Sutton to Hope, 12 November 1845, MNHL, GOCB 09845/1/5, ff. 61-4.
456. Hope to Manners-Sutton, 30 December 1845, MNHL, GOCB 09845/1/5, ff. 64-85.
457. *Manx Liberal*, 28 August 1847.
458. Three memorials to Grey, 1846 and 1847, memorials and correspondence on reform of the House of Keys, PP 1847 (141), pp. 1-5.
459. Grey to Hope, 18 January 1847, memorials and correspondence on reform of the House of Keys, PP 1847 (141), p. 5.
460. *Isle of Man Times*, 5 June 1847.
461. *Parliamentary Debates*, volume 97, 2 March 1848, p. 126.
462. *Statutes of the Isle of Man*, volume 2, 'Commutation of Tithes', 1839, pp. 114-23. Moore, *A History*, pp. 576, 932, 949-51 and 967-8. Terry Cringle, in Gordon N. Kniveton, editor, *Here is the News: An Illustrated Manx History*, (Douglas, 1992), pp. 93-9.
463. Memorials and correspondence regarding harbour improvements at Castletown, PP 1851 (651), pp. 1-36.
464. Forster, 'Constitutional and Financial Movements', p 27.
465. Wright, *Treasury Control of the Civil Service*, pp. 1-4. Henry Roseveare, *The Treasury: The Foundations of Control*, (London, 1973), pp. 22-7. Samuel H. Beer, *Treasury Control: The co-ordination of financial and economic policy in Great Britain*, (London, 1956), p. 16.
466. Hope to Trevellyan, 23 August 1852, MNHL, GOCB 09845/1/6, ff. 363-7.
467. Wilson to Hope, 7 February 1853, and Treasury minute, 1 February 1853 MNHL, GOCB 09845/1/6, ff. 402-6. Customs report, minutes and correspondence between Treasury and Isle of Man on customs reform, 14 April 1853, PP 1852-53 (982), pp. 1-7.
468. James Wilson (1805-60), founder of *The Economist* 1843, MP 1847, Financial Secretary of the Treasury 1853-58, Vice-President of the Board of Trade 1859, political economist and advocate of free trade and repeal of the Corn Laws and Navigation Acts.
469. Bridges, *The Treasury*, p. 225.
470. Hope to Wilson, 12 February 1853, MNHL, GOCB 09845/1/6, ff. 406-19.
471. Report, 14 April 1853, minutes and correspondence between Treasury and Isle of Man on customs reform, PP 1852-53 (982), pp. 5-7.
472. *Mona's Herald*, 27 April 1853, commenting on report in *The Times*.
473. *Mona's Herald*, 4 and 11 May 1853.
474. *Manx Sun*, 30 April 1853, commenting on reports in *The Times* and *Morning Post*.
475. *Manx Sun*, 30 April and 7 May 1853. *Mona's Herald*, 4 May 1853.
476. Speaker John Moore to Hope, 30 April 1853, MNHL, GOCB 09845/1/6, ff. 433-5. Minutes of meeting, 6 May 1853, MNHL, LCJ 09191/4/3, f. 255. *Manx Sun*, 7 May 1853.
477. Acting Speaker Gawne to Hope and reply, and Hope to Wilson, enclosing Keys letter, 7 May 1853, MNHL, GOCB 09845/1/6, ff. 433-40. *Manx Sun*, 7 May 1853.

478. Sir Robert Harry Inglis, Baronet (1786-1855), MP 1824.
479. William Ewart (1798-1869), MP 1828-37 and 1839-68, advocate of repeal of the Corn Laws. *Manx Sun*, 7 and 14 May 1853.
480. Hope to Wilson enclosing letter from Keys, 16 May 1853, MNHL, GOCB 09845/1/6, ff. 442-4. *Manx Sun*, 21 May 1853.
481. *Mona's Herald*, 1 June and 6 July 1853. Moore to Wilson, 21 July 1853, minutes and correspondence between Treasury and Isle of Man on customs reform, PP 1852-53 (982), pp. 22-3.
482. Henry John Temple, third Viscount Palmerston (1784-1865), MP 1807, Home Secretary 1852-55, Prime Minister 1855-58 and 1859-65.
483. Sir Joshua Walmsley (1794-1871), MP 1849, advocated repeal of the Corn Laws, worked with Cobden and Bright in Anti-Corn Law League.
484. *Mona's Herald*, 2 May 1866.
485. *Manx Sun*, 21 May 1853. *Mona's Herald*, 1 June and 6 July 1853. Return of gross revenue of customs of the Isle of Man, 1805-53, PP 1852-53 (501), pp. 1-3.
486. *Mona's Herald*, 1 June 1853.
487. Wilson to Hope, 7 and 16 June 1853, MNHL, GOCB 09845/1/6, ff. 447-53.
488. House of Keys and Legislative Council correspondence and minutes, 20 June 1853, MNHL, GOCB 09845/1/6, ff. 453-67. *Manx Sun*, 8 July 1854.
489. *Mona's Herald*, 22 June 1853.
490. *Manx Sun*, 25 June and 2, 9 and 23 July 1853. *Mona's Herald*, 6 and 13 July 1853.
491. Hope to Wilson and Fitzroy, 20 June 1853, MNHL, GOCB 09845/1/6, ff. 456-67.
492. *Manx Sun*, 2 July 1853. *Mona's Herald*, 6 July 1853.
493. William Callister (1808-72), MHK 1847-69, worked for reform of the House of Keys, timber merchant and founder director of Isle of Man Banking Company Ltd, one daughter married Edward Curphey Farrant, MHK, and another married John Thomas Clucas, Secretary to the Governor, Clerk to the Council and Treasurer of the Isle of Man. John Moore, Speaker, to Hope, and Hope to Palmerston, 6 July 1853, MNHL, GOCB 09845/1/6, ff. 472-4. *Manx Sun*, 9 July 1853. *Mona's Herald*, 13 July 1853.
494. *Manx Sun*, 16 and 23 July 1853. *Mona's Herald*, 20 July 1853.
495. Douglas committee to Palmerston, 6 July 1853, minutes and correspondence between Treasury and Isle of Man on customs reform, PP 1852-53 (982), p. 36.
496. Fielde to Palmerston and Wilson, 9, 12, 16, 19 and 27 July 1853, minutes and correspondence between Treasury and Isle of Man on customs reform, PP 1852-53 (982), pp. 38-41. *Mona's Herald*, 28 June 1854.
497. Wilson to Hope, 5 July 1853, and Hope to Palmerston and Wilson, 9 July 1853, MNHL, GOCB 09845/1/6, ff. 471 and 475-9. *Manx Sun*, 22 July 1854.
498. Treasury minute on proposed alteration of customs duties, 8 July 1853, PP 1852-53 (746), pp. 1-7. Wilson to Hope, 9 July 1853, MNHL, GOCB 09845/1/6, ff. 479-503. Minutes of meeting, 14 July 1853, MNHL, LCJ 09191/4/3, ff. 282-306.
499. Minutes of meetings, 14 and 19 July 1853, MNHL, LCJ 09191/4/3, ff. 306-24. *Mona's Herald* (supplement), 15 July 1853. *Manx Sun*, 22 June 1854.
500. Observations from Dumbell and Callister, 16 July 1853, minutes and correspondence between Treasury and Isle of Man on customs reform, PP 1852-53 (982), pp. 44-50. Minutes of meeting, 19 July 1853, MNHL, LCJ 09191/4/3, ff. 324-7. *Manx Sun*, 22 June 1854.

501. *The Economist*, 16 July 1853, p. 786.
502. *Punch*, volume 25, July-December 1853, p. 34.
503. Wilson to Dumbell and Callister and Hope, 22, 23 and 25 July 1853, MNHL, GOCB 09845/1/6, ff. 523-41. *Mona's Herald* (supplement), 28 July 1853. *Manx Sun*, 30 July 1853.
504. Treasury letter on proposed alteration of customs duties, 23 July 1853, PP 1852-53 (847), pp. 1-6. *Manx Sun*, 30 July 1853.
505. Minutes of meeting, 28 July 1853, MNHL, GOCB 09845/1/6, ff. 557-8. Minutes of meeting, 15 March and 22 June 1866, MNHL, HKJ 09191/2/5.
506. *Mona's Herald*, 3 August 1853.
507. Dumbell and Callister to Palmerston, 2 August 1853, and H. Waddington, Home Office, to Hope, 8 August 1853, MNHL, GOCB 09845/1/6, ff. 566-7.
508. Hope to Fitzroy, 26 August 1853, MNHL, GOCB 09845/1/6, ff. 578-95.
509. Hope to Wilson, 29 July 1853, MNHL, GOCB 09845/1/6, ff. 544-5.
510. Waddington to Hope, 8 August 1853, MNHL, GOCB 09845/1/6, ff. 566-71. Loch to Grey, 21 March 1865, MNHL, GOCB 09845/1/11, ff. 26-43. Correspondence between Wilson and Dumbell and Callister, August 1853, minutes and correspondence between Treasury and Isle of Man on customs reform, PP 1852-53 (982), pp. 57-64.
511. *Mona's Herald*, 10 August 1853. *Manx Sun*, 13 August 1853.
512. *Acts of Parliament*, 16 and 17 Victoria, chapters 106 and 107, see appendix 2. Wilson to Hope, 26 August 1853, MNHL, GOCB 09845/1/6, f. 577. *Mona's Herald*, 7 September 1853.
513. Moore, *A History*, p. 622.
514. *Manx Sun*, 28 January, 1 and 4 February and 27 May 1854. *Mona's Herald*, 8 February 1854.
515. Trevelyan to Hope, 27 April 1854, MNHL, GOCB 09845/1/7, ff. 34-5. Minutes of meeting, 5 May 1854, MNHL, LCJ 09191/4/3, ff. 390-3, and HKJ 09191/2/3. *Manx Sun*, 13 May 1854.
516. Correspondence between Wilson and Hope, 2 June to 7 July 1854, MNHL, GOCB 09845/1/7, ff. 50-3. *Manx Sun*, 10 June 1854.
517. Hope to Wilson and Wilson to Hope, 6 June 1854, MNHL, GOCB 09845/1/7, ff. 58-60.
518. Correspondence between Aberdeen, Fitzroy, Wilson and Hope, 2 June to 7 July 1854, MNHL, GOCB 09845/1/7, ff. 50-80. Minutes of meeting, 8 June 1854, MNHL, HKJ 09191/2/3. Minutes of meetings, MNHL, LCJ 09191/4/3, 8 and 28 June 1854, ff. 398-405 and 408-14. *Manx Sun*, 10 June and 1 July 1854. *Mona's Herald*, 14 June 1854.
519. Correspondence between Wilson and Hope, 2 June to 7 July 1854, MNHL, GOCB 09845/1/7, ff. 50-80.
520. J. J. Moore to Wilson, 23 June 1854, Granville, 22 July 1854, and Palmerston, 26 July 1854, appropriation of customs revenues for construction of harbour, and redress of grievances, PP 1864 (553), pp. 12 and 23-5.
521. Wilson to Hope and reply, 7 and 11 August 1854, MNHL, GOCB 09845/1/7, ff. 105-7. Minutes of meeting, 22 November 1854, MNHL, LCJ 09191/4/3, ff. 429-30. Minutes of meeting, 13 December 1854, MNHL, HKJ 09191/2/3.
522. *Act of Parliament*, 17 and 18 Victoria, chapter 122.
523. Waddington to Hope, 20 September 1854, enclosing letter from Wilson, 25 August 1854, MNHL, GOCB 09845/1/7, ff. 114-16.
524. Speaker Gawne to Aberdeen, 14 December 1854, MNHL, GOCB 09845/1/7, ff. 155-8.
525. Kneale, 'Trials of a Manx Radical', p. 93.

526. Mark Quayle, Clerk of the Rolls, to Sir George Grey, 24 January 1863, NA, HO 45/7434.
527. Henry Brougham Loch, first Baron Loch of Drylaw (1827-1900), Governor of the Isle of Man 1863-92, see appendix 7.
528. George Grey, second Baronet (1799-1882), MP 1832, Home Secretary 1846, a position he held intermittently for the next twenty years.
529. Royal Commission document relating to Loch as Governor, 29 January 1863, and Royal instructions for Loch, 29 January 1863, National Archives of Scotland, GD 268/118/30 and GD 268/118/2.
530. Loch to Sir George Grey, 21 March 1865, MNHL GOCB 09845/1/11, ff. 42-3. Customs returns 1863-66, 25 April 1867, MNHL, MB Finance and Customs D154/4x/3a. Government minute, June 1870, MNHL GOP 09845/1/4, ff. 104-5. William Thwaite, *Isle of Man: Its Civil and Ecclesiastical History*, (Sheffield, 1863), p. 7. Moore, *A History*, pp. 576, 646-7 and 712.
531. 'A. K.' writing in *The Echo*, 9 May 1892.
532. *Slater's Royal National Commercial Directory and Topography of the Isle of Man*, (London, 1857), p. 12.
533. Messrs Walker, Burgess & Cooper to Secretary of the Admiralty, 2 January 1861, and Hawkshaw's report to Public Works Loan Office, 28 October 1863, MNHL, GOP D151/11x/5, ff. 63 and 65-70.
534. Moore, *A History*, pp. 629-32.
535. Hawkshaw's report to Public Works Loan Office, 28 October 1863, MNHL, GOP D151/11x/5, ff. 65-70. *Manx Sun*, 3 September 1864. W. B. Kinley, 'The Development of Douglas Harbour: A Mariner's View', in Joyce Wareham, editor, *IOMNHAS*, volume 10, number 2, (Kendal, 1994), pp. 78-9.
536. *Brown's Isle of Man Directory* (Douglas, 1881), pp. 57-8.
537. *Manx Sun*, 26 November 1864.
538. *Mona's Herald*, 26 October 1864.
539. *Mona's Herald*, 1 February 1865. *Brown's Directory* (1881), pp. 57-8.
540. *Mona's Herald*, 8 February 1865.
541. Loch to Horatio Waddington, Under Secretary of State of the Home Office, 4 March 1865, MNHL, GOCB 09845/1/10, ff. 612-13.
542. Frederick Peel, Financial Secretary of the Treasury, to Loch, 17 March 1865, MNHL, GOCB 09845/1/11, f. 12.
543. Abernethy to Loch, 31 March 1865, MNHL, GOCB 09845/1/11, ff. 61-5.
544. Treasury to Loch, 26 April 1865, and reply, 27 April 1865, MNHL, GOCB 09845/1/11, ff. 95-6.
545. Moore to Loch, 23 March 1863, appropriation of customs revenues for construction of harbour and redress of grievances, PP 1864 (553), pp. 43-51.
546. James Brown (1815-81), see appendix 8.
547. *Statutes of the Isle of Man*, volume 3, 'Douglas Town (Amendment) Act', 1864, pp. 114-24. *Brown's Directory* (1881), pp. 52-6. Martin Faragher, 'The Browns of the Times: An Instance of Black Social Mobility in the 19th Century', in John Manley, editor, *North West Labour History*, issue 20, (Salford, 1996), pp. 44-9.
548. *Mona's Herald*, 2 March 1864.
549. Minutes of meeting, 15 and 16 March 1864, MNHL, HKJ 09191/2/4. *Mona's Herald*, 16 March 1864. *Brown's Directory* (1881), pp. 52-6.
550. Faragher, 'The Browns of the Times', p. 47.
551. Milner, *Manx Law Reports*, pp. 134-41. Minutes of meeting, 17 May 1864, MNHL, HKJ 09191/2/4. *Brown's Directory* (1881), pp. 52-6.

552. *Act of Parliament*, 25 and 26 Victoria, chapter 20.
553. *Manx Sun*, 24 June 1865.
554. Minutes of meeting, 22 November 1865, MNHL, HKJ 09191/2/5.
555. Loch to Grey, 21 March 1865, MNHL, GOCB 09845/1/11, ff. 22-6.
556. Loch to Grey, 21 March 1865, MNHL, GOCB, 09845/1/11, ff. 26-43.
557. Loch to Grey, 21 March 1865, MNHL, GOCB 09845/1/11, ff. 25-6.
558. Waddington to Loch, 27 March 1865, MNHL, GOCB 09845/1/11, f. 53.
559. Loch to Gladstone, 5 May 1865, MNHL, GOCB 09845/1/11, ff. 97-9.
560. Sir Llewellyn Woodward, *The Age of Reform*, 1815-1870, (Oxford, 1938), p. 181.
561. For in-depth details of the proposals, see C. W. Gawne, *Development of the Fiscal Relationship between the Isle of Man and Britain: Revestment Act to Common Purse Arrangement, 1765-1895*, (unpublished PhD thesis, University of Liverpool, 2005), pp. 160-3.
562. Hugh Culling Eardley Childers (1827-96), MP 1860, Financial Secretary of the Treasury 1865-66, First Lord of the Admiralty 1868-71, Secretary of State for War 1880-82, Chancellor of the Exchequer 1882-85, Home Secretary 1886. Loch to Childers, 14 November 1865, supplementary correspondence relative to financial measures for the Isle of Man, PP 1866 (115), pp. 1-3.
563. Childers to Loch, 26 November 1865, and Loch to Childers, 28 November 1865, supplementary correspondence relative to financial measures for the Isle of Man, PP 1866 (115), pp. 3-6.
564. Waddington to Loch, 2 February 1866, referring to Childers to Thomas George Baring, Under Secretary of State of the Home Office, 28 December 1865, and Treasury minute, 21 December 1865, MNHL, GOCB 09845/1/11, ff. 436-52.
565. Correspondence between Loch and Childers, 14 and 22 February, 1, 3 and 6 March 1866, supplementary correspondence relative to financial measures for the Isle of Man, PP 1866 (115), pp. 6-13. Loch to Waddington, 8 March 1866, MNHL, GOCB 09845/1/11, ff. 538-40.
566. Minutes of meetings, 14 and 15 March 1866, MNHL, LCJ 09191/4/4, ff. 226-8.
567. Minutes of meeting 15 March 1866, MNHL, HKJ 09191/2/5.
568. Minutes of meetings, 20 March 1866, MNHL, LCJ 09191/4/4, ff. 234-5. *Mona's Herald*, 21 March 1866.
569. Tynwald resolution, 20 March 1866, correspondence relative to financial measures for the Isle of Man, PP 1866 (115), p. 22.
570. Loch to Grey, 22 March 1866, and Waddington to Loch, 27 March 1866, MNHL, GOCB 09845/1/11, ff. 557 and 569. Minutes of meeting, April 1866, MNHL, HKJ 09191/2/5.
571. *Manx Sun*, 24 March 1866.
572. *Act of Parliament*, 29 Victoria, chapter 23, see appendix 2.
573. *Bill of Parliament*, 91, 23 March 1866. *Mona's Herald*, 2 May 1866.
574. Treasury to Loch, 7 July 1866, enclosing minute, 5 July 1866, MNHL, GOCB 09845/1/12, ff. 143-9.
575. Waddington to Loch, 11 July 1866, and Hunt to Loch, 6 August 1866, MNHL, GOCB 09845/1/12, ff. 154 and 180-3.
576. Loch to Sir Edward Lugard, Under Secretary of State for the War Office, 17 April 1865, MNHL, GOCB 09845/1/11, ff. 87-8. Clucas had succeeded James Burman as Clerk of the 'Lieutenancy' in 1864, hence the War Office involvement in the appointment.
577. See appendix 1.
578. *Statutes of the Isle of Man*, volume 3, 'House of Keys Election Act', 1866, pp. 372-421.

579. Minutes of meeting, 23 May 1866, MNHL, HKJ 09191/2/5. *Mona's Herald*, 30 May 1866.
580. Minutes of meeting, 8 June 1866, MNHL, HKJ 09191/2/5.
581. *Manx Sun*, 30 June 1866.
582. Minutes of meeting, 22 June 1866, MNHL, HKJ 09191/2/5.
583. *Brown's Directory* (1881), pp. 58-62.
584. *Census 1901*, total male population: 1861 - 24,727, 1871 - 25,914, 1881 - 25,760, males over 20: 1881 - 13,358, pp. 1 and 6. Return of the probable number of voters, June 1866, MNHL, MB Elections D155/2x.
585. Minutes of meeting, 17 July 1866, MNHL, HKJ 09191/4/4, ff. 256-7. *Brown's Directory* (1881), pp. 60-2.
586. *Brown's Directory* (1881), pp. 58-62.
587. R. E. Forster, 'The First Election of the House of Keys - 1867', in, A. M. Cubbon and Ann M. Harrison, editors, *JMM*, volume 7, number 83, (Douglas, 1967), p. 46.
588. Loch to Home Secretary, Spencer Horatio Walpole, 16 August 1866, MNHL, GOCB 09845/1/12, f. 202. Minutes of meeting, MNHL, HKJ 09191/2/5, 20 December 1866.
589. *Mona's Herald*, 10 November 1866.
590. *Manx Sun*, 2 and 16 February 1867.
591. *Manx Sun*, 6 April 1867.
592. See appendix 9.
593. *Mona's Herald*, 17 April 1867.
594. C. W. Gawne, 'Reforming Lieutenant Governor', in Dollin Kelly, editor, *New Manx Worthies*, (Douglas 2006), p. 288.
595. Report by Loch to Home Office, Printed Confidential Documents, 17 November 1873, MNHL, GOP 09845/Box 37.
596. Ibid., 13 September 1879.
597. MNHL, Government Office Correspondence Books and Papers, 1863-82, 09845.
598. Loch to Home Office, 25 March 1868, MNHL, GOCB 09845/1/13, f. 543, Loch to Treasury, 1 March 1872, MNHL, GOCB 09845/1/19, ff. 204-5, 31 March 1877, MNHL, GOCB 09845/1/32, ff. 23-5, and 27 January 1882, MNHL, GOCB 09845/1/37, ff. 573-4.
599. Moore, *A History*, pp. 720-1. David G. Kermode, *Offshore Island Politics: The Constitutional and Political Development of the Isle of Man in the Twentieth Century*, (Liverpool, 2001), p. 16. See appendix 1, 'Detailed Customs Duties Revenue, 1867-1900'.
600. Exchange of correspondence between Loch, Treasury and Home Office, 16 February to 16 December 1871, MNHL, GOCB 09845/1/16, ff. 239-627.
601. Loch to Harcourt, 15 March 1882, NA, HO 45/9619/A14728.
602. Moore, *A History*, pp. 958-9. Birch, *Economic Geography*, p. 184. Vaughan Robinson and Danny McCarroll, editors, *The Isle of Man: Celebrating a Sense of Place*, (Liverpool, 1990), pp. 204-5.
603. Sir Spencer Walpole (1839-1907), Governor of Isle of Man 1882-93, see appendix 10.
604. *Statutes of the Isle of Man*, volumes 3-6. There were 1,240 pages of legislation during Loch's nineteen years of office (1863-82) and 990 during Walpole's eleven (1882-93).
605. Walpole to Godfrey Lushington, Permanent Under Secretary of State of the Home Office, 20 May 1885, and John Hibbert to Lushington, 11 June 1885, NA, HO 45/9654/A40068.
606. Walpole, *Land of Home Rule*, p. 274.
607. Moore, *A History*, pp. 813-14.

608. *Act of Parliament*, 50 Victoria, chapter 5. The annual resolution was only ceased in 1955.
609. Walpole, *Land of Home Rule*, p. 254.
610. *Debates of Tynwald*, volume 6, 22 April 1890, pp. 616-19.
611. Loch to Treasury, 18 June 1867, and George Ward Hunt, Financial Secretary of the Treasury, to Loch, 26 June 1867, MNHL, GOCB 09845/1/13, ff. 71-2 and 82-6.
612. *Debates of Tynwald*, volume 6, 30 April 1890, pp. 679-706.
613. *Mona's Herald*, 7 May 1890.
614. Walpole to Welby, 5 and 17 July 1890, MNHL, GOCB 09845/1/41, ff. 150-1 and 169.
615. Walpole to Welby, 23 September 1890, MNHL, GOCB 09845/1/41, ff. 274-5.
616. Reginald Earle Welby, first Baronet (1832-1915), joined Treasury 1856, Assistant Financial Secretary of the Treasury 1880, Permanent Secretary of the Treasury 1885-94.
617. Walpole to Welby, 11 October 1890, MNHL, GOCB 09845/1/41, ff. 308-12.
618. Ibid.
619. Walpole to Murray, 12 November 1890, MNHL, GOCB 09845/1/41, ff. 374-5.
620. W. Jackson, Treasury, to Walpole, 18 December 1890, Isle of Man customs duties papers 1890-94, MNHL, MB Finance and Customs D154/4x/25, pp. 2-3.
621. Sir James Gell (1823-1905), High Bailiff of Castletown 1854, Attorney General 1866, First Deemster 1898, Clerk of the Rolls 1900, edited a number of works dealing with laws and constitution of the Island. Walpole to Gell, 20 and 22 December 1890, MNHL, GOCB 09845/1/41, ff. 454-9.
622. Minutes of meeting, 13 January 1891, MNHL, LCJ 09191/4/6, ff. 134-5.
623. For in-depth details of the various lengthy negotiations between 1891 and 1893, see Gawne, *Development of the Fiscal Relationship*, pp. 202-25.
624. Welby to Walpole, enclosing extract from a report by Dick, 19 February 1891, Isle of Man customs duties papers 1890-94, MNHL, MB Finance and Customs D154/4x/25, pp. 7-8.
625. Walpole to Welby, 24 February 1891, MNHL, GOCB 09845/1/41, f. 615.
626. Welby to Walpole, 17 March 1891, Isle of Man customs duties papers 1890-94, MNHL, MB Finance and Customs D154/4x/25, p. 11.
627. *Debates of Tynwald*, volume 8, 7 April 1891, pp. 360-3.
628. *Debates of Tynwald*, volume 9, 9 July 1891, pp. 46-54.
629. Sir Alured Dumbell (1835-1900), High Bailiff of Ramsey 1873, second Deemster 1880, Clerk of the Rolls 1883, son of George William Dumbell.
630. *Debates of Tynwald*, volume 9, 17 November 1891, pp. 133-210.
631. *Debates of Tynwald*, volume 9, 28 January 1892, pp. 366-419.
632. *Act of Parliament*, 55 and 56 Victoria, chapter 28, see appendix 2.
633. *Statutes of the Isle of Man*, 'An Act to consolidate and amend the Laws as to Public Education and Industrial Schools', 1893.
634. Moore, *A History*, p. 687.
635. Thomas Thurman, record of an 1895 holiday, MNHL 09370/1.
636. Moore, *A History*, pp. 687-8.
637. *Isle of Man Times*, 19 November 1887.
638. *Statutes of the Isle of Man*, volume 6, 'Poor Relief Act', 1888, pp. 55-62.
639. Douglas Poor Relief Committee minute book, 1888-95, MNHL 0511.

640. Douglas Poor Relief General Purposes Subcommittee minute book, 1888-94, 6 July 1892, MNHL 05110.
641. Walpole, *Land of Home Rule*, p. 274.
642. Walpole to Home Office, 17 April 1889, MNHL, GOCB 09845/1/40, ff. 282-304.
643. Sir Joseph West Ridgeway (1844-1930), Governor of Isle of Man 1893-95, see appendix II.
644. For in-depth details of the various lengthy negotiations between 1893 and 1895, see Gawne, *Development of the Fiscal Relationship*, pp. 226-40.
645. *Statutes of the Isle of Man*, volume 6, 'An Act with respect to returns of tea and tobacco imported into the Isle of Man', 1894, pp. 602-5.
646. Ridgeway to Under Secretary of State of the Home Office, 16 May 1895, MNHL, GOCB 09845/1/45, f. 172. Richard Prowse, Secretary to the Customs, to Ridgeway, 14 June 1895, Isle of Man customs duties papers 1894-95, MNHL, MB Finance and Customs D154/4x/28, pp. 6-13. Minutes of meeting, 29 June 1895, MNHL, LCJ 09191/4/6, f. 225.
647. *Debates of Tynwald*, volume 12, 5 July 1895, pp. 546-52.
648. *Statutes of the Isle of Man*, volume 7, 'An Act to amend the Revenue Returns Act, 1894', 1895, pp. 6-8. *Debates of Tynwald*, volume 13, 9 July and 13 August 1895, pp. 6-9. Ridgeway to Secretary to the Customs, 11 July 1895, MNHL, GOCB 09845/1/45, ff. 223-4.
649. Committee report on the petition of the Duke of Atholl, PP 1805 (139), pp. 1-9. Various accounts and papers relating to the petition of the Duke of Atholl, PP 1805, (11, 29, 79, 143, 159 and 160).
650. The document containing this information is listed online at British National Archives as '1859/60, Isle of Man, contribution from customs', NA, HO45/6745, but after an extensive search it was confirmed on 15 August 2005 that the original was unable to be traced.
651. Whilst it has been possible to abstract the customs revenue figures from the Isle of Man's general revenue for the construction of appendix I, 'Customs Duties Revenue, 1867-1900', it has not been possible to separate the customs expenditure figures as they were merged with the other items of general expenditure from 1866/67.
652. A. W. Moore, *Manx Worthies, or Biographies of notable Manx Men and Women*, (Douglas, 1901), p. 186. Kneale, 'Trials of a Manx Radical', pp. 89-93. Harrison, 'Reform from the North', pp. 403-12.
653. Judy Drake and Iris Green, *John Courtney Bluett*, (Basingstoke, 1989).
654. Robert Kelly, *For those in Peril*, (Onchan, 1979).
655. *Dictionary of National Biography*, (London, 1886), pp. 76-80. *Oxford Dictionary of National Biography*, (Oxford, 2004), pp.987-90.
656. Gawne, 'Reforming Lieutenant Governor', pp. 286-9.
657. Faragher, 'The Browns of the Times', pp. 44-9.
658. List of Members of the House of Keys 26 July 1866, MNHL, HKJ 09191/2/5, and elected 3-5 April 1867, 09191/2/6. Minutes of meeting, 18 April 1867, MNHL, LCJ 09191/2/4, ff. 285-6. Spicer, 'The Worthiest Men in the Land during Five Centuries', pp. 143-7.
659. Winterbottom, *Governors of the Isle of Man*, pp. 96-106.
660. Ibid., pp. 106-11.

Bibliography

PRIMARY SOURCES

Manx Parliamentary Proceedings
Debates of Tynwald
Statutes of the Isle of Man

British Parliamentary Proceedings
Acts of Parliament
Bills of Parliament
Debrett's Parliamentary Register
Parliamentary Debates
Parliamentary Papers

Manx Newspapers and Periodicals
Isle of Man Examiner
Isle of Man Times
Manks Advertiser
Manx Liberal
Manx Sun
Mona's Herald
Peel City Guardian and Chronicle
Rising Sun
Brown's Isle of Man Directory, (Douglas, 1881 and 1894)
Isle of Man Examiner Almanac, (Douglas, 1883-97)
Isle of Man Examiner Annual, (Douglas, 1898-1900)
Quiggin's Illustrated Guide and Visitor's Companion, (Douglas, 1841)
Slater's Royal National Commercial Directory and Topography of the Isle of Man, (London, 1857)

British Newspapers and Periodicals
The Echo
The Economist

Gentlemen's Magazine
Morning Chronicle and London Advertiser
Pigot and Co.'s Directory, (London, 1824)
Pigot and Slater's Directory, (London, 1837)
Punch
Slater's Directory, (London, 1867)

Reports
The Report of the Commissioners of Inquiry for the Isle of Man, 1792, (London, 1805)
Report of the Departmental Committee on the constitution, etc. of the Isle of Man, Cd. 5950, (London, 1911)
Report of the Commission on the Isle of Man Constitution, volume I, (Douglas, 1959)
Report of the Finance Board on Customs and the Common Purse Arrangement, (Douglas, 1966)
Relationships between the United Kingdom and the Channel Islands and the Isle of Man, (London, 1969-73).
PA International: Review of the Isle of Man-United Kingdom Common Purse Agreement, (London, 1976)
First Interim Report of the Tynwald Select Committee on the Common Purse, (Douglas, 1978)

Statistics
Composite Price Index, 1750-2003, Office for National Statistics, (London, 2004)
Islands in the British Seas, Enumerator's Schedule, Census 1841, microfilm
Islands in the British Seas, Isle of Man, Jersey, Guernsey and adjacent Isles, Census 1881, 1891 and *1901*, (London, 1883, 1893 and 1903)
Isle of Man, Isle of Man Government Treasury, (Douglas, 1995)
Isle of Man Census 2006, Isle of Man Government Treasury, (Douglas, 2007).
Isle of Man, Sheet 95, Landranger Series, Ordnance Survey, (Southampton, 2002).
Isle of Man Summer Passenger Arrivals, 1887-2003, fourth edition, Economic Affairs Division of the Treasury, (Douglas, 2004)

Reference Works
Dictionary of National Biography
Microsoft Encarta 96 Encyclopaedia
Oxford Dictionary of National Biography
The New Collins Concise English Dictionary

BIBLIOGRAPHY

The Oxford English Dictionary
Who was Who

Manx National Heritage Library and Archives
Atholl Papers 09707
Duke of Atholl's collections of letters 01996 and 09979
Bluett Papers 09566
Bridge House Papers
Sir Wadsworth Busk's correspondence 10362
Castle Rushen Papers 09782
Civil Records, *Libri Irrotulamentorum* 09864
Civil Records, *Libri Scaccarii* 10071
Derby Papers 01719
Records of the Diocese of Sodor and Man 09309
Douglas Poor Relief Committee minute book, 1888-95 05111
Douglas Poor Relief General Purposes Subcommittee minute book, 1888-94 05110
Drinkwater Papers 09771
Election Association minute book 000290
Sir James Gell to Governor Henniker 01058C
Goldie-Taubman Papers 09591
Government Office Correspondence Books 09845
Government Office Papers 09845
House of Keys Journals 09191
Canon Edward William Kissack's diary, historical notes and matters of antiquarian interest 10907
Legislative Council Journals 09191
Manx Books: Constitution D151, Finance and Customs D154, Elections D155 and Atholl Family F70
Melville collection of manuscripts 01798
George Moore Letter Books, 1750-60 00501C and 1766-78 00499C
Mortgage and Deeds series 09494
Papers relating to the sale of the Isle of Man 00576C
Papers relating to St George's church 01989
Thomas Thurman, record of an 1895 holiday 09370
Unknown to the Marquis of Rockingham 05966
Colonel Mark Wilks Papers 00332

British National Archives
Customs Papers 143
Home Office Papers 45, 98 and 99
Privy Council Papers 1
Treasury Papers 1

National Archives of Scotland
Papers of the Loch family GD 268/118

SECONDARY SOURCES

Ashworth, William J., *Customs and Excise: Trade, production and consumption in England, 1640-1845*, (Oxford, 2003)

Atholl, Murray, John, seventh Duke of, editor, *Chronicles of the Atholl and Tullibardine Families*, volume 4, (Edinburgh, 1908)

Bagley, J. J., *The Earls of Derby, 1485-1985*, (London, 1985)

Bawden, T. A., editor, *Tynwald Companion*, (Douglas, 2000)

Beer, Samuel H., *Treasury Control: The co-ordination of financial and economic policy in Great Britain*, (London, 1956)

Begg, David, Fischer, Stanley, and Dornbusch, Rudiger, *Economics: Fifth Edition*, (Maidenhead, 1984)

Belchem, J. C., 'Radical Entrepreneur: William Shirrefs and the Manx Free Press of the 1840s', in Warham, Joyce, editor, *Proceedings of the Isle of Man Natural History and Antiquarian Society*, volume 10, number 1, (Kendal, 1992)

Belchem, John, editor, *A New History of the Isle of Man, volume 5: The Modern Period, 1830-1999*, (Liverpool, 2000)

Birch, J. W., *The Isle of Man: A Study in Economic Geography*, (Cambridge, 1964)

Bird, Hinton, *An Island that led: The History of Manx Education*, (two volumes, Port St Mary, 1991 and 1995)

Blundell, William, 'A History of the Isle of Man, (1648-56)', in Harrison, William, editor, *The Manx Society*, volume 25, (Douglas, 1876)

Bowring, John, 'Free Trade Recollections', in *Howitt's Journal*, volume 11, (30 January 1847)

Bowring, John, *Autobiographical Recollections*, (London, 1877)

Bridges, The Rt Hon Lord, *The Treasury*, (London, 1964)

Bridson, Eric, 'A Disturbance at Douglas', in Cubbon, A. M., and Serjeant, W. R., editors, *Journal of the Manx Museum*, volume 6, number 77, (Douglas, 1961)

Broderick, George, translator, *Cronica Regum Mannie et Insularum: Chronicles of the Kings of Man and the Isles*, (Douglas, 1979)

Broderick, George, *Tynwald: a Manx cult-site and institution of pre-Scandinavian origin?*, (paper presented as a Centre for Manx Studies seminar in February 2003)

Bullock, H. A., *History of the Isle of Man*, (London, 1816)

Butler, Weeden, Reverend, *Memoirs of Mark Hildesley, Lord Bishop of Sodor and Man*, (London, 1799)

Cain, P. J., *Hobson and Imperialism: Radicalism, New Liberalism and Finance, 1887-1938*, (Oxford, 2002)

Cain, T. W., Deemster, 'Constitutional Reform in the Twentieth Century', in Critchlow, M. J., editor, *Proceedings of the Isle of Man Natural History and Antiquarian Society*, volume 10, number 3, (Kendal, 1996)

Canny, Nicholas, editor, *Oxford History of the British Empire: The Origins of Empire*, (Oxford, 1998)

Chaloner, James, 'A Short Treatise of the Isle of Man', in King, Daniel, *The Vale-Royal of England*, (London, 1656)

Coakley, Frances, editor, *A Manx Note Book*, CD-ROM, (Peel, 2006)

Connery, Chappel, *The Dumbell Affair*, (Prescot, 1981)

Craine, David, 'A Manx Merchant of the Eighteenth Century', in Gill, W. Walter, and Moore, Ramsey B., editors, *Proceedings of the Isle of Man Natural History and Antiquarian Society*, volume 4, number 4, (Douglas, 1945)

Craine, David, 'The Potato Riots, 1825', in Gill, W. Walter, and Moore, Ramsey B., editors, *Proceedings of the Isle of Man Natural History and Antiquarian Society*, volume 4, number 4, (Douglas, 1945)

Craine, Leonard, 'The Castle Mona Estate', R. A. Curphey, editor, *Proceedings of the Isle of Man Natural History and Antiquarian Society*, volume 8, number 1, (Douglas, 1976)

Creer, Hampton, *Never to Return: The Story of Manx Prisoners Transported to the Penal Colonies*, (Douglas, 2000)

Cringle, Terry, in Kniveton, Gordon N., editor, *Here is the News: An Illustrated Manx History*, (Douglas, 1992)

Cubbon, A. M., *Early Maps of the Isle of Man*, (fourth edition, reprinted Douglas, 1994)

Cubbon, W., *A Bibliographical Account of Works relating to the Isle of Man*, (two volumes, Oxford, 1933 and 1939)

Cubbon, W., editor, 'The Baptism of the Castle Mona', *Journal of the Manx Museum*, volume 3, number 45, (Douglas, 1935)

Cubbon, W., editor, 'Centenary of Erection of Smelt Monument', *Journal of the Manx Museum*, volume 3, number 53, (Douglas, 1937)

Dickinson, H. T., editor, *Britain and the American Revolution*, (Harlow, 1998)

Dickinson, J. R., *The Lordship of Man Under the Stanleys: Government and Economy in the Isle of Man, 1580-1704*, (Preston, 1997)

Dolley, Michael, 'Procurator Extraordinary - Sir Wadsworth Busk (1730-1811)', in Curphey, R. A., editor, *Proceedings of the Isle of Man Natural History and Antiquarian Society*, volume 8, number 3, (Douglas, 1976-78)

Donnelly, Graham, *A Foundation in Economics*, (Cheltenham, 1991)

Drake, Judy, and Green, Iris, *John Courtney Bluett*, (Basingstoke, 1989)

Faragher, Martin, 'The Browns of the Times: An Instance of Black Social Mobility in the 19th Century', in Manley, John, editor, *North West Labour History*, issue 20, (Salford, 1996)

Feltham, John, 'A Tour through the Isle of Man in 1797 and 1798', in Airey, Robert, Reverend, editor, *The Manx Society*, volume 6, (Douglas, 1861)

Fieldhouse, D. K., *Economics and Empire, 1830-1914*, (London, 1973)

Forster, R. E., *A Study of the Constitutional and Financial Movements in the Isle of Man, 1833-1866*, (unpublished BA thesis, University of Birmingham, 1951)

Forster, R. E., 'The Reformist Movements in 1837', in Forster, R. E., editor, *Proceedings of the Isle of Man Natural History and Antiquarian Society*, volume 6, number 3, (Kendal, 1964)

Forster, R. E., 'The First Election of the House of Keys - 1867', in Cubbon, A. M., and Harrison, Ann M., editors, *Journal of the Manx Museum*, volume 7, number 83, (Douglas, 1967)

Forster, R. E., 'Aspects of Manx Emigration: 1750-1990', in Warham, Joyce, editor, *Proceedings of the Isle of Man Natural History and Antiquarian Society*, volume 10, number 1, (Kendal, 1992)

Friedman, Milton, *Essays in Positive Economics*, (Chicago, 1953)

Fyson, R. C. M., 'Bronterre O'Brien: A Chartist in the Isle of Man 1844-1847', in Critchlow, M. J., editor, *Proceedings of the Isle of Man Natural History and Antiquarian Society*, volume 10, number 4, (Kendall, 1998)

Gawne, C. W., *The Isle of Man's Annual Financial 'Imperial Contribution' to Britain, in particular, The British Parliament's Privy Council Committee Report, 1925-26*, (unpublished MA thesis, University of Liverpool, 1999).

Gawne, C. W., *Development of the Fiscal Relationship between the Isle of Man and Britain: Revestment Act to Common Purse Arrangement, 1765-1895*, (unpublished PhD thesis, University of Liverpool, 2005).

Gawne, C. W., 'Reforming Lieutenant Governor', in Kelly, Dollin, editor, *New Manx Worthies*, (Douglas 2006)

Gelling, Canon John, *A History of the Manx Church, 1698-1911*, (Douglas, 1998).
Grindley, Thomas, *The Story of Revestment: A Sketch of Manx History in the eighteenth century*, (Douglas, 1903)
Grindley, Thomas, *The Story of the Manx Crown Revenue*, (Douglas, 1903)
Harrison, Ann, 'Economic Opportunities, 1700', in Cubbon, A. M. and Harrison, Ann M., editors, *Journal of the Manx Museum*, volume 7, number 83, (Douglas, 1967)
Harrison, Ann M., 'Reform from the North, 1844-47', in Curphey, R. A., editor, *Proceedings of the Isle of Man Natural History and Antiquarian Society*, volume 8, number 4, (Douglas, 1982)
Harrison, Ann M., 'Richard Sherwood in Manx Politics, 1867-83', in Curphey, R. A., editor, *Proceedings of the Isle of Man Natural History and Antiquarian Society*, volume 8, number 4, (Douglas, 1982)
Harrison, S., editor, *100 Years of Heritage*, (Douglas, 1986)
Harrison, William, 'Mona Miscellany', in Harrison, William, editor, *The Manx Society*, volume 16, (Edinburgh, 1869)
Harrison, William, 'Records of the Tynwald and St John's Chapel in the Isle of Man', *The Manx Society*, volume 19, (Douglas, 1871)
Hill, C. P., *British Economic and Social History, 1700-1982*, (London, 1985)
Hobsbawm, E. J., *Industry and Empire - An Economic History of Britain since 1750*, (London, 1968)
Hoon, E. E., *The organisation of the English customs system, 1696-1786*, (Newton Abbot, 1968)
Howe, Anthony, 'Restoring free trade: the British experience, 1776-1873', in Winch, Donald, and O'Brien, Patrick K., editors, *The Political Economy of British Historical Experience, 1688-1914*, (Oxford, 2002)
Jarvis, R. C. *Manx Smuggling in the Eighteenth Century*, (Board of Customs, 1955/56)
Kelly, Robert, *For those in Peril*, (Onchan, 1979)
Kermode, D. G., *Devolution at Work: A Case Study of the Isle of Man*, (Farnborough, 1979)
Kermode, David G., *Offshore Island Politics: The Constitutional and Political Development of the Isle of Man in the Twentieth Century*, (Liverpool, 2001)
Kinley, W. B., 'The Development of Douglas Harbour: A Mariner's View', in Wareham, Joyce, editor, *Proceedings of the Isle of Man Natural History and Antiquarian Society*, volume 10, number 2, (Kendal, 1994)
Kinvig, R. H., *The Isle of Man: A social, cultural and political history*, (Liverpool, 1975)
Kneale, W. T., 'The Trials of a Manx Radical: The Life and Times of Robert Fargher, 1803-63', in Cubbon, A. M., and Serjeant, W. R., editors, *Journal of the Manx Museum*, volume 6, number 76, (Douglas, 1960)
Kniveton, Gordon N., editor, *Douglas Centenary, 1896-1996*, (Douglas, 1996)

Laughton, Alfred, *High Bailiff Laughton's Reminiscences*, (Douglas, 1916)
Laughton, J. B., *A New Historical Topographical and Parochial Guide to the Isle of Man*, (Douglas, 1842)
Leneman, Leah, *Living in Athol: A Social History of the Estates, 1685-1785*, (Edinburgh, 1986)
Loch, Gordon, *The Family of Loch*, (Edinburgh, 1934)
Marshall, P. J., editor, *Oxford History of the British Empire: The Eighteenth Century*, (Oxford, 1998)
Mathieson, N., 'The Governors during the Atholl Lordship', in West, J. I., editor, *Proceedings of the Isle of Man Natural History and Antiquarian Society*, volume 6, number 1, (Kendal, 1959)
May, Trevor, *An Economic and Social History of Britain, 1760-1970*, (Harlow, 1987)
Miller, Peter N., *Defining the Common Good: Empire, religion and philosophy in eighteenth-century Britain*, (Cambridge, 1994)
Milner, Alan, editor-in-chief, *The Manx Law Reports, 1522-1920*, (Oxford, 2004)
Mitchell, B. R., *Abstract of British Historical Statistics*, (London, 1962)
Moore, A. W., *Extracts from the Journals of the Self-elected House of Keys*, (Douglas, 1890)
Moore, A. W., editor, *Manx Ballads and Music*, (Douglas, 1896)
Moore, A. W., *A History of the Isle of Man*, (two volumes, London, 1900, reprinted Douglas, 1977)
Moore, A. W., *Manx Worthies, or Biographies of notable Manx Men and Women*, (Douglas, 1901)
Moore, George, 'The Effect of the Act of 1765', in Forster, R. E., editor, *Proceedings of the Isle of Man Natural History and Antiquarian Society*, volume 7, number 1, (Douglas, 1967)
Morgan, Kenneth, 'Mercantilism and the British empire, 1688-1815', in Winch, Donald, and O'Brien, Patrick K., editors, *The Political Economy of British Historical Experience, 1688-1914*, (Oxford, 2002)
Morrison, Sophia, editor, *Mannin: a Journal of Matters Past and Present relating to Mann*, volume 6, (Douglas, 1915)
Norris, Samuel, *Manx Memories and Movements*, (third edition, reprinted Douglas, 1994)
Oliver, J. R., 'A Collection of National Documents Relating to the Isle of Man: Respecting Concessions to the People and Subjects of the Isle of Man', in Oliver, J. R., editor, *The Manx Society*, volume 9, (Douglas, 1863)
Parr, John, 'An Abstract of the Laws, Customs and Ordinances of the Isle of Man', in Gell, James, editor, *The Manx Society*, volume 12, (Douglas, 1867)
Paterson, David, *Liberalism and Conservatism, 1846-1905*, (Oxford, 2001)
Payne, E. J., editor, *Select Works of Edmund Burke, and Miscellaneous Writings*, (three volumes, Oxford, 1874-78)
Pickard, Chris, 'Eighteenth Century Manx Merchantmen and Privateers', in Warham, Joyce, editor, *Proceedings of the Isle of Man Natural History and Antiquarian Society*, volume 9, number 4,

(Douglas, 1980-89)

Porter, Andrew, editor, *Oxford History of the British Empire: The Nineteenth Century*, (Oxford, 1999)

Postlethwayt, Malachy, *The Universal Dictionary of Trade and Commerce*, (two volumes, London, 1751 and 1755)

Qualtrough, J. K. and Scatchard, W. J., *That Island*, (Douglas, 1965)

Robertson, David, *A Tour through the Isle of Man*, (London, 1794)

Robinson, Vaughan, and McCarroll, Danny, editors, *The Isle of Man: Celebrating a Sense of Place*, (Liverpool, 1990)

Roeder, C., editor, *Manx Notes and Queries: With an Account of Francois Thurot*, (Douglas, 1904).

Roper, William, *A Short History of the Transactions in the Isle of Man on which the House of Keys founded their late Petition to the House of Commons against His Grace the Duke of Atholl*, (Douglas, 1825).

Roseveare, Henry, *The Treasury: The Foundations of Control*, (London, 1973)

Sacheverell, William, 'An Account of the Isle of Man', (c.1692), in Cumming, J. G., Reverend, editor, *The Manx Society*, volume 1, (Douglas, 1859)

Sargeaunt, B. E., *An Outline of the Financial System of the Isle of Man Government*, (Douglas, 1925)

Searle, Charles ('An Impartial Hand'), *A Short View of the Present State of the Isle of Man*, (1767)

Slack, Stuart, *Streets of Douglas - Old and New*, (Douglas, 1996)

Sloman, John, and Sutcliffe, Mark, *Economics*, (Hemel Hempstead, 1997)

Smith, Adam, *The Wealth of the Nations: Books 1-3*, (1776, reprinted London, 1986)

Smith, Anthony, *National Identity*, (London, 1991)

Smith, Graham, *Something to declare: 1000 years of Customs and Excise*, (London 1980)

Solly, M., *Government and Law in the Isle of Man*, (Castletown, 1994)

Speed, P. F, *The Growth of the British Economy, 1700-1850*, (Exeter, 1980)

Spicer, J. Inglis, 'The Worthiest Men in the Land during Five Centuries', in Cubbon, W., editor, *Journal of the Manx Museum*, volume 2, number 37, (Douglas, 1933)

Stanley, James, seventh Earl of Derby, 'History and Antiquities of the Isle of Man', in Mackenzie, William, Reverend, editor, *The Manx Society*, volume 3, (Douglas, 1860)

Stenning, E. H., *Portrait of the Isle of Man*, (London, 1958)

Stott, Ros, 'A Brief Encounter: The Duke of Atholl and the Isle of Man 1736-1764', in Davey, Peter, and Finlayson, David, editors, *Mannin Revisited*, (Edinburgh, 2002)

Thwaite, William, *Isle of Man: Its Civil and Ecclesiastical History*, (Sheffield, 1863)

Townley, Richard, *A Journal kept in the Isle of Man*, (two volumes, Whitehaven, 1791)

Train, Joseph, *An Historical and Statistical Account of the Isle of Man*, (two volumes, Douglas, 1845)
Waldron, G., *The History and Description of the Isle of Man*, (London, 1744)
Walker, John, *The Queen Has Been Pleased: The British Honours System at Work*, (London, 1986)
Walpole, Spencer, *Land of Home Rule: An Essay on the History and Constitution of the Isle of Man*, (London, 1893)
Watson, J. Steven, *The Reign of George III, 1760-1815*, (Oxford, 1960)
Webber, Captain, 'An Impartial Enquiry, c.1760', in Wood, G. W., *An Account of Manx Smuggling*, (Douglas, c.1917)
Webber, David T., *An Illustrated Encyclopedia of the Isle of Man*, (Douglas, 1997)
Welch, John ('A Stranger'), *A Six Day's Tour through the Isle of Man*, (Douglas, 1836)
Wilkins, Frances, *The Isle of Man in Smuggling History*, (Kidderminster, 1992)
Wilkins, Frances, *George Moore and Friends: Letters from a Manx Merchant (1750-1760)*, (Kidderminster, 1994)
Wilkins, Frances, *The Smuggling Trade Revisited*, (Kidderminster, 2004)
Winch, Donald, and O'Brien, Patrick K., editors, *The Political Economy of British Historical Experience, 1688-1914*, (Oxford, 2002)
Winterbottom, Derek, *Governors of the Isle of Man since 1765*, (Douglas, 1999)
Winterbottom, Derek, (script of a talk given to Castletown Heritage Society in 2003)
Woods, G., *An Account of the Past and Present State of the Isle of Man*, (London, 1811)
Woodward, Llewellyn, Sir, *The Age of Reform, 1815-1870*, (Oxford, 1938)
Wright, Maurice, *Treasury Control of the Civil Service*, (London, 1969)
Young, G. V. C., and Foster, Caroline, *Captain François Thurot*, (Peel, 1986)

INDEX

Bold page numbers refer to illustrations.

Aberdeen, Earl of, Prime Minister 143, 144, 145
Abernethy, James 150-2
'Abernethy's bird-cage' 150-3, **152**
Acts, British (in date order):
  Goods from Foreign parts by whom to be imported (1651) 17-18
  An Act for the Encouraging and Increasing of Shipping and Navigation (1660) 17-18
  An Act for the Encouragement of Trade (1663) 17-18
  An Act for the Planting of Tobacco in England, and for regulating the Plantation Trade (1670) 17-18
  An Act for the Encouragement of the Greenland and Eastland Trades, and for the better Securing the Trade (1672) 17-18
  An Act for better securing the duties of East India goods (1706) 22
  An Act for the Further preventing His Majesty's subjects from trading to the East Indies under Foreign Commissions (1721) 23
  An Act for the Improvement His Majesty's Revenues of Customs, Excise and Inland Duties (1726) 23, 40
  An Act for carrying into execution a contract made, pursuant to the Act of Parliament of the twelfth of His late Majesty King George the First and the Duke and Duchess of Atholl, the proprietors of the Isle of Man, and their trustees, for the purchase of the said Island and its dependencies, under certain exceptions therein particularly mentioned ('Revestment Act') (1765) 11, 43, 45, **46**, 48, 49, 50, 58, 60, 78, 79, 87, 132, 200, 201
  An Act for more effectually preventing the mischiefs arising to the revenue and commerce of Great Britain and Ireland from the illicit and clandestine trade to and from the Isle of Man ('Mischief Act') (1765) 42, 45, 48, 49, 50, 60, 200, 201
  An Act for encouraging and regulating the trade and manufactures of the Isle of Man (1767) 54-6, 69-70, 87, 201
  An Act for granting to His Majesty several additional duties upon certain goods imported into the Isle of Man; and for the better regulating the trade and securing the revenue of the said Island (1780) 57
  An Act for the further encouragement of the trade and manufacturers of the Isle of Man, for improving the revenue thereof; and for the more effectual prevention of smuggling to and from the said Island (1798) 67-8, 70
  An Act for settling and securing a certain Annuity on John, now Duke of Atholl, and the heirs general of the seventh Earl of Derby (1805) 70, 79
  An Act for regulating and encouraging the trade, for the improvement of the revenue, and prevention of smuggling to and from the Isle of Man (1805) 70
  An Act to repeal certain Acts regulating the importation and exportation of corn, grain, meal and flour (1821) 72
  An Act to empower the Commissioners of His Majesty's Treasury to purchase a certain Annuity in respect of Duties of Customs levied in the Isle of Man, and any reserved Sovereign Rights in the said Island, belonging to John, Duke of Atholl (1825) 77
  An Act for regulating the trade of the Isle of Man (1825) 78
  An Act to amend laws relating to the importation of corn (1828) 87
  An Act for regulating the trade of the Isle of Man (1833) 85

An Act for granting Duties of Customs (1833) 85
An Act to regulate the importation of corn into the Isle of Man (1835) 87
An Act to Amend the Laws relating to the Customs in the Isle of Man (1844) 118, 128, 135, 137, 160
An Act for Consolidating Customs Duties Acts (1853) 142
An Act to amend and consolidate the Laws relating to the Customs of the United Kingdom and of the Isle of Man, and certain Laws relating to Trade and Navigation and the British Possessions (1853) 142, 150, 156, 160
An Act for the further Alteration and Amendment of the Laws and Duties of Customs (1854) 145
An Act respecting the issue of Writs of Habeas Corpus out of England into Her Majesty's Possessions Abroad (1862) 155
An Act to alter certain Duties of Customs in the Isle of Man, and for other purposes ('Customs, Harbours and Public Purposes Act') (1866) **164**, 164-5, 166, 172, 173, 186, 205
An Act to amend the law respecting the Customs Duties of the Isle of Man (1887) 179
An Act to amend the law respecting the Customs Duties in the Isle of Man (1892) 189
Acts, Manx (in date order):
Customary Laws (1417) 15, (1422) 10, 21, (1429) 21, (1523) 17, (1577), (1582) and (1593)14, (1609) 15, 16
Regulations for the Castles, &c, and Ordinances &c (1561) 15
Customs Duties (1577) 15, 17
Herring Fishery (1610) and (1613) 15
Ordinances (1636) 15
Customary Lands (1645) 15
An Act Against Non-residence (1697) 21
Act of Settlement (1704) 21
An Act for Preventing Frauds in Her Majesty's Customes by the Exportation of forraigne Goods from this Island (1711) 22

Customs Act (1714) 22
Statute Laws, Book of Rates of 1692 confirmed by Keys (1737) 17, 20-1, 26
Act for affording Relief to Insolvent Debtors in the Isle of Man (1814) 71
Douglas Town (Amendment) Act (1864) 153
House of Keys Election Act (1866) 165-70, **168**, **169**, 172, 205
Poor Relief Act (1888) 192
Act to consolidate and amend the Laws as to Public Education and Industrial Schools (1893) 189-90
An Act with respect to returns of tea and tobacco imported into the Isle of Man (1894) 193-4
An Act to amend the Revenue Returns Act, 1894 (1895) 198
Addington, Henry *see* Viscount Sidmouth
Admiralty 150, 152
Africa 18, 29
agriculture *see* farming
alms houses **192**
America 28, 29, 31, 56, 113, 201
asylum 153, 156, 182
Atholl, Dukes of, Lords of Man 10, 129, 161, 200
Blair Atholl and Dunkeld, ducal properties 57, 79, 80
succession to lordship from Earls of Derby 11, 23-6
suzerain and other rights of Isle of Man by Britain, purchase of 11, 37-48, 57-60, 63-5, 67, 68-70, 79-80, 199, 201, 202
see also smuggling
Attorney General 7, 8, 45
Ayre 167, 170

Bacon, John Joseph 29
Ballamoore 29, 35
Ballaugh coast, battle off, (1760) 33-5, **34**
Bank of Mona 148, 175
Battle of Sky Hill (1079) **9**, 9-10
Belchem, John 5
Berail, Peter 33
Bill for confirming the Sale and Conveyances made to His Majesty, of the Isle, Castle, Peel, and

Lordship of Man, and other Estates in the said Island of Man, lately belonging to John, Duke of Atholl (1829) 80
Birch, J. W. 5
Bishop of Sodor and Man 7, 8, 10, 24-5, 149, 205
Black Watch (*Freiceadan Dubh*) 47
Blamire, William, MP 98
Bluett, John Courtney 12, 83, 89, 90, 91, 92, 93, 94-8, **97**, 142, 203, 226
    Mrs Bluett 98
Blundell, William 3
Board of Trade 97, 108-10, 116, 131, 151
Bosanquet, John Bernard 78
Bowring, Dr Sir John, MP 12, **109**, 124, 203, 228
    customs and licence system 110-11, 116, 117, 118
    Mrs Bowring 119-20
    visit to Isle of Man 118-20, 121
Braddan 7, 94
brandy 28, 31, 32, 33, 39, 65, 85, 87, 91, 92, 101, 117, 118, 128, 134, 180
Bridson, Captain Paul 27
Brig *Caesar* **55**
Britain:
    Consolidated Fund 70, 77, 79, 91, 135, 142, 160, 209
    Crown 2, 7, 8, 54, 72, 74, 77, 99, 148, 149, 153, 166, 176, 205
    economic policies 21-2
    Exchequer 22, 23, 36, 40, 51, 54, 55, 79, 80, 83, 89, 121, 129, 134, 135, 137, 142, 143, 160, 161, 164-5, 185, 200
    'First Industrial Nation' 105
    free trade policy 105-6
    navigation and trade Acts 11, 17-18, 22
    sovereign rights, Isle of Man 1, 2, 4, 10-11, 12, 23, 37, 40-5, 47-8, 63-5, 79-80, 155, 199, 200, 201, 202
    see also Lords of Man: suzerain rights
    wars with France 22, 33
Brown, James 12, 230
    constitutional reform 153-6, **155**, 167
Bullock, Mrs Hannah 4, 51-2

Burke, Edmund 56
Busk, Wadsworth 58-9

Calcraft, Mrs 60
Callan, Catherine (Mrs George Moore) 29
Callister, William, MHK **133**, 136-7, 139, 140, 165, 166-7
Callow, Daniel, MHK 59
Campbell, Colin 39
Canada 103
Captains of parishes 45, 91, 116
Captains of towns 17, 45
Carrickfergus, Ireland, French attack on (1760) 34-5
'Castle Maze' 15
Castle Mona 77, **78**, 84, 120
Castle Rushen **19**, **20**, 24, 27, 28, 42, **45**, 73, 76, 85, 115, **126**, 154, **155**, 175, 176, 193
Castletown 7, **16**, **19**, 24, 28, 32, 46, 52, 66, 76, 93, 108, 115, 120, 125, **126**, 167, 170, 173
    transfer of capital to Douglas 175
Chaloner, James 3-4, 17
Charlotte, Lady, Baroness Strange 37, **38**, 40, 43, 57
Childers, Hugh Culling Eardley, MP **159**, 159-60, 164
Christian, Deemster Ewan 15
Christian, Ewan, MHK (of Milntown and Unrigg) 21
Christian, Ewan, MHK (of Lewaigue) 21
Christian, Deemster John 74, 98
Christian, John Edward 170
Christian, Captain Matthew 27-8
Christian, Reverend William Bell, MHK 172
Chronicles of the Kings of Man and the Isles (*Cronica Regum Mannie et Insularum*) 9
Churchill, Winston 48-9
Clerk of the Rolls 24, 108
'clique' 63, 82, 83, 101-3, 121, 123, 146, 202, 204, 206
Clucas, Captain John, MHK 102-3
Clucas, John Thomas 165
coasting trade 13, 67, 89, 98, 99, 111, 117, 120, 203
Cochrane, Governor Basil 31-2, 37
Cockburn, Lord Chief Justice 155
coffee 39, 54, 66, 85, 98, 117, 157, 183

271

Collector of Customs, Douglas 106, 140, 142, 181
Commissioners of Customs:
    England 18-19, 26, 66
    Scotland 38, 66
    Britain 94, 101, 107, 128, 129, 130
    see also Customs Department
Common Purse Arrangement 1-2, 177, 182, 183-90, 193-8, 206-7
Corlett, Thomas Arthur 94, 96, 98
Corn Laws 105
Cosnahan, Hugh, MHK 42
Cosnahan, John, MHK 58, 61
cottage, Manx 13, **14**, 16
Courtenay, William 78
Cowell, John Robert, MHK 181, 183, 184
Craigie, Lawrence 98
Crigan, Bishop Claudius 60
Crosse, John 57
Crovan, Godred **9**, 9-10
Crown see Britain
Cubbin, Henry, Thomas and Richard 108-9
Cunningham, Patrick Taubman, MHK 167, 169
Curphy, Captain 50
Curwen, John Christian, MP, MHK 59, 61, 67, **68**, 70
Cust, Sir John 51
customs see public finances
Customs Department 78, 96, 129, 130, 142, 159-60, 173, 175, 179, 183, 187, 188, 194-7, 198, 201
    see also Commissioners of Customs
'Customs, Harbours and Public Purposes Act' (1866) see British Acts

Darling, Alistair 207
Dawson, Lieutenant Governor Richard 60
debtors 26-7, 52, 71
Deemster 7, 8, 20, 24, 26, 45, 47, 108
Denmark 27, 28, 33
Department of Constitutional Affairs 8
Derby, Earls of, Lords of Man 10, 11, 18, 21, 23, 199, 200
    succession to lordship by Dukes of Atholl 11, 23
Derbyhaven 24, 27

Dickinson, Roger 5
diet 13
Disraeli, Benjamin 4
Dixon, Thomas 71
Douglas 7, 16, 18, 24, 27, 28, 29, 49, **52**, 54, 66, 75, 77, 84-5, **95**, 100, 113, 114, 115, **119**, 147, 153, **174**, 175, **192**, **197**
    breakwater and harbour **52**, 79, 96, 125, 150-3, **152**, 158, 173
    Customs House **106**, **119**
    election (1867) 167, 170-2, **171**
    fiscal reform 88, 92, 93, 94, 97, 108, 109, 116, 118, 119, 120, 130, 131, 133, 181, **196**
    Poor Relief Committee 192-3
    riots 72-3
    tourism 71, 182, 190, **196**
    Town Commissioners 153, 154, 167, 170
    transfer of capital from Castletown 175
Douglas (servant to George Moore and François Thurot) 35
Dow, Captain George 27-8
Drinkwater, Sir George 85
Drinkwater, Deemster William 156, 163
Duff, John 90
Duff, Robert 116
Dumbell, Alured 188
Dumbell banknote **148**
Dumbell, George William, MHK 90, 92, 115, 116-17, 131, **133**, 136-7, 138, 139, 140, 170, 172
Dumbell, Son & Howard 148
Dundas, Henry, Lord Melville 63, 67
Dunkirk 28, 33
Dutch East Indies 28

East India Company 27, 38
East Indies 18, 22, 23
Economist, The, 135-6
education 162, 174-5, 188-90, 192
Elizabeth, Lady, Countess of Derby 15
Ellenborough, Lord 70
Elliot, Captain James 33-5
Ellis, Everington & Company 108

INDEX

emigration 49-50
English Civil War 3, 10
Ennett, Margaret (Sally Innett) 115
'Espionage' 107
Europe, trade with 8, 17-18, 29, 30
European Union 8, 207-8
Ewart, William, MP 131, 132

Faeroe Islands 27, 33, 54
Fairfax, Lord 3, 17
Fargher, John Christian 154
Fargher, Robert 12, **82**, 83, 107, 114-15, 116, 130, 131, 147, 202, 225
Fargher, Thomas 170
farming 8, 13-15, 21, 22, 49, 52, 71, 72, 91, 94, 106, 125, 177, 199
Farrant, Edward Curphey MHK 167, 169
Fell, Captain Thomas 74-5
Feltham, George 48
Fielde, Matthew Henry 133-4
fiscal reform *see* public finances
fishing 13, 14, 15-16, **16**, 17, 22, 25, 31, 42, 49, **52**, 55, 57, 66, 68, 72, 78, 91, 94, 105, 106, 125, 148-9, 177, 199
Forster, Robert 4-5
Fowler, Mr 107
France 28, 30, 31, 39
    wars with Britain 22, 33
free trade 8, 12, 22, 81, 92, 96, 105-6, 109, 111, 112, 116, 120, 130, 187

Garff 167, 170
Garrett, Dr Philip 98
Garrett, Thomas 74, 116, 131
Gawne, Edward, MHK 61
Gawne, Edward Moore, Speaker of the House of Keys 154, 167, 169, 170
Gawne, Thomas, MHK 61
Gawne, Deemster Thomas 72, 74-5
Gell, Deemster Sir James 4, 185-6, **187**
Geneste, Mr 71
George III, King 40, 43, 45, 47

Germany 39
Gillie, James 33
gin 65, 85, 91, 92, 117, 118, 128
Gladstone, William Ewart 109-10, 117, 118, 133, 136, 144, 151, 158
Glenfaba 167
Goldie, General Thomas 72
Goldie Taubman, Captain John, MHK 94, 98
Goldie-Taubman, John Senhouse, Speaker of the House of Keys 165-6, 170, 172
Goschen, George, MP 180
Graham, Sir James, MP 139
Grant, William, MP 63
Granville, Earl 144
Grellier, James 114
Grenville, George, MP 40, **41**, 42, 56, 57
Grey, Sir George, MP 147, **157**, 176, 205
    constitutional reform 123, 124, 153, 158
    fiscal reform 153, 156, 158, 164
Grindley, Thomas 4, 48
Guernsey 8, 54

Halsall, John 15
Harbour Commissioners 118, 120, 125, 128, 142, 145, 150, 152, 160, 203, 204
harbour dues 66, 117, 118, 129
Harcourt, Sir William Vernon, MP 177
Hardwicke, Lord 201
Harris, Samuel 90, 131
Harrison, Ann 5
Harrison, John, MHK 61
Harrison, John Caesar Tobin 170
Harrison, Thomas, MHK 61
Harrison, William 78
Hawkshaw, John Clarke 151
Hebrides 9
Henry IV, King 10
Henry VII, King 11
Heron, George 84
High Bailiff 91, 108, 115
Hildesley, Mark, Bishop of Sodor and Man 35, 49-50
Hillary, Sir William 12, 83, 84, 88-9, **90**, 94, 95, 96,

273

97, 98, 100, 116, 118, 119, 203, 227
Holland 28, 30, 33, 38, 39
Holmes, James 93, 94
Home Office 3, 8, 72, 76-7, 89, 93, 101, 116, 117, 121, 132, 134, 139, 146, 150, 162, 165, 169, 175, 176, 177, 179, 188, 192, 201, 203, 204
   Commissioners' Report on the Isle of Man (1792) 63-7
Hope, Governor Charles **122**, 132, 134, 135, 143, 144, 145, 146
   constitutional reform 121-3, 139, 204
   fiscal reform 121, 122, 127-9, 130, 140, 204
House of Commons 42, 51, 58, 69, 70, 77, 80, 87, 132, 136, 204
   constitutional reform 153
   fiscal reform 85, 88-9, 109, 117-18, 129, 131, 143, 164, 188
   Reform Act (1832) 81, 82, 137
House of Industry 193
House of Keys 2, 7, 10, 21, 24, 25, 26, 42, 45, 49, 51, 55, **61**, 72, 94, 132-5, 141-5, 176, 177, 199, 200, 202-6
   action against James Brown 153-6
   Bishop Wilson's library 42, **61**
   constitutional reform 81-3, 87-8, 103-4, 120, 121-4, 125-6, 135-40, 145-6, 153-6, 158, 161-3, 165-72, 173, 204-5
   Election Act (1866) 165-70, **168**, **169**
   election qualifications 167, 175
   elections (1867) 165-72, **168**, **169**, **171**, 231-2
   fiscal reform 87-8, 89, 90-1, 93, 94, 98-101, 107, 110, 116, 118, 120, 125-6, 130-1, 137-8, 140, 145-6, 161-2, 183, 202
   fourth Duke of Atholl 58, 59, 60, 68, 69, 74, 75, 76, 77
   self-election 12, 20, 74, 81, 82, 92-3, 101-3, 121, 122, 123, 149-50, 153, 158, **169**
   Speaker 7
   see also 'Hunt the Keys'; Legislative Council; Tynwald
House of Lords 58, 69
Hudgeon, William 74

Hume, James 95-6
'Hunt the Keys' 102-3, 110
Hutchins, Reverend James 74

Imperial Contribution 161, 206
'ingates' and 'outgates' (imports and exports) 17
industry 13-14, 17, 55
Inglis, Sir Robert, MP 131, 132
Innett, Sally *see* Margaret Ennett
Ireland 7, 17, 18, 19, 28, 30, 33, 34, 38, 39, 43, 51, 65, 72, 93, 135, 140, 147, 199
Isle of Man:
   annexation threat 12, 37, 81, 83, 103-4, 105, 123-4, 201, 206
   constitution 3, 7-9, 11, 144, 199, 201
   description 7-12
   map **6**
   origin of government 10
Isle of Man Building Society 93
Isle of Man Commercial Banking Company 110
Isle of Man Directory 167
Isle of Man Examiner **182**
Isle of Man Joint Stock Bank 115, 121, 123
Isle of Man Steam Packet Company 93, **95**, 119, 125, 150
Isle of Man Times 123-4, 153, **155**

Jackson, Thomas 151-3
Jamaica 103
Jeffcott, John Moore 154
Jefferson, George 94, 113-14
Jersey 8
Johnson, Charles 115

Kaupthing Singer and Friedlander (Isle of Man) Ltd 207
Kelly, James, MHK 61
Kelly, John 34
Kelly, John, MHK, 102
Kelly, Miss Maggie 35
Kelly, William, MHK 102-3, 110, 120
Kermode, David 5

Index

Kermode, John 74
Kerwin, Thomas, MHK 61
Kewin, Elizabeth 74-5
Kingdom of Man and the Isles 9-10
Kneale, Thomas 94

Lace, Deemster 50
Lace, John, MHK 60
Lamothe, Frederick John, MHK 156
land tenancy ('straw tenure') 13, 14-15, 21
Laxey 125, **127**
Legislative Council 7, 74, 76, 132, 143-4, 146, 149, 201, 204, 205, 206
    constitutional reform 161, 165, 167
    fiscal reform 91, 98, 101, 107, 116, 135, 137, 140, 161, 183
    see also House of Keys; Tynwald
Lidderdale, William 32
Lindesay, Governor Patrick 26
Loch, Governor Sir Henry Brougham 12, 147, **149**, 174-7, 178, 179, 198, 206, 229
    constitutional reform 153, 156, 158, 161, 162, 163, 165-70, 172, 173, 205
    Douglas breakwater construction 150-1, **152**
    fiscal reform 156-65, 166, 172, 173, 205
London Custom House 96
Lord's Council 10, 14, 20, 24, 26, 47, 200-1
Lords of Man 2, 13, 18, 26, 84, 199, 201, 202, 208
    Castle Rushen 20
    fishing catch ('Castle Maze') 15
    land tenancy ('straw tenure') 13, 14-15
    suzerain rights 4, 10-11, 12, 23, 42, 47-8, 54, 59, 60, 64, 65, 79, 80
        see also Britain: sovereign rights
    transfer of Lordship to Crown 43
Lowther, Lord 97
Lutwidge, Charles 39, 50, 51, 58-9
MacDonnell, Lord 49
Macquire, Richard 23
mail service 173-4
Manks Advertiser 113-14, 115
Manners-Sutton, John Henry Thomas, MP 111, **112**, 121-3
Mansfield, Lord 41
Manx language 7, 8, 46
Manx Liberal 113, 114, 115
    constitutional reform 123
    fiscal reform 92, 107
Manx Sun **113**, 114, 133, **189**
    constitutional reform 87, 92-3
    fiscal reform 87, 92, 110, 118, 130, 163
Manx Yeoman Cavalry 72
Matthews, Francis, MHK 90, 107
Maule, Fox, MP 89, 91
McBride, Catherine 74-5
McCrone, James 73, 74
McGuffog, Robert 93, 94
McHutchin, John 93, 94, 98
merchants and 'merchant strangers' 16, 17, 18, 21, 23, 24, 31-6, 39, 40, 49, 51, 54, 61-2, 63, 66, 68, 69, 83, 93-4, 101, 107-10, 117, 180, 203
Michael 167, 170, 172
Middle 167, 170
mining 106, 125, **127**, 177
'Mischief Act' (1765) 42, 45, 48, 49, 50, 60, 200, 201
    see also British Acts; revestment; 'Revestment Act'
Mona's Herald 102-3, **113**, 114-15, 202, 225
    constitutional reform 83, 101, 131, 138, 153-4, 170
    fiscal reform 87, 89, 92, 100, 101, 106, 107, 110, 112, 118, 130, 131-2, 133-4, 164, 183
Mona's Isle **95**
Montgomerie, Captain Pat 31, 35
Montgomerie, Captain Robert 31
Moore, A. W., Speaker of the House of Keys 4, 48, 50, 142
Moore, Sir George 12, **30**, 35-6, 51, 58, 59, 63
    merchant 29-31, 32
    ships *Peggy* and *Lilly* 31, 35
    smuggling 12, 32-3
Moore, John James, MHK 94, 98, 102-3, 116, 131, 142, 144-5, 153, 164
Moore, John Thomas, MHK 94, 98

Moore, Margaret 31
Moore, Norris, MHK 61
Moore, Phil 30
Moore, Reverend Philip 50
Moore, Robert John, MHK 165
Moore, Thomas, MHK 42, 51
Moore, William Fine, MHK 170-2
Moss, James 28
Mullin-e-Cloie 26
Murray, Captain 31-2
Murray, George, Bishop of Sodor and Man 71-4, **73**, 77
Murray, General James, MP 59
Murray, Governor James 24, 26
Murray, James, second Duke of Atholl 23-5, **25**, 28-9, 37
   investiture as Lord of Man 24-5
   succession to title 23
Murray, John, third Duke of Atholl **38**, 47, 50, 51, 57, 64, 79
   Britain's arrangements for purchase back of Isle of Man rights 40-7
   succession to title 37-8
Murray, John, fourth Duke of Atholl 4, 57, **58**, 71, 81, 201
   compensation for Isle of Man rights 12, 57, 58, 59, 63, 64, 65, 67-70, 77-80
   feud with Cornelius Smelt 75-7
   relationship with House of Keys 58, 59, 60, 68, 69, 74, 75, 76, 77
Murray, Captain Mungo 75
Murray, William *see* Lord Mansfield

newspaper rivalry 113-16
National Institution for the Preservation of Life from Shipwreck 90
Norway 8, 9-10, 27, 28, 33

Oates, James, MHK 61
Onchan 7, 93
'One of the Proscribed' 107-8
Organisation for Economic Cooperation and Development 207

Orr, John 33
Osgoode, William 63
Ostend 28
Oswald, Dr 75
Owens, William 28

Palmerston, Viscount 131, 133, 139, 144, 145
Parr, Deemster John 4
Patrick 29, 93
Peel 7, 24, 28, 29-30, 31-2, 33, 35, 52, **53**, 66, 80, 108, 120, 125, 151, 167, 170, 173, 174, 182, 190
   riots 72
Peel, Sir Robert, MP 74, 75, 76, 105, 108, 118
Penrice, John 115
Phillips, James 28
Pitt the Younger, William, MP 59-60, 63, 67, 68, 69, 70
Poole, Josiah 23
population 7, 29, 39, 49-50, 120, 128, 148, 167, 182, 195-7
Port Erin 7, 125, 174, 176
Port St Mary 125, 173, 182
Portugal 27
Poulett Thomson, Charles Edward, MP 85-6, **88**, 89, 97, 98-101
privateers 33
Privy Council 3, 8, 68, 69, 72, 89
protectionism 105
public finances 66, 70-1, 201-7
   Accumulated/Consolidated Fund 161, 173, 185, 186
   Book of Rates (1692) 20-1, 26
   customs imposition by Britain 54-6
   customs tariffs and allowances 85, 209-24
   'fiscal population' 181-2, 193-8
   fiscal reform:
      'Revestment' 43-56
      'Financial Threat' 81-3, 85-101
      'Free Trade' 105-12, 116-24
      'Britain's Continuing Authority' 125-46
      'Fiscal and Constitutional Reform' 153, 156-65,

172
'Common Purse' 177, 179-90, 193-8
licence system 12, 54, 65, 66, 68, 120, 124, 202, 203
  opposition 83, 85, 87, 94, 96, 98, 99, 101, 105, 106-8, 110-2, 116, 117
  abolition 127-9, 133, 140-2, **141**
Public Works Loan Commissioners 151
Punch **136**

Quayle family 60, 63
Quayle, George, MHK 61, **62**
Quayle, John 32
Quayle, John, MHK 61
Quayle, John, Clerk of the Rolls **62**
Quayle, Robert, MHK 61
Quayle, Thomas 57, 59
Queen's Bench 155
Quiggin family 114
Quiggin, J. 94
Quiggin, William 108
Quiggin, William, & Company 94
Quillin, John 46

railway **174**
Ramsey 7, 27, 28, 35, 52, 66, 93, 108, 120, 121, 125, 151, 167, 170, 172, 173, 174, 182
Ready, Governor Lieutenant Colonel John **86**
  constitutional reform 103, 121
  fiscal reform 85-6, 89, 91, 94, 107, 110, 111, 117, 203
Red Pier, Douglas 79
Reid, David 63
Report of the Commissioners of Inquiry for the Isle of Man (1792) 63-7, **64**, 117
Report of the Departmental Committee on the Constitution etc. of the Isle of Man (1911) 48-9
revenue *see* public finances
revestment 59, 63, 66, 68, 71, 79, 80, 129, 144, 177, 179, 201, 205
  lead up to 37-43
  process of transfer 43-8

impact 49-56
see also 'Mischief Act'; 'Revestment Act'
'Revestment Act' (1765) 11, 43, 45, **46**, 48, 49, 50, 58, 60, 78, 87, 132, 200, 201
see also British Acts; revestment; 'Mischief Act'
Richard III, King 11
Richardson, Mr 66
Ridgeway, Governor Joseph West 12, 193-4, **194**, 197-8, 207, 234
riots 72-4
Robertson, David 65
Rockingham, Marquis of 58-9
Roe, William 63
Rogers, Samuel 116
Roper, William 75
Royal Assent 8, 139, 153, 169, 205
rum 28, 31, 32, 33, 39, 65, 85, 117, 128
Rushen 167
Russell, Lord John 81, 82, 86, 93, 100, 101, 103

Sacheverell, Governor William 19
Salisbury, Lord 180
Sandon, Lord, MP 85
Sankey, Governor Nicholas 21
Scotland 7, 8, 10, 22, 28, 29, 30, 31, 33, 38-9, 57, 63, 65, 79, 135
Scott, Sir Walter 4
Searle, Charles 4
Seven Years War 33, 39-40
Shaw, Lieutenant Governor Alexander 67
Shaw-Lefevre, John, 111, 117
Sherwood, Richard 170, 172
Shetland 27
Shimmin, Thomas 72
shipbuilding **52**, 87, 98, 125, **126**
Shirrefs, William 124
Sidmouth, Viscount (Henry Addington) 68, 69, 72, 75, 76
slave trade 18, 28, 29, 63
Smelt, Colonel Cornelius, Lieutenant Governor 72, 73, **76**
  feud with fourth Duke of Atholl 75-7

Smith, Governor Major General Edward 67
Smuggling ('the trade') 1, 2, 11, 12, 13, 60, 63, 64, 65, 85, 129, 160, 179, 199, 200
    beginnings 17-20, **19**, 21-3
    height 26-36, 37, 38-40
    end 40-3, 45-56
    remnants 57, 59, 65, 67, 68, 70, 81, 83, 87, 100, 111, 116, 117, 120, 127, 128, 130, 147, 202
    see also various Lords of Man; 'Mischief Act'; revestment; 'Revestment Act'
Snaefell 7
Spain 28, 31, 35, 39
spirits 39, 54, 65, 66, 68, 89, 92, 94, 111, 117, 140, 157-8, 163, 180-1, 183, 198
Spranger, John 63
St George's chapel 49
St John's 8, 24
St Kilda 33
St Mark's 73
Stainsby-Conant-Pigott, Governor Francis 147
Stanley, Sir Edward 23
Stanley, Ferdinando, fifth Earl of Derby 14
Stanley, James, seventh Earl of Derby (*Yn Stanlagh Mooar*: 'The Great Stanley') 10, 17, 18, 23
Stanley, James, tenth Earl of Derby 21, 23
Stanley, Sir John 10, 59
Stanley, Sir Thomas, first Baron Stanley 10
Stanley, Thomas, first Earl of Derby 10-11
Stanley, William, sixth Earl of Derby 15
    Elizabeth, Lady, Countess of Derby 15
Stanley, William, ninth Earl of Derby 19, 21, 26
Statutes *see* Acts
Steuart, George 77
Stevenson, Frederick, MHK 61
Stevenson, John, MHK 21
Stevenson, Richard, MHK 59
Stewart, Major David, MHK 94, 102-3
Strange, Lord Charles 17
'straw tenure' 13, 14-15, 21
sugar 85, 89, 91, 98, 111, 117, 118, 140, 157, 163
Sweden 27, 28, 33, 39

Taubman family 60-1, 63
Taubman, John, (senior) Speaker of House of Keys 57, 59, 60, **61**, **62**
Taubman, John, (junior), Speaker of House of Keys 60, 61, **62**
tax haven 207
Taylor, Thomas 31
tea 27, 28, 31, 32, 38, 39, 54, 65, 66, 89, 91, 98, 101, 111, 117, 118, 140, 157, 158, 159, 180-3, 183-8, **182**, 194, 195, 197
Tellett, Daniel, MHK 61
Thurman, Thomas 190-1, **191**, 193
Thurot, Captain François 33-5
Times, The 107, 143
timber 17, 87, 89, 91, 93, 94, 98, 117, 140, 157
tithes, Church 15, 71, 72-4
tobacco 28, 31, 32, 39, 54, 65, 66, 85, 89, 91, 94, 111, 117, 128, 134, 140, 157, 158, 163, 183, 188-9, **189**, 194, 195, 197
Torrance, Gavin 94
tourism 12, **191**, **196**, 205, 206
    beginnings 71, 83-4, 93, 106, 116, 120
    height 148, 150, 154, 163, 174, 177, 190-2, 194-8, 203
    seasonal workers 191-2
    tea drinking 182, 185, 187, 188
    visitors, total 149, 157, 177, 182, 185, 195-6
Townley, Richard 65
'trade, the' *see* smuggling
Train, Joseph 4, 86-7, 120-1
Treasury 66, 69, 125, 132, 143-5, 150, 151, 173, 175-6, 177, 179, 200, 201
    fiscal reform 55, 56, 92, 107, 111, 126-8, 130-1, 132-5, 136, 138, 139, 142, 146, 156, 158-61, 162, 163, 164-5, 166, 179, 183-6, 188, 193, 198, 201-2, 205
    minute on customs revenue 160-1
    purchase back of Isle of Man sovereign rights 23, 37, 40, 41, 42-3, 50, 51, 77, 78, 79, 161
    smuggling 38, 39
Trevelyan, Sir Charles Edward 127, 143
Tyldesley, Edward 18-19

Tyldesley, Thomas 18
Tynwald 1-2, 3, 4, 10, 16, 17, 20, 21, 22, 72, 73, 75, 82, 143-6, 150-1, 153, 166, 176-7, 192, 193, 204, 208
　Book of Rates (1692) 20-1, 26
　constitution:
　　legitimacy 1, 7, 10, 11
　　Lords of Man and Britain 26, 43, 48, 54, 63-5, 139, 149, 199-200, 201, 205
　education 174-5, 188-90
　fiscal reform 85, 86, 89, 91, 92, 95, 98, 99, 101, 104, 111, 116, 127, 130, 132, 134, 135, 137-8, 140, 142, 143, 156, 158, 160-3, 164-5, 166, 172, 173, 179, 180-3, 184, 186-9, 193-8, 203, 204, 205, 207
　House of Keys reform 153, 158, 166-72, 173, 204-5
　President 7
　transfer from Castletown to Douglas **175**
　see also House of Keys; Legislative Council
Tynwald Day 8, 24, 85
Tynwald Hill 8, 24, 26

Union of England and Scotland (1707) 22

Victoria, Queen 101, 153
votes for women 175

wages 15, 16-17
Waldron, George 4, 27
Wales 7, 28, 38
Walker, Burgess & Cooper 150
Walker, James 150
Wallace, Alexander 33
Wallace, Joseph Ritson 114, 115
Wallace, Robert, MP 97
Walls, William 114
Walmsley, Sir Joshua, MP 131, 132
Walpole, Robert, MP 23, 178
Walpole, Governor Spencer 4, 12, 48, 70, **178**, 192, 193, 198, 206, 207, 233
　fiscal reform 178-89

Water Bailiff 15, 17, 108
Wattleworth, Margaret 29
Webber, Captain 27
Welby, Reginald Earle **184**, 185, 187, 188
Welch, John 83-5, 87, 103
West Indies 18, 29, 31, 39, 201
whisky 57, 170, 181
White, John Meadows 98, 118, 131
Wilks, Reverend James 51
William IV, King 101, 203
Wilson, James, MP 128-30, **129**, 131-2, 134, 136, 137-40, 143-5
Wilson, John 93-4
Wilson, Susan 193
Wilson, Thomas 93-4
Wilson, Thomas, Bishop of Sodor and Man 21, 22-3
wine 17, 28, 32, 52, 57, 65, 85, 89, 91, 94, 117, 118, 148, 157, 194, 195, 197, 198
Winram, John 108
Winterbottom, Derek 5
Wood, Governor John 45-7, 50